1995

The Complete Poems of
CHRISTINA ROSSETTI

The Complete Poems of CHRISTINA ROSSETTI

A VARIORUM EDITION

VOLUME II

Edited, with Textual Notes and Introductions, by

R. W. CRUMP

LOUISIANA STATE UNIVERSITY PRESS
BATON ROUGE & LONDON

Manufactured in the United States of America

Designer: Christopher Wilcox
Typeface: Baskerville
Typesetter: G&S Typesetters
Printer: Thomson-Shore, Inc.

1991 printing

LIBRARY OF CONGRESS CATALOGING IN PUBLICATION DATA

(Revised for volume 2)

Rossetti, Christina Georgina, 1830–1894.
  The complete poems of Christina Rossetti.

  Includes bibliographical references and indexes.
  I. Crump, R. W. (Rebecca W.), 1944–
II. Title.
PR5237.A1   1979   821'.8   78-5571
ISBN 0-8071-0358-6 (v. 1)
ISBN 0-8071-1246-1 (v. 2)

Table of Contents

I Sing-Song: A Nursery Rhyme Book (1872)

II   Poems Added in *Sing-Song: A Nursery Rhyme Book* (1893)

III   *A Pageant and Other Poems* (1881)

IV Poems Added in *Poems* (1888, 1890)

THE WORLD. SELF-DESTRUCTION

DIVERS WORLDS. TIME AND
ETERNITY

Acknowledgments

To all of the libraries, institutions, and private collectors named in the list of holograph poems, I would again like to express my gratitude for their courteous help and kind permission to use their books and manuscripts. I am especially grateful to Harold Rossetti for permission to print the unpublished material of Christina Rossetti, as well as to Mrs. Geoffrey Dennis and Mrs. Roderic O'Conor. I remain indebted to all others whose help is acknowledged in Volume I particularly Catherine Barton, managing editor of Louisiana State University Press, for valuable assistance in producing this volume. In addition, I am grateful to Brad Grissom, editor, the *Kentucky Review*, for bringing to my attention the acquisition of the manuscript of "Roses and Roses" ["Where shall I find a white rose blowing"] by the University of Kentucky Library. I am also indebted to Professor Lewis Simpson, Louisiana State University, and especially Professor Jerome McGann, California Institute of Technology, for support of my work on a number of occasions. The John Simon Guggenheim Memorial Foundation awarded me a fellowship that enabled me to complete this volume.

The Complete Poems of
CHRISTINA ROSSETTI

Holograph Poems

Beinecke Rare Book and Manuscript Library, Yale University, New Haven, Connecticut
  Manuscript of "A Bird Song"
  Fourteen numbered pages containing six poems: "Symbols," "Something like Truth" ["Sleep at Sea"], "Easter Even," "The Watchers," "Once," and "Song Enough"

Henry W. and Albert A. Berg Collection, New York Public Library, New York City
  Manuscript of "I love very well the first blossoming"

Bodleian Library, Oxford, England
  Nine notebooks of poems, 1845–1856
  Manuscripts of "The Offering of the New Law, the One Oblation Once Offered" and "Heaven Overarches"

British Library, London, England
  Seven notebooks of poems, 1842–1845, 1856–1866
  Bound holograph volume of *Sing-Song*
  Bound holograph of *Il Rosseggiar dell' Oriente*
  Manuscripts of "Valentines to My Mother," 1876–1886
  Manuscripts of "Sleeping at Last," "Love's Compass," "A Song of Flight," "An Apple-Gathering," "By Way of Remembrance," "Counterblast on Penny Trumpet," "He and She," "Hymn after Gabriele Rossetti," "Mirrors of Life and Death," "My Mouse," and "To My Mother on Her Birthday"
  Manuscript of "Hear what the mournful linnets say" in Maria Rossetti's handwriting

Brown University Library, Providence, Rhode Island
  Manuscript of "A Year's Windfalls"

Mrs. Geoffrey Dennis, Woodstock, England
  Notebook of poems, 1859–1860

One of Christina's copies of *Sing-Song* (1872) with her
holographs of the poems added in the second edition of
Sing-Song (1893)
Manuscript of "Michael F. M. Rossetti"

Duke University Library, Durham, North Carolina
Manuscript of "Methinks the ills of life I fain would shun"

Christopher Erb, Bayonne, New Jersey
Manuscript of "One Sea-Side Grave"

Historical Society of Pennsylvania, Philadelphia
Letter containing the first stanza of "Passing Away"

Houghton Library, Harvard University, Cambridge,
Massachusetts
Manuscript of "A Ballad of Boding"

Humanities Research Center, University of Texas at Austin
Notebook containing *A Pageant and Other Poems*
Manuscripts of "Song" ["She sat and sang alway"], "Three
Seasons," "An Echo from Willowwood," and "The Way of
the World"
Letter containing the first stanza of "Up-Hill"

Huntington Library, San Marino, California
Notebook containing *Maude: Prose and Verse*
Manuscripts of *Later Life: A Double Sonnet of Sonnets*
Manuscripts of "Behold the Man," "Up-Hill," and part of
"At Home"

Iowa State Department of History and Archives, Des Moines
Two pages from Christina's rough draft of "The Months: A
Pageant"

Mrs. Roderic O'Conor, Henley-on-Thames, England
One of Christina's copies of *Sing-Song* (1872), containing her
Italian translations of the poems, and the poems added in
the second edition of *Sing-Song* (1893)

Pierpont Morgan Library, New York City
Manuscript of "A Dirge"
Manuscript of "Song" ["When I am dead my dearest"] and
part of "What Sappho Would Have Said Had Her Leap
Cured Instead of Killed Her"

Open Collection, Princeton University Library, Princeton, New Jersey
> Manuscripts of "Autumn," "A Coast Nightmare," "A Discovery," "An Escape," "A Hopeless Case," "My Old Friends," "A Prospective Meeting," "Reflection," "A Return," "Rivals," "River Thames," "Ruin," "Solitude," "A Study," "Summer," "Sunshine," "Winter. A Christmas Carol," "A Year's Windfalls," "4th May morning," and "Gone to his rest"

Rossetti Collection of Janet Camp Troxell, Princeton University Library
> Rough drafts of eighteen *bouts-rimés* sonnets
> Manuscripts of "A Christmas Carol" ["A Holy Heavenly Chime"], "Cor Mio," "De Profundis," "Hadrian's Death-Song Translated," "Heaven Over Arches," "Husband and Wife," "Imitated from the Arpa Evangelica: Page 121" ["Hymn after Gabriele Rossetti: Second Version"], "In resurrection is it awfuller" ["By Way of Remembrance"], "L'Uommibatto," "Meeting," "Parted," "Si Rimanda la tocca-caldaja," "Time and Opportunity," "Hope in Grief," "O Ptimogenita," and "The Succession of Kings"
> Manuscript containing deleted partial stanzas of three poems, including "The Key-Note"
> Manuscript of the first three stanzas of "A Christmas Carol" ["Before the paling of the stars"]
> Manuscript of the first stanza of "Up-Hill"
> Manuscript of the short story "Commonplace," containing "In July no goodbye" and "Love hath a name of death" ["Love's Name"]

Harold F. Rossetti, London, England
> Manuscript of "Sonnets are full of love"

Kenneth Spencer Research Library, University of Kansas, Lawrence
> Manuscript of "The whole head is sick and the whole heart faint" and the last three lines of "The Trees' Counselling"

Robert H. Taylor Collection, Princeton University Library, New Jersey

Letter containing "Mr. and Mrs. Scott and I" (on indefinite
deposit at the Princeton University Library)

University of British Columbia Library, Vancouver, Canada
Letters containing Christina's Italian translations of "Bread
and milk for breakfast," "Hear what the mournful linnets
say," "O sailor come ashore," "The horses of the sea," "Oh
fair to see," and "If a pig wore a wig"
Letters containing "A roundel seems to fit a round of days,"
"My first is a donkey," "Pity the sorrows of a poor old
dog," "The two Rossettis (brothers they)" ["The P.R.B."],
"In Progress," and part of "A sonnet and a love sonnet
from me"

University of Kentucky Libraries, Lexington
Manuscript of "Roses and Roses" ["Where shall I find a
white rose blowing"]

Editions and Reprints

In order to be certain that the absence of end-of-line punctuation was not the result of imperfect inking in each printed text recorded in the notes, I collated several copies of each text. A complete list including anthologies, journals, newspapers, and other works containing authoritative texts that are used in this volume would be very long; the list below is therefore limited to the editions and reprints of collections of Christina Rossetti's poems. An *a* after the date of publication indicates an American edition, and parentheses enclose the dates of reprints. Reprints are cited in the textual notes only where they show a new variant; the variants designated 1885r and 1896s are recorded only if they differ from the first editions published in those years (r = Christina Rossetti's own annotated copy, s = special edition).

SING-SONG

1872   *Sing-Song. A Nursery Rhyme Book.* London: George Routledge and Sons, 1872.

        Copy owned by Mrs. Geoffrey Dennis, with Christina Rossetti's holographs of the poems added in the second edition of *Sing-Song* (1893)

        Copy owned by Mrs. Roderic O'Conor, with Christina Rossetti's Italian translations of the poems, and the poems added in the second edition of *Sing-Song* (1893)

        University of Chicago Library, PZ163.R78S6.1872

        University of North Carolina Library, RBC.PR5237.S5

1872a   *Sing-Song. A Nursery Rhyme Book.* Boston: Roberts Brothers, 1872.

        Philadelphia Free Library, A821.R732

        Library of Congress, PR5237.S5

1893   *Sing-Song. A Nursery Rhyme Book.* London and New York:
        Macmillan, 1893.
            British Library,)11652.g.16
            Harvard University Library, Typ 805.93.7520
            Stanford University Library, PR5237.55.1893

1904   *The Poetical Works of Christina Georgina Rossetti, with Memoir
        and Notes by William Michael Rossetti.* London: Macmillan,
        1904.
            Louisiana State University Library, 828.R734pXr
            The editor's own copy

A PAGEANT AND OTHER POEMS

1881   *A Pageant and Other Poems.* London: Macmillan, 1881.
            Harvard University Library, EC.85.R7354.881p
            University of Chicago Library, PR5237.P2.1881
            University of Georgia Library, PR5237.P3.1881a

1881a   *A Pageant and Other Poems.* Boston: Roberts Brothers,
        1881.
            Harvard University Library, 23473.25
            Stanford University Library, 821.6.R83p
            Yale University Library, Ip.R734.881b

(1882a) *Poems.* Boston: Roberts Brothers, 1882.
            British Library, 11609.dd.18

(1888a) *Poems.* Boston: Roberts Brothers, 1888. 208 pp.
            Case Western Reserve University Library, 821.89.R82ea
            Library of Congress, PR5237.A.1.1888

1888a   *Poems.* Boston: Roberts Brothers, 1888. 231 pp.
            Harvard University Library, 23473.26.20
            Wheaton College Library, PR5237.A1.1888

1890   *Poems, New and Enlarged Edition.* London and New York:
        Macmillan, 1890.
            Harvard University Library, KD 5818 Hilles Library
            Princeton University Library, 3913.1.1890

(1891) *Poems, New and Enlarged Edition.* London and New York:
        Macmillan, 1891.
            Harvard University Library, KPD 5493

(1892) *Poems, New and Enlarged Edition.* London and New York: Macmillan, 1892.
    Princeton University Library, Ex3913.1.1892

1896 *New Poems, Hitherto Unpublished or Uncollected.* Edited by William Michael Rossetti. London and New York: Macmillan, 1896.
    Harvard University Library, Keats *EC8 K2262 Za895rb
    Princeton University Library, 3913.1.367
    University of Texas Library, ApR 734 896nba

1896s *New Poems, Hitherto Unpublished or Uncollected.* Edited by William Michael Rossetti. London: Macmillan, 1896. Special edition of one hundred large paper copies printed in January, 1896.
    Princeton University Library, 3913.1.367.11 (#35)
    University of Texas Library, HANLEY R734n (#76)

1904 *The Poetical Works of Christina Georgina Rossetti, with Memoir and Notes by William Michael Rossetti.* London: Macmillan, 1904.
    Louisiana State University Library, , 828.R734pXr
    The editor's own copy

VERSES

1881 *Called to be Saints: The Minor Festivals Devotionally Studied.* London: Society for Promoting Christian Knowledge; New York: E. and J. B. Young, [1881].
    Boston University Theology Library, 242.3.R73c
    Harvard University Library, *EC.85.R7354.881c
    Yale University Library, Mrg78.R73

1885 *Time Flies: A Reading Diary.* London: Society for Promoting Christian Knowledge, 1885.
    University of Georgia Library, BV832.R74.1885
    University of Virginia, BV832.R74

1885r *Time Flies: A Reading Diary.* London: Society for Promoting Christian Knowledge, 1885.
    University of Texas Library, MS file (Rossetti, CG) Works B [Contains author's holograph marginalia]

1886a   *Time Flies: A Reading Diary.* Boston: Roberts Brothers.
        Oberlin College Library, 242.R735
        University of Chicago Library, PR5237.T5.1886

(1890) *Time Flies: A Reading Diary.* London: Society for Promoting Christian Knowledge, 1890.
        Library of Congress, BV4832.R74.1890
        Yale University Library, Ip.R734.885Tb

1892   *The Face of the Deep: A Devotional Commentary on the Apocalypse.* London: Society for Promoting Christian Knowledge; New York: E. and J. B. Young, 1892.
        Florida State University, Hum.BS.2825.R65
        Harvard University Library, *EC85.R7354.892f
        University of Wisconsin Library, BS.2825.R65

(1893) *The Face of the Deep: A Devotional Commentary on the Apocalypse.* Second edition. London: Society for Promoting Christian Knowledge; New York: E. and J. B. Young, 1893.
        Princeton University Library, Ex5298.786.1893
        College of Puget Sound Library, 228.R735f

1893   *Verses. Reprinted from "Called to be Saints," "Time Flies," "The Face of the Deep."* London: Society for Promoting Christian Knowledge; New York: E. and J. B. Young, 1893.
        Cincinnati University Library, PR5237.V4.1893
        Duke University Library, 821.89.R829V
        Harvard University Library, *EC85.R7354.D893v
        University of Wisconsin Library, PR5237.V4
        The editor's own copy

(1894) *Verses. Reprinted from "Called to be Saints," "Time Flies," "The Face of the Deep."* Sixth Edition. London: Society for Promoting Christian Knowledge; New York: E. and J. B. Young, 1894
        Copy owned by E. E. Bissell
        Gonzaga University Library, 821.89.R735v.c.1

(1895) *The Face of the Deep: A Devotional Commentary on the Apocalypse.* Third edition. London: Society for Promoting Christian Knowledge; New York: E. and J. B. Young, 1895.
        British Library, 3188.b.27

1904   *The Poetical Works of Christina Georgina Rossetti, with Memoir
        and Notes by William Michael Rossetti.* London: Macmillan,
        1904.
            Louisiana State University Library, 828.R734pXr
            The editor's own copy

Introduction

The printing histories of *Sing-Song, A Pageant and Other Poems*, and *Verses* during Christina's lifetime are critical to the determination of the text of this volume.[1] *Sing-Song* and *A Pageant and Other Poems* underwent two lines of development—the English and the American. In England, George Routledge published *Sing-Song* in 1872. Comparison of the first edition and Christina's manuscript notebook reveals that Christina maintained close control over the poems, although some house practices were imposed on punctuation and spelling. In the second edition of *Sing-Song*, published by Macmillan in 1893, Christina lengthened six poems and added five new ones to the collection.[2] In America, Roberts Brothers of Boston, who had already published *Goblin Market and Other Poems* and *The Prince's Progress and Other Poems*, issued an edition of *Sing-Song* in 1872, the text of which is almost identical with that of the Routledge edition.

Christina returned to her usual publisher, Macmillan, for *A Pageant and Other Poems* in 1881. As with *Sing-Song*, the text of the first edition closely parallels the manuscript notebook. Roberts Brothers published an American edition of *A Pageant and Other Poems* in 1881 and later combined it with Christina's first two collections (*Goblin Market and Other Poems* and *The Prince's Progress and Other Poems*) in a volume entitled *Poems*, which appeared in 1882 and again in 1888. Some of the 1888 copies contain seventeen previously unpublished poems, added at the end of the *Pageant* collection. In 1890 those new poems were incorporated into the Macmillan edi-

---

1. For a description of the organization of poems and statement of my editorial principles, see Volume I, pp. xi–xiii.
2. She lengthened "I caught a little ladybird," "I have a little husband," "The dear old woman in the lane," "I have a Poll parrot," "Clever little Willie wee," and "The peach tree on the southern wall" (originally "A peach for brothers, one for each").

tion of *Poems*.[3] Roberts Brothers imposed the usual American house spellings on Christina's poems, but there were noticeably fewer punctuation changes than was the case with the *Goblin Market* and *Prince's Progress* collections.

Christina's final collection, *Verses* (1893), is a combination of poems drawn largely from three earlier books of prose and poetry— *Called to be Saints: The Minor Festivals Devotionally Studied* (1881), *Time Flies: A Reading Diary* (1885), and *The Face of the Deep: A Devotional Commentary on the Apocalypse* (1892)—although four of the poems in *Verses* are new.[4] Published by the Society for Promoting Christian Knowledge, the *Verses* text shows numerous variations from the earlier versions in punctuation, spelling, paragraphing, and even some wording; furthermore, Christina added titles to many of the previously untitled poems and divided the poems into eight groups (see Table of Contents herein). I have been unable to trace the whereabouts of the manuscript notebook of *Verses* since its sale in 1931 by Maggs Brothers of London, but the kinds of changes seen in the 1893 text appear to me to be authorial.[5]

For each of the three collections in the present volume, I chose as the copy-text the first English edition because that text appeared to come closest to the final intentions of the author. I emended the first editions in the following ways: I restored house spellings to manuscript spellings; where the printed paragraphing violated Christina's usual practices, as seen in her manuscripts, I adopted the manuscript paragraphing; and I corrected typesetting errors to

3. See Appendix B, herein, for a comparison of the arrangements of poems in her 1888 and 1890 collections.

4. The new poems are "O mine enemy," "Passiontide," "Good Friday Morning," and "Love is strong as Death" ["As flames that consume the mountains, as winds that coerce the sea"].

5. *Books Manuscripts Bindings and Autograph Letters Remarkable for Their Interest & Rarity Being the Five Hundred and Fiftyfifth Catalogue Issued by Maggs Bros* (London: Maggs Bros, 1931) gives, on page 183, the following description:

ROSSETTI (Christina G.).

THE COMPLETE AUTOGRAPH MANUSCRIPT OF HER POEMS AS PREPARED BY HER FOR THE EDITION PUBLISHED IN 1893, COMPRISING 389 PAGES, THE WHOLE ENTIRELY IN HER AUTOGRAPH.

£250

4to. Preserved in buckrum case.

The whole of this Manuscript is in Christina Rossetti's Autograph, and comprises Title-page; Contents I page; Manuscript of the Poems pp. 4–373; and Index of First Lines 374–389.

the manuscript reading. Occasionally the principles just enumerated were inadequate to determine the reading; deviations from these principles are recorded in the textual notes. The present edition thus furnishes an eclectic text, which, unlike any single authoritative version, is based on a consideration of Christina's extant manuscripts, letters, editions, and individual printings of her poems in journals and anthologies.

I Sing-Song
A Nursery Rhyme Book
(1872)

RHYMES
DEDICATED
WITHOUT PERMISSION
TO
THE BABY
WHO
SUGGESTED
THEM

Angels at the foot,
  And Angels at the head,
And like a curly little lamb
  My pretty babe in bed.

Love me,—I love you,
  Love me, my baby;
Sing it high, sing it low,
  Sing it as may be.
5 Mother's arms under you,
  Her eyes above you;
Sing it high, sing it low,
  Love me,—I love you.

My baby has a father and a mother,
    Rich little baby!
Fatherless, motherless, I know another
    Forlorn as may be:
5   Poor little baby!

Our little baby fell asleep,
    And may not wake again
For days and days, and weeks and weeks;
    But then he'll wake again,
5   And come with his own pretty look,
    And kiss Mamma again.

"Kookoorookoo! kookoorookoo!"
    Crows the cock before the morn;
"Kikirikee! kikirikee!"
    Roses in the east are born.
5   "Kookoorookoo! kookoorookoo!"
    Early birds begin their singing;
"Kikirikee! kikirikee!"
    The day, the day, the day is springing.

    Baby cry—
    Oh fie!—
At the physic in the cup:
    Gulp it twice
5   And gulp it thrice,
Baby gulp it up.

Eight o'clock;
The postman's knock!
Five letters for Papa;
    One for Lou,
5   And none for you,
And three for dear Mamma.

Bread and milk for breakfast,
    And woollen frocks to wear,
And a crumb for robin redbreast
    On the cold days of the year.

There's snow on the fields,
    And cold in the cottage,
While I sit in the chimney nook
    Supping hot pottage.

5   My clothes are soft and warm,
      Fold upon fold,
But I'm so sorry for the poor
    Out in the cold.

Dead in the cold, a song-singing thrush,
Dead at the foot of a snowberry bush,—
Weave him a coffin of rush,
Dig him a grave where the soft mosses grow,
5   Raise him a tombstone of snow.

I dug and dug amongst the snow,
And thought the flowers would never grow;
I dug and dug amongst the sand,
And still no green thing came to hand.

5   Melt, O snow! the warm winds blow
To thaw the flowers and melt the snow;
But all the winds from every land
Will rear no blossom from the sand.

A city plum is not a plum;
A dumb-bell is no bell, though dumb;
A party rat is not a rat;
A sailor's cat is not a cat;
5   A soldier's frog is not a frog;
A captain's log is not a log.

Your brother has a falcon,
    Your sister has a flower;
But what is left for mannikin,
    Born within an hour?

5   I'll nurse you on my knee, my knee,
        My own little son;
     I'll rock you, rock you, in my arms,
        My least little one.

     Hear what the mournful linnets say:
        "We built our nest compact and warm,
     But cruel boys came round our way
        And took our summerhouse by storm.
5   "They crushed the eggs so neatly laid;
        So now we sit with drooping wing,
     And watch the ruin they have made,
        Too late to build, too sad to sing."

     A baby's cradle with no baby in it,
        A baby's grave where autumn leaves drop sere;
     The sweet soul gathered home to Paradise,
        The body waiting here.

     Hop-o'-my-thumb and little Jack Horner,
        What do you mean by tearing and fighting?
     Sturdy dog Trot close round the corner,
        I never caught him growling and biting.

     Hope is like a harebell trembling from its birth,
     Love is like a rose the joy of all the earth;
     Faith is like a lily lifted high and white,
     Love is like a lovely rose the world's delight;
5   Harebells and sweet lilies show a thornless growth,
     But the rose with all its thorns excels them both.

     O wind, why do you never rest,
        Wandering, whistling to and fro,

Bringing rain out of the west,
  From the dim north bringing snow?

Crying, my little one, footsore and weary?
  Fall asleep, pretty one, warm on my shoulder:
I must tramp on through the winter night dreary,
  While the snow falls on me colder and colder.
5 You are my one, and I have not another;
    Sleep soft, my darling, my trouble and treasure;
  Sleep warm and soft in the arms of your mother,
    Dreaming of pretty things, dreaming of pleasure.

Growing in the vale
  By the uplands hilly,
Growing straight and frail,
  Lady Daffadowndilly.
5 In a golden crown,
And a scant green gown
  While the spring blows chilly,
Lady Daffadown,
  Sweet Daffadowndilly.

A linnet in a gilded cage,—
  A linnet on a bough,—
In frosty winter one might doubt
  Which bird is luckier now.
5 But let the trees burst out in leaf,
  And nests be on the bough,
Which linnet is the luckier bird,
  Oh who could doubt it now?

Wrens and robins in the hedge,
  Wrens and robins here and there;

Building, perching, pecking, fluttering,
    Everywhere!

My baby has a mottled fist,
   My baby has a neck in creases;
My baby kisses and is kissed,
   For he's the very thing for kisses.

Why did baby die,
Making Father sigh,
Mother cry?

Flowers, that bloom to die,
5 Make no reply
Of "why?"
But bow and die.

If all were rain and never sun,
   No bow could span the hill;
If all were sun and never rain,
   There'd be no rainbow still.

O wind, where have you been,
   That you blow so sweet?
Among the violets
   Which blossom at your feet.

5 The honeysuckle waits
   For Summer and for heat.
But violets in the chilly Spring
   Make the turf so sweet.

On the grassy banks
Lambkins at their pranks;
Woolly sisters, woolly brothers

Jumping off their feet
5   While their woolly mothers
Watch by them and bleat.

Rushes in a watery place,
And reeds in a hollow;
A soaring skylark in the sky,
A darting swallow;
5   And where pale blossom used to hang
Ripe fruit to follow.

Minnie and Mattie
And fat little May,
Out in the country,
Spending a day.

5   Such a bright day,
With the sun glowing,
And the trees half in leaf,
And the grass growing.

Pinky white pigling
10   Squeals through his snout,
Woolly white lambkin
Frisks all about.

Cluck! cluck! the nursing hen
Summons her folk,—
15   Ducklings all downy soft
Yellow as yolk.

Cluck! cluck! the mother hen
Summons her chickens
To peck the dainty bits
20   Found in her pickings.

Minnie and Mattie
And May carry posies,
Half of sweet violets,
Half of primroses.

25 Give the sun time enough,
    Glowing and glowing,
He'll rouse the roses
    And bring them blowing.

Don't wait for roses
30   Losing today,
O Minnie, Mattie,
    And wise little May.

Violets and primroses
    Blossom today
35 For Minnie and Mattie
    And fat little May.

Heartsease in my garden bed,
    With sweetwilliam white and red,
Honeysuckle on my wall:—
    Heartsease blossoms in my heart
5 When sweet William comes to call,
    But it withers when we part,
And the honey-trumpets fall.

If I were a Queen,
    What would I do?
I'd make you King,
    And I'd wait on you.

5 If I were a King,
    What would I do?
I'd make you Queen,
    For I'd marry you.

What are heavy? sea-sand and sorrow:
What are brief? today and tomorrow:
What are frail? Spring blossoms and youth:
What are deep? the ocean and truth.

There is but one May in the year,
  And sometimes May is wet and cold;
There is but one May in the year
  Before the year grows old.

5 Yet though it be the chilliest May,
  With least of sun and most of showers,
Its wind and dew, its night and day,
  Bring up the flowers.

The summer nights are short
  ˙Where northern days are long:
For hours and hours lark after lark
  Trills out his song.

5 The summer days are short
  Where southern nights are long:
Yet short the night when nightingales
  Trill out their song.

The days are clear,
  Day after day,
When April's here,
  That leads to May,
5 And June
Must follow soon:
  Stay, June, stay!—
If only we could stop the moon
And June!

Twist me a crown of wind-flowers;
  That I may fly away
To hear the singers at their song,
  And players at their play.

5 Put on your crown of wind-flowers:
  But whither would you go?

Beyond the surging of the sea
    And the storms that blow.

Alas! your crown of wind-flowers
10   Can never make you fly:
I twist them in a crown today,
    And tonight they die.

Brown and furry
Caterpillar in a hurry,
Take your walk
To the shady leaf, or stalk,
5   Or what not,
Which may be the chosen spot.
No toad spy you,
Hovering bird of prey pass by you;
Spin and die,
10   To live again a butterfly.

A toadstool comes up in a night,—
    Learn the lesson, little folk:—
An oak grows on a hundred years,
    But then it is an oak.

A pocket handkerchief to hem—
    Oh dear, oh dear, oh dear!
How many stitches it will take
    Before it's done, I fear.

5   Yet set a stitch and then a stitch,
    And stitch and stitch away,
Till stitch by stitch the hem is done—
    And after work is play!

If a pig wore a wig,
    What could we say?

Treat him as a gentleman,
And say "Good day."
5 If his tail chanced to fail,
What could we do?—
Send him to the tailoress
To get one new.

Seldom "can't,"
Seldom "don't;"
Never "shan't,"
Never "won't."

1 and 1 are 2—
That's for me and you.

2 and 2 are 4—
That's a couple more.

5 3 and 3 are 6
Barley-sugar sticks.

4 and 4 are 8
Tumblers at the gate.

5 and 5 are 10
10 Bluff seafaring men.

6 and 6 are 12
Garden lads who delve.

7 and 7 are 14
Young men bent on sporting.

15 8 and 8 are 16
Pills the doctor's mixing.

9 and 9 are 18
Passengers kept waiting.

10 and 10 are 20
20 Roses—pleasant plenty!

11 and 11 are 22
Sums for brother George to do.

12 and 12 are 24
Pretty pictures, and no more.

How many seconds in a minute?
Sixty, and no more in it.

How many minutes in an hour?
Sixty for sun and shower.

5   How many hours in a day?
Twenty-four for work and play.

How many days in a week?
Seven both to hear and speak.

How many weeks in a month?
10   Four, as the swift moon runn'th.

How many months in a year?
Twelve the almanack makes clear.

How many years in an age?
One hundred says the sage.

15   How many ages in time?
No one knows the rhyme.

What will you give me for my pound?
Full twenty shillings round.
What will you give me for my shilling?
Twleve pence to give I'm willing.
5   What will you give me for my penny?
Four farthings, just so many.

January cold desolate;
February all dripping wet;
March wind ranges;
April changes;

5   Birds sing in tune
             To flowers of May,
         And sunny June
             Brings longest day;
         In scorched July
10   The storm-clouds fly
         Lightning torn;
         August bears corn,
         September fruit;
         In rough October
15   Earth must disrobe her;
         Stars fall and shoot
         In keen November;
         And night is long
         And cold is strong
20   In bleak December.

         What is pink? a rose is pink
         By the fountain's brink.
         What is red? a poppy's red
         In its barley bed.
5   What is blue? the sky is blue
         Where the clouds float thro'.
         What is white? a swan is white
         Sailing in the light.
         What is yellow? pears are yellow,
10   Rich and ripe and mellow.
         What is green? the grass is green,
         With small flowers between.
         What is violet? clouds are violet
         In the summer twilight.
15   What is orange? why, an orange,
         Just an orange!

         Mother shake the cherry-tree,
             Susan catch a cherry;

Oh how funny that will be,
  Let's be merry!

5   One for brother, one for sister,
  Two for mother more,
Six for father, hot and tired,
  Knocking at the door.

A pin has a head, but has no hair;
A clock has a face, but no mouth there;
Needles have eyes, but they cannot see;
A fly has a trunk without lock or key;
5   A timepiece may lose, but cannot win;
A corn-field dimples without a chin;
A hill has no leg, but has a foot;
A wine-glass a stem, but not a root;
A watch has hands, but no thumb or finger;
10 A boot has a tongue, but is no singer;
Rivers run, though they have no feet;
A saw has teeth, but it does not eat;
Ash-trees have keys, yet never a lock;
And baby crows, without being a cock.

Hopping frog, hop here and be seen,
  I'll not pelt you with stick or stone:
Your cap is laced and your coat is green;
  Good bye, we'll let each other alone.

5   Plodding toad, plod here and be looked at,
You the finger of scorn is crooked at:
But though you're lumpish, you're harmless too;
You won't hurt me, and I won't hurt you.

Where innocent bright-eyed daisies are,
  With blades of grass between,
Each daisy stands up like a star
  Out of a sky of green.

The city mouse lives in a house;—
    The garden mouse lives in a bower,
He's friendly with the frogs and toads,
    And sees the pretty plants in flower.

5   The city mouse eats bread and cheese;—
    The garden mouse eats what he can;
We will not grudge him seeds and stalks,
    Poor little timid furry man.

What does the donkey bray about?
What does the pig grunt through his snout?
What does the goose mean by a hiss?
Oh, Nurse, if you can tell me this,
5   I'll give you such a kiss.

The cockatoo calls "cockatoo,"
The magpie chatters "how d'ye do?"
The jackdaw bids me "go away,"
Cuckoo cries "cuckoo" half the day:
10   What do the others say?

Three plum buns
    To eat here at the stile
In the clover meadow,
    For we have walked a mile.

5   One for you, and one for me,
    And one left over:
Give it to the boy who shouts
    To scare sheep from the clover.

A motherless soft lambkin
    Alone upon a hill;
No mother's fleece to shelter him
    And wrap him from the cold:—
5   I'll run to him and comfort him,
    I'll fetch him, that I will;

I'll care for him and feed him
    Until he's strong and bold.

Dancing on the hill-tops,
    Singing in the valleys,
Laughing with the echoes,
    Merry little Alice.

5   Playing games with lambkins
    In the flowering valleys,
Gathering pretty posies,
    Helpful little Alice.

If her father's cottage
10   Turned into a palace,
And he owned the hill-tops
    And the flowering valleys,
She'd be none the happier,
    Happy little Alice.

When fishes set umbrellas up
    If the rain-drops run,
Lizards will want their parasols
    To shade them from the sun.

The peacock has a score of eyes,
    With which he cannot see;
The cod-fish has a silent sound,
    However that may be;
5   No dandelions tell the time,
    Although they turn to clocks;
Cat's-cradle does not hold the cat,
    Nor foxglove fit the fox.

Pussy has a whiskered face,
Kitty has such pretty ways;

Doggie scampers when I call,
And has a heart to love us all.

The dog lies in his kennel,
   And Puss purrs on the rug,
And baby perches on my knee
   For me to love and hug.
5   Pat the dog and stroke the cat,
   Each in its degree;
And cuddle and kiss my baby,
   And baby kiss me.

If hope grew on a bush,
   And joy grew on a tree,
What a nosegay for the plucking
   There would be!
5   But oh! in windy autumn,
   When frail flowers wither,
What should we do for hope and joy,
   Fading together?

I planted a hand
   And there came up a palm,
I planted a heart
   And there came up balm.
5   Then I planted a wish,
   But there sprang a thorn,
While heaven frowned with thunder
   And earth sighed forlorn.

Under the ivy bush
   One sits sighing,
And under the willow tree
   One sits crying:—

5   Under the ivy bush
        Cease from your sighing,
     But under the willow tree
        Lie down a-dying.

     There is one that has a head without an eye,
        And there's one that has an eye without a head:
     You may find the answer if you try;
        And when all is said,
5   Half the answer hangs upon a thread!

     If a mouse could fly,
        Or if a crow could swim,
     Or if a sprat could walk and talk,
        I'd like to be like him.
5   If a mouse could fly,
        He might fly away;
     Or if a crow could swim,
        It might turn him grey;
     Or if a sprat could walk and talk,
10   What would he find to say?

     Sing me a song—
        What shall I sing?—
     Three merry sisters
        Dancing in a ring,
5   Light and fleet upon their feet
        As birds upon the wing.

     Tell me a tale—
        What shall I tell?—
     Two mournful sisters,
10   And a tolling knell,
     Tolling ding and tolling dong,
        Ding dong bell.

The lily has an air,
  And the snowdrop a grace,
And the sweetpea a way,
  And the heartsease a face,—
5 Yet there's nothing like the rose
  When she blows.

Margaret has a milking-pail,
  And she rises early;
Thomas has a threshing-flail,
  And he's up betimes.
5 Sometimes crossing through the grass
  Where the dew lies pearly,
They say "Good morrow" as they pass
  By the leafy limes.

In the meadow—what in the meadow?
Bluebells, buttercups, meadowsweet,
And fairy rings for the children's feet
  In the meadow.
5 In the garden—what in the garden?
Jacob's-ladder and Solomon's-seal,
And Love-lies-bleeding beside All-heal
  In the garden.

A frisky lamb
And a frisky child
Playing their pranks
  In a cowslip meadow:
5 The sky all blue
And the air all mild
And the fields all sun
  And the lanes half shadow.

Mix a pancake,
Stir a pancake,
    Pop it in the pan;
Fry the pancake,
5   Toss the pancake,—
    Catch it if you can.

The wind has such a rainy sound
    Moaning through the town,
The sea has such a windy sound,—
    Will the ships go down?

5   The apples in the orchard
    Tumble from their tree.—
Oh will the ships go down, go down,
    In the windy sea?

Three little children
    On the wide wide earth,
Motherless children—
    Cared for from their birth
5   By tender Angels.
Three little children
    On the wide wide sea,
Motherless children—
    Safe as safe can be
10   With guardian Angels.

Fly away, fly away over the sea,
    Sun-loving swallow, for summer is done;
Come again, come again, come back to me,
    Bringing the summer and bringing the sun.

Minnie bakes oaten cakes,
    Minnie brews ale,

All because her Johnny's coming
    Home from sea.
5   And she glows like a rose,
    Who was so pale,
And "Are you sure the church clock goes?"
    Says she.

A white hen sitting
    On white eggs three:
Next, three speckled chickens
    As plump as plump can be.
5   An owl, and a hawk,
    And a bat come to see:
But chicks beneath their mother's wing
    Squat safe as safe can be.

Currants on a bush,
    And figs upon a stem,
And cherries on a bending bough,
    And Ned to gather them.

I have but one rose in the world,
    And my one rose stands a-drooping:
Oh when my single rose is dead
    There'll be but thorns for stooping.

Rosy maiden Winifred,
With a milkpail on her head,
Tripping through the corn,
    While the dew lies on the wheat
5   In the sunny morn.
Scarlet shepherd's-weatherglass
    Spreads wide open at her feet
      As they pass;

Cornflowers give their almond smell
10   While she brushes by,
        And a lark sings from the sky
          "All is well."

When the cows come home the milk is coming,
Honey's made while the bees are humming;
Duck and drake on the rushy lake,
And the deer live safe in the breezy brake;
5   And timid, funny, brisk little bunny,
Winks his nose and sits all sunny.

Roses blushing red and white,
        For delight;
Honeysuckle wreaths above,
        For love;
5   Dim sweet-scented heliotrope,
        For hope;
Shining lilies tall and straight,
        For royal state;
Dusky pansies, let them be
10   For memory;
With violets of fragrant breath,
        For death.

"Ding a ding,"
The sweet bells sing,
And say:
"Come, all be gay"
5   For a wedding day.

"Dong a dong,"
The bells sigh long,
And call:
"Weep one, weep all"
10   For a funeral.

A ring upon her finger,
    Walks the bride,
With the bridegroom tall and handsome
    At her side.

5   A veil upon her forehead,
    Walks the bride,
With the bridegroom proud and merry
    At her side.

Fling flowers beneath the footsteps
10   Of the bride;
Fling flowers before the bridegroom
    At her side.

"Ferry me across the water,
    Do, boatman, do."
"If you've a penny in your purse
    I'll ferry you."

5   "I have a penny in my purse,
    And my eyes are blue;
So ferry me across the water,
    Do, boatman, do."

"Step into my ferry-boat,
10   Be they black or blue,
And for the penny in your purse
    I'll ferry you."

When a mounting skylark sings
    In the sunlit summer morn,
I know that heaven is up on high,
    And on earth are fields of corn.

5   But when a nightingale sings
    In the moonlit summer even,
I know not if earth is merely earth,
    Only that heaven is heaven.

Who has seen the wind?
    Neither I nor you:
But when the leaves hang trembling
    The wind is passing thro'.

5   Who has seen the wind?
    Neither you nor I:
But when the trees bow down their heads
    The wind is passing by.

The horses of the sea
    Rear a foaming crest,
But the horses of the land
    Serve us the best.

5   The horses of the land
    Munch corn and clover,
While the foaming sea-horses
    Toss and turn over.

O sailor, come ashore,
    What have you brought for me?
Red coral, white coral,
    Coral from the sea.

5   I did not dig it from the ground,
    Nor pluck it from a tree;
Feeble insects made it
    In the stormy sea.

A diamond or a coal?
    A diamond, if you please:
Who cares about a clumsy coal
    Beneath the summer trees?

5   A diamond or a coal?
    A coal, sir, if you please:
One comes to care about the coal
    What time the waters freeze.

An emerald is as green as grass;
   A ruby red as blood;
A sapphire shines as blue as heaven;
   A flint lies in the mud.

5   A diamond is a brilliant stone,
   To catch the world's desire;
An opal holds a fiery spark;
   But a flint holds fire.

Boats sail on the rivers,
   And ships sail on the seas;
But clouds that sail across the sky
   Are prettier far than these.

5   There are bridges on the rivers,
   As pretty as you please;
But the bow that bridges heaven,
   And overtops the trees,
And builds a road from earth to sky,
10   Is prettier far than these.

The lily has a smooth stalk,
   Will never hurt your hand;
But the rose upon her briar
   Is lady of the land.

5   There's sweetness in an apple tree,
   And profit in the corn;
But lady of all beauty
   Is a rose upon a thorn.

When with moss and honey
10   She tips her bending briar,
And half unfolds her glowing heart,
   She sets the world on fire.

Hurt no living thing:
   Ladybird, nor butterfly,

Nor moth with dusty wing,
   Nor cricket chirping cheerily,
5   Nor grasshopper so light of leap,
   Nor dancing gnat, nor beetle fat,
Nor harmless worms that creep.

I caught a little ladybird
   That flies far away;
I caught a little lady wife
   That is both staid and gay.

5   Come back, my scarlet ladybird,
   Back from far away;
I weary of my dolly wife,
   My wife that cannot play.

She's such a senseless wooden thing
10   She stares the livelong day;
Her wig of gold is stiff and cold
   And cannot change to grey.

All the bells were ringing
And all the birds were singing,
When Molly sat down crying
   For her broken doll:
5   O you silly Moll!
Sobbing and sighing
   For a broken doll,
When all the bells are ringing,
And all the birds are singing.

Wee wee husband,
   Give me some money,
I have no comfits,
   And I have no honey.

5   Wee wee wifie,
   I have no money,

Milk, nor meat, nor bread to eat,
    Comfits, nor honey.

I have a little husband
    And he is gone to sea,
The winds that whistle round his ship
    Fly home to me.
5   The winds that sigh about me
    Return again to him;
So I would fly, if only I
    Were light of limb.

The dear old woman in the lane
    Is sick and sore with pains and aches,
We'll go to her this afternoon,
    And take her tea and eggs and cakes.
5   We'll stop to make the kettle boil,
    And brew some tea, and set the tray,
And poach an egg, and toast a cake,
    And wheel her chair round, if we may.

Swift and sure the swallow,
    Slow and sure the snail:
Slow and sure may miss his way,
    Swift and sure may fail.

"I dreamt I caught a little owl
    And the bird was blue—"

"But you may hunt for ever
And not find such an one."
5   "I dreamt I set a sunflower,
    And red as blood it grew—"

"But such a sunflower never
Bloomed beneath the sun."

What does the bee do?
　　Bring home honey.
And what does Father do?
　　Bring home money.
5　And what does Mother do?
　　Lay out the money.
And what does baby do?
　　Eat up the honey.

I have a Poll parrot,
　　And Poll is my doll,
And my nurse is Polly,
　　And my sister Poll.

5　"Polly!" cried Polly,
"Don't tear Polly dolly"—
While softhearted Poll
Trembled for the doll.

A house of cards
　　Is neat and small:
Shake the table,
　　It must fall.

5　Find the Court cards
　　One by one;
Raise it, roof it,—
　　Now it's done:—
Shake the table!
10　　That's the fun.

The rose with such a bonny blush,
　　What has the rose to blush about?
If it's the sun that makes her flush,
　　What's in the sun to flush about?

The rose that blushes rosy red,
　　She must hang her head;
The lily that blows spotless white,
　　She may stand upright.

Oh fair to see
Bloom-laden cherry tree,
　　Arrayed in sunny white;
　　An April day's delight,
5　Oh fair to see!

Oh fair to see
Fruit-laden cherry tree,
　　With balls of shining red
　　Decking a leafy head,
10　Oh fair to see!

Clever little Willie wee,
　　Bright eyed, blue eyed little fellow;
Merry little Margery
　　With her hair all yellow.

5　Little Willie in his heart
　　Is a sailor on the sea,
And he often cons a chart
　　With sister Margery.

The peach tree on the southern wall
　　Has basked so long beneath the sun,
Her score of peaches great and small
　　Bloom rosy, every one.

5　A peach for brothers, one for each,
　　A peach for you and a peach for me;
But the biggest, rosiest, downiest peach
　　For Grandmamma with her tea.

A rose has thorns as well as honey,
I'll not have her for love or money;
An iris grows so straight and fine,
That she shall be no friend of mine;
5   Snowdrops like the snow would chill me;
Nightshade would caress and kill me;
Crocus like a spear would fright me;
Dragon's-mouth might bark or bite me;
Convolvulus but blooms to die;
10   A wind-flower suggests a sigh;
Love-lies-bleeding makes me sad;
And poppy-juice would drive me mad:—
But give me holly, bold and jolly,
Honest, prickly, shining holly;
15   Pluck me holly leaf and berry
For the day when I make merry.

Is the moon tired? she looks so pale
Within her misty veil:
She scales the sky from east to west,
And takes no rest.

5   Before the coming of the night
The moon shows papery white;
Before the dawning of the day
She fades away.

If stars dropped out of heaven,
    And if flowers took their place,
The sky would still look very fair,
    And fair earth's face.

5   Winged Angels might fly down to us
    To pluck the stars,
But we could only long for flowers
    Beyond the cloudy bars.

Sing-Song: A Nursery Rhyme Book

"Goodbye in fear, goodbye in sorrow,
     Goodbye, and all in vain,
Never to meet again, my dear—"
     "Never to part again."
5   "Goodbye today, goodbye tomorrow,
     Goodbye till earth shall wane,
Never to meet again, my dear—"
     "Never to part again."

If the sun could tell us half
     That he hears and sees,
Sometimes he would make us laugh,
     Sometimes make us cry:
5   Think of all the birds that make
     Homes among the trees;
Think of cruel boys who take
     Bird that cannot fly.

If the moon came from heaven,
     Talking all the way,
What could she have to tell us,
     And what could she say?
5   "I've seen a hundred pretty things,
     And seen a hundred gay;
But only think: I peep by night
     And do not peep by day!"

O Lady Moon, your horns point toward the east:
          Shine, be increased;
O Lady Moon, your horns point toward the west:
          Wane, be at rest.

What do the stars do
     Up in the sky,

Higher than the wind can blow,
    Or the clouds can fly?

5   Each star in its own glory
        Circles, circles still;
    As it was lit to shine and set,
        And do its Maker's Will.

Motherless baby and babyless mother,
Bring them together to love one another.

Crimson curtains round my mother's bed,
    Silken soft as may be;
Cool white curtains round about my bed,
    For I am but a baby.

Baby lies so fast asleep
    That we cannot wake her:
Will the Angels clad in white
    Fly from heaven to take her?

5   Baby lies so fast asleep
        That no pain can grieve her;
    Put a snowdrop in her hand,
        Kiss her once and leave her.

I know a baby, such a baby,—
    Round blue eyes and cheeks of pink,
Such an elbow furrowed with dimples,
    Such a wrist where creases sink.

5   "Cuddle and love me, cuddle and love me"
        Crows the mouth of coral pink:
    Oh the bald head, and oh the sweet lips,
        And oh the sleepy eyes that wink!

        Lullaby, oh lullaby!
Flowers are closed and lambs are sleeping;
        Lullaby, oh lullaby!
Stars are up, the moon is peeping;
5   Lullaby, oh lullaby!
While the birds are silence keeping,
        (Lullaby, oh lullaby!)
Sleep, my baby, fall a-sleeping,
        Lullaby, oh lullaby!

Lie a-bed,
Sleepy head,
Shut up eyes, bo-peep;
Till daybreak
5 Never wake:—
Baby, sleep.

II Poems Added in
Sing-Song
A Nursery Rhyme Book
(1893)

Brownie, Brownie, let down your milk
White as swansdown and smooth as silk,
Fresh as dew and pure as snow:
For I know where the cowslips blow,
5   And you shall have a cowslip wreath
No sweeter scented than your breath.

Stroke a flint, and there is nothing to admire:
Strike a flint, and forthwith flash out sparks of fire.

I am a King,
   Or an Emperor rather,
I wear crown-imperial
   And prince's-feather;
5   Golden-rod is the sceptre
   I wield and wag,
And a broad purple flag flower
   Waves for my flag.

Elder the pithy
10   With old-man and sage,
These are my councillors
   Green in old age;
Lords-and-ladies in silence
   Stand round me and wait,
15 While gay ragged-robin
   Makes bows at my gate.

Playing at bob cherry
   Tom and Nell and Hugh:
Cherry bob! cherry bob!
   There's a bob for you.

5   Tom bobs a cherry
   For gaping snapping Hugh,
While curly-pated Nelly
   Snaps at it too.

Look, look, look—
10   Oh what a sight to see!
The wind is playing cherry bob
   With the cherry tree.

Blind from my birth,
Where flowers are springing
I sit on earth
All dark.
5   Hark! hark!
A lark is singing,
His notes are all for me,
For me his mirth:—
Till some day I shall see
10   Beautiful flowers
And birds in bowers
Where all Joy Bells are ringing.

III A Pageant and Other Poems

(1881)

Sonnets are full of love, and this my tome
  Has many sonnets: so here now shall be
  One sonnet more, a love sonnet, from me
To her whose heart is my heart's quiet home,
5   To my first Love, my Mother, on whose knee
I learnt love-lore that is not troublesome;
  Whose service is my special dignity,
And she my loadstar while I go and come.
And so because you love me, and because
10   I love you, Mother, I have woven a wreath
    Of rhymes wherewith to crown your honoured name:
    In you not fourscore years can dim the flame
Of love, whose blessed glow transcends the laws
  Of time and change and mortal life and death.

THE KEY-NOTE.

Where are the songs I used to know,
  Where are the notes I used to sing?
  I have forgotten everything
I used to know so long ago;
5 Summer has followed after Spring;
  Now Autumn is so shrunk and sere,
I scarcely think a sadder thing
  Can be the Winter of my year.

Yet Robin sings thro' Winter's rest,
10   When bushes put their berries on;
    While they their ruddy jewels don,
He sings out of a ruddy breast;

The hips and haws and ruddy breast
    Make one spot warm where snowflakes lie,
15 They break and cheer the unlovely rest
    Of Winter's pause—and why not I?

THE MONTHS:
A PAGEANT.

PERSONIFICATIONS.

Boys.	Girls.
JANUARY.	FEBRUARY.
MARCH.	APRIL.
JULY.	MAY.
AUGUST.	JUNE.
OCTOBER.	SEPTEMBER.
DECEMBER.	NOVEMBER.

ROBIN REDBREASTS; LAMBS AND SHEEP; NIGHTINGALE AND
NESTLINGS.

Various Flowers, Fruits, etc.

Scene: A COTTAGE WITH ITS GROUNDS.

[A room in a large comfortable cottage; a fire burning on the
   hearth; a table on which the breakfast things have been left
   standing. January discovered seated by the fire.]

   JANUARY.

Cold the day and cold the drifted snow,
Dim the day until the cold dark night.

                                [Stirs the fire.

Crackle, sparkle, faggot; embers glow:
Some one may be plodding thro' the snow
5 Longing for a light,
For the light that you and I can show.
If no one else should come,
Here Robin Redbreast's welcome to a crumb,
And never troublesome:
10 Robin, why don't you come and fetch your crumb?

Here's butter for my hunch of bread,
   And sugar for your crumb;
Here's room upon the hearthrug,
   If you'll only come.

15   In your scarlet waistcoat,
   With your keen bright eye,
Where are you loitering?
   Wings were made to fly!

Make haste to breakfast,
20   Come and fetch your crumb,
For I'm as glad to see you
   As you are glad to come.

[Two Robin Redbreasts are seen tapping with their beaks at the lattice, which January opens. The birds flutter in, hop about the floor, and peck up the crumbs and sugar thrown to them. They have scarcely finished their meal, when a knock is heard at the door. January hangs a guard in front of the fire, and opens to February, who appears with a bunch of snowdrops in her hand.]

JANUARY.

Good-morrow, sister.

FEBRUARY.

                Brother, joy to you!
25 I've brought some snowdrops; only just a few,
But quite enough to prove the world awake,
Cheerful and hopeful in the frosty dew
   And for the pale sun's sake.

[She hands a few of her snowdrops to January, who retires into the background. While February stands arranging the remaining snowdrops in a glass of water on the window-sill, a soft butting and bleating are heard outside. She opens the door, and sees one foremost lamb, with other sheep and lambs bleating and crowding towards her.]

FEBRUARY.

O you, you little wonder, come—come in,
30 You wonderful, you woolly soft white lamb:
You panting mother ewe, come too,
And lead that tottering twin
Safe in:
Bring all your bleating kith and kin,
35 Except the horny ram.

[February opens a second door in the background, and
    the little flock files thro' into a warm and sheltered
    compartment out of sight.]

The lambkin tottering in its walk
    With just a fleece to wear;
The snowdrop drooping on its stalk
    So slender,—
40 Snowdrop and lamb, a pretty pair,
Braving the cold for our delight,
    Both white,
    Both tender.

[A rattling of doors and windows; branches seen without,
    tossing violently to and fro.]

How the doors rattle, and the branches sway!
45 Here's brother March comes whirling on his way
With winds that eddy and sing:—

[She turns the handle of the door, which bursts open, and
    discloses March hastening up, both hands full of violets
    and anemones.]

FEBRUARY.

Come, show me what you bring;
For I have said my say, fulfilled my day,
And must away.

MARCH.

[Stopping short on the threshold.]

50   I blow an arouse
        Thro' the world's wide house
        To quicken the torpid earth:
        Grappling I fling
        Each feeble thing,
55   But bring strong life to the birth.
        I wrestle and frown,
        And topple down;
        I wrench, I rend, I uproot;
        Yet the violet
60   Is born where I set
        The sole of my flying foot,

[Hands violets and anemones to February, who retires into the
    background.]

        And in my wake
        Frail windflowers quake,
        And the catkins promise fruit.
65   I drive ocean ashore
        With rush and roar,
        And he cannot say me nay:
        My harpstrings all
        Are the forests tall,
70   Making music when I play.
        And as others perforce,
        So I on my course
        Run and needs must run,
        With sap on the mount
75   And buds past count
        And rivers and clouds and sun,
        With seasons and breath
        And time and death
        And all that has yet begun.

[Before March has done speaking, a voice is heard
    approaching accompanied by a twittering of birds. April
    comes along singing, and stands outside and out of sight
    to finish her song.]

APRIL.

[Outside.]

80   Pretty little three
        Sparrows in a tree,
            Light upon the wing;
            Tho' you cannot sing
            You can chirp of Spring:
85   Chirp of Spring to me,
        Sparrows, from your tree.

        Never mind the showers,
        Chirp about the flowers
            While you build a nest:
90   Straws from east and west,
            Feathers from your breast,
        Make the snuggest bowers
        In a world of flowers.

        You must dart away
95   From the chosen spray,
            You intrusive third
            Extra little bird;
            Join the unwedded herd!
        These have done with play,
100   And must work today.

    APRIL.

[Appearing at the open door.]

Good-morrow and good-bye: if others fly,
Of all the flying months you're the most flying.

    MARCH.

You're hope and sweetness, April.

APRIL.

Birth means dying,

105 As wings and wind mean flying;
So you and I and all things fly or die;
And sometimes I sit sighing to think of dying.
But meanwhile I've a rainbow in my showers,
And a lapful of flowers,
110 And these dear nestlings aged three hours;
And here's their mother sitting,
Their father's merely flitting
To find their breakfast somewhere in my bowers.

[As she speaks April shows March her apron full of flowers
and nest full of birds. March wanders away into the grounds.
April, without entering the cottage, hangs over the hungry
nestlings watching them.]

APRIL.

What beaks you have, you funny things,
115   What voices shrill and weak;
Who'd think that anything that sings
   Could sing thro' such a beak?
Yet you'll be nightingales one day,
   And charm the country side,
120 When I'm away and far away
   And May is queen and bride.

[May arrives unperceived by April, and gives her a kiss. April
starts and looks round.]

APRIL.

Ah May, good-morrow May, and so good-bye.

MAY.

That's just your way, sweet April, smile and sigh:
Your sorrow's half in fun,

125 Begun and done
And turned to joy while twenty seconds run.
I've gathered flowers all as I came along,
At every step a flower
Fed by your last bright shower,—

[She divides an armful of all sorts of flowers with April, who
strolls away thro' the garden.]

MAY.

130 And gathering flowers I listened to the song
Of every bird in bower.

The world and I are far too full of bliss
To think or plan or toil or care;
The sun is waxing strong,
135 The days are waxing long,
And all that is,
Is fair.

Here are my buds of lily and of rose,
And here's my namesake blossom may;
140 And from a watery spot
See here forget-me-not,
With all that blows
Today.

Hark to my linnets from the hedges green,
145 Blackbird and lark and thrush and dove,
And every nightingale
And cuckoo tells its tale,
And all they mean
Is love.

[June appears at the further end of the garden, coming
slowly towards May, who, seeing her, exclaims]

MAY.

150 Surely you're come too early, sister June.

JUNE.

Indeed I feel as if I came too soon
To round your young May moon
And set the world a-gasping at my noon.
Yet come I must. So here are strawberries
155   Sun-flushed and sweet, as many as you please;
And here are full-blown roses by the score,
More roses, and yet more.

[May, eating strawberries, withdraws among the flower beds.]

JUNE.

The sun does all my long day's work for me,
   Raises and ripens everything;
160   I need but sit beneath a leafy tree
      And watch and sing.

            [Seats herself in the shadow of a laburnum.

Or if I'm lulled by note of bird and bee,
   Or lulled by noontide's silence deep,
I need but nestle down beneath my tree
165   And drop asleep.

[June falls asleep; and is not awakened by the voice of July,
   who behind the scenes is heard half singing, half calling.]

JULY.

[Behind the scenes.]

Blue flags, yellow flags, flags all freckled,
Which will you take? yellow, blue, speckled!
Take which you will, speckled, blue, yellow,
Each in its way has not a fellow.

[Enter July, a basket of many-coloured irises slung upon his
   shoulders, a bunch of ripe grass in one hand, and a plate
   piled full of peaches balanced upon the other. He steals up
   to June, and tickles her with the grass. She wakes.]

JUNE.

170 What, here already?

JULY.

Nay, my tryst is kept;
The longest day slipped by you while you slept.
I've brought you one curved pyramid of bloom,

[Hands her the plate.

Not flowers but peaches, gathered where the bees,
175 As downy, bask and boom
In sunshine and in gloom of trees.
But get you in, a storm is at my heels;
The whirlwind whistles and wheels,
Lightning flashes and thunder peals,
180 Flying and following hard upon my heels.

[June takes shelter in a thickly-woven arbour.]

JULY.

The roar of a storm sweeps up
    From the east to the lurid west,
The darkening sky, like a cup,
    Is filled with rain to the brink;
185 The sky is purple and fire,
    Blackness and noise and unrest;
The earth, parched with desire,
    Opens her mouth to drink.

Send forth thy thunder and fire,
190   Turn over thy brimming cup,
O sky, appease the desire
    Of earth in her parched unrest;
Pour out drink to her thrist,
    Her famishing life lift up;
195 Make thyself fair as at first,
    With a rainbow for thy crest.

Have done with thunder and fire,
    O sky with the rainbow crest;
O earth, have done with desire,
200   Drink, and drink deep, and rest.

[Enter August, carrying a sheaf made up of different kinds of grain.]

JULY.

Hail, brother August, flushed and warm
And scatheless from my storm.
Your hands are full of corn, I see,
As full as hands can be:
205 And earth and air both smell as sweet as balm
In their recovered calm,
And that they owe to me.

[July retires into a shrubbery.]

AUGUST.

Wheat sways heavy, oats are airy,
    Barley bows a graceful head,
210   Short and small shoots up canary,
    Each of these is some one's bread;
Bread for man or bread for beast,
    Or at very least
    A bird's savoury feast.

215 Men are brethren of each other,
    One in flesh and one in food;
And a sort of foster brother
    Is the litter, or the brood,
Of that folk in fur or feather,
220   Who, with men together,
    Breast the wind and weather.

[August descries September toiling across the lawn.]

AUGUST.

My harvest home is ended; and I spy
September drawing nigh
With the first thought of Autumn in her eye,
225   And the first sigh
Of Autumn wind among her locks that fly.

[September arrives, carrying upon her head a basket heaped
    high with fruit.]

SEPTEMBER.

Unload me, brother. I have brought a few
Plums and these pears for you,
A dozen kinds of apples, one or two
230   Melons, some figs all bursting thro'
Their skins, and pearled with dew
These damsons violet-blue.

[While September is speaking, August lifts the basket to the
    ground, selects various fruits, and withdraws slowly along
    the gravel walk, eating a pear as he goes.]

SEPTEMBER.

        My song is half a sigh
        Because my green leaves die;
235   Sweet are my fruits, but all my leaves are dying;
            And well may Autumn sigh,
                And well may I
        Who watch the sere leaves flying.

        My leaves that fade and fall,
240   I note you one and all;
        I call you, and the Autumn wind is calling,
            Lamenting for your fall,
                And for the pall
        You spread on earth in falling.

245   And here's a song of flowers to suit such hours:
        A song of the last lilies, the last flowers,
        Amid my withering bowers.

In the sunny garden bed
　　Lilies look so pale,
250　Lilies droop the head
　　In the shady grassy vale;
If all alike they pine
In shade and in shine,
If everywhere they grieve,
255　Where will lilies live?

[October enters briskly, some leafy twigs bearing different
sorts of nuts in one hand, and a long ripe hop-bine trailing
after him from the other. A dahlia is stuck in his bottonhole.]

OCTOBER.

Nay, cheer up sister. Life is not quite over,
Even if the year has done with corn and clover,
With flowers and leaves; besides, in fact it's true,
Some leaves remain and some flowers too,
260　For me and you.
Now see my crops:

　　　　　　[Offering his produce to September.

　　　　I've brought you nuts and hops;
And when the leaf drops, why, the walnut drops.

[October wreaths the hop-bine about September's neck, and
gives her the nut twigs. They enter the cottage together, but
without shutting the door. She steps into the background:
he advances to the hearth, removes the guard, stirs up the
smouldering fire, and arranges several chestnuts ready to
roast.]

OCTOBER.

Crack your first nut and light your first fire,
265　Roast your first chestnut crisp on the bar;
Make the logs sparkle, stir the blaze higher,
　　Logs are cheery as sun or as star,
　　Logs we can find wherever we are.

Spring one soft day will open the leaves,
270   `Spring one bright day will lure back the flowers;
Never fancy my whistling wind grieves,
    Never fancy I've tears in my showers;
    Dance, nights and days! and dance on, my hours!

                      [Sees November approaching.

OCTOBER.

Here comes my youngest sister, looking dim
275   And grim,
With dismal ways.
What cheer, November?

NOVEMBER.

[Entering and shutting the door.]

Nought have I to bring
Tramping a-chill and shivering,
280   Except these pine-cones for a blaze,—
Except a fog which follows,
And stuffs up all the hollows,—
Except a hoar frost here and there,—
Except some shooting stars
285   Which dart their luminous cars
Trackless and noiseless thro' the keen night air.

[October, shrugging his shoulders, withdraws into the
    background, while November throws her pine cones
    on the fire, and sits down listlessly.]

NOVEMBER.

    The earth lies fast asleep, grown tired
        Of all that's high or deep;
    There's nought desired and nought required
290   Save a sleep.

    I rock the cradle of the earth,
        I lull her with a sigh;

And know that she will wake to mirth
  By and by.

[Thro' the window December is seen running and leaping in
  the direction of the door. He knocks.]

NOVEMBER.

[Calls out without rising.]

295   Ah, here's my youngest brother come at last:
Come in, December.

[He opens the door and enters, loaded with evergreens in
  berry, etc.]

NOVEMBER.

                    Come, and shut the door,
For now it's snowing fast;
It snows, and will snow more and more;
300   Don't let it drift in on the floor.
But you, you're all aglow; how can you be
Rosy and warm and smiling in the cold?

DECEMBER.

Nay, no closed doors for me,
But open doors and open hearts and glee
305   To welcome young and old.
    Dimmest and brightest month am I;
My short days end, my lengthening days begin;
What matters more or less sun in the sky,
    When all is sun within?

                    [He begins making a wreath as he sings.

310   Ivy and privet dark as night,
I weave with hips and haws a cheerful show,
And holly for a beauty and delight,
    And milky mistletoe.

While high above them all I set
315 Yew twigs and Christmas roses pure and pale;
Then Spring her snowdrop and her violet
    May keep, so sweet and frail;

May keep each merry singing bird,
Of all her happy birds that singing build:
320 For I've a carol which some shepherds heard
    Once in a wintry field.

[While December concludes his song all the other Months
troop in from the garden, or advance out of the background.
The Twelve join hands in a circle, and begin dancing round
to a stately measure as the Curtain falls.]

PASTIME.

A boat amid the ripples, drifting, rocking,
    Two idle people, without pause or aim;
While in the ominous west there gathers darkness
    Flushed with flame.

5 A haycock in a hayfield backing, lapping,
    Two drowsy people pillowed round about;
While in the ominous west across the darkness
    Flame leaps out.

Better a wrecked life than a life so aimless,
10   Better a wrecked life than a life so soft;
The ominous west glooms thundering, with its fire
    Lit aloft.

"ITALIA, IO TI SALUTO!"

To come back from the sweet South, to the North
    Where I was born, bred, look to die;
Come back to do my day's work in its day,
    Play out my play—
5   Amen, amen, say I.

To see no more the country half my own,
　　Nor hear the half familiar speech,
Amen, I say; I turn to that bleak North
　　　Whence I came forth—
10　　The South lies out of reach.

But when our swallows fly back to the South,
　　To the sweet South, to the sweet South,
The tears may come again into my eyes
　　　On the old wise,
15　　And the sweet name to my mouth.

MIRRORS OF LIFE AND DEATH.

The mystery of Life, the mystery
Of Death, I see
Darkly as in a glass;
Their shadows pass,
5　And talk with me.

As the flush of a Morning Sky,
As a Morning Sky colourless—
Each yields its measure of light
To a wet world or a dry;
10　Each fares thro' day to night
With equal pace,
And then each one
Is done.

As the Sun with glory and grace
15　In his face,
Benignantly hot,
Graciously radiant and keen,
Ready to rise and to run,—
Not without spot,
20　Not even the Sun.

As the Moon
On the wax, on the wane,
With night for her noon;

Vanishing soon,
25   To appear again.

As Roses that droop
Half warm, half chill, in the languid May,
And breathe out a scent
Sweet and faint;
30   Till the wind gives one swoop
To scatter their beauty away.

As Lilies a multitude,
One dipping, one rising, one sinking,
On rippling waters, clear blue
35   And pure for their drinking;
One new dead, and one opened anew,
And all good.

As a cankered pale Flower,
With death for a dower,
40   Each hour of its life half dead;
With death for a crown
Weighing down
Its head.

As an Eagle, half strength and half grace,
45   Most potent to face
Unwinking the splendour of light;
Harrying the East and the West,
Soaring aloft from our sight;
Yet one day or one night dropped to rest,
50   On the low common earth
Of his birth.

As a Dove,
Not alone,
In a world of her own
55   Full of fluttering soft noises
And tender sweet voices
Of love.

As a Mouse
Keeping house

60 In the fork of a tree,
    With nuts in a crevice,
    And an acorn or two;
    What cares he
    For blossoming boughs,
65 Or the song-singing bevies
    Of birds in their glee,
    Scarlet, or golden, or blue?

    As a Mole grubbing underground;
    When it comes to the light
70 It grubs its way back again,
    Feeling no bias of fur
    To hamper it in its stir,
    Scant of pleasure and pain,
    Sinking itself out of sight
75 Without sound.

    As Waters that drop and drop,
    Weariness without end,
    That drop and never stop,
    Wear that nothing can mend,
80 Till one day they drop—
    Stop—
    And there's an end,
    And matters mend.

    As Trees, beneath whose skin
85 We mark not the sap begin
    To swell and rise,
    Till the whole bursts out in green:
    We mark the falling leaves
    When the wide world grieves
90 And sighs.

    As a Forest on fire,
    Where maddened creatures desire
    Wet mud or wings
    Beyond all those things
95 Which could assauge desire
    On this side the flaming fire.

As Wind with a sob and sigh
To which there comes no reply
But a rustle and shiver
100 From rushes of the river;
As Wind with a desolate moan,
Moaning on alone.

As a Desert all sand,
Blank, neither water nor land
105 For solace, or dwelling, or culture,
Where the storms and the wild creatures howl;
Given over to lion and vulture,
To ostrich, and jackal, and owl:
Yet somewhere an oasis lies;
110 There waters arise
To nourish one seedling of balm,
Perhaps, or one palm.

As the Sea,
Murmuring, shifting, swaying;
115 One time sunnily playing,
One time wrecking and slaying;
In whichever mood it be,
Worst or best,
Never at rest.

120 As still Waters and deep,
As shallow Waters that brawl,
As rapid Waters that leap
To their fall.

As Music, as Colour, as Shape,
125 Keys of rapture and pain
Turning in vain
In a lock which turns not again,
While breaths and moments escape.

As Spring, all bloom and desire;
130 As Summer, all gift and fire;
As Autumn, a dying glow;
As Winter, with nought to show:

Winter which lays its dead all out of sight,
All clothed in white,
135 All waiting for the long-awaited light.

A BALLAD OF BODING.

There are sleeping dreams and waking dreams;
What seems is not always as it seems.

I looked out of my window in the sweet new morning,
And there I saw three barges of manifold adorning
5 Went sailing toward the East:
The first had sails like fire,
The next like glittering wire,
But sackcloth were the sails of the least;
And all the crews made music, and two had spread a
        feast.

10 The first choir breathed in flutes,
And fingered soft guitars;
The second won from lutes
Harmonious chords and jars,
With drums for stormy bars:
15 But the third was all of harpers and scarlet trumpeters;
Notes of triumph, then
An alarm again,
As for onset, as for victory, rallies, stirs,
Peace at last and glory to the vanquishers.

20 The first barge showed for figurehead a Love with wings;
The second showed for figurehead a Worm with stings;
The third, a Lily tangled to a Rose which clings.
The first bore for freight gold and spice and down;
The second bore a sword, a sceptre, and a crown;
25 The third, a heap of earth gone to dust and brown.
Winged Love meseemed like Folly in the face;
Stinged Worm meseemed loathly in his place;
Lily and Rose were flowers of grace.

Merry went the revel of the fire-sailed crew,
30 Singing, feasting, dancing to and fro:
Pleasures ever changing, ever graceful, ever new;
Sighs, but scarce of woe;
All the sighing
Wooed such sweet replying;
35 All the sighing, sweet and low,
Used to come and go
For more pleasure, merely so.
Yet at intervals some one grew tired
Of everything desired,
40 And sank, I knew not whither, in sorry plight,
Out of sight.

The second crew seemed ever
Wider-visioned, graver,
More distinct of purpose, more sustained of will;
45 With heads erect and proud,
And voices sometimes loud;
With endless tacking, counter-tacking,
All things grasping, all things lacking,
It would seem;
50 Ever shifting helm, or sail, or shroud,
Drifting on as in a dream.
Hoarding to their utmost bent,
Feasting to their fill,
Yet gnawed by discontent,
55 Envy, hatred, malice, on their road they went.
Their freight was not a treasure,
Their music not a pleasure;
The sword flashed, cleaving thro' their bands,
Sceptre and crown changed hands.

60 The third crew as they went
Seemed mostly different;
They toiled in rowing, for to them the wind was contrary,
As all the world might see.
They laboured at the oar,
65 While on their heads they bore
The fiery stress of sunshine more and more.

They laboured at the oar hand-sore,
Till rain went splashing,
And spray went dashing,
70   Down on them, and up on them, more and more.
They sails were patched and rent,
Their masts were bent,
In peril of their lives they worked and went.
For them no feast was spread,
75   No soft luxurious bed
Scented and white,
No crown or sceptre hung in sight;
In weariness and painfulness,
In thirst and sore distress,
80   They rowed and steered from left to right
With all their might.
Their trumpeters and harpers round about
Incessantly played out,
And sometimes they made answer with a shout;
85   But oftener they groaned or wept,
And seldom paused to eat, and seldom slept.
I wept for pity watching them, but more
I wept heart-sore
Once and again to see
90   Some weary man plunge overboard, and swim
To Love or Worm ship floating buoyantly:
And there all welcomed him.

The ships steered each apart and seemed to scorn each
            other,
Yet all the crews were interchangeable;
95   Now one man, now another,
—Like bloodless spectres some, some flushed by health,—
Changed openly, or changed by stealth,
Scaling a slippery side, and scaled it well.
The most left Love ship, hauling wealth
100   Up Worm ship's side;
While some few hollow-eyed
Left either for the sack-sailed boat;
But this, tho' not remote,

Was worst to mount, and whoso left it once
105   Scarce ever came again,
But seemed to loathe his erst companions,
And wish and work them bane.

Then I knew (I know not how) there lurked quicksands
            full of dread,
Rocks and reefs and whirlpools in the water bed,
110   Whence a waterspout
Instantaneously leaped out,
Roaring as it reared its head.
Soon I spied a something dim,
Many-handed, grim,
115   That went flitting to and fro the first and second ship;
It puffed their sails full out
With puffs of smoky breath
From a smouldering lip,
And cleared the waterspout
120   Which reeled roaring round about
Threatening death.
With a horny hand it steered,
And a horn appeared
On its sneering head upreared
125   Haughty and high
Against the blackening lowering sky.
With a hoof it swayed the waves;
They opened here and there,
Till I spied deep ocean graves
130   Full of skeletons
That were men and women once
Foul or fair;
Full of things that creep
And fester in the deep
135   And never breathe the clean life-nurturing air.

The third bark held aloof
From the Monster with the hoof,
Despite his urgent beck,
And fraught with guile
140   Abominable his smile;

Till I saw him take a flying leap on to that deck.
Then full of awe,
With these same eyes I saw
His head incredible retract its horn
145   Rounding like babe's new born,
While silvery phosphorescence played
About his dis-horned head.
The sneer smoothed from his lip,
He beamed blandly on the ship;
150   All winds sank to a moan,
All waves to a monotone
(For all these seemed his realm),
While he laid a strong caressing hand upon the helm.

Then a cry well nigh of despair
155   Shrieked to heaven, a clamour of desperate prayer.
The harpers harped no more,
While the trumpeters sounded sore,
An alarm to wake the dead from their bed:
To the rescue, to the rescue, now or never,
160   To the rescue, O ye living, O ye dead,
Or no more help or hope for ever!—
The planks strained as tho' they must part asunder,
The masts bent as tho' they must dip under,
And the winds and the waves at length
165   Girt up their strength,
And the depths were laid bare,
And heaven flashed fire and volleyed thunder
Thro' the rain-choked air,
And sea and sky seemed to kiss
170   In the horror and the hiss
Of the whole world shuddering everywhere.

Lo! a Flyer swooping down
With wings to span the globe,
And splendour for his robe
175   And splendour for his crown.
He lighted on the helm with a foot of fire,
And spun the Monster overboard:
And that monstrous thing abhorred,

Gnashing with balked desire,
180 Wriggled like a worm infirm
Up the Worm
Of the loathly figurehead.
There he crouched and gnashed;
And his head re-horned, and gashed
185 From the other's grapple, dripped bloody red.

I saw that thing accurst
Wreak his worst
On the first and second crew:
Some with baited hook
190 He angled for and took,
Some dragged overboard in a net he threw,
Some he did to death
With hoof or horn or blasting breath.

I heard a voice of wailing
195 Where the ships went sailing,
A sorrowful voice prevailing
Above the sound of the sea,
Above the singers' voices,
And musical merry noises;
200 All songs had turned to sighing,
The light was failing,
The day was dying—
Ah me,
That such a sorrow should be!

205 There was sorrow on the sea and sorrow on the land
When Love ship went down by the bottomless quicksand
To its grave in the bitter wave.
There was sorrow on the sea and sorrow on the land
When Worm ship went to pieces on the rock-bound
strand,
210 And the bitter wave was its grave.
But land and sea waxed hoary
In whiteness of a glory
Never told in story
Nor seen by mortal eye,
215 When the third ship crossed the bar

Where whirls and breakers are,
And steered into the splendours of the sky;
That third bark and that least
Which had never seemed to feast,
220 Yet kept high festival above sun and moon and star.

YET A LITTLE WHILE.

I dreamed and did not seek: today I seek
     Who can no longer dream;
But now am all behindhand, waxen weak,
     And dazed amid so many things that gleam
5   Yet are not what they seem.

I dreamed and did not work: today I work
     Kept wide awake by care
And loss, and perils dimly guessed to lurk;
     I work and reap not, while my life goes bare
10   And void in wintry air.

I hope indeed; but hope itself is fear
     Viewed on the sunny side;
I hope, and disregard the world that's here,
     The prizes drawn, the sweet things that betide;
15   I hope, and I abide.

HE AND SHE.

"Should one of us remember,
     And one of us forget,
I wish I knew what each will do—
     But who can tell as yet?"

5   "Should one of us remember,
     And one of us forget,
I promise you what I will do—
And I'm content to wait for you,
     And not be sure as yet."

MONNA INNOMINATA.
A SONNET OF SONNETS.

Beatrice, immortalized by "altissimo poeta . . . cotanto
amante"; Laura, celebrated by a great tho' an inferior bard,—
have alike paid the exceptional penalty of exceptional honour,
and have come down to us resplendent with charms, but (at
least, to my apprehension) scant of attractiveness.

These heroines of world-wide fame were preceded by a
bevy of unnamed ladies "donne innominate" sung by a school
of less conspicuous poets; and in that land and that period
which gave simultaneous birth to Catholics, to Albigenses,
and to Troubadours, one can imagine many a lady as sharing
her lover's poetic aptitude, while the barrier between them
might be one held sacred by both, yet not such as to render
mutual love incompatible with mutual honour.

Had such a lady spoken for herself, the portrait left us
might have appeared more tender, if less dignified, than any
drawn even by a devoted friend. Or had the Great Poetess of
our own day and nation only been unhappy instead of happy,
her circumstances would have invited her to bequeath to us,
in lieu of the "Portuguese Sonnets," an inimitable "donna
innominata" drawn not from fancy but from feeling, and
worthy to occupy a niche beside Beatrice and Laura.

I.

"Lo dì che han detto a' dolci amici addio."—DANTE.
"Amor, con quanto sforzo oggi mi vinci!"—PETRARCA.

Come back to me, who wait and watch for you:—
   Or come not yet, for it is over then,
   And long it is before you come again,
So far between my pleasures are and few.
5 While, when you come not, what I do I do
   Thinking "Now when he comes," my sweetest "when:"
   For one man is my world of all the men
This wide world holds; O love, my world is you.
Howbeit, to meet you grows almost a pang
10 Because the pang of parting comes so soon;

My hope hangs waning, waxing, like a moon
    Between the heavenly days on which we meet:
Ah me, but where are now the songs I sang
    When life was sweet because you called them sweet?

2.

"Era già l'ora che volge il desio."—DANTE.
"Ricorro al tempo ch'io vi vidi prima."—PETRARCA.

I wish I could remember, that first day,
    First hour, first moment of your meeting me,
    If bright or dim the season, it might be
Summer or Winter for aught I can say;
5   So unrecorded did it slip away,
    So blind was I to see and to foresee,
    So dull to mark the budding of my tree
That would not blossom yet for many a May.
If only I could recollect it, such
10   A day of days! I let it come and go
    As traceless as a thaw of bygone snow;
It seemed to mean so little, meant so much;
If only now I could recall that touch,
    First touch of hand in hand—Did one but know!

3.

"O ombre vane, fuor che ne l'aspetto!"—DANTE.
"Immaginata guida la conduce."—PETRARCA.

I dream of you to wake: would that I might
    Dream of you and not wake but slumber on;
    Nor find with dreams the dear companion gone,
As Summer ended Summer birds take flight.
5   In happy dreams I hold you full in sight,
    I blush again who waking look so wan;
    Brighter than sunniest day that ever shone,
In happy dreams your smile makes day of night.
Thus only in a dream we are at one,
10   Thus only in a dream we give and take
    The faith that maketh rich who take or give;

If thus to sleep is sweeter than to wake,
    To die were surely sweeter than to live,
Tho' there be nothing new beneath the sun.

    4.

    "Poca favilla gran fiamma seconda."—DANTE.
    "Ogni altra cosa, ogni pensier va fore,
      E sol ivi con voi rimansi amore."—PETRARCA.

I loved you first: but afterwards your love
    Outsoaring mine, sang such a loftier song
As drowned the friendly cooings of my dove.
    Which owes the other most? my love was long,
5   And yours one moment seemed to wax more strong;
I loved and guessed at you, you construed me
And loved me for what might or might not be—
    Nay, weights and measures do us both a wrong.
For verily love knows not "mine" or "thine;"
10   With separate "I" and "thou" free love has done,
    For one is both and both are one in love:
Rich love knows nought of "thine that is not mine;"
    Both have the strength and both the length thereof,
Both of us, of the love which makes us one.

    5.

    "Amor che a nulla amato amar perdona."—DANTE.
    "Amor m'addusse in sì gioiosa spene."—PETRARCA.

O my heart's heart, and you who are to me
    More than myself myself, God be with you,
    Keep you in strong obedience leal and true
To Him whose noble service setteth free,
5   Give you all good we see or can foresee,
    Make your joys many and your sorrows few,
    Bless you in what you bear and what you do,
Yea, perfect you as He would have you be.
So much for you; but what for me, dear friend?
10   To love you without stint and all I can

Today, tomorrow, world without an end;
   To love you much and yet to love you more,
   As Jordan at his flood sweeps either shore;
Since woman is the helpmeet made for man.

6.

"Or puoi la quantitate
Comprender de l'amor che a te mi scalda."—DANTE.
"Non vo'che da tal nodo amor mi scioglia."—PETRARCA.

Trust me, I have not earned your dear rebuke,
   I love, as you would have me, God the most;
   Would lose not Him, but you, must one be lost,
Nor with Lot's wife cast back a faithless look
5   Unready to forego what I forsook;
   This say I, having counted up the cost,
   This, tho' I be the feeblest of God's host,
The sorriest sheep Christ shepherds with His crook.
Yet while I love my God the most, I deem
10   That I can never love you overmuch;
   I love Him more, so let me love you too;
   Yea, as I apprehend it, love is such
I cannot love you if I love not Him,
   I cannot love Him if I love not you.

7.

"Qui primavera sempre ed ogni frutto."—DANTE.
"Ragionando con meco ed io con lui."—PETRARCA.

"Love me, for I love you"—and answer me,
   "Love me, for I love you"—so shall we stand
   As happy equals in the flowering land
Of love, that knows not a dividing sea.
5   Love builds the house on rock and not on sand,
   Love laughs what while the winds rave desperately;
And who hath found love's citadel unmanned?
   And who hath held in bonds love's liberty?
My heart's a coward tho' my words are brave—

10 We meet so seldom, yet we surely part
  So often; there's a problem for your art!
   Still I find comfort in his Book, who saith,
  Tho' jealousy be cruel as the grave,
   And death be strong, yet love is strong as death.

8.

"Come dicesse a Dio: D'altro non calme."—Dante.
"Spero trovar pietà non che perdono."—Petrarca.

"I, if I perish, perish"—Esther spake:
  And bride of life or death she made her fair
  In all the lustre of her perfumed hair
 And smiles that kindle longing but to slake.
5 She put on pomp of loveliness, to take
  Her husband thro' his eyes at unaware;
  She spread abroad her beauty for a snare,
 Harmless as doves and subtle as a snake.
 She trapped him with one mesh of silken hair,
10 She vanquished him by wisdom of her wit,
   And built her people's house that it should stand:—
   If I might take my life so in my hand,
 And for my love to Love put up my prayer,
 And for love's sake by Love be granted it!

9.

"O dignitosa coscienza e netta!"—Dante.
"Spirto più acceso di virtuti ardenti."—Petrarca.

Thinking of you, and all that was, and all
  That might have been and now can never be,
  I feel your honoured excellence, and see
 Myself unworthy of the happier call:
5 For woe is me who walk so apt to fall,
  So apt to shrink afraid, so apt to flee,
  Apt to lie down and die (ah, woe is me!)
 Faithless and hopeless turning to the wall.
 And yet not hopeless quite nor faithless quite,

10   Because not loveless; love may toil all night,
             But take at morning; wrestle till the break
                 Of day, but then wield power with God and man:—
                 So take I heart of grace as best I can,
             Ready to spend and be spent for your sake.

             10.
             "Con miglior corso e con migliore stella."—DANTE.
             "La vita fugge e non s'arresta un' ora."—PETRARCA.

         Time flies, hope flags, life plies a wearied wing;
             Death following hard on life gains ground apace;
             Faith runs with each and rears an eager face,
         Outruns the rest, makes light of everything,
5   Spurns earth, and still finds breath to pray and sing;
             While love ahead of all uplifts his praise,
             Still asks for grace and still gives thanks for grace,
         Content with all day brings and night will bring.
         Life wanes; and when love folds his wings above
10   Tired hope, and less we feel his conscious pulse,
                 Let us go fall asleep, dear friend, in peace:
                 A little while, and age and sorrow cease;
             A little while, and life reborn annuls
         Loss and decay and death, and all is love.

             11.
             "Vien dietro a me e lascia dir le genti."—DANTE.
             "Contando i casi della vita nostra."—PETRARCA.

         Many in aftertimes will say of you
             "He loved her"—while of me what will they say?
             Not that I loved you more than just in play,
         For fashion's sake as idle women do.
5   Even let them prate; who know not what we knew
             Of love and parting in exceeding pain,
             Of parting hopeless here to meet again,
         Hopeless on earth, and heaven is out of view.
         But by my heart of love laid bare to you,

10   My love that you can make not void nor vain,
     Love that foregoes you but to claim anew
        Beyond this passage of the gate of death,
        I charge you at the Judgment make it plain
        My love of you was life and not a breath.

        12.

     "Amor, che ne la mente mi ragiona."—DANTE.
     "Amor vien nel bel viso di costei."—PETRARCA.

     If there be any one can take my place
        And make you happy whom I grieve to grieve,
        Think not that I can grudge it, but believe
     I do commend you to that nobler grace,
5   That readier wit than mine, that sweeter face;
        Yea, since your riches make me rich, conceive
        I too am crowned, while bridal crowns I weave,
     And thread the bridal dance with jocund pace.
     For if I did not love you, it might be
10   That I should grudge you some one dear delight;
        But since the heart is yours that was mine own,
        Your pleasure is my pleasure, right my right,
     Your honourable freedom makes me free,
        And you companioned I am not alone.

        13.

     "E drizzeremo glí occhi al Primo Amore."—DANTE.
     "Ma trovo peso non da le mie braccia."—PETRARCA.

     If I could trust mine own self with your fate,
        Shall I not rather trust it in God's hand?
        Without Whose Will one lily doth not stand,
     Nor sparrow fall at his appointed date;
5   Who numbereth the innumerable sand,
     Who weighs the wind and water with a weight,
     To Whom the world is neither small nor great,
        Whose knowledge foreknew every plan we planned.
     Searching my heart for all that touches you,
10   I find there only love and love's goodwill

Helpless to help and impotent to do,
    Of understanding dull, of sight most dim;
    And therefore I commend you back to Him
Whose love your love's capacity can fill.

    14.

    "E la Sua Volontade è nostra pace."—DANTE.
    "Sol con questi pensier, con altre chiome."—PETRARCA.

Youth gone, and beauty gone if ever there
    Dwelt beauty in so poor a face as this;
    Youth gone and beauty, what remains of bliss?
I will not bind fresh roses in my hair,
5   To shame a cheek at best but little fair,—
    Leave youth his roses, who can bear a thorn,—
I will not seek for blossoms anywhere,
    Except such common flowers as blow with corn.
Youth gone and beauty gone, what doth remain?
10   The longing of a heart pent up forlorn,
    A silent heart whose silence loves and longs;
    The silence of a heart which sang its songs
While youth and beauty made a summer morn,
Silence of love that cannot sing again.

"LUSCIOUS AND SORROWFUL."

Beautiful, tender, wasting away for sorrow;
Thus today; and how shall it be with thee tomorrow?
    Beautiful, tender—what else?
        A hope tells.

5   Beautiful, tender, keeping the jubilee
In the land of home together, past death and sea;
    No more change or death, no more
        Salt sea-shore.

DE PROFUNDIS.

Oh why is heaven built so far,
  Oh why is earth set so remote?
I cannot reach the nearest star
  That hangs afloat.

5   I would not care to reach the moon,
  One round monotonous of change;
Yet even she repeats her tune
  Beyond my range.

I never watch the scattered fire
10 Of stars, or sun's far-trailing train,
But all my heart is one desire,
  And all in vain:

For I am bound with fleshly bands,
  Joy, beauty, lie beyond my scope;
15 I strain my heart, I stretch my hands,
  And catch at hope.

TEMPUS FUGIT.

Lovely Spring,
A brief sweet thing,
Is swift on the wing;
Gracious Summer,
5   A slow sweet comer,
Hastens past;
Autumn while sweet
Is all incomplete
With a moaning blast,—
10 Nothing can last,
Can be cleaved unto,
Can be dwelt upon;
It is hurried thro',
It is come and gone,
15 Undone it cannot be done,
It is ever to do,

Ever old, ever new,
Ever waxing old
And lapsing to Winter cold.

GOLDEN GLORIES.

The buttercup is like a golden cup,
    The marigold is like a golden frill,
The daisy with a golden eye looks up,
    And golden spreads the flag beside the rill,
5   And gay and golden nods the daffodil,
The gorsey common swells a golden sea,
    The cowslip hangs a head of golden tips,
And golden drips the honey which the bee
    Sucks from sweet hearts of flowers and stores and sips.

JOHNNY.
FOUNDED ON AN ANECDOTE OF THE FIRST FRENCH REVOLUTION.

Johnny had a golden head
    Like a golden mop in blow,
Right and left his curls would spread
    In a glory and a glow,
5 And they framed his honest face
Like stray sunbeams out of place.

Long and thick, they half could hide
    How threadbare his patched jacket hung;
They used to be his Mother's pride;
10   She praised them with a tender tongue,
And stroked them with a loving finger
That smoothed and stroked and loved to linger.

On a doorstep Johnny sat,
    Up and down the street looked he;
15 Johnny did not own a hat,
    Hot or cold tho' days might be;

Johnny did not own a boot
To cover up his muddy foot.

Johnny's face was pale and thin,
20   Pale with hunger and with crying;
For his Mother lay within,
       Talked and tossed and seemed a-dying,
While Johnny racked his brains to think
How to get her help and drink,

25   Get her physic, get her tea,
       Get her bread and something nice;
Not a penny piece had he,
       And scarce a shilling might suffice;
No wonder that his soul was sad,
30   When not one penny piece he had.

As he sat there thinking, moping,
       Because his Mother's wants were many,
Wishing much but scarcely hoping
       To earn a shilling or a penny,
35   A friendly neighbour passed him by
And questioned him: Why did he cry?

Alas! his trouble soon was told:
       He did not cry for cold or hunger,
Tho' he was hungry both and cold;
40   He only felt more weak and younger,
Because he wished so to be old
And apt at earning pence or gold.

Kindly that neighbour was, but poor,
       Scant coin had he to give or lend;
45   And well he guessed there needed more
       Than pence or shillings to befriend
The helpless woman in her strait,
So much loved, yet so desolate.

One way he saw, and only one:
50   He would—he could not—give the advice,
And yet he must: the widow's son
       Had curls of gold would fetch their price;

Long curls which might be clipped, and sold
For silver, or perhaps for gold.

55 Our Johnny, when he understood
    Which shop it was that purchased hair,
Ran off as briskly as he could,
    And in a trice stood cropped and bare,
Too short of hair to fill a locket,
60 But jingling money in his pocket.

Precious money—tea and bread,
    Physic, ease, for Mother dear,
Better than a golden head:
    Yet our hero dropped one tear
65 When he spied himself close shorn,
Barer much than lamb new born.

His Mother throve upon the money,
    Ate and revived and kissed her son:
But oh! when she perceived her Johnny,
70   And understood what he had done
All and only for her sake,
She sobbed as if her heart must break.

"HOLLOW-SOUNDING AND MYSTERIOUS."

There's no replying
To the Wind's sighing,
Telling, foretelling,
Dying, undying,
5 Dwindling and swelling,
Complaining, droning,
Whistling and moaning,
Ever beginning,
Ending, repeating,
10 Hinting and dinning,
Lagging and fleeting—
We've no replying
Living or dying
To the Wind's sighing.

15   What are you telling,
    Variable Wind-tone?
    What would be teaching,
    O sinking, swelling,
    Desolate Wind-moan?
20   Ever for ever
    Teaching and preaching,
    Never, ah never
    Making us wiser—
    The earliest riser
25   Catches no meaning,
    The last who hearkens
    Garners no gleaning
    Of wisdom's treasure,
    While the world darkens:—
30   Living or dying,
    In pain, in pleasure,
    We've no replying
    To wordless flying
    Wind's sighing.

MAIDEN MAY.

Maiden May sat in her bower,
In her blush rose bower in flower,
    Sweet of scent;
Sat and dreamed away an hour,
5   Half content, half uncontent.

"Why should rose blossoms be born,
Tender blossoms, on a thorn
    Tho' so sweet?
Never a thorn besets the corn
10   Scentless in its strength complete.

"Why are roses all so frail,
At the mercy of a gale,
    Of a breath?

Yet so sweet and perfect pale,
15   Still so sweet in life and death."

Maiden May sat in her bower,
In her blush rose bower in flower,
          Where a linnet
Made one bristling branch the tower
20   For her nest and young ones in it.

"Gay and clear the linnet trills;
Yet the skylark only, thrills
          Heaven and earth
When he breasts the height, and fills
25   Height and depth with song and mirth.

"Nightingales which yield to night
Solitary strange delight,
          Reign alone:
But the lark for all his height
30   Fills no solitary throne;

"While he sings, a hundred sing;
Wing their flight below his wing
          Yet in flight;
Each a lovely joyful thing
35   To the measure of its delight.

"Why then should a lark be reckoned
One alone, without a second
          Near his throne?
He in skyward flight unslackened,
40   In his music, not alone."

Maiden May sat in her bower;
Her own face was like a flower
          Of the prime,
Half in sunshine, half in shower,
45   In the year's most tender time.

Her own thoughts in silent song
Musically flowed along,
          Wise, unwise,

Wistful, wondering, weak or strong:
50   As brook shallows sink or rise.

Other thoughts another day,
Maiden May, will surge and sway
          Round your heart;
Wake, and plead, and turn at bay,
55   Wisdom part, and folly part.

Time not far remote will borrow
Other joys, another sorrow,
          All for you;
Not today, and yet tomorrow
60   Reasoning false and reasoning true.

Wherefore greatest? Wherefore least?
Hearts that starve and hearts that feast?
          You and I?
Stammering Oracles have ceased,
65   And the whole earth stands at "why?"

Underneath all things that be
Lies an unsolved mystery;
          Over all
Spreads a veil impenetrably,
70   Spreads a dense unlifted pall.

Mystery of mysteries:
This creation hears and sees
          High and low—
Vanity of vanities:
75   *This* we test and *this* we know.

Maiden May, the days of flowering
Nurse you now in sweet embowering,
          Sunny days;
Bright with rainbows all the showering,
80   Bright with blossoms all the ways.

Close the inlet of your bower,
Close it close with thorn and flower,
          Maiden May;
Lengthen out the shortening hour,—
85   Morrows are not as today.

Stay today which wanes too soon,
Stay the sun and stay the moon,
    Stay your youth;
Bask you in the actual noon,
90   Rest you in the present truth.

Let today suffice today:
For itself tomorrow may
    Fetch its loss,
Aim and stumble, say its say,
95   Watch and pray and bear its cross.

TILL TOMORROW.

    Long have I longed, till I am tired
        Of longing and desire;
Farewell my points in vain desired,
        My dying fire;
5   Farewell all things that die and fail and tire.

Springtide and youth and useless pleasure
        And all my useless scheming,
My hopes of unattainable treasure,
        Dreams not worth dreaming,
10   Glow-worms that gleam but yield no warmth in gleaming,

Farewell all shows that fade in showing:
        My wish and joy stand over
Until tomorrow; Heaven is glowing
        Thro' cloudy cover,
15   Beyond all clouds loves me my Heavenly Lover.

DEATH-WATCHES.

The Spring spreads one green lap of flowers
    Which Autumn buries at the fall,
No chilling showers of Autumn hours
    Can stay them or recall;

5   Winds sing a dirge, while earth lays out of sight
      Her garment of delight.

    The cloven East brings forth the sun,
       The cloven West doth bury him
    What time his gorgeous race is run
10   And all the world grows dim;
    A funeral moon is lit in heaven's hollow,
    And pale the star-lights follow.

TOUCHING "NEVER."

    Because you never yet have loved me, dear,
       Think you you never can nor ever will?
       Surely while life remains hope lingers still,
    Hope the last blossom of life's dying year.
5   Because the season and mine age grow sere,
       Shall never Spring bring forth her daffodil,
       Shall never sweeter Summer feast her fill
    Of roses with the nightingales they hear?
    If you had loved me, I not loving you,
10   If you had urged me with the tender plea
    Of what our unknown years to come might do
    (Eternal years, if Time should count too few),
       I would have owned the point you pressed on me,
    Was possible, or probable, or true.

BRANDONS BOTH.

    Oh fair Milly Brandon, a young maid, a fair maid!
       All her curls are yellow and her eyes are blue,
    And her cheeks were rosy red till a secret care made
       Hollow whiteness of their brightness as a care will do.
5   Still she tends her flowers, but not as in the old days,
       Still she sings her songs, but not the songs of old:
    If now it be high Summer her days seem brief and cold
          days,
       If now it be high Summer her nights are long and cold.

If you have a secret keep it, pure maid Milly;
10   Life is filled with troubles and the world with scorn;
And pity without love is at best times hard and chilly,
      Chilling sore and stinging sore a heart forlorn.

Walter Brandon, do you guess Milly Brandon's secret?
      Many things you know, but not everything,
15   With your locks like raven's plumage, and eyes like an egret,
      And a laugh that is music, and such a voice to sing.

Nelly Knollys, she is fair, but she is not fairer
      Than fairest Milly Brandon was before she turned so
         pale:
Oh, but Nelly's dearer if she be not rarer,
20   She need not keep a secret or blush behind a veil.

Beyond the first green hills, beyond the nearest valleys,
      Nelly dwells at home beneath her mother's eyes:
Her home is neat and homely, not a cot and not a palace,
      Just the home where love sets up his happiest
         memories.

25   Milly has no mother; and sad beyond another
      Is she whose blessed mother is vanished out of call:
Truly comfort beyond comfort is stored up in a Mother
      Who bears with all, and hopes thro' all, and loves us all.

Where peacocks nod and flaunt up and down the terrace,
30   Furling and unfurling their scores of sightless eyes,
To and fro among the leaves and buds and flowers and
         berries
      Maiden Milly strolls and pauses, smiles and sighs.

On the hedged-in terrace of her father's palace
      She may stroll and muse alone, may smile or sigh alone,
35   Letting thoughts and eyes go wandering over hills and
         valleys
      Today her father's, and one day to be all her own.

If her thoughts go coursing down lowlands and up
         highlands,
      It is because the startled game are leaping from their
         lair;

If her thoughts dart homeward to the reedy river islands,
40   It is because the waterfowl rise startled here or there.

At length a footfall on the steps: she turns, composed and
          steady,
    All the long-descended greatness of her father's house
    Lifting up her head; and there stands Walter keen and
          ready
    For hunting or for hawking, a flush upon his brows.

45 "Good-morrow, fair cousin." "Good-morrow, fairest
          cousin:
    The sun has started on his course, and I must start
          today.
    If you have done me one good turn you've done me many
          a dozen,
    And I shall often think of you, think of you away."

    "Over hill and hollow what quarry will you follow,
50   Or what fish will you angle for beside the river's edge?
    There's cloud upon the hill-top and there's mist deep
          down the hollow,
    And fog among the rushes and the rustling sedge."

    "I shall speed well enough be it hunting or hawking,
    Or casting a bait toward the shyest daintiest fin.
55 But I kiss your hands, my cousin; I must not loiter
          talking,
    For nothing comes of nothing, and I'm fain to seek and
          win."

    "Here's a thorny rose: will you wear it an hour,
    Till the petals drop apart still fresh and pink and sweet?
    Till the petals drop from the drooping perished flower,
60   And only the graceless thorns are left of it."

    "Nay, I have another rose sprung in another garden,
    Another rose which sweetens all the world for me.
    Be you a tenderer mistress and be you a warier warden
    Of your rose, as sweet as mine, and full as fair to see."

65 "Nay, a bud once plucked there is no reviving,
    Nor is it worth your wearing now, nor worth indeed my
          own;

The dead to the dead, and the living to the living.
　　It's time I go within, for it's time now you were gone."

"Good-bye, Milly Brandon, I shall not forget you,
70　　Tho' it be good-bye between us for ever from today;
　　I could almost wish today that I had never met you,
　　　And I'm true to you in this one word that I say."

"Good-bye, Walter. I can guess which thornless rose you
　　　covet;
　　Long may it bloom and prolong its sunny morn:
75　Yet as for my one thorny rose, I do not cease to love it,
　　And if it is no more a flower I love it as a thorn."

A LIFE'S PARALLELS.

Never on this side of the grave again,
　　On this side of the river,
On this side of the garner of the grain,
　　　Never,—
5　Ever while time flows on and on and on,
　　That narrow noiseless river,
Ever while corn bows heavy-headed, wan,
　　　Ever,—
Never despairing, often fainting, rueing,
10　　But looking back, ah never!
Faint yet pursuing, faint yet still pursuing
　　　Ever.

AT LAST.

Many have sung of love a root of bane:
　　While to my mind a root of balm it is,
　　For love at length breeds love; sufficient bliss
For life and death and rising up again.
5　Surely when light of Heaven makes all things plain,
　　Love will grow plain with all its mysteries;
　　Nor shall we need to fetch from over seas

Wisdom or wealth or pleasure safe from pain.
Love in our borders, love within our heart,
10   Love all in all, we then shall bide at rest,
        Ended for ever life's unending quest,
            Ended for ever effort, change and fear:
Love all in all;—no more that better part
        Purchased, but at the cost of all things here.

GOLDEN SILENCES.

There is silence that saith, "Ah me!"
    There is silence that nothing saith;
        One the silence of life forlorn,
    One the silence of death;
5   One is, and the other shall be.

One we know and have known for long,
    One we know not, but we shall know,
        All we who have ever been born;
    Even so, be it so,—
10 There is silence, despite a song.

Sowing day is a silent day,
    Resting night is a silent night;
        But whoso reaps the ripened corn
    Shall shout in his delight,
15 While silences vanish away.

IN THE WILLOW SHADE.

I sat beneath a willow tree,
    Where water falls and calls;
While fancies upon fancies solaced me,
    Some true, and some were false.

5   Who set their heart upon a hope
        That never comes to pass,
    Droop in the end like fading heliotrope
        The sun's wan looking-glass.

Who set their will upon a whim
10   Clung to thro' good and ill,
Are wrecked alike whether they sink or swim,
    Or hit or miss their will.

All things are vain that wax and wane,
    For which we waste our breath;
15   Love only doth not wane and is not vain,
    Love only outlives death.

A singing lark rose toward the sky,
    Circling he sang amain;
He sang, a speck scarce visible sky-high,
20   And then he sank again.

A second like a sunlit spark
    Flashed singing up his track;
But never overtook that foremost lark,
    And songless fluttered back.

25   A hovering melody of birds
    Haunted the air above;
They clearly sang contentment without words,
    And youth and joy and love.

O silvery weeping willow tree
30   With all leaves shivering,
Have you no purpose but to shadow me
    Beside this rippled spring?

On this first fleeting day of Spring,
    For Winter is gone by,
35   And every bird on every quivering wing
    Floats in a sunny sky;

On this first Summer-like soft day,
    While sunshine steeps the air,
And every cloud has gat itself away,
40   And birds sing everywhere.

Have you no purpose in the world
    But thus to shadow me
With all your tender drooping twigs unfurled,
    O weeping willow tree?

45   With all your tremulous leaves outspread
      Betwixt me and the sun,
   While here I loiter on a mossy bed
      With half my work undone;

   My work undone, that should be done
50   At once with all my might;
   For after the long day and lingering sun
      Comes the unworking night.

   This day is lapsing on its way,
      Is lapsing out of sight;
55   And after all the chances of the day
      Comes the resourceless night.

   The weeping willow shook its head
      And stretched its shadow long;
   The west grew crimson, the sun smouldered red,
60   The birds forbore a song.

   Slow wind sighed thro' the willow leaves,
      The ripple made a moan,
   The world drooped murmuring like a thing that grieves;
      And then I felt alone.

65   I rose to go, and felt the chill,
      And shivered as I went;
   Yet shivering wondered, and I wonder still,
      What more that willow meant;

   That silvery weeping willow tree
70   With all leaves shivering,
   Which spent one long day overshadowing me
      Beside a spring in Spring.

FLUTTERED WINGS.

   The splendour of the kindling day,
      The splendour of the setting sun,
   These move my soul to wend its way,
      And have done
5   With all we grasp and toil amongst and say.

The paling roses of a cloud,
    The fading bow that arches space,
These woo my fancy toward my shroud;
    Toward the place
10 Of faces veiled, and heads discrowned and bowed.

The nation of the steadfast stars,
    The wandering star whose blaze is brief,
These make me beat against the bars
    Of my grief;
15 My tedious grief, twin to the life it mars.

O fretted heart tossed to and fro,
    So fain to flee, so fain to rest!
All glories that are high or low,
    East or west,
20 Grow dim to thee who art so fain to go.

A FISHER-WIFE.

The soonest mended, nothing said;
    And help may rise from east or west;
But my two hands are lumps of lead,
    My heart sits leaden in my breast.

5 O north wind swoop not from the north,
    O south wind linger in the south,
Oh come not raving raging forth,
    To bring my heart into my mouth;

For I've a husband out at sea,
10   Afloat on feeble planks of wood;
He does not know what fear may be;
    I would have told him if I could.

I would have locked him in my arms,
    I would have hid him in my heart;
15 For oh! the waves are fraught with harms,
    And he and I so far apart.

WHAT'S IN A NAME?

Why has Spring one syllable less
Than any its fellow season?
There may be some other reason,
And I'm merely making a guess;
5   But surely it hoards such wealth
Of happiness, hope and health,
Sunshine and musical sound,
It may spare a foot from its name
Yet all the same
10   Superabound.

Soft-named Summer,
Most welcome comer,
Brings almost everything
Over which we dream or sing
15   Or sigh;
But then summer wends its way,
Tomorrow,—today,—
Good-bye!

Autumn,—the slow name lingers,
20   While we likewise flag;
It silences many singers;
Its slow days drag,
Yet hasten at speed
To leave us in chilly need
25   For Winter to strip indeed.

In all-lack Winter,
Dull of sense and of sound,
We huddle and shiver
Beside our splinter
30   Of crackling pine,
Snow in sky and snow on ground.
Winter and cold
Can't last for ever!
Today, tomorrow, the sun will shine;
35   When we are old,
But some still are young,

Singing the song
Which others have sung,
Ringing the bells
40 Which others have rung,—
Even so!
We ourselves, who else?
We ourselves long
Long ago.

MARIANA.

Not for me marring or making,
Not for me giving or taking;
   I love my Love and he loves not me,
I love my Love and my heart is breaking.

5 Sweet is Spring in its lovely showing,
Sweet the violet veiled in blowing,
   Sweet it is to love and be loved;
Ah, sweet knowledge beyond my knowing!

Who sighs for love sighs but for pleasure,
10 Who wastes for love hoards up a treasure;
   Sweet to be loved and take no count,
Sweet it is to love without measure.

Sweet my Love whom I loved to try for,
Sweet my Love whom I love and sigh for,
15   Will you once love me and sigh for me,
You my Love whom I love and die for?

MEMENTO MORI.

Poor the pleasure
Doled out by measure,
Sweet tho' it be, while brief
As falling of the leaf;
5 Poor is pleasure
By weight and measure.

Sweet the sorrow
Which ends tomorrow;
Sharp tho' it be and sore,
10   It ends for evermore:
Zest of sorrow,
What ends tomorrow.

"ONE FOOT ON SEA, AND ONE ON SHORE."

"Oh tell me once and tell me twice
    And tell me thrice to make it plain,
When we who part this weary day,
    When we who part shall meet again."

5   "When windflowers blossom on the sea
    And fishes skim along the plain,
Then we who part this weary day,
    Then you and I shall meet again."

"Yet tell me once before we part,
10   Why need we part who part in pain?
If flowers must blossom on the sea,
    Why, we shall never meet again.

"My cheeks are paler than a rose,
    My tears are salter than the main,
15   My heart is like a lump of ice
    If we must never meet again."

"Oh weep or laugh, but let me be,
    And live or die, for all's in vain;
For life's in vain since we must part,
20   And parting must not meet again

"Till windflowers blossom on the sea
    And fishes skim along the plain;
Pale rose of roses let me be,
    Your breaking heart breaks mine again."

BUDS AND BABIES.

A million buds are born that never blow,
    That sweet with promise lift a pretty head
    To blush and wither on a barren bed
        And leave no fruit to show.

5   Sweet, unfulfilled. Yet have I understood
    One joy, by their fragility made plain:
    Nothing was ever beautiful in vain,
        Or all in vain was good.

BOY JOHNNY.

"If you'll busk you as a bride
    And make ready,
It's I will wed you with a ring,
    O fair lady."

5   "Shall I busk me as a bride,
    I so bonny,
For you to wed me with a ring,
    O boy Johnny?"

"When you've busked you as a bride
10   And made ready,
Who else is there to marry you,
    O fair lady?"

"I will find my lover out,
    I so bonny,
15   And you shall bear my wedding-train,
    O boy Johnny."

FREAKS OF FASHION.

Such a hubbub in the nests,
    Such a bustle and squeak!

Nestlings, guiltless of a feather,
   Learning just to speak,
5   Ask—"And how about the fashions?"
   From a cavernous beak.

Perched on bushes, perched on hedges,
   Perched on firm hahas,
Perched on anything that holds them,
10   Gay papas and grave mammas
Teach the knowledge-thirsty nestlings:
   Hear the gay papas.

Robin says: "A scarlet waistcoat
   Will be all the wear,
15 Snug, and also cheerful-looking
   For the frostiest air,
Comfortable for the chest too
   When one comes to plume and pair."

"Neat gray hoods will be in vogue,"
20   Quoth a Jackdaw: "Glossy gray,
Setting close, yet setting easy,
   Nothing fly-away;
Suited to our misty mornings,
   À la negligée."

25 Flushing salmon, flushing sulphur,
   Haughty Cockatoos
Answer—"Hoods may do for mornings,
   But for evenings choose
High head-dresses, curved like crescents,
30   Such as well-bred persons use."

"Top-knots, yes; yet more essential
   Still, a train or tail,"
Screamed the Peacock: "Gemmed and lustrous,
   Not too stiff, and not too frail;
35 Those are best which rearrange as
   Fans, and spread or trail."

Spoke the Swan, entrenched behind
   An inimitable neck:

"After all, there's nothing sweeter
40   For the lawn or lake
Than simple white, if fine and flaky
    And absolutely free from speck."

"Yellow," hinted a Canary,
    "Warmer, not less *distingué*."
45   "Peach colour," put in a Lory,
    "Cannot look *outré*."
"All the colours are in fashion,
    And are right," the Parrots say.

"Very well. But do contrast
50   Tints harmonious,"
Piped a Blackbird, justly proud
    Of bill aurigerous;
"Half the world may learn a lesson
    As to that from us."

55   Then a Stork took up the word:
    "Aim at height and *chic*:
Not high heels, they're common; somehow,
    Stilted legs, not thick,
Nor yet thin:" he just glanced downward
60   And snapped to his beak.

Here a rustling and a whirring,
    As of fans outspread,
Hinted that mammas felt anxious
    Lest the next thing said
65   Might prove less than quite judicious,
    Or even underbred.

So a mother Auk resumed
    The broken thread of speech:
"Let colours sort themselves, my dears,
70   Yellow, or red, or peach;
The main points, as it seems to me,
    We mothers have to teach,

"Are form and texture, elegance,
    An air reserved, sublime;

75   The mode of wearing what we wear
         With due regard to month and clime.
      But now, let's all compose ourselves,
         It's almost breakfast-time."

      A hubbub, a squeak, a bustle!
80   Who cares to chatter or sing
      With delightful breakfast coming?
         Yet they whisper under the wing:
      "So we may wear whatever we like,
         Anything, everything!"

AN OCTOBER GARDEN.

      In my Autumn garden I was fain
         To mourn among my scattered roses;
         Alas for that last rosebud which uncloses
      To Autumn's languid sun and rain
5   When all the world is on the wane!
         Which has not felt the sweet constraint of June,
         Nor heard the nightingale in tune.

      Broad-faced asters by my garden walk,
         You are but coarse compared with roses:
10   More choice, more dear that rosebud which uncloses
      Faint-scented, pinched, upon its stalk,
      That least and last which cold winds balk;
         A rose it is tho' least and last of all,
         A rose to me tho' at the fall.

"SUMMER IS ENDED."

      To think that this meaningless thing was ever a rose,
         Scentless, colourless, *this*!
         Will it ever be thus (who knows?)
            Thus with our bliss,
5   If we wait till the close?

Tho' we care not to wait for the end, there comes the end
      Sooner, later, at last,
   Which nothing can mar, nothing mend:
      An end locked fast,
10   Bent we cannot re-bend.

PASSING AND GLASSING.

    All things that pass
    Are woman's looking-glass;
They show her how her bloom must fade,
And she herself be laid
5   With withered roses in the shade;
    With withered roses and the fallen peach,
    Unlovely, out of reach
      Of summer joy that was.

    All things that pass
10   Are woman's tiring-glass;
The faded lavender is sweet,
Sweet the dead violet
Culled and laid by and cared for yet;
    The dried-up violets and dried lavender
15   Still sweet, may comfort her,
      Nor need she cry Alas!

    All things that pass
    Are wisdom's looking-glass;
Being full of hope and fear, and still
20 Brimful of good or ill,
According to our work and will;
    For there is nothing new beneath the sun;
    Our doings have been done,
      And that which shall be was.

"I WILL ARISE."

Weary and weak,—accept my weariness;
　　Weary and weak and downcast in my soul,
With hope growing less and less,
　　And with the goal
5　　Distant and dim,—accept my sore distress.
I thought to reach the goal so long ago,
　　At outset of the race I dreamed of rest,
Not knowing what now I know
　　Of breathless haste,
10　　Of long-drawn straining effort across the waste.

One only thing I knew, Thy love of me;
　　One only thing I know, Thy sacred same
Love of me full and free,
　　A craving flame
15　　Of selfless love of me which burns in Thee.
How can I think of Thee, and yet grow chill;
　　Of Thee, and yet grow cold and nigh to death?
Re-energize my will,
　　Rebuild my faith;
20　　I will arise and run, Thou giving me breath.

I will arise, repenting and in pain;
　　I will arise, and smite upon my breast
And turn to Thee again;
　　Thou choosest best,
25　　Lead me along the road Thou makest plain.
Lead me a little way, and carry me
　　A little way, and hearken to my sighs,
And store my tears with Thee,
　　And deign replies
30　　To feeble prayers;—O Lord, I will arise.

A PRODIGAL SON.

Does that lamp still burn in my Father's house,
　　Which he kindled the night I went away?

I turned once beneath the cedar boughs,
    And marked it gleam with a golden ray;
5   Did he think to light me home some day?

Hungry here with the crunching swine,
    Hungry harvest have I to reap;
In a dream I count my Father's kine,
    I hear the tinkling bells of his sheep,
10   I watch his lambs that browse and leap.

There is plenty of bread at home,
    His servants have bread enough and to spare;
The purple wine-fat froths with foam,
    Oil and spices make sweet the air,
15   While I perish hungry and bare.

Rich and blessed those servants, rather
    Than I who see not my Father's face!
I will arise and go to my Father:—
    "Fallen from sonship, beggared of grace,
20   Grant me, Father, a servant's place."

SOEUR LOUISE DE LA MISÉRICORDE.
(1674.)

I have desired, and I have been desired;
    But now the days are over of desire,
    Now dust and dying embers mock my fire;
Where is the hire for which my life was hired?
5   Oh vanity of vanities, desire!

Longing and love, pangs of a perished pleasure,
    Longing and love, a disenkindled fire,
    And memory a bottomless gulf of mire,
And love a fount of tears outrunning measure;
10   Oh vanity of vanities, desire!

Now from my heart, love's deathbed, trickles, trickles,
    Drop by drop slowly, drop by drop of fire,
    The dross of life, of love, of spent desire;

Alas, my rose of life gone all to prickles,—
15　　Oh vanity of vanities, desire!

Oh vanity of vanities, desire;
　　Stunting my hope which might have strained up higher,
　　Turning my garden plot to barren mire;
Oh death-struck love, oh disenkindled fire,
20　　Oh vanity of vanities, desire!

AN "IMMURATA" SISTER.

Life flows down to death; we cannot bind
　　That current that it should not flee:
Life flows down to death, as rivers find
　　The inevitable sea.

5　Men work and think, but women feel;
　　And so (for I'm a woman, I)
　　And so I should be glad to die
And cease from impotence of zeal,
And cease from hope, and cease from dread,
10　　And cease from yearnings without gain,
　　And cease from all this world of pain,
And be at peace among the dead.

Hearts that die, by death renew their youth,
　　Lightened of this life that doubts and dies;
15　Silent and contented, while the Truth
　　Unveiled makes them wise.

Why should I seek and never find
　　That something which I have not had?
　　Fair and unutterably sad
20　The world hath sought time out of mind;
The world hath sought and I have sought,—
　　Ah, empty world and empty I!
　　For we have spent our strength for nought,
And soon it will be time to die.

25   Sparks fly upward toward their fount of fire,
         Kindling, flashing, hovering:—
      Kindle, flash, my soul; mount higher and higher,
         Thou whole burnt-offering!

"IF THOU SAYEST, BEHOLD, WE KNEW IT NOT."
      —Proverbs xxiv. 11, 12.

         1.

      I have done I know not what,—what have I done?
         My brother's blood, my brother's soul, doth cry:
         And I find no defence, find no reply,
      No courage more to run this race I run
5   Not knowing what I have done, have left undone;
         Ah me, these awful unknown hours that fly
         Fruitless it may be, fleeting fruitless by
      Rank with death-savour underneath the sun.
      For what avails it that I did not know
10   The deed I did? what profits me the plea
      That had I known I had not wronged him so?
         Lord Jesus Christ, my God, him pity Thou;
         Lord, if it may be, pity also me:
         In judgment pity, and in death, and now.

         2.

      Thou Who hast borne all burdens, bear our load,
         Bear Thou our load whatever load it be;
         Our guilt, our shame, our helpless misery,
      Bear Thou Who only canst, O God my God.
5   Seek us and find us, for we cannot Thee
      Or seek or find or hold or cleave unto:
      We cannot do or undo; Lord, undo
         Our self-undoing, for Thine is the key
      Of all we are not tho' we might have been.
10   Dear Lord, if ever mercy moved Thy mind,
         If so be love of us can move Thee yet,

If still the nail-prints in Thy Hands are seen,
    Remember us,—yea, how shouldst Thou forget?
    Remember us for good, and seek, and find.

3.

Each soul I might have succoured, may have slain,
    All souls shall face me at the last Appeal,
    That great last moment poised for woe or weal,
That final moment for man's bliss or bane.
5   Vanity of vanities, yea all is vain
    Which then will not avail or help or heal:
    Disfeatured faces, worn-out knees that kneel,
Will more avail than strength or beauty then.
Lord, by Thy Passion,—when Thy Face was marred
10   In sight of earth and hell tumultuous,
    And Thy heart failed in Thee like melting wax,
And Thy Blood dropped more precious than the nard,—
    Lord, for Thy sake, not our's, supply our lacks,
    For Thine own sake, not our's, Christ, pity us.

THE THREAD OF LIFE.

1.

The irresponsive silence of the land,
    The irresponsive sounding of the sea,
    Speak both one message of one sense to me:—
Aloof, aloof, we stand aloof, so stand
5   Thou too aloof bound with the flawless band
    Of inner solitude; we bind not thee;
    But who from thy self-chain shall set thee free?
What heart shall touch thy heart? what hand thy hand?—
And I am sometimes proud and sometimes meek,
10   And sometimes I remember days of old
When fellowship seemed not so far to seek
    And all the world and I seemed much less cold,
    And at the rainbow's foot lay surely gold,
And hope felt strong and life itself not weak.

2.

Thus am I mine own prison. Everything
   Around me free and sunny and at ease:
   Or if in shadow, in a shade of trees
Which the sun kisses, where the gay birds sing
5   And where all winds make various murmuring;
   Where bees are found, with honey for the bees;
   Where sounds are music, and where silences
Are music of an unlike fashioning.
Then gaze I at the merrymaking crew,
10   And smile a moment and a moment sigh
Thinking: Why can I not rejoice with you?
   But soon I put the foolish fancy by:
I am not what I have nor what I do;
   But what I was I am, I am even I.

3.

Therefore myself is that one only thing
   I hold to use or waste, to keep or give;
   My sole possession every day I live,
And still mine own despite Time's winnowing.
5   Ever mine own, while moons and seasons bring
   From crudeness ripeness mellow and sanative;
   Ever mine own, till Death shall ply his sieve;
And still mine own, when saints break grave and sing.
And this myself as king unto my King
10   I give, to Him Who gave Himself for me;
Who gives Himself to me, and bids me sing
   A sweet new song of His redeemed set free;
He bids me sing: O death, where is thy sting?
   And sing: O grave, where is thy victory?

AN OLD-WORLD THICKET.

    . . . "Una selva oscura."—DANTE.

Awake or sleeping (for I know not which)
   I was or was not mazed within a wood

       Where every mother-bird brought up her brood
          Safe in some leafy niche
5   Of oak or ash, of cypress or of beech,

       Of silvery aspen trembling delicately,
          Of plane or warmer-tinted sycomore,
          Of elm that dies in secret from the core,
            Of ivy weak and free,
10   Of pines, of all green lofty things that be.

       Such birds they seemed as challenged each desire;
          Like spots of azure heaven upon the wing,
          Like downy emeralds that alight and sing,
            Like actual coals on fire,
15   Like anything they seemed, and everything.

       Such mirth they made, such warblings and such chat
          With tongue of music in a well-tuned beak,
          They seemed to speak more wisdom than we speak,
            To make our music flat
20   And all our subtlest reasonings wild or weak.

       Their meat was nought but flowers like butterflies,
          With berries coral-coloured or like gold;
          Their drink was only dew, which blossoms hold
            Deep where the honey lies;
25   Their wings and tails were lit by sparkling eyes.

       The shade wherein they revelled was a shade
          That danced and twinkled to the unseen sun;
          Branches and leaves cast shadows one by one,
            And all their shadows swayed
30   In breaths of air that rustled and that played.

       A sound of waters neither rose nor sank,
          And spread a sense of freshness through the air;
          It seemed not here or there, but everywhere,
            As if the whole earth drank,
35   Root fathom deep and strawberry on its bank.

       But I who saw such things as I have said,
          Was overdone with utter weariness;
          And walked in care, as one whom fears oppress
            Because above his head

40 Death hangs, or damage, or the dearth of bread.

Each sore defeat of my defeated life
    Faced and outfaced me in that bitter hour;
    And turned to yearning palsy all my power,
        And all my peace to strife,
45 Self stabbing self with keen lack-pity knife.

Sweetness of beauty moved me to despair,
    Stung me to anger by its mere content,
    Made me all lonely on that way I went,
        Piled care upon my care,
50 Brimmed full my cup, and stripped me empty and bare:

For all that was but showed what all was not,
    But gave clear proof of what might never be;
    Making more destitute my poverty,
        And yet more blank my lot,
55 And me much sadder by its jubilee.

Therefore I sat me down: for wherefore walk?
    And closed mine eyes: for wherefore see or hear?
    Alas, I had no shutter to mine ear,
        And could not shun the talk
60 Of all rejoicing creatures far or near.

Without my will I hearkened and I heard
    (Asleep or waking, for I know not which),
    Till note by note the music changed its pitch;
        Bird ceased to answer bird,
65 And every wind sighed softly if it stirred.

The drip of widening waters seemed to weep,
    All fountains sobbed and gurgled as they sprang,
Somewhere a cataract cried out in its leap
        Sheer down a headlong steep;
70 High over all cloud-thunders gave a clang.

Such universal sound of lamentation
    I heard and felt, fain not to feel or hear;
    Nought else there seemed but anguish far and near;
        Nought else but all creation
75 Moaning and groaning wrung by pain or fear,

Shuddering in the misery of its doom:
   My heart then rose a rebel against light,
   Scouring all earth and heaven and depth and height,
    Ingathering wrath and gloom,
80   Ingathering wrath to wrath and night to night.

Ah me, the bitterness of such revolt,
   All impotent, all hateful, and all hate,
That kicks and breaks itself against the bolt
    Of an imprisoning fate,
85   And vainly shakes, and cannot shake the gate.

Agony to agony, deep called to deep,
   Out of the deep I called of my desire;
   My strength was weakness and my heart was fire;
    Mine eyes that would not weep
90   Or sleep, scaled height and depth, and could not sleep;

The eyes, I mean, of my rebellious soul,
   For still my bodily eyes were closed and dark:
   A random thing I seemed without a mark,
    Racing without a goal,
95   Adrift upon life's sea without an ark.

More leaden than the actual self of lead
   Outer and inner darkness weighed on me.
   The tide of anger ebbed. Then fierce and free
    Surged full above my head
100 The moaning tide of helpless misery.

Why should I breathe, whose breath was but a sigh?
   Why should I live, who drew such painful breath?
Oh weary work, the unanswerable why!—
    Yet I, why should I die,
105 Who had no hope in life, no hope in death?

Grasses and mosses and the fallen leaf
   Make peaceful bed for an indefinite term;
   But underneath the grass there gnaws a worm—
    Haply, there gnaws a grief—
110 Both, haply always; not, as now, so brief.

The pleasure I remember, it is past;
   The pain I feel, is passing passing by;

Thus all the world is passing, and thus I:
    All things that cannot last
115   Have grown familiar, and are born to die.

And being familiar, have so long been borne
    That habit trains us not to break but bend:
Mourning grows natural to us who mourn
    In foresight of an end,
120   But that which ends not who shall brave or mend?

Surely the ripe fruits tremble on their bough,
    They cling and linger trembling till they drop:
I, trembling, cling to dying life; for how
    Face the perpetual Now?
125   Birthless and deathless, void of start or stop,

Void of repentance, void of hope and fear,
    Of possibility, alternative,
    Of all that ever made us bear to live
    From night to morning here,
130   Of promise even which has no gift to give.

The wood, and every creature of the wood,
    Seemed mourning with me in an undertone;
Soft scattered chirpings and a windy moan,
    Trees rustling where they stood
135 And shivered, showed compassion for my mood.

Rage to despair; and now despair had turned
    Back to self-pity and mere weariness,
With yearnings like a smouldering fire that burned,
    And might grow more or less,
140   And might die out or wax to white excess.

Without, within me, music seemed to be;
    Something not music, yet most musical,
Silence and sound in heavenly harmony;
    At length a pattering fall
145   Of feet, a bell, and bleatings, broke through all.

Then I looked up. The wood lay in a glow
    From golden sunset and from ruddy sky;
The sun had stooped to earth though once so high;
    Had stooped to earth, in slow

150   Warm dying loveliness brought near and low.

    Each water drop made answer to the light,
       Lit up a spark and showed the sun his face;
       Soft purple shadows paved the grassy space
          And crept from height to height,
155   From height to loftier height crept up apace.

    While opposite the sun a gazing moon
       Put on his glory for her coronet,
    Kindling her luminous coldness to its noon,
          As his great splendour set;
160   One only star made up her train as yet.

    Each twig was tipped with gold, each leaf was edged
       And veined with gold from the gold-flooded west;
    Each mother-bird, and mate-bird, and unfledged
          Nestling, and curious nest,
165   Displayed a gilded moss or beak or breast.

    And filing peacefully between the trees,
       Having the moon behind them, and the sun
    Full in their meek mild faces, walked at ease
          A homeward flock, at peace
170   With one another and with every one.

    A patriarchal ram with tinkling bell
       Led all his kin; sometimes one browsing sheep
       Hung back a moment, or one lamb would leap
          And frolic in a dell;
175   Yet still they kept together, journeying well,

    And bleating, one or other, many or few,
       Journeying together toward the sunlit west;
    Mild face by face, and woolly breast by breast,
          Patient, sun-brightened too,
180   Still journeying toward the sunset and their rest.

"ALL THY WORKS PRAISE THEE, O LORD."
A PROCESSIONAL OF CREATION.

ALL.

I all-creation sing my song of praise
To God Who made me and vouchsafes my days,
And sends me forth by multitudinous ways.

SERAPH.

I, like my Brethren, burn eternally
5   With love of Him Who is Love, and loveth me;
The Holy, Holy, Holy Unity.

CHERUB.

I, with my Brethren, gaze eternally
On Him Who is Wisdom, and Who knoweth me;
The Holy, Holy, Holy Trinity.

ALL ANGELS.

10 We rule, we serve, we work, we store His treasure,
Whose vessels are we brimmed with strength and
            pleasure;
Our joys fulfil, yea, overfill our measure.

HEAVENS.

We float before the Presence Infinite,
We cluster round the Throne in our delight,
15 Revolving and rejoicing in God's sight.

FIRMAMENT.

I, blue and beautiful, and framed of air,
At sunrise and at sunset grow most fair;
His glory by my glories I declare.

POWERS.

We Powers are powers because He makes us strong;
20   Wherefore we roll all rolling orbs along,
We move all moving things, and sing our song.

SUN.

I blaze to Him in mine engarlanding
Of rays, I flame His whole burnt-offering,
While as a bridegroom I rejoice and sing.

MOON.

25   I follow, and am fair, and do His Will;
Thro' all my changes I am faithful still,
Full-orbed or strait His mandate to fulfil.

STARS.

We Star-hosts numerous, innumerous,
Throng space with energy untumultuous,
30   And work His Will Whose eye beholdeth us.

GALAXIES AND NEBULAE.

No thing is far or near; and therefore we
Float neither far nor near; but where we be
Weave dances round the Throne perpetually.

COMETS AND METEORS.

Our lights dart here and there, whirl to and fro,
35   We flash and vanish, we die down and glow;
All doing His Will Who bids us do it so.

SHOWERS.

We give ourselves; and be we great or small,
Thus are we made like Him Who giveth all,
Like Him Whose gracious pleasure bids us fall.

DEWS.

40   We give ourselves in silent secret ways,
Spending and spent in silence full of grace;
And thus are made like God, and show His praise.

WINDS.

We sift the air and winnow all the earth;
And God Who poised our weights and weighs our worth
45   Accepts the worship of our solemn mirth.

FIRE.

My power and strength are His Who fashioned me,
Ordained me image of His Jealousy,
Forged me His weapon fierce exceedingly.

HEAT.

I glow unto His glory, and do good:
50   I glow, and bring to life both bud and brood;
I glow, and ripen harvest-crops for food.

WINTER AND SUMMER.

Our wealth and joys and beauties celebrate
His wealth of beauty Who sustains our state,
Before Whose changelessness we alternate.

SPRING AND AUTUMN.

55   I hope,—
        And I remember,—
                We give place
Either to other with contented grace,
Acceptable and lovely all our days.

FROST.

60   I make the unstable stable, binding fast
      The world of waters prone to ripple past:
      Thus praise I God, Whose mercies I forecast.

COLD.

      I rouse and goad the slothful apt to nod,
      I stir and urge the laggards with my rod:
65   My praise is not of men, yet I praise God.

SNOW.

      My whiteness shadoweth Him Who is most fair,
      All spotless: yea, my whiteness which I wear
      Exalts His Purity beyond compare.

VAPOURS.

      We darken sun and moon, and blot the day,
70   The good Will of our Maker to obey:
      Till to the glory of God we pass away.

NIGHT.

      Moon and all stars I don for diadem
      To make me fair: I cast myself and them
      Before His feet, Who knows us gem from gem.

DAY.

75   I shout before Him in my plentitude
      Of light and warmth, of hope and wealth and food;
      Ascribing all good to the Only Good.

LIGHT AND DARKNESS.

      I am God's dwelling-place,—
                              And also I

80   Make His pavilion,—
                    Lo, we bide and fly
      Exulting in the Will of God Most High.

        LIGHTNING AND THUNDER.

      We indivisible flash forth His Fame,
      We thunder forth the glory of His Name,
85   In harmony of resonance and flame.

        CLOUDS.

      Sweet is our store, exhaled from sea or river:
      We wear a rainbow, praising God the Giver
      Because His mercy is for ever and ever.

        EARTH.

      I rest in Him rejoicing: resting so
90   And so rejoicing, in that I am low;
      Yet known of Him, and following on to know.

        MOUNTAINS.

      Our heights which laud Him, sink abased before
      Him higher than the highest evermore:
      God higher than the highest we adore.

        HILLS.

95   We green-tops praise Him, and we fruitful heads,
      Whereon the sunshine and the dew He sheds:
      We green-tops praise Him, rising from our beds.

        GREEN THINGS.

      We all green things, we blossoms bright or dim,
      Trees, bushes, brushwood, corn and grasses slim,
100   We lift our many-favoured lauds to Him.

ROSE,—LILY,—VIOLET.

I praise Him on my thorn which I adorn,—
And I, amid my world of thistle and thorn,—
And I, within my veil where I am born.

APPLE,—CITRON,—POMEGRANATE.

We Apple-blossom, Citron, Pomegranate,
105   We clothed of God without our toil and fret,
We offer fatness where His Throne is set.

VINE,—CEDAR,—PALM.

I proffer Him my sweetness, who am sweet,—
I bow my strength in fragrance at His feet,—
I wave myself before His Judgment Seat.

MEDICINAL HERBS.

110   I bring refreshment,—
                    I bring ease and calm,—
I lavish strength and healing,—
                    I am balm,—
We work His pitiful Will and chant our psalm.

A SPRING.

115   Clear my pure fountain, clear and pure my rill,
My fountain and mine outflow deep and still,
I set His semblance forth and do His Will.

SEA.

Today I praise God with a sparkling face,
My thousand thousand waves all uttering praise:
120   Tomorrow I commit me to His Grace.

FLOODS.

We spring and swell meandering to and fro,
From height to depth, from depth to depth we flow,
We fertilize the world, and praise Him so.

WHALES AND SEA MAMMALS.

We Whales and Monsters gambol in His sight
125 Rejoicing every day and every night,
Safe in the tender keeping of His Might.

FISHES.

Our fashions and our colours and our speeds
Set forth His praise Who framed us and Who feeds,
Who knows our number and regards our needs.

BIRDS.

130 Winged Angels of this visible world, we fly
To sing God's praises in the lofty sky;
We scale the height to praise our Lord most High.

EAGLE AND DOVE.

I the sun-gazing Eagle,—
                              I the Dove
135 With plumes of softness and a note of love,—
We praise by divers gifts One God above.

BEASTS AND CATTLE.

We forest Beasts,—
                              We Beasts of hill or cave,—
We border-loving Creatures of the wave,—
140 We praise our King with voices deep and grave.

SMALL ANIMALS.

God forms us weak and small, but pours out all
We need, and notes us while we stand or fall:
Wherefore we praise Him, weak and safe and small.

LAMB.

I praise my loving Lord, Who maketh me
145   His type by harmless sweet simplicity:
Yet He the Lamb of lambs incomparably.

LION.

I praise the Lion of the Royal Race,
Strongest in fight and swiftest in the chase:
With all my might I leap and lavish praise.

ALL MEN.

150   All creatures sing around us, and we sing:
We bring our own selves as our offering,
Our very selves we render to our King.

ISRAEL.

Flock of our Shepherd's pasture and His fold,
Purchased and well-beloved from days of old,
155   We tell His praise which still remains untold.

PRIESTS.

We free-will Shepherds tend His sheep and feed;
We follow Him while caring for their need;
We follow praising Him, and them we lead.

SERVANTS OF GOD.

We love God, for He loves us; we are free
160   In serving Him, who serve Him willingly:
As kings we reign, and praise His Majesty.

HOLY AND HUMBLE PERSONS.

All humble souls He calls and sanctifies;
All holy souls He calls to make them wise;
Accepting all, His free-will sacrifice.

BABES.

165 He maketh me,—
            And me,—
                   And me,—
                         To be
His blessed little ones around His knee,
170 Who praise Him by mere love confidingly.

WOMEN.

God makes our service love, and makes our wage
Love: so we wend on patient pilgrimage,
Extolling Him by love from age to age.

MEN.

God gives us power to rule: He gives us power
175 To rule ourselves, and prune the exuberant flower
Of youth, and worship Him hour after hour.

SPIRITS AND SOULS—

Lo, in the hidden world we chant our chant
To Him Who fills us that we nothing want,
To Him Whose bounty leaves our craving scant.

OF BABES—

180 With milky mouths we praise God, from the breast
Called home betimes to rest the perfect rest,
By love and joy fulfilling His behest.

OF WOMEN—

We praise His Will which made us what He would,
His Will which fashioned us and called us good,
185   His Will our plenary beatitude.

OF MEN.

We praise His Will Who bore with us so long,
Who out of weakness wrought us swift and strong,
Champions of right and putters-down of wrong.

ALL.

Let everything that hath or hath not breath,
190   Let days and endless days, let life and death,
Praise God, praise God, praise God, His creature saith.

LATER LIFE: A DOUBLE SONNET OF SONNETS.

1.

Before the mountains were brought forth, before
    Earth and the world were made, then God was God:
And God will still be God, when flames shall roar
    Round earth and heaven dissolving at His nod:
5   And this God is our God, even while His rod
Of righteous wrath falls on us smiting sore:
And this God is our God for evermore
    Thro' life, thro' death, while clod returns to clod.
For tho' He slay us we will trust in Him;
10   We will flock home to Him by divers ways:
    Yea, tho' He slay us we will vaunt His praise,
Serving and loving with the Cherubim,
Watching and loving with the Seraphim,
    Our very selves His praise thro' endless days.

2.

Rend hearts and rend not garments for our sins;
   Gird sackcloth not on body but on soul;
   Grovel in dust with faces toward the goal
Nor won, nor neared: he only laughs who wins.
5   Not neared the goal, the race too late begins;
   All left undone, we have yet to do the whole;
   The sun is hurrying west and toward the pole
Where darkness waits for earth with all her kins.
Let us today while it is called today
10   Set out, if utmost speed may yet avail—
   The shadows lengthen and the light grows pale:
     For who thro' darkness and the shadow of death,
Darkness that may be felt, shall find a way,
     Blind-eyed, deaf-eared, and choked with failing
       breath?

3.

Thou Who didst make and knowest whereof we are
     made,
   Oh bear in mind our dust and nothingness,
   Our wordless tearless dumbness of distress:
Bear Thou in mind the burden Thou hast laid
5   Upon us, and our feebleness unstayed
   Except Thou stay us: for the long long race
   Which stretches far and far before our face
Thou knowest,—remember Thou whereof we are made.
If making makes us Thine then Thine we are,
10   And if redemption we are twice Thine own:
If once Thou didst come down from heaven afar
     To seek us and to find us, how not save?
   Comfort us, save us, leave us not alone,
     Thou Who didst die our death and fill our grave.

4.

So tired am I, so weary of today,
   So unrefreshed from foregone weariness,

So overburdened by foreseen distress,
So lagging and so stumbling on my way,
5   I scarce can rouse myself to watch or pray,
      To hope, or aim, or toil for more or less,—
      Ah, always less and less, even while I press
Forward and toil and aim as best I may.
Half-starved of soul and heartsick utterly,
10   Yet lift I up my heart and soul and eyes
      (Which fail in looking upward) toward the prize:
Me, Lord, Thou seest tho' I see not Thee;
      Me now, as once the Thief in Paradise,
Even me, O Lord my Lord, remember me.

5.

Lord, Thou Thyself art Love and only Thou;
      Yet I who am not love would fain love Thee;
      But Thou alone being Love canst furnish me
With that same love my heart is craving now.
5   Allow my plea! for if Thou disallow,
      No second fountain can I find but Thee;
      No second hope or help is left to me,
No second anything, but only Thou.
O Love accept, according my request;
10   O Love exhaust, fulfilling my desire:
      Uphold me with the strength that cannot tire,
Nerve me to labour till Thou bid me rest,
      Kindle my fire from Thine unkindled fire,
And charm the willing heart from out my breast.

6.

We lack, yet cannot fix upon the lack:
      Not this, nor that; yet somewhat, certainly.
      We see the things we do not yearn to see
Around us: and what see we glancing back?
5   Lost hopes that leave our hearts upon the rack,
      Hopes that were never ours yet seemed to be,
      For which we steered on life's salt stormy sea

Braving the sunstroke and the frozen pack.
If thus to look behind is all in vain,
10   And all in vain to look to left or right,
Why face we not our future once again,
Launching with hardier hearts across the main,
    Straining dim eyes to catch the invisible sight,
And strong to bear ourselves in patient pain?

    7.

To love and to remember; that is good:
    To love and to forget; that is not well:
    To lapse from love to hatred; that is hell
And death and torment, rightly understood.
5   Soul dazed by love and sorrow, cheer thy mood;
    More blest art thou than mortal tongue can tell:
    Ring not thy funeral but thy marriage bell,
And salt with hope thy life's insipid food.
Love is the goal, love is the way we wend,
10   Love is our parallel unending line
    Whose only perfect Parallel is Christ,
Beginning not begun, End without end:
    For He Who hath the Heart of God sufficed,
Can satisfy all hearts,—yea, thine and mine.

    8.

We feel and see with different hearts and eyes:—
    Ah Christ, if all our hearts could meet in Thee
    How well it were for them and well for me,
Our hearts Thy dear accepted sacrifice.
5   Thou, only Life of hearts and Light of eyes,
    Our life, our light, if once we turn to Thee,
    So be it, O Lord, to them and so to me;
Be all alike Thine own dear sacrifice.
Thou Who by death hast ransomed us from death,
10   Thyself God's sole well-pleasing Sacrifice,
    Thine only sacred Self I plead with Thee:
    Make Thou it well for them and well for me

That Thou hast given us souls and wills and breath,
And hearts to love Thee, and to see Thee eyes.

9.

Star Sirius and the Pole Star dwell afar
    Beyond the drawings each of other's strength:
    One blazes thro' the brief bright summer's length
Lavishing life-heat from a flaming car;
5   While one unchangeable upon a throne
    Broods o'er the frozen heart of earth alone,
Content to reign the bright particular star
    Of some who wander or of some who groan.
They own no drawings each of other's strength,
10   Nor vibrate in a visible sympathy,
       Nor veer along their courses each toward each:
    Yet are their orbits pitched in harmony
Of one dear heaven, across whose depth and length
    Mayhap they talk together without speech.

10.

Tread softly! all the earth is holy ground.
    It may be, could we look with seeing eyes,
    This spot we stand on is a Paradise
Where dead have come to life and lost been found,
5   Where Faith has triumphed, Martyrdom been crowned,
    Where fools have foiled the wisdom of the wise;
    From this same spot the dust of saints may rise,
And the King's prisoners come to light unbound.
O earth, earth, earth, hear thou thy Maker's Word:
10   "Thy dead thou shalt give up, nor hide thy slain"—
    Some who went weeping forth shall come again
    Rejoicing from the east or from the west,
As doves fly to their windows, love's own bird
    Contented and desirous to the nest.[1]

> [1] "Quali colombe dal disio chiamate
> Con l'ali aperte e ferme al dolce nido
> Volan per l'aer dal voler portate."
> DANTE.

11.

Lifelong our stumbles, lifelong our regret,
    Lifelong our efforts failing and renewed,
    While lifelong is our witness, "God is good:"
Who bore with us till now, bears with us yet,
5   Who still remembers and will not forget,
        Who gives us light and warmth and daily food;
        And gracious promises half understood,
And glories half unveiled, whereon to set
Our heart of hearts and eyes of our desire;
10   Uplifting us to longing and to love,
Luring us upward from this world of mire,
    Urging us to press on and mount above
Ourselves and all we have had experience of,
Mounting to Him in love's perpetual fire.

12.

A dream there is wherein we are fain to scream,
    While struggling with ourselves we cannot speak:
    And much of all our waking life, as weak
And misconceived, eludes us like the dream.
5   For half life's seemings are not what they seem,
        And vain the laughs we laugh, the shrieks we shriek;
        Yea, all is vain that mars the settled meek
Contented quiet of our daily theme.
When I was young I deemed that sweets are sweet:
10   But now I deem some searching bitters are
    Sweeter than sweets, and more refreshing far,
        And to be relished more, and more desired,
And more to be pursued on eager feet,
    On feet untired, and still on feet tho' tired.

13.

Shame is a shadow cast by sin: yet shame
    Itself may be a glory and a grace,
    Refashioning the sin-disfashioned face;
A nobler bruit than hollow-sounded fame,

5   A new-lit lustre on a tarnished name,
           One virtue pent within an evil place,
           Strength for the fight, and swiftness for the race,
       A stinging salve, a life-requickening flame.
       A salve so searching we may scarcely live,
10   A flame so fierce it seems that we must die,
           An actual cautery thrust into the heart:
           Nevertheless, men die not of such smart;
       And shame gives back what nothing else can give,
       Man to himself,—then sets him up on high.

14.

       When Adam and when Eve left Paradise
           Did they love on and cling together still,
           Forgiving one another all that ill
       The twain had wrought on such a different wise?
5   She propped upon his strength, and he in guise
           Of lover tho' of lord, girt to fulfil
           Their term of life and die when God should will;
       Lie down and sleep, and having slept arise.
       Boast not against us, O our enemy!
10   Today we fall, but we shall rise again;
       We grope today, tomorrow we shall see:
           What is today that we should fear today?
           A morrow cometh which shall sweep away
       Thee and thy realm of change and death and pain.

15.

       Let woman fear to teach and bear to learn,
           Remembering the first woman's first mistake.
           Eve had for pupil the inquiring snake,
       Whose doubts she answered on a great concern;
5   But he the tables so contrived to turn,
           It next was his to give and her's to take;
           Till man deemed poison sweet for her sweet sake,
       And fired a train by which the world must burn.
       Did Adam love his Eve from first to last?

10   I think so; as we love who works us ill,
         And wounds us to the quick, yet loves us still.
         Love pardons the unpardonable past:
         Love in a dominant embrace holds fast
            His frailer self, and saves without her will.

16.

         Our teachers teach that one and one make two:
            Later, Love rules that one and one make one:
            Abstruse the problems! neither need we shun,
         But skilfully to each should yield its due.
5   The narrower total seems to suit the few,
            The wider total suits the common run;
            Each obvious in its sphere like moon or sun;
         Both provable by me, and both by you.
         Befogged and witless, in a wordy maze
10   A groping stroll perhaps may do us good;
            If cloyed we are with much we have understood,
         If tired of half our dusty world and ways,
            If sick of fasting, and if sick of food;—
         And how about these long still-lengthening days?

17.

         Something this foggy day, a something which
            Is neither of this fog nor of today,
            Has set me dreaming of the winds that play
         Past certain cliffs, along one certain beach,
5   And turn the topmost edge of waves to spray:
            Ah pleasant pebbly strand so far away,
         So out of reach while quite within my reach,
            As out of reach as India or Cathay!
         I am sick of where I am and where I am not,
10   I am sick of foresight and of memory,
            I am sick of all I have and all I see,
            I am sick of self, and there is nothing new;
         Oh weary impatient patience of my lot!—
            Thus with myself: how fares it, Friends, with you?

18.

So late in Autumn half the world's asleep,
   And half the wakeful world looks pinched and pale;
   For dampness now, not freshness, rides the gale;
And cold and colourless comes ashore the deep
5   With tides that bluster or with tides that creep;
   Now veiled uncouthness wears an uncouth veil
   Of fog, not sultry haze; and blight and bale
Have done their worst, and leaves rot on the heap.
So late in Autumn one forgets the Spring,
10   Forgets the Summer with its opulence,
The callow birds that long have found a wing,
   The swallows that more lately gat them hence:
Will anything like Spring, will anything
   Like Summer, rouse one day the slumbering sense?

19.

Here now is Winter. Winter, after all,
   Is not so drear as was my boding dream
   While Autumn gleamed its latest watery gleam
On sapless leafage too inert to fall.
5   Still leaves and berries clothe my garden wall
   Where ivy thrives on scantiest sunny beam;
   Still here a bud and there a blossom seem
Hopeful, and robin still is musical.
Leaves, flowers and fruit and one delightful song
10   Remain; these days are short, but now the nights
   Intense and long, hang out their utmost lights;
Such starry nights are long, yet not too long;
Frost nips the weak, while strengthening still the strong
   Against that day when Spring sets all to rights.

20.

A hundred thousand birds salute the day:—
   One solitary bird salutes the night:
Its mellow grieving wiles our grief away,
   And tunes our weary watches to delight;

5   It seems to sing the thoughts we cannot say,
       To know and sing them, and to set them right;
     Until we feel once more that May is May,
       And hope some buds may bloom without a blight.
     This solitary bird outweighs, outvies,
10   The hundred thousand merry-making birds
     Whose innocent warblings yet might make us wise
     Would we but follow when they bid us rise,
       Would we but set their notes of praise to words
     And launch our hearts up with them to the skies.

21.

A host of things I take on trust: I take
     The nightingales on trust, for few and far
     Between those actual summer moments are
When I have heard what melody they make.
5   So chanced it once at Como on the Lake:
     But all things, then, waxed musical; each star
     Sang on its course, each breeze sang on its car,
All harmonies sang to senses wide awake.
All things in tune, myself not out of tune,
10   Those nightingales were nightingales indeed:
     Yet truly an owl had satisfied my need,
And wrought a rapture underneath that moon,
     Or simple sparrow chirping from a reed;
For June that night glowed like a doubled June.

22.

The mountains in their overwhelming might
     Moved me to sadness when I saw them first,
And afterwards they moved me to delight;
     Struck harmonies from silent chords which burst
5   Out into song, a song by memory nursed;
For ever unrenewed by touch or sight
Sleeps the keen magic of each day or night,
     In pleasure and in wonder then immersed.
All Switzerland behind us on the ascent,

10   All Italy before us we plunged down
            St. Gothard, garden of forget-me-not:
            Yet why should such a flower choose such a spot?
        Could we forget that way which once we went
            Tho' not one flower had bloomed to weave its crown?

            23.

        Beyond the seas we know, stretch seas unknown
            Blue and bright-coloured for our dim and green;
            Beyond the lands we see, stretch lands unseen
        With many-tinted tangle overgrown;
5   And icebound seas there are like seas of stone,
            Serenely stormless as death lies serene;
            And lifeless tracts of sand, which intervene
        Betwixt the lands where living flowers are blown.
        This dead and living world befits our case
10   Who live and die: we live in wearied hope,
        We die in hope not dead; we run a race
        Today, and find no present halting-place;
            All things we see lie far within our scope,
        And still we peer beyond with craving face.

            24.

        The wise do send their hearts before them to
            Dear blessed Heaven, despite the veil between;
            The foolish nurse their hearts within the screen
        Of this familiar world, where all we do
5   Or have is old, for there is nothing new:
            Yet elder far that world we have not seen;
            God's Presence antedates what else hath been:
        Many the foolish seem, the wise seem few.
        Oh foolishest fond folly of a heart
10   Divided, neither here nor there at rest!
                That hankers after Heaven, but clings to earth;
                That neither here nor there knows thorough mirth,
        Half-choosing, wholly missing, the good part:—
            Oh fool among the foolish, in thy quest.

25.

When we consider what this life we lead
　Is not, and is: how full of toil and pain,
　How blank of rest and of substantial gain,
Beset by hunger earth can never feed,
5　And propping half our hearts upon a reed;
　　We cease to mourn lost treasures, mourned in vain,
　　Lost treasures we are fain and yet not fain
To fetch back for a solace of our need.
For who that feel this burden and this strain,
10　This wide vacuity of hope and heart,
Would bring their cherished well-beloved again:
　　To bleed with them and wince beneath the smart,
To have with stinted bliss such lavish bane,
　　To hold in lieu of all so poor a part?

26.

This Life is full of numbness and of balk,
　Of haltingness and baffled short-coming,
　Of promise unfulfilled, of everything
That is puffed vanity and empty talk:
5　Its very bud hangs cankered on the stalk,
　　Its very song-bird trails a broken wing,
　　Its very Spring is not indeed like Spring,
But sighs like Autumn round an aimless walk.
This Life we live is dead for all its breath;
10　Death's self it is, set off on pilgrimage,
　　Travelling with tottering steps the first short stage:
　　The second stage is one mere desert dust
　　Where Death sits veiled amid creation's rust:—
Unveil thy face, O Death who art not Death.

27.

I have dreamed of Death:—what will it be to die
　Not in a dream, but in the literal truth
　With all Death's adjuncts ghastly and uncouth,

The pang that is the last and the last sigh?
5   Too dulled, it may be, for a last good-bye,
          Too comfortless for any one to soothe,
          A helpless charmless spectacle of ruth
       Thro' long last hours, so long while yet they fly.
       So long to those who hopeless in their fear
10   Watch the slow breath and look for what they dread:
       While I supine with ears that cease to hear,
             With eyes that glaze, with heart pulse running down
             (Alas! no saint rejoicing on her bed),
          May miss the goal at last, may miss a crown.

          28.

       In life our absent friend is far away:
          But death may bring our friend exceeding near,
          Show him familiar faces long so dear
       And lead him back in reach of words we say.
5   He only cannot utter yea or nay
          In any voice accustomed to our ear;
          He only cannot make his face appear
       And turn the sun back on our shadowed day.
       The dead may be around us, dear and dead;
10   The unforgotten dearest dead may be
             Watching us with unslumbering eyes and heart;
       Brimful of words which cannot yet be said,
             Brimful of knowledge they may not impart,
             Brimful of love for you and love for me.

"FOR THINE OWN SAKE, O MY GOD."

       Wearied of sinning, wearied of repentance,
          Wearied of self, I turn, my God, to Thee;
       To Thee, my Judge, on Whose all-righteous sentence
          Hangs mine eternity:
5   I turn to Thee, I plead Thyself with Thee,—
          Be pitiful to me.

Wearied I loathe myself, I loathe my sinning,
  My stains, my festering sores, my misery:
Thou the Beginning, Thou ere my beginning
10   Didst see and didst foresee
Me miserable, me sinful, ruined me,—
  I plead Thyself with Thee.

I plead Thyself with Thee Who art my Maker,
  Regard Thy handiwork that cries to Thee;
15 I plead Thyself with Thee Who wast partaker
      Of mine infirmity,
Love made Thee what Thou art, the love of me,—
  I plead Thyself with Thee.

UNTIL THE DAY BREAK.

When will the day bring its pleasure?
  When will the night bring its rest?
Reaper and gleaner and thresher
  Peer toward the east and the west:—
5   The Sower He knoweth, and He knoweth best.

Meteors flash forth and expire,
  Northern lights kindle and pale;
These are the days of desire,
  Of eyes looking upward that fail;
10   Vanishing days as a finishing tale.

Bows down the crop in its glory
  Tenfold, fiftyfold, hundredfold;
The millet is ripened and hoary,
  The wheat ears are ripened to gold:—
15   Why keep us waiting in dimness and cold?

The Lord of the harvest, He knoweth
  Who knoweth the first and the last:
The Sower Who patiently soweth,
  He scanneth the present and past:
20   He saith, "What thou hast, what remaineth, hold fast."

Yet, Lord, o'er Thy toil-wearied weepers
  The storm-clouds hang muttering and frown:
On threshers and gleaners and reapers,
  O Lord of the harvest, look down;
25   Oh for the harvest, the shout, and the crown!

"Not so," saith the Lord of the reapers,
  The Lord of the first and the last:
"O My toilers, My weary, My weepers,
  What ye have, what remaineth, hold fast.
30   Hide in My heart till the vengeance be past."

"OF HIM THAT WAS READY TO PERISH."

Lord, I am waiting, weeping, watching for Thee:
  My youth and hope lie by me buried and dead,
  My wandering love hath not where to lay its head
    Except Thou say "Come to Me."

5   My noon is ended, abolished from life and light,
  My noon is ended, ended and done away,
  My sun went down in the hours that still were day,
    And my lingering day is night.

How long, O Lord, how long in my desperate pain
10   Shall I weep and watch, shall I weep and long for
        Thee?
  Is Thy grace ended, Thy love cut off from me?
    How long shall I long in vain?

O God Who before the beginning hast seen the end,
  Who hast made me flesh and blood, not frost and not
      fire,
15   Who hast filled me full of needs and love and desire
    And a heart that craves a friend,

Who hast said "Come to Me and I will give thee rest,"
  Who hast said "Take on thee My yoke and learn of Me,"
  Who calledst a little child to come to Thee,
20   And pillowedst John on Thy breast;

Who spak'st to women that followed Thee sorrowing,
    Bidding them weep for themselves and weep for their
        own;
    Who didst welcome the outlaw adoring Thee all alone,
      And plight Thy word as a King,—
25 By Thy love of these and of all that ever shall be,
    By Thy love of these and of all the born and unborn,
    Turn Thy gracious eyes on me and think no scorn
      Of me, not even of me.

Beside Thy Cross I hang on my cross in shame,
30   My wounds, weakness, extremity cry to Thee:
    Bid me also to Paradise, also me
      For the glory of Thy Name.

"BEHOLD THE MAN!"

Shall Christ hang on the Cross, and we not look?
    Heaven, earth and hell stood gazing at the first,
    While Christ for long-cursed man was counted cursed;
Christ, God and Man, Whom God the Father strook
5 And shamed and sifted and one while forsook:—
    Cry shame upon our bodies we have nursed
    In sweets, our souls in pride, our spirits immersed
In wilfulness, our steps run all acrook.
Cry shame upon us! for He bore our shame
10   In agony, and we look on at ease
With neither hearts on flame nor cheeks on flame:
    What hast thou, what have I, to do with peace?
Not to send peace but send a sword He came,
    And fire and fasts and tearful night-watches.

THE DESCENT FROM THE CROSS.

Is this the Face that thrills with awe
    Seraphs who veil their face above?

Is this the Face without a flaw,
   The Face that is the Face of Love?
5 Yea, this defaced, a lifeless clod,
   Hath all creation's love sufficed,
Hath satisfied the love of God,
   This Face the Face of Jesus Christ.

"IT IS FINISHED."

Dear Lord, let me recount to Thee
Some of the great things Thou hast done
    For me, even me
    Thy little one.

5 It was not I that cared for Thee,—
But Thou didst set Thy heart upon
    Me, even me
    Thy little one.

And therefore was it sweet to Thee
10 To leave Thy Majesty and Throne,
    And grow like me
    A Little One,

A swaddled Baby on the knee
Of a dear Mother of Thine own,
15   Quite weak like me
    Thy little one.

Thou didst assume my misery,
And reap the harvest I had sown,
    Comforting me
20   Thy little one.

Jerusalem and Galilee,—
Thy love embraced not those alone,
    But also me
    Thy little one.

25   Thy unblemished Body on the Tree
     Was bared and broken to atone
          For me, for me
          Thy little one.

     Thou lovedst me upon the Tree,—
30   Still me, hid by the ponderous stone,—
          Me always,—me
          Thy little one.

     And love of me arose with Thee
     When death and hell lay overthrown:
35   Thou lovedst me
          Thy little one.

     And love of me went up with Thee
     To sit upon Thy Father's Throne:
          Thou lovest me
40   Thy little one.

     Lord, as Thou me, so would I Thee
     Love in pure love's communion,
          For Thou lov'st me
          Thy little one:

45   Which love of me bring back with Thee
     To Judgment when the Trump is blown,
          Still loving me
          Thy little one.

AN EASTER CAROL.

          Spring bursts today,
     For Christ is risen and all the earth's at play.

          Flash forth, thou Sun,
     The rain is over and gone, its work is done.

5   Winter is past,
     Sweet Spring is come at last, is come at last.

Bud, Fig and Vine,
Bud, Olive, fat with fruit and oil and wine.

Break forth this morn
10   In roses, thou but yesterday a Thorn.

Uplift thy head,
O pure white Lily thro' the Winter dead.

Beside your dams
Leap and rejoice, you merry-making Lambs.

15   All Herds and Flocks
Rejoice, all Beasts of thickets and of rocks.

Sing, Creatures, sing,
Angels and Men and Birds and everything,

All notes of Doves
20   Fill all our world: this is the time of loves.

"BEHOLD A SHAKING."

1.

Man rising to the doom that shall not err,—
    Which hath most dread: the arouse of all or each;
    All kindreds of all nations of all speech,
Or one by one of *him* and *him* and *her*?
5   While dust reanimate begins to stir
    Here, there, beyond, beyond, reach beyond reach;
    While every wave refashions on the beach
Alive or dead-in-life some seafarer.
Now meeting doth not join or parting part;
10   True meeting and true parting wait till then,
        When whoso meet are joined for evermore,
Face answering face and heart at rest in heart:—
        God bring us all rejoicing to the shore
Of happy Heaven, His sheep home to the pen.

2.

Blessed that flock safe penned in Paradise;
 Blessed this flock which tramps in weary ways;
 All form one flock, God's flock; all yield Him praise
By joy or pain, still tending toward the prize.
5 Joy speaks in praises there, and sings and flies
 Where no night is, exulting all its days;
 Here, pain finds solace, for, behold, it prays;
In both love lives the life that never dies.
Here life is the beginning of our death,
10 And death the starting-point whence life ensues;
 Surely our life is death, our death is life:
 Nor need we lay to heart our peace or strife,
But calm in faith and patience breathe the breath
God gave, to take again when He shall choose.

ALL SAINTS.

They are flocking from the East
And the West,
They are flocking from the North
And the South,
5 Every moment setting forth
From realm of snake or lion,
Swamp or sand,
Ice or burning;
Greatest and least,
10 Palm in hand
And praise in mouth,
They are flocking up the path
To their rest,
Up the path that hath
15 No returning.

Up the steeps of Zion
They are mounting,
Coming, coming,
Throngs beyond man's counting;

20   With a sound
      Like innumerable bees
      Swarming, humming
      Where flowering trees
      Many tinted,
25   Many scented,
      All alike abound
      With honey,—
      With a swell
      Like a blast upswaying unrestrainable
30   From a shadowed dell
      To the hill-tops sunny,—
      With a thunder
      Like the ocean when in strength
      Breadth and length
35   It sets to shore;
      More and more
      Waves on waves redoubled pour
      Leaping flashing to the shore
      (Unlike the under
40   Drain of ebb that loseth ground
      For all its roar).

      They are thronging
      From the East and West,
      From the North and South,
45   Saints are thronging, loving, longing,
      To their land
      Of rest,
      Palm in hand
      And praise in mouth.

"TAKE CARE OF HIM."

"Thou whom I love, for whom I died,
    Lovest thou Me, My bride?"—
Low on my knees I love Thee, Lord,
    Believed in and adored.

5   "That I love thee the proof is plain:
       How dost thou love again?"—
    In prayer, in toil, in earthly loss,
       In a long-carried cross.

    "Yea, thou dost love: yet one adept
10   Brings more for Me to accept."—
    I mould my will to match with Thine,
       My wishes I resign.

    "Thou givest much: then give the whole
       For solace of My soul."—
15   More would I give, if I could get:
       But, Lord, what lack I yet?

    "In Me thou lovest Me: I call
       Thee to love Me in all."—
    Brim full my heart, dear Lord, that so
20   My love may overflow.

    "Love Me in sinners and in saints,
       In each who needs or faints."—
    Lord, I will love Thee as I can
       In every brother man.

25   "All sore, all crippled, all who ache,
       Tend all for My dear sake."—
    All for Thy sake, Lord: I will see
       In every sufferer Thee.

    "So I at last, upon My Throne
30   Of glory, Judge alone,
    So I at last will say to thee:
       Thou diddest it to Me."

A MARTYR.
THE VIGIL OF THE FEAST.

    Inner not outer, without gnash of teeth
       Or weeping, save quiet sobs of some who pray
       And feel the Everlasting Arms beneath,—

Blackness of darkness this, but not for aye;
5   Darkness that even in gathering fleeteth fast,
       Blackness of blackest darkness close to day.
Lord Jesus, thro' Thy darkened pillar cast,
       Thy gracious eyes all-seeing cast on me
       Until this tyranny be overpast.
10   Me, Lord, remember who remember Thee,
       And cleave to Thee, and see Thee without sight,
       And choose Thee still in dire extremity,
And in this darkness worship Thee my Light,
       And Thee my Life adore in shadow of death,
15   Thee loved by day, and still beloved by night.
It is the Voice of my Beloved that saith:
       "I am the Way, the Truth, the Life, I go
       Whither that soul knows well that followeth"—
O Lord, I follow, little as I know;
20   At this eleventh hour I rise and take
       My life into my hand, and follow so,
With tears and heart-misgivings and heart-ache;
       Thy feeblest follower, yet Thy follower
       Indomitable for Thine only sake.
25   Tonight I gird my will afresh, and stir
       My strength, and brace my heart to do and dare,
       Marvelling: Will tomorrow wake the whirr
Of the great rending wheel, or from his lair
       Startle the jubilant lion in his rage,
30   Or clench the headsman's hand within my hair,
Or kindle fire to speed my pilgrimage,
       Chariot of fire and horses of sheer fire
       Whirling me home to heaven by one fierce stage?—
Thy Will I will, I Thy desire desire;
35   Let not the waters close above my head,
       Uphold me that I sink not in this mire:
For flesh and blood are frail and sore afraid;
       And young I am, unsatisfied and young,
       With memories, hopes, with cravings all unfed,
40   My song half sung, its sweetest notes unsung,
       All plans cut short, all possibilities,
       Because my cord of life is soon unstrung.

Was I a careless woman set at ease
   That this so bitter cup is brimmed for me?
45   Had mine own vintage settled on the lees?
A word, a puff of smoke, would set me free;
   A word, a puff of smoke, over and gone: . . .
   Howbeit, whom have I, Lord, in heaven but Thee?
Yea, only Thee my choice is fixed upon
50   In heaven or earth, eternity or time:—
Lord, hold me fast, Lord, leave me not alone,
   Thy silly heartless dove that sees the lime
   Yet almost flutters to the tempting bough:
Cover me, hide me, pluck me from this crime.
55   A word, a puff of smoke, would save me now: . . .
   But who, my God, would save me in the day
   Of Thy fierce anger? only Saviour Thou.
Preoccupy my heart, and turn away
   And cover up mine eyes from frantic fear,
60   And stop mine ears lest I be driven astray:
For one stands ever dinning in mine ear
   How my gray Father withers in the blight
   Of love for me, who cruel am and dear;
And how my Mother thro' this lingering night
65   Until the day, sits tearless in her woe,
Loathing for love of me the happy light
Which brings to pass a concourse and a show
   To glut the hungry faces merciless,
   The thousand faces swaying to and fro,
70   Feasting on me unveiled in helplessness
   Alone,—yet not alone: Lord, stand by me
   As once by lonely Paul in his distress.
As blossoms to the sun I turn to Thee;
   Thy dove turns to her window, think no scorn;
75   As one dove to an ark on shoreless sea,
To Thee I turn mine eyes, my heart forlorn;
   Put forth Thy scarred right Hand, kind Lord, take hold
   Of me Thine all-forsaken dove who mourn:
For Thou hast loved me since the days of old,
80   And I love Thee Whom loving I will love
Thro' life's short fever-fits of heat and cold;

Thy Name will I extol and sing thereof,
　　Will flee for refuge to Thy Blessed Name.
　　Lord, look upon me from Thy bliss above:
85　Look down on me, who shrink from all the shame
　　And pangs and desolation of my death,
　　Wrenched piecemeal or devoured or set on flame,
While all the world around me holds its breath
　　With eyes glued on me for a gazing-stock,
90　Pitiless eyes, while no man pitieth.
The floods are risen, I stagger in their shock,
　　My heart reels and is faint, I fail, I faint:
　　My God, set Thou me up upon the rock,
Thou Who didst long ago Thyself acquaint
95　With death, our death; Thou Who didst long ago
　　Pour forth Thy soul for sinner and for saint.
Bear me in mind, whom no one else will know;
　　Thou Whom Thy friends forsook, take Thou my part,
　　Of all forsaken in mine overthrow;
100　Carry me in Thy bosom, in Thy heart,
　　Carry me out of darkness into light,
　　Tomorrow make me see Thee as Thou art.
Lover and friend Thou hidest from my sight:—
　　Alas, alas, mine earthly love, alas,
105　For whom I thought to don the garments white
And white wreath of a bride, this rugged pass
　　Hath utterly divorced me from thy care;
　　Yea, I am to thee as a shattered glass
Worthless, with no more beauty lodging there,
110　Abhorred, lest I involve thee in my doom:
　　For sweet are sunshine and this upper air,
And life and youth are sweet, and give us room
　　For all most sweetest sweetnesses we taste:
　　Dear, what hast thou in common with a tomb?
115　I bow my head in silence, I make haste
　　Alone, I make haste out into the dark,
　　My life and youth and hope all run to waste.
Is this my body cold and stiff and stark,
　　Ashes made ashes, earth becoming earth,
120　Is this a prize for man to make his mark?

Am I that very I who laughed in mirth
    A while ago, a little little while,
    Yet all the while a-dying since my birth?
Now am I tired, too tired to strive or smile;
125   I sit alone, my mouth is in the dust:
    Look Thou upon me, Lord, for I am vile.
In Thee is all my hope, is all my trust,
    On Thee I centre all my self that dies,
    And self that dies not with its mortal crust,
130 But sleeps and wakes, and in the end will rise
    With hymns and hallelujahs on its lips,
    Thee loving with the love that satisfies.
As once in Thine unutterable eclipse
    The sun and moon grew dark for sympathy,
135   And earth cowered quaking underneath the drips
Of Thy slow Blood priceless exceedingly,
    So now a little spare me, and show forth
    Some pity, O my God, some pity of me.
If trouble comes not from the south or north,
140   But meted to us by Thy tender hand,
    Let me not in Thine eyes be nothing worth:
Behold me where in agony I stand,
    Behold me no man caring for my soul,
    And take me to Thee in the far-off land,
145 Shorten the race and lift me to the goal.

WHY?

Lord, if I love Thee and Thou lovest me,
    Why need I any more these toilsome days;
    Why should I not run singing up Thy ways
Straight into heaven, to rest myself with Thee?
5   What need remains of death-pang yet to be,
    If all my soul is quickened in Thy praise;
    If all my heart loves Thee, what need the amaze,
Struggle and dimness of an agony?—
Bride whom I love, if thou too lovest Me,

10   Thou needs must choose My Likeness for thy dower:
            So wilt thou toil in patience, and abide
            Hungering and thirsting for that blessed hour
        When I My Likeness shall behold in thee,
            And thou therein shalt waken satisfied.

        "LOVE IS STRONG AS DEATH."

        "I have not sought Thee, I have not found Thee,
            I have not thirsted for Thee:
        And now cold billows of death surround me,
        Buffeting billows of death astound me,—
5   Wilt Thou look upon, wilt Thou see
            Thy perishing me?"

        "Yea, I have sought thee, yea, I have found thee,
            Yea, I have thirsted for thee,
        Yea, long ago with love's bands I bound thee:
10   Now the Everlasting Arms surround thee,—
            Thro' death's darkness I look and see
            And clasp thee to Me."

IV Poems Added in Poems
(1888)

BIRCHINGTON CHURCHYARD.

A lowly hill which overlooks a flat,
    Half sea, half country side;
    A flat-shored sea of low-voiced creeping tide
Over a chalky weedy mat.

5   A hill of hillocks, flowery and kept green
    Round Crosses raised for hope,
    With many-tinted sunsets where the slope
Faces the lingering western sheen.

A lowly hope, a height that is but low,
10   While Time sets solemnly,
    While the tide rises of Eternity,
Silent and neither swift nor slow.

ONE SEA-SIDE GRAVE.

Unmindful of the roses,
    Unmindful of the thorn,
A reaper tired reposes
    Among his gathered corn:
5   So might I, till the morn!

Cold as the cold Decembers,
    Past as the days that set,
While only one remembers
    And all the rest forget,—
10   But one remembers yet.

BROTHER BRUIN.

A dancing Bear grotesque and funny
Earned for his master heaps of money,
Gruff yet good-natured, fond of honey,
And cheerful if the day was sunny.
5   Past hedge and ditch, past pond and wood
He tramped, and on some common stood;
There cottage children circling gaily,
He in their midmost footed daily.
Pandean pipes and drum and muzzle
10   Were quite enough his brain to puzzle:
But like a philosophic bear
He let alone extraneous care
And danced contented anywhere.

Still, year on year, and wear and tear,
15   Age even the gruffest bluffest bear.
A day came when he scarce could prance,
And when his master looked askance
On dancing Bear who would not dance.
To looks succeeded blows; hard blows
20   Battered his ears and poor old nose.
From bluff and gruff he waxed curmudgeon;
He danced indeed, but danced in dudgeon,
Capered in fury fast and faster:—
Ah, could he once but hug his master
25   And perish in one joint disaster!
But deafness, blindness, weakness growing,
Not fury's self could keep him going.
One dark day when the snow was snowing
His cup was brimmed to overflowing:
30   He tottered, toppled on one side,
Growled once, and shook his head, and died.
The master kicked and struck in vain,
The weary drudge had distanced pain
And never now would wince again.
35   The master growled: he might have howled
Or coaxed—that slave's last growl was growled.

So gnawed by rancour and chagrin
One thing remained: he sold the skin.

What next the man did is not worth
40 Your notice or my setting forth,
But hearken what befell at last.
His idle working days gone past,
And not one friend and not one penny
Stored up (if ever he had any
45 Friends: but his coppers had been many),
All doors stood shut against him, but
The workhouse door which cannot shut.
There he droned on—a grim old sinner
Toothless and grumbling for his dinner,
50 Unpitied quite, uncared for much
(The ratepayers not favouring such),
Hungry and gaunt, with time to spare:
Perhaps the hungry gaunt old Bear
Danced back, a haunting memory.
55 Indeed I hope so: for you see
If once the hard old heart relented
The hard old man may have repented.

"A HELPMEET FOR HIM."

Woman was made for man's delight;
    Charm, O woman, be not afraid!
His shadow by day, his moon by night,
    Woman was made.

5   Her strength with weakness is overlaid;
    Meek compliances veil her might;
Him she stays, by whom she is stayed.

World-wide champion of truth and right,
    Hope in gloom and in danger aid,
10 Tender and faithful, ruddy and white,
    Woman was made.

A SONG OF FLIGHT.

While we slumber and sleep
The sun leaps up from the deep
—Daylight born at the leap!—
Rapid, dominant, free,
5   Athirst to bathe in the uttermost sea.

While we linger at play
—If the year would stand at May!—
Winds are up and away
Over land, over sea,
10   To their goal wherever their goal may be.

It is time to arise,
To race for the promised prize,
—The Sun flies, the Wind flies—
We are strong, we are free,
15   And home lies beyond the stars and the sea.

A WINTRY SONNET.

A Robin said: The Spring will never come,
    And I shall never care to build again.
A Rosebush said: These frosts are wearisome,
    My sap will never stir for sun or rain.
5   The half Moon said: These nights are fogged and slow,
    I neither care to wax nor care to wane.
The Ocean said: I thirst from long ago,
    Because earth's rivers cannot fill the main.—
When Springtime came, red Robin built a nest,
10   And trilled a lover's song in sheer delight.
    Gray hoarfrost vanished, and the Rose with might
Clothed her in leaves and buds of crimson core.
The dim Moon brightened. Ocean sunned his crest,
    Dimpled his blue, yet thirsted evermore.

RESURGAM.

From depth to height, from height to loftier height,
　　The climber sets his foot and sets his face,
　　Tracks lingering sunbeams to their halting-place,
And counts the last pulsations of the light.
5　Strenuous thro' day and unsurprised by night
　　He runs a race with Time and wins the race,
　　Emptied and stripped of all save only Grace,
Will, Love, a threefold panoply of might.
Darkness descends for light he toiled to seek:
10　He stumbles on the darkened mountain-head,
　　Left breathless in the unbreathable thin air,
　　Made freeman of the living and the dead:—
He wots not he has topped the topmost peak,
　　But the returning sun will find him there.

TODAY'S BURDEN.

"Arise, depart, for this is not your rest."—
　　Oh burden of all burdens, still to arise
　　And still depart, nor rest in any wise!
Rolling, still rolling thus to east from west
5　Earth journeys on her immemorial quest,
　　Whom a moon chases in no different guise:
　　Thus stars pursue their courses, and thus flies
The sun, and thus all creatures manifest.
Unrest the common heritage, the ban
10　Flung broadcast on all humankind, on all
　　Who live; for living, all are bound to die:
That which is old, we know that it is man:
　　These have no rest who sit and dream and sigh,
　　Nor have those rest who wrestle and who fall.

"THERE IS A BUDDING MORROW IN MIDNIGHT."

Wintry boughs against a wintry sky;
    Yet the sky is partly blue
        And the clouds are partly bright:—
Who can tell but sap is mounting high
5   Out of sight,
Ready to burst through?

Winter is the mother-nurse of Spring,
    Lovely for her daughter's sake,
        Not unlovely for her own:
10 For a future buds in everything;
        Grown, or blown,
Or about to break.

EXULTATE DEO.

Many a flower hath perfume for its dower,
    And many a bird a song,
And harmless lambs milkwhite beside their dams
    Frolic along;
5 Perfume and song and whiteness offering praise
    In humble, peaceful ways.

Man's high degree hath will and memory,
    Affection and desire,
By loftier ways he mounts of prayer and praise;
10   Fire unto fire,
Deep unto deep responsive, height to height,
    Until he walk in white.

A HOPE CAROL.

A night was near, a day was near,
    Between a day and night
I heard sweet voices calling clear,
    Calling me:

5   I heard a whirr of wing on wing,
        But could not see the sight;
    I long to see my birds that sing,
        I long to see.

    Below the stars, beyond the moon,
10   Between the night and day
    I heard a rising falling tune
        Calling me:
    I long to see the pipes and strings
        Whereon such minstrels play;
15   I long to see each face that sings,
        I long to see.

    Today or may be not today,
        Tonight or not tonight,
    All voices that command or pray
20   Calling me,
    Shall kindle in my soul such fire
    And in my eyes such light
    That I shall see that heart's desire
        I long to see.

CHRISTMAS CAROLS.

1.

Whoso hears a chiming for Christmas at the nighest,
    Hears a sound like Angels chanting in their glee,
Hears a sound like palm boughs waving in the highest,
    Hears a sound like ripple of a crystal sea.
5   Sweeter than a prayer-bell for a saint in dying,
    Sweeter than a death-bell for a saint at rest,
Music struck in Heaven with earth's faint replying
    "Life is good, and death is good, for Christ is Best."

2.

A holy, heavenly chime
Rings fulness in of time,
And on His Mother's breast
Our Lord God ever-Blest
5   Is laid a Babe at rest.

Stoop, Spirits unused to stoop,
Swoop, Angels, flying swoop,
Adoring as you gaze,
Uplifting hymns of praise:—
10 "Grace to the Full of Grace!"

The cave is cold and strait
To hold the angelic state:
More strait it is, more cold,
To foster and infold
15 Its Maker one hour old.

Thrilled thro' with awestruck love,
Meek Angels poised above,
To see their God, look down:
"What, is there never a Crown
20 For Him in swaddled gown?

"How comes He soft and weak
With such a tender cheek,
With such a soft small hand?—
The very Hand which spann'd
25 Heaven when its girth was plann'd.

"How comes He with a voice
Which is but baby-noise?—
That Voice which spake with might
—'Let there be light'—and light
30 Sprang out before our sight.

"What need hath He of flesh
Made flawless now afresh?
What need of human heart?—
Heart that must bleed and smart
35 Choosing the better part.

"But see: His gracious smile
Dismisses us a while
To serve Him in His kin.
Haste we, make haste, begin
40   To fetch His brethren in."

Like stars they flash and shoot,
The Shepherds they salute:
"Glory to God" they sing:
"Good news of peace we bring,
45   For Christ is born a King."

3.

Lo! newborn Jesus
    Soft and weak and small,
Wrapped in baby's bands
By His Mother's hands,
5   Lord God of all.

Lord God of Mary,
    Whom His Lips caress
While He rocks to rest
On her milky breast
10   In helplessness.

Lord God of shepherds
    Flocking through the cold,
Flocking through the dark
To the only Ark,
15   The only Fold.

Lord God of all things
    Be they near or far,
Be they high or low;
Lord of storm and snow,
20   Angel and star.

Lord God of all men,—
    My Lord and my God!
Thou who lovest me,
Keep me close to Thee
25   By staff and rod.

> Lo! newborn Jesus
>   Loving great and small,
> Love's free Sacrifice,
> Opening Arms and Eyes
> 30   To one and all.

A CANDLEMAS DIALOGUE.

"Love brought Me down: and cannot love make thee
Carol for joy to Me?
Hear cheerful robin carol from his tree,
Who owes not half to Me
5   I won for thee."

"Yea, Lord, I hear his carol's wordless voice;
And well may he rejoice
Who hath not heard of death's discordant noise.
So might I too rejoice
10   With such a voice."

"True, thou hast compassed death: but hast not thou
The tree of life's own bough?
Am I not Life and Resurrection now?
My Cross balm-bearing bough
15   For such as thou."

"Ah me, Thy Cross!—but that seems far away;
Thy Cradle-song today
I too would raise and worship Thee and pray:
Not empty, Lord, today
20   Send me away."

"If thou wilt not go empty, spend thy store;
And I will give thee more,
Yea, make thee ten times richer than before.
Give more and give yet more
25   Out of thy store."

"Because Thou givest me Thyself, I will
Thy blessed word fulfil,
Give with both hands, and hoard by giving still:
Thy pleasure to fulfil,
30   And work Thy Will."

MARY MAGDALENE AND THE OTHER MARY.
A SONG FOR ALL MARIES.

Our Master lies asleep and is at rest:
    His Heart has ceased to bleed, His Eye to weep:
The sun ashamed has dropt down in the west:
    Our Master lies asleep.

5   Now we are they who weep, and trembling keep
Vigil, with wrung heart in a sighing breast,
    While slow time creeps, and slow the shadows creep.

Renew Thy youth, as eagle from the nest;
    O Master, who hast sown, arise to reap:—
10   No cock-crow yet, no flush on eastern crest:
    Our Master lies asleep.

PATIENCE OF HOPE.

The flowers that bloom in sun and shade
        And glitter in the dew,
    The flowers must fade.
The birds that build their nest and sing
5   When lovely Spring is new,
        Must soon take wing.

The sun that rises in his strength
    To wake and warm the world,
        Must set at length.
10   The sea that overflows the shore
    With billows frothed and curled,
        Must ebb once more.

All come and go, all wax and wane,
    O Lord, save only Thou
15   Who dost remain
The Same to all eternity.
    All things which fail us now
        We trust to Thee.

V Verses

(1893)

"OUT OF THE DEEP
HAVE I CALLED UNTO THEE,
O LORD."

Alone Lord God, in Whom our trust and peace,
  Our love and our desire, glow bright with hope;
  Lift us above this transitory scope
Of earth, these pleasures that begin and cease,
5 This moon which wanes, these seasons which decrease:
  We turn to Thee; as on an eastern slope
  Wheat feels the dawn beneath night's lingering cope,
Bending and stretching sunward ere it sees.
Alone Lord God, we see not yet we know;
10 By love we dwell with patience and desire,
    And loving so and so desiring pray;
    Thy will be done in earth as heaven today;
As yesterday it was, tomorrow so;
  Love offering love on love's self-feeding fire.

Seven vials hold Thy wrath: but what can hold
  Thy mercy save Thine own Infinitude
  Boundlessly overflowing with all good,
All lovingkindness, all delights untold?
5 Thy Love, of each created love the mould;
  Thyself, of all the empty plenitude;
  Heard of at Ephrata, found in the Wood,
For ever One, the Same, and Manifold.

Lord, give us grace to tremble with that dove
10   Which Ark-bound winged its solitary way
And overpast the Deluge in a day,
    Whom Noah's hand pulled in and comforted:
For we who much more hang upon Thy Love
    Behold its shadow in the deed he did.

"Where neither rust nor moth doth corrupt."

Nerve us with patience, Lord, to toil or rest,
    Toiling at rest on our allotted level;
    Unsnared, unscared by world or flesh or devil,
Fulfilling the good Will of Thy behest:
5   Not careful here to hoard, not here to revel;
But waiting for our treasure and our zest
Beyond the fading splendour of the west,
    Beyond this deathstruck life and deathlier evil.
Not with the sparrow building here a house:
10   But with the swallow tabernacling so
    As still to poise alert to rise and go
        On eager wings with wing-outspeeding wills
Beyond earth's gourds and past her almond boughs,
    Past utmost bound of the everlasting hills.

"As the sparks fly upwards."

Lord, grant us wills to trust Thee with such aim
    Of hope and passionate craving of desire,
    That we may mount aspiring, and aspire
Still while we mount; rejoicing in Thy Name
5   Yesterday, this day, day by day the Same:
    So sparks fly upward scaling heaven by fire,
    Still mount and still attain not, yet draw nigher
While they have being to their fountain flame.

To saints who mount, the bottomless abyss
10   Is as mere nothing, they have set their face
    Onward and upward toward that blessèd place
      Where man rejoices with his God, and soul
With soul, in the unutterable kiss
    Of peace for every victor at the goal.

Lord, make us all love all: that when we meet
    Even myriads of earth's myriads at Thy Bar,
    We may be glad as all true lovers are
Who having parted count reunion sweet.
5 Safe gathered home around Thy blessèd Feet,
    Come home by different roads from near or far,
    Whether by whirlwind or by flaming car,
From pangs or sleep, safe folded round Thy seat.
Oh, if our brother's blood cry out at us,
10   How shall we meet Thee Who hast loved us all,
      Thee Whom we never loved, not loving him?
    The unloving cannot chant with Seraphim,
Bear harp of gold or palm victorious,
    Or face the Vision Beatifical.

O Lord, I am ashamed to seek Thy Face
    As tho' I loved Thee as Thy saints love Thee:
    Yet turn from those Thy lovers, look on me,
Disgrace me not with uttermost disgrace;
5 But pour on me ungracious, pour Thy grace
    To purge my heart and bid my will go free,
    Till I too taste Thy hidden Sweetness, see
Thy hidden Beauty in the holy place.
O Thou Who callest sinners to repent,
10   Call me Thy sinner unto penitence,
      For many sins grant me the greater love:
    Set me above the waterfloods, above
Devil and shifting world and fleshly sense,
Thy Mercy's all-amazing monument.

It is not death, O Christ, to die for Thee:
   Nor is that silence of a silent land
   Which speaks Thy praise so all may understand:
Darkness of death makes Thy dear lovers see
5   Thyself Who Wast and Art and Art to Be;
     Thyself, more lovely than the lovely band
     Of saints who worship Thee on either hand,
Loving and loved thro' all eternity.
Death is not death, and therefore do I hope:
10   Nor silence silence; and I therefore sing
     A very humble hopeful quiet psalm,
   Searching my heart-field for an offering;
A handful of sun-courting heliotrope,
     Of myrrh a bundle, and a little balm.

Lord, grant us eyes to see and ears to hear,
   And souls to love and minds to understand,
   And steadfast faces toward the Holy Land,
And confidence of hope, and filial fear,
5   And citizenship where Thy saints appear
     Before Thee heart in heart and hand in hand,
     And Alleluias where their chanting band
As waters and as thunders fill the sphere.
Lord, grant us what Thou wilt, and what Thou wilt
10   Deny, and fold us in Thy peaceful fold:
     Not as the world gives, give to us Thine own:
Inbuild us where Jerusalem is built
   With walls of jasper and with streets of gold,
     And Thou Thyself, Lord Christ, for Corner Stone.

"Cried out with Tears."

Lord, I believe, help Thou mine unbelief:
   Lord, I repent, help mine impenitence:
   Hide not Thy Face from me, nor spurn me hence,
Nor utterly despise me in my grief;

5   Nor say me nay, who worship with the thief
        Bemoaning my so long lost innocence:—
        Ah me! my penitence a fresh offence,
    Too tardy and too tepid and too brief.
    Lord, must I perish, I who look to Thee?
10   Look Thou upon me, bid me live, not die;
            Say "Come," say not "Depart," tho' Thou art just:
            Yea, Lord, be mindful how out of the dust
        I look to Thee while Thou dost look on me,
        Thou Face to face with me and Eye to eye.

    O Lord, on Whom we gaze and dare not gaze,
        Increase our faith that gazing we may see,
        And seeing love, and loving worship Thee
    Thro' all our days, our long and lengthening days.
5   O Lord, accessible to prayer and praise,
        Kind Lord, Companion of the two or three,
        Good Lord, be gracious to all men and me,
    Lighten our darkness and amend our ways.
    Call up our hearts to Thee, that where Thou art
10   Our treasure and our heart may dwell at one:
            Then let the pallid moon pursue her sun,
        So long as it shall please Thee, far apart,—
            Yet art Thou with us, Thou to Whom we run,
        We hand in hand with Thee and heart in heart.

"I will come and heal him."

    O Lord God, hear the silence of each soul,
        Its cry unutterable of ruth and shame,
        Its voicelessness of self-contempt and blame:
    Nor suffer harp and palm and aureole
5   Of multitudes who praise Thee at the goal,
        To set aside Thy poor and blind and lame;
        Nor blazing Seraphs utterly to outflame
    The spark that flies up from each earthly coal.

My price Thy priceless Blood; and therefore I
10   Price of Thy priceless Blood am precious so
        That good things love me in their love of Thee:
    I comprehend not why Thou lovedst me
    With Thy so mighty Love; but this I know,
No man hath greater love than thus to die.

    Ah Lord, Lord, if my heart were right with Thine
        As Thine with mine, then should I rest resigned
        Awaiting knowledge with a quiet mind
Because of heavenly wisdom's anodyne.
5   Then would Thy Love be more to me than wine,
        Then should I seek being sure at length to find,
        Then should I trust to Thee all humankind
Because Thy Love of them is more than mine.
Then should I stir up hope and comfort me
10   Remembering Thy Cradle and Thy Cross;
        How Heaven to Thee without us had been loss,
        How Heaven with us is Thy one only Heaven,
Heaven shared with us thro' all eternity,
        With us long sought, long loved, and much forgiven.

"The gold of that land is good."

I long for joy, O Lord, I long for gold,
    I long for all Thou profferest to me,
I long for the unimagined manifold
    Abundance laid up in Thy treasury.
5   I long for pearls, but not from mundane sea;
I long for palms, but not from earthly mould;
    Yet in all else I long for, long for Thee,
Thyself to hear and worship and behold.
For Thee, beyond the splendour of that day
10   Where all is day and is not any night;
        For Thee, beyond refreshment of that rest
    To which tired saints press on for its delight:—

Or if not thus for Thee, yet Thee I pray
  To make me long so till Thou make me blest.

Weigh all my faults and follies righteously,
  Omissions and commissions, sin on sin;
  Make deep the scale, O Lord, to weigh them in;
Yea, set the Accuser vulture-eyed to see
5   All loads ingathered which belong to me:
  That so in life the judgement may begin,
  And Angels learn how hard it is to win
One solitary sinful soul to Thee.
I have no merits for a counterpoise:
10   Oh vanity my work and hastening day,
What can I answer to the accusing voice?
    Lord, drop Thou in the counterscale alone
    One Drop from Thine own Heart, and overweigh
    My guilt, my folly, even my heart of stone.

Lord, grant me grace to love Thee in my pain,
  Thro' all my disappointment love Thee still,
  Thy love my strong foundation and my hill,
Tho' I be such as cometh not again,
5   A fading leaf, a spark upon the wane:
  So evermore do Thou Thy perfect Will
  Beloved thro' all my good, thro' all mine ill,
Beloved tho' all my love beside be vain.
If thus I love Thee, how wilt Thou love me,
10   Thou Who art greater than my heart? (Amen!)
    Wilt Thou bestow a part, withhold a part?
The longing of my heart cries out to Thee,
    The hungering thirsting longing of my heart:
    What I forewent wilt Thou not grant me then?

Lord, make me one with Thine own faithful ones,
  Thy Saints who love Thee and are loved by Thee;
  Till the day break and till the shadows flee,

At one with them in alms and orisons;
5   At one with him who toils and him who runs,
And him who yearns for union yet to be;
At one with all who throng the crystal sea
And wait the setting of our moons and suns.
Ah, my beloved ones gone on before,
10   Who looked not back with hand upon the plough!
If beautiful to me while still in sight,
How beautiful must be your aspects now;
Your unknown, well-known aspects in that light
Which clouds shall never cloud for evermore.

"Light of Light."

O Christ our Light, Whom even in darkness we
(So we look up) discern and gaze upon,
O Christ, Thou loveliest Light that ever shone,
Thou Light of Light, Fount of all lights that be,
5   Grant us clear vision of Thy Light to see,
Tho' other lights elude us, or begone
Into the secret of oblivion,
Or gleam in places higher than man's degree.
Who looks on Thee looks full on his desire,
10   Who looks on Thee looks full on Very Love:
Looking, he answers well, "What lack I yet?"
His heat and cold wait not on earthly fire,
His wealth is not of earth to lose or get;
Earth reels, but he has stored his store above.

CHRIST OUR ALL IN ALL.

"The ransomed of the Lord."

Thy lovely saints do bring Thee love,
Incense and joy and gold;

Fair star with star, fair dove with dove,
  Beloved by Thee of old.
5 I, Master, neither star nor dove,
  Have brought Thee sins and tears;
Yet I too bring a little love
  Amid my flaws and fears.
A trembling love that faints and fails
10 Yet still is love of Thee,
A wondering love that hopes and hails
  Thy boundless Love of me;
Love kindling faith and pure desire,
  Love following on to bliss,
15 A spark, O Jesu, from Thy fire,
  A drop from Thine abyss.

Lord, we are rivers running to Thy sea,
Our waves and ripples all derived from Thee:
A nothing we should have, a nothing be,
  Except for Thee.
5 Sweet are the waters of Thy shoreless sea,
Make sweet our waters that make haste to Thee;
Pour in Thy sweetness, that ourselves may be
  Sweetness to Thee.

"An exceeding bitter cry."

Contempt and pangs and haunting fears—
  Too late for hope, too late for ease,
  Too late for rising from the dead;
  Too late, too late to bend my knees,
5   Or bow my head,
Or weep, or ask for tears.

Hark! . . . One I hear Who calls to me:
  "Give Me thy thorn and grief and scorn,
  Give Me thy ruin and regret.

10   Press on thro' darkness toward the morn:
          One loves thee yet:
      Have I forgotten thee?"

      Lord, Who art Thou? Lord, is it Thou
          My Lord and God Lord Jesus Christ?
15   How said I that I sat alone
      And desolate and unsufficed?
              Surely a stone
      Would raise Thy praises now!

      O Lord, when Thou didst call me, didst Thou know
          My heart disheartened thro' and thro',
          Still hankering after Egypt full in view
      Where cucumbers and melons grow?
5   —"Yea, I knew."—

      But, Lord, when Thou didst choose me, didst Thou know
          How marred I was and withered too,
          Nor rose for sweetness nor for virtue rue,
      Timid and rash, hasty and slow?
10   —"Yea, I knew."—

      My Lord, when Thou didst love me, didst Thou know
          How weak my efforts were, how few,
          Tepid to love and impotent to do,
      Envious to reap while slack to sow?
15   —"Yea, I knew."—

      Good Lord, Who knowest what I cannot know
          And dare not know, my false, my true,
          My new, my old; Good Lord, arise and do
      If loving Thou hast known me so.
20   —"Yea, I knew."—

"Thou, God, seest me."

      Ah me, that I should be
      Exposed and open evermore to Thee!—
          "Nay, shrink not from My light,

    And I will make thee glorious in My sight
5   With the overcoming Shulamite."—
    Yea, Lord, Thou moulding me.

    . . . Without a hiding-place
    To hide me from the terrors of Thy Face.—
      "Thy hiding-place is here
10   In Mine own heart, wherefore the Roman spear
      For thy sake I accounted dear."—
    My Jesus! King of Grace.

    . . . Without a veil, to give
    Whiteness before Thy Face that I might live.—
15   "Am I too poor to dress
      Thee in My royal robe of righteousness?
      Challenge and prove My Love's excess."—
    Give, Lord, I will receive.

    . . . Without a pool wherein
20   To wash my piteous self and make me clean.—
      "My Blood hath washed away
      Thy guilt, and still I wash thee day by day:
      Only take heed to trust and pray."—
    Lord, help me to begin.

    Lord Jesus, who would think that I am Thine?
      Ah, who would think
    Who sees me ready to turn back or sink,
      That Thou art mine?
5   I cannot hold Thee fast tho' Thou art mine:
      Hold Thou me fast,
    So earth shall know at last and heaven at last
      That I am Thine.

"The Name of Jesus."

Jesus, Lord God from all eternity,
    Whom love of us brought down to shame,

I plead Thy Life with Thee,
   I plead Thy Death, I plead Thy Name.

5   Jesus, Lord God of every living soul,
      Thy Love exceeds its uttered fame,
   Thy Will can make us whole,
      I plead Thyself, I plead Thy Name.

Lord God of Hosts, most Holy and most High,
   What made Thee tell Thy Name of Love to me?
What made Thee live our life? what made Thee die?
   "My love of thee."

5   I pitched so low, Thou so exceeding high,
      What was it made Thee stoop to look at me
   While flawless sons of God stood wondering by?
      "My love of thee."

   What is there which can lift me up on high
10   That we may dwell together, Thou with me,
   When sin and death and suffering are gone by?
      "My love of thee."

   O Lord, what is that best thing hid on high
      Which makes heaven heaven as Thou hast promised
         me,
15   Yea, makes it Christ to live and gain to die?
      "My love of thee."

Lord, what have I that I may offer Thee?
Look, Lord, I pray Thee, and see.—

What is it thou hast got?
Nay, child, what is it thou hast not?
5   Thou hast all gifts that I have given to thee:
   Offer them all to Me,
   The great ones and the small,
   I will accept them one and all.—

   I have a will, good Lord, but it is marred;
10   A heart both crushed and hard:

Not such as these the gift
Clean-handed lovely saints uplift.—

Nay, child, but wilt thou judge for Me?
I crave not thine, but thee.—

15   Ah, Lord, Who lovest me!
Such as I have now give I Thee.

If I should say "my heart is in my home,"
I turn away from that high halidom
    Where Jesus sits: for nowhere else
    But with its treasure dwells
5   The heart: this Truth and this experience tells.

If I should say "my heart is in a grave,"
I turn away from Jesus risen to save:
    I slight that death He died for me;
    I, too, deny to see
10   His beauty and desirability.

O Lord, Whose Heart is deeper than my heart,
Draw mine to Thine to worship where Thou art;
    For Thine own glory join the twain
    Never to part again,
15   Nor to have lived nor to have died in vain.

Leaf from leaf Christ knows;
Himself the Lily and the Rose:

Sheep from sheep Christ tells;
Himself the Shepherd, no one else:

5   Star and star He names,
Himself outblazing all their flames:

Dove by dove, He calls
To set each on the golden walls:

Drop by drop, He counts
10   The flood of ocean as it mounts:

Grain by grain, His hand
Numbers the innumerable sand.

Lord, I lift to Thee
In peace what is and what shall be:

15   Lord, in peace I trust
To Thee all spirits and all dust.

Lord, carry me.—Nay, but I grant thee strength
To walk and work thy way to Heaven at length.—

Lord, why then am I weak?—Because I give
Power to the weak, and bid the dying live.—

5   Lord, I am tired.—He hath not much desired
The goal, who at the starting-point is tired.—

Lord, dost Thou know?—I know what is in man;
What the flesh can, and what the spirit can.—

Lord, dost Thou care?—Yea, for thy gain or loss
10   So much I cared, it brought Me to the Cross.—

Lord, I believe; help Thou mine unbelief.—
Good is the word; but rise, for life is brief.

The follower is not greater than the Chief:
Follow thou Me along My way of grief.

Lord, I am here.—But, child, I look for thee
        Elsewhere and nearer Me.—
Lord, that way moans a wide insatiate sea:
        How can I come to Thee?—
5   Set foot upon the water, test and see
        If thou canst come to Me.—
Couldst Thou not send a boat to carry me,
        Or dolphin swimming free?—
Nay, boat nor fish if thy will faileth thee:
10   For My Will too is free.—
O Lord, I am afraid.—Take hold on Me:
        I am stronger than the sea.—

Save, Lord, I perish.—I have hold of thee,
  I made and rule the sea,
15 I bring thee to the haven where thou wouldst be.

New creatures; the Creator still the Same
  For ever and for ever: therefore we
  Win hope from God's unsearchable decree
And glorify His still unchanging Name.
5 We too are still the same: and still our claim,
  Our trust, our stay, is Jesus, none but He:
  He still the Same regards us, and still we
Mount toward Him in old love's accustomed flame.
We know Thy wounded Hands: and Thou dost know
10   Our praying hands, our hands that clasp and cling
To hold Thee fast and not to let Thee go.
    All else be new then, Lord, as Thou hast said:
    Since it is Thou, we dare not be afraid,
  Our King of old and still our Self-same King.

"King of kings and Lord of lords."

Is this that Name as ointment poured forth
  For which the virgins love Thee; King of kings
  And Lord of lords? All Seraphs clad in wings;
All Cherubs and all Wheels which south and north,
5 Which east and west turn not in going forth;
  All many-semblanced ordered Spirits, as rings
  Of rainbow in unwonted fashionings,
Might answer, Yes. But we from south and north,
From east and west, a feeble folk who came
10   By desert ways in quest of land unseen,
  A promised land of pasture ever green
    And ever springing ever singing wave,
Know best Thy Name of Jesus: Blessed Name,
  Man's life and resurrection from the grave.

Thy Name, O Christ, as incense streaming forth
  Sweetens our names before God's Holy Face;
Luring us from the south and from the north
    Unto the sacred place.
5   In Thee God's promise is Amen and Yea.
  What art Thou to us? Prize of every lot,
Shepherd and Door, our Life and Truth and Way:—
    Nay, Lord, what art Thou not?

"The Good Shepherd."

O Shepherd with the bleeding Feet,
  Good Shepherd with the pleading Voice,
    What seekest Thou from hill to hill?
Sweet were the valley pastures, sweet
5   The sound of flocks that bleat their joys,
    And eat and drink at will.
Is one worth seeking, when Thou hast of Thine
    Ninety and nine?—

How should I stay My bleeding Feet,
10   How should I hush My pleading Voice?
    I Who chose death and clomb a hill,
Accounting gall and wormwood sweet,
  That hundredfold might bud My joys
    For love's sake and good will.
15 I seek My one, for all there bide of Mine
    Ninety and nine.

"Rejoice with Me."

Little Lamb, who lost thee?—
  I myself, none other.—
Little Lamb, who found thee?—
  Jesus, Shepherd, Brother.
5 Ah, Lord, what I cost Thee!
  Canst Thou still desire?—

Still Mine arms surround thee,
    Still I lift thee higher,
    Draw thee nigher.

Shall not the Judge of all the earth do right?
    Yea, Lord, altho' Thou say me nay:
Shall not His Will be to me life and light?
    Yea, Lord, altho' Thou slay.
5   Yet, Lord, remembering turn and sift and see,
    Remember tho' Thou sift me thro',
Remember my desire, remember me,
    Remember, Lord, and do.

Me and my gift: kind Lord, behold,
    Be not extreme to test or sift;
Thy Love can turn to fire and gold
    Me and my gift.
5   Myself and mine to Thee I lift:
Gather us to Thee from the cold
    Dead outer world where dead things drift.

If much were mine, then manifold
    Should be the offering of my thrift:
10   I am but poor, yet love makes bold
    Me and my gift.

"He cannot deny Himself."

Love still is Love, and doeth all things well,
Whether He show me heaven or hell
    Or earth in her decay
    Passing away
5   On a day.

Love still is Love, tho' He should say, "Depart,"
And break my incorrigible heart,
  And set me out of sight
  Widowed of light
10 In the night.

Love still is Love, is Love, if He should say,
"Come," on that uttermost dread day;
  "Come," unto very me,
  "Come where I be,
15 Come and see."

Love still is Love, whatever comes to pass:
O Only Love, make me Thy glass,
  Thy pleasure to fulfil
  By loving still
20 Come what will.

"Slain from the foundation of the world."

Slain for man, slain for me, O Lamb of God, look down;
 Loving to the end look down, behold and see:
Turn Thine Eyes of pity, turn not on us Thy frown,
 O Lamb of God, slain for man, slain for me.

5 Mark the wrestling, mark the race for indeed a crown;
 Mark our chariots how we drive them heavily;
Mark the foe upon our track blasting thundering down,
 O Lamb of God, slain for man, slain for me.

Set as a Cloudy Pillar against them Thy frown,
10 Thy Face of Light toward us gracious utterly;
Help granting, hope granting, until Thou grant a crown,
 O Lamb of God, slain for man, slain for me.

Lord Jesu, Thou art sweetness to my soul:
 I to myself am bitterness:

Regard my fainting struggle toward the goal,
   Regard my manifold distress,
5   O Sweet Jesu.

Thou art Thyself my goal, O Lord my King:
   Stretch forth Thy hand to save my soul:
What matters more or less of journeying?
   While I touch Thee I touch my goal,
10   O Sweet Jesu.

I, Lord, Thy foolish sinner low and small,
Lack all.
His heart too high was set
Who asked, What lack I yet?
5 Woe's me at my most woeful pass!
I, Lord, who scarcely dare adore,
Weep sore:
Steeped in this rotten world I fear to rot.
Alas! what lack I not?
10 Alas! alas for me! alas
More and yet more!—

Nay, stand up on thy feet, betaking thee
To Me.
Bring fear; but much more bring
15 Hope to thy patient King:
What, is My pleasure in thy death?
I loved that youth who little knew
The true
Width of his want, yet worshipped with goodwill:
20 So love I thee, and still
Prolong thy day of grace and breath.
Rise up and do.—

Lord, let me know mine end, and certify
When I
25 Shall die and have to stand
Helpless on Either Hand,
Cut off, cut off, my day of grace.—
Not so: for what is that to thee?

I see
30   The measure and the number of thy day:
     Keep patience, tho' I slay;
     Keep patience till thou see My Face.
     Follow thou Me.

"Because He first loved us."

I was hungry, and Thou feddest me;
    Yea, Thou gavest drink to slake my thirst:
O Lord, what love gift can I offer Thee
    Who hast loved me first?—

5   Feed My hungry brethren for My sake;
        Give them drink, for love of them and Me:
    Love them as I loved thee, when Bread I brake
        In pure love of thee.—

    Yea, Lord, I will serve them by Thy grace;
10   Love Thee, seek Thee, in them; wait and pray:
    Yet would I love Thyself, Lord, face to face,
        Heart to heart, one day.—

    Let today fulfil its daily task,
        Fill thy heart and hand to them and Me:
15 Tomorrow thou shalt ask, and shalt not ask
        Half I keep for thee.

    Lord, hast Thou so loved us, and will not we
        Love Thee with heart and mind and strength and soul,
        Desiring Thee beyond our glorious goal,
    Beyond the heaven of heavens desiring Thee?
5   Each saint, all saints cry out: Yea me, yea me,
        Thou hast desired beyond an aureole,
        Beyond Thy many Crowns, beyond the whole
    Ninety and nine unwandering family.
    Souls in green pastures of the watered land,

10   Faint pilgrim souls wayfaring thro' the sand,
        Abide with Thee and in Thee are at rest:
        Yet evermore, kind Lord, renew Thy quest
    After new wanderers; such as once Thy Hand
        Gathered, Thy Shoulders bore, Thy Heart caressed.

    As the dove which found no rest
        For the sole of her foot, flew back
    To the ark her only nest
        And found safety there;
5   Because Noah put forth his hand,
        Drew her in from ruin and wrack,
    And was more to her than the land
        And the air:

    So my spirit, like that dove,
10   Fleeth away to an ark
    Where dwelleth a Heart of Love,
        A Hand pierced to save,
    Tho' the sun and the moon should fail,
        Tho' the stars drop into the dark,
15   And my body lay itself pale
        In a grave.

"Thou art Fairer than the children of men."

    A rose, a lily, and the Face of Christ
        Have all our hearts sufficed:
    For He is Rose of Sharon nobly born,
        Our Rose without a thorn;
5   And He is Lily of the Valley, He
        Most sweet in purity.
    But when we come to name Him as He is,
        Godhead, Perfection, Bliss,
    All tongues fall silent, while pure hearts alone
10   Complete their orison.

"As the Apple Tree among the trees of the wood."

As one red rose in a garden where all other roses are
    white
  Blossoms alone in its glory, crowned all alone
In a solitude of own sweetness and fragrance of own
    delight,
  With loveliness not another's and thorns its own;
5 As one ruddy sun amid million orbs comely and
    colourless,
  Among all others, above all others is known;
As it were alone in the garden, alone in the heavenly
    place,
  Chief and centre of all, in fellowship yet alone.

None other Lamb, none other Name,
  None other Hope in heaven or earth or sea,
None other Hiding-place from guilt and shame,
  None beside Thee.

5 My faith burns low, my hope burns low,
  Only my heart's desire cries out in me
By the deep thunder of its want and woe,
  Cries out to Thee.

Lord, Thou art Life tho' I be dead,
10 Love's Fire Thou art however cold I be:
Nor heaven have I, nor place to lay my head,
  Nor home, but Thee.

"Thy Friend and thy Father's Friend forget not."

Friends, I commend to you the narrow way:
  Not because I, please God, will walk therein,
  But rather for the Love Feast of that day,
The exceeding prize which whoso will may win.
5   Earth is half spent and rotting at the core,
    Here hollow death's heads mock us with a grin,

Here heartiest laughter leaves us tired and sore.
  Men heap up pleasures and enlarge desire,
  Outlive desire, and famished evermore
10 Consume themselves within the undying fire.
  Yet not for this God made us: not for this
  Christ sought us far and near to draw us nigher,
Sought us and found and paid our penalties.
  If one could answer "Nay" to God's command,
15 Who shall say "Nay" when Christ pleads all He is
For us, and holds us with a wounded Hand?

"Surely He hath borne our griefs."

Christ's Heart was wrung for me, if mine is sore;
  And if my feet are weary, His have bled;
  He had no place wherein to lay His Head;
If I am burdened, He was burdened more.
5 The cup I drink, He drank of long before;
  He felt the unuttered anguish which I dread;
  He hungered Who the hungry thousands fed,
And thirsted Who the world's refreshment bore.
If grief be such a looking-glass as shows
10 Christ's Face and man's in some sort made alike,
    Then grief is pleasure with a subtle taste:
    Wherefore should any fret or faint or haste?
Grief is not grievous to a soul that knows
  Christ comes,—and listens for that hour to strike.

"They toil not, neither do they spin."

Clother of the lily, Feeder of the sparrow,
  Father of the fatherless, dear Lord,
Tho' Thou set me as a mark against Thine arrow,
  As a prey unto Thy sword,
5 As a ploughed up field beneath Thy harrow,
  As a captive in Thy cord,
Let that cord be love; and some day make my narrow
  Hallowed bed according to Thy Word.   Amen.

Darkness and light are both alike to Thee:
   Therefore to Thee I lift my darkened face;
Upward I look with eyes that fail to see,
   Athirst for future light and present grace.
5   I trust the Hand of Love I scarcely trace.
With breath that fails I cry, Remember me:
   Add breath to breath, so I may run my race
That where Thou art there may Thy servant be.
For Thou art gulf and fountain of my love,
10   I unreturning torrent to Thy sea,
      Yea, Thou the measureless ocean for my rill:
      Seeking I find, and finding seek Thee still:
And oh! that I had wings as hath a dove,
   Then would I flee away to rest with Thee.

"And now why tarriest thou?"

Lord, grant us grace to mount by steps of grace
   From grace to grace nearer, my God, to Thee;
     Not tarrying for tomorrow,
     Lest we lie down in sorrow
5   And never see
Unveiled Thy Face.

Life is a vapour vanishing in haste;
   Life is a day whose sun grows pale to set;
     Life is a stint and sorrow,
10   One day and not the morrow;
     Precious, while yet
It runs to waste.

Lord, strengthen us; lest fainting by the way
   We come not to Thee, we who come from far;
15   Lord, bring us to that morrow
     Which makes an end of sorrow,
     Where all saints are
On holyday.

Where all the saints rest who have heard Thy call,
20   Have risen and striven and now rejoice in rest:
  Call us too home from sorrow
  To rest in Thee tomorrow;
 In Thee our Best,
In Thee our All.

Have I not striven, my God, and watched and prayed?
 Have I not wrestled in mine agony?
 Wherefore still turn Thy Face of Grace from me?
Is Thine Arm shortened that Thou canst not aid?
5   Thy silence breaks my heart: speak tho' to upbraid,
 For Thy rebuke yet bids us follow Thee.
 I grope and grasp not; gaze, but cannot see.
When out of sight and reach my bed is made,
And piteous men and women cease to blame
10   Whispering and wistful of my gain or loss;
 Thou Who for my sake once didst feel the Cross,
  Lord, wilt Thou turn and look upon me then,
And in Thy Glory bring to nought my shame,
 Confessing me to angels and to men?

"God is our Hope and Strength."

Tempest and terror below; but Christ the Almighty
  above.
 Tho' the depth of the deep overflow, tho' fire run
  along on the ground,
Tho' all billows and flames make a noise,—and where
  is an Ark for the dove?—
 Tho' sorrows rejoice against joys, and death and
  destruction abound:
5   Yet Jesus abolisheth death, and Jesus Who loves us we
  love;

His dead are renewed with a breath, His lost are the
  sought and the found.
Thy wanderers call and recall, Thy dead men lift out of
    the ground;
  O Jesus, Who lovest us all, stoop low from Thy Glory
    above:
Where sin hath abounded make grace to abound and to
  superabound,
10   Till we gaze on Thee face unto Face, and respond to
    Thee love unto Love.

Day and night the Accuser makes no pause,
Day and night protest the Righteous Laws,
Good and Evil witness to man's flaws;
Man the culprit, man's the ruined cause,
5   Man midway to death's devouring jaws
  And the worm that gnaws.

Day and night our Jesus makes no pause,
Pleads His own fulfilment of all laws,
Veils with His Perfections mortal flaws,
10   Clears the culprit, pleads the desperate cause,
Plucks the dead from death's devouring jaws
  And the worm that gnaws.

O mine enemy
Rejoice not over me!
  Jesus waiteth to be gracious:
    I will yet arise,
5   Mounting free and far,
Past sun and star,
  To a house prepared and spacious
    In the skies.

Lord, for Thine own sake
10   Kindle my heart and break;
  Make mine anguish efficacious
    Wedded to Thine own:

Be not Thy dear pain,
Thy Love in vain,
15   Thou Who waitest to be gracious
     On Thy Throne.

Lord, dost Thou look on me, and will not I
    Launch out my heart to Heaven to look on Thee?
    Here if one loved me I should turn to see,
And often think on him and often sigh,
5   And by a tender friendship make reply
    To love gratuitous poured forth on me,
    And nurse a hope of happy days to be,
And mean "until we meet" in each good-bye.
Lord, Thou dost look and love is in Thine Eyes,
10   Thy Heart is set upon me day and night,
    Thou stoopest low to set me far above:
O Lord, that I may love Thee make me wise;
    That I may see and love Thee grant me sight;
    And give me love that I may give Thee love.

"Peace I leave with you."

Tumult and turmoil, trouble and toil,
    Yet peace withal in a painful heart;
Never a grudge and never a broil,
    And ever the better part.
5   O my King and my heart's own choice,
    Stretch Thy Hand to Thy fluttering dove;
Teach me, call to me with Thy Voice,
    Wrap me up in Thy Love.

O Christ our All in each, our All in all!
    Others have this or that, a love, a friend,
    A trusted teacher, a long worked for end:

But what to me were Peter or were Paul
5   Without Thee? fame or friend if such might be?
            Thee wholly will I love, Thee wholly seek,
Follow Thy foot-track, hearken for Thy call.
            O Christ mine All in all, my flesh is weak,
            A trembling fawning tyrant unto me:
10   Turn, look upon me, let me hear Thee speak:
            Tho' bitter billows of Thine utmost sea
Swathe me, and darkness build around its wall,
Yet will I rise, Thou lifting when I fall,
            And if Thou hold me fast, yet cleave to Thee.

Because Thy Love hath sought me,
            All mine is Thine and Thine is mine:
Because Thy Blood hath bought me,
            I will not be mine own but Thine.

5   I lift my heart to Thy Heart,
            Thy Heart sole resting-place for mine:
Shall Thy Heart crave for my heart,
            And shall not mine crave back for Thine?

Thy fainting spouse, yet still Thy spouse;
            Thy trembling dove, yet still Thy dove;
Thine own by mutual vows,
            By mutual love.

5   Recall Thy vows, if not her vows;
            Recall Thy Love, if not her love:
For weak she is, Thy spouse,
            And tired, Thy dove.

"Like as the hart desireth the water brooks."

My heart is yearning:
            Behold my yearning heart,

And lean low to satisfy
  Its lonely beseeching cry,
5   For Thou its fulness art.

Turn, as once turning
  Thou didst behold Thy Saint
    In deadly extremity;
    Didst look, and win back to Thee
10   His will frighted and faint.

Kindle my burning
  From Thine unkindled Fire;
    Fill me with gifts and with grace
    That I may behold Thy Face,
15   For Thee I desire.

My heart is yearning,
  Yearning and thrilling thro'
    For Thy Love mine own of old,
    For Thy Love unknown, untold,
20   Ever old, ever new.

"That where I am, there ye may be also."

How know I that it looms lovely that land I have never
    seen,
With morning-glories and heartsease and unexampled
    green,
With neither heat nor cold in the balm-redolent air?
  Some of this, not all, I know; but this is so;
5   Christ is there.

How know I that blessedness befalls who dwell in
    Paradise,
The outwearied hearts refreshing, rekindling the
    worn-out eyes,
All souls singing, seeing, rejoicing everywhere?
  Nay, much more than this I know; for this is so;
10   Christ is there.

O Lord Christ, Whom having not seen I love and desire
    to love,
O Lord Christ, Who lookest on me uncomely yet still Thy
    dove,
Take me to Thee in Paradise, Thine own made fair;
    For whatever else I know, this thing is so;
15   Thou art there.

"Judge not according to the appearance."

Lord, purge our eyes to see
Within the seed a tree,
    Within the glowing egg a bird,
      Within the shroud a butterfly:
5   Till taught by such, we see
Beyond all creatures Thee,
    And hearken for Thy tender word,
      And hear it, "Fear not: it is I."

My God, wilt Thou accept, and will not we
    Give aught to Thee?
The kept we lose, the offered we retain
    Or find again.
5   Yet if our gift were lost, we well might lose
    All for Thy use:
Well lost for Thee, Whose Love is all for us
    Gratuitous.

A chill blank world. Yet over the utmost sea
The light of a coming dawn is rising to me,
    No more than a paler shade of darkness as yet;
While I lift my heart, O Lord, my heart unto Thee
5   Who hast not forgotten me, yea, Who wilt not forget.

Forget not Thy sorrowful servant, O Lord my God,
Weak as I cry, faint as I cry underneath Thy rod,

Soon to lie dumb before Thee a body devoid of breath,
Dust to dust, ashes to ashes, a sod to the sod:
10   Forget not my life, O my Lord, forget not my death.

"The Chiefest among ten thousand."

O Jesu, better than Thy gifts
  Art Thou Thine only Self to us!
Palm branch its triumph, harp uplifts
  Its triumph-note melodious:
5   But what are such to such as we?
O Jesu, better than Thy saints
  Art Thou Thine only Self to us!
The heart faints and the spirit faints
  For only Thee all-Glorious,
10   For Thee, O only Lord, for Thee.

SOME FEASTS AND FASTS.

ADVENT SUNDAY.

Behold, the Bridegroom cometh: go ye out
With lighted lamps and garlands round about
To meet Him in a rapture with a shout.

It may be at the midnight, black as pitch,
5   Earth shall cast up her poor, cast up her rich.

It may be at the crowing of the cock
Earth shall upheave her depth, uproot her rock.

For lo, the Bridegroom fetcheth home the Bride:
His Hands are Hands she knows, she knows His Side.

10   Like pure Rebekah at the appointed place,
Veiled, she unveils her face to meet His Face.

Like great Queen Esther in her triumphing,
She triumphs in the Presence of her King.

His Eyes are as a Dove's, and she's Dove-eyed;
15   He knows His lovely mirror, sister, Bride.

He speaks with Dove-voice of exceeding love,
And she with love-voice of an answering Dove.

Behold, the Bridegroom cometh: go we out
With lamps ablaze and garlands round about
20   To meet Him in a rapture with a shout.

ADVENT.

Earth grown old, yet still so green,
        Deep beneath her crust of cold
Nurses fire unfelt, unseen:
        Earth grown old.

5   We who live are quickly told:
Millions more lie hid between
        Inner swathings of her fold.

When will fire break up her screen?
        When will life burst thro' her mould?
10   Earth, earth, earth, thy cold is keen,
        Earth grown old.

Sooner or later: yet at last
The Jordan must be past;

It may be he will overflow
His banks the day we go;

5   It may be that his cloven deep
Will stand up on a heap.

Sooner or later: yet one day
We all must pass that way;

Each man, each woman, humbled, pale,
10   Pass veiled within the veil;

Child, parent, bride, companion,
Alone, alone, alone.

For none a ransom can be paid,
A suretyship be made:
15 I, bent by mine own burden, must
Enter my house of dust;

I, rated to the full amount,
Must render mine account.

When earth and sea shall empty all
20 Their graves of great and small;

When earth wrapped in a fiery flood
Shall no more hide her blood;

When mysteries shall be revealed;
All secrets be unsealed;

25 When things of night, when things of shame,
Shall find at last a name,

Pealed for a hissing and a curse
Throughout the universe:

Then Awful Judge, most Awful God,
30 Then cause to bud Thy rod,

To bloom with blossoms, and to give
Almonds; yea, bid us live.

I plead Thyself with Thee, I plead
Thee in our utter need:

35 Jesus, most Merciful of Men,
Show mercy on us then;

Lord God of Mercy and of men,
Show mercy on us then.

CHRISTMAS EVE.

Christmas hath a darkness
    Brighter than the blazing noon,

Christmas hath a chillness
    Warmer than the heat of June,
5 Christmas hath a beauty
    Lovelier than the world can show:
For Christmas bringeth Jesus,
    Brought for us so low.

Earth, strike up your music,
10   Birds that sing and bells that ring;
Heaven hath answering music
    For all Angels soon to sing:
Earth, put on your whitest
    Bridal robe of spotless snow:
15 For Christmas bringeth Jesus,
    Brought for us so low.

CHRISTMAS DAY.

A baby is a harmless thing
    And wins our hearts with one accord,
And Flower of Babies was their King,
    Jesus Christ our Lord:
5 Lily of lilies He
Upon His Mother's knee;
Rose of roses, soon to be
Crowned with thorns on leafless tree.

A lamb is innocent and mild
10   And merry on the soft green sod;
And Jesus Christ, the Undefiled,
    Is the Lamb of God:
Only spotless He
Upon His Mother's knee;
15 White and ruddy, soon to be
Sacrificed for you and me.

Nay, lamb is not so sweet a word,
    Nor lily half so pure a name;
Another name our hearts hath stirred,
20   Kindling them to flame:

"Jesus" certainly
Is music and melody:
Heart with heart in harmony
Carol we and worship we.

CHRISTMASTIDE.

Love came down at Christmas,
    Love all lovely, Love Divine;
Love was born at Christmas,
    Star and Angels gave the sign.

5   Worship we the Godhead,
    Love Incarnate, Love Divine;
Worship we our Jesus:
    But wherewith for sacred sign?

Love shall be our token,
10   Love be yours and love be mine,
Love to God and all men,
    Love for plea and gift and sign.

ST. JOHN, APOSTLE.

Earth cannot bar flame from ascending,
Hell cannot bind light from descending,
Death cannot finish life never ending.

Eagle and sun gaze at each other,
5   Eagle at sun, brother at Brother,
Loving in peace and joy one another.

O St. John, with chains for thy wages,
Strong thy rock where the storm-blast rages,
Rock of refuge, the Rock of Ages.

10   Rome hath passed with her awful voice,
Earth is passing with all her joys,
Heaven shall pass away with a noise.

So from us all follies that please us,
So from us all falsehoods that ease us,—
15 Only all saints abide with their Jesus.

Jesus, in love looking down hither,
Jesus, by love draw us up thither,
That we in Thee may abide together.

"Beloved, let us love one another," says St. John,
   Eagle of eagles calling from above:
Words of strong nourishment for life to feed upon,
   "Beloved, let us love."

5   Voice of an eagle, yea, Voice of the Dove:
If we may love, winter is past and gone;
   Publish we, praise we, for lo! it is enough.

More sunny than sunshine that ever yet shone,
   Sweetener of the bitter, smoother of the rough,
10 Highest lesson of all lessons for all to con,
   "Beloved, let us love."

HOLY INNOCENTS.

They scarcely waked before they slept,
   They scarcely wept before they laughed;
   They drank indeed death's bitter draught,
But all its bitterest dregs were kept
5 And drained by Mothers while they wept.

From Heaven the speechless Infants speak:
   Weep not (they say), our Mothers dear,
   For swords nor sorrows come not here.
Now we are strong who were so weak,
10 And all is ours we could not seek.

We bloom among the blooming flowers,
   We sing among the singing birds;
   Wisdom we have who wanted words:

Here morning knows not evening hours,
15   All's rainbow here without the showers.

And softer than our Mother's breast,
  And closer than our Mother's arm,
  Is here the Love that keeps us warm
And broods above our happy nest.
20   Dear Mothers, come: for Heaven is best.

Unspotted lambs to follow the one Lamb,
  Unspotted doves to wait on the one Dove;
To whom Love saith, "Be with Me where I am,"
  And lo! their answer unto Love is love.

5   For tho' I know not any note they know,
    Nor know one word of all their song above,
I know Love speaks to them, and even so
  I know the answer unto Love is love.

EPIPHANY.

"Lord Babe, if Thou art He
We sought for patiently,
Where is Thy court?
Hither may prophecy and star resort;
5   Men heed not their report."—
    "Bow down and worship, righteous man:
    This Infant of a span
    Is He man sought for since the world began!"—
"Then, Lord, accept my gold, too base a thing
10   For Thee, of all kings King."—

"Lord Babe, despite Thy youth
I hold Thee of a truth
Both Good and Great:
But wherefore dost Thou keep so mean a state,
15   Low-lying desolate?"—
    "Bow down and worship, righteous seer:

The Lord our God is here
Approachable, Who bids us all draw near."—
"Wherefore to Thee I offer frankincense,
20   Thou Sole Omnipotence."—

"But I have only brought
Myrrh; no wise afterthought
Instructed me
To gather pearls or gems, or choice to see
25   Coral or ivory."—
    "Not least thine offering proves thee wise:
    For myrrh means sacrifice,
    And He that lives, this Same is He that dies."—
"Then here is myrrh: alas! yea, woe is me
30   That myrrh befitteth Thee."—

Myrrh, frankincense, and gold:
And lo! from wintry fold
Good-will doth bring
A Lamb, the innocent likeness of this King
35   Whom stars and seraphs sing:
    And lo! the bird of love, a Dove
    Flutters and coos above:
    And Dove and Lamb and Babe agree in love:—
Come all mankind, come all creation hither,
40   Come, worship Christ together.

EPIPHANYTIDE.

Trembling before Thee we fall down to adore Thee,
    Shamefaced and trembling we lift our eyes to Thee:
O First and with the last! annul our ruined past,
    Rebuild us to Thy glory, set us free
5   From sin and from sorrow to fall down and worship
        Thee.

Full of pity view us, stretch Thy sceptre to us,
    Bid us live that we may give ourselves to Thee:

O faithful Lord and True! stand up for us and do,
   Make us lovely, make us new, set us free—
10   Heart and soul and spirit—to bring all and worship
      Thee.

SEPTUAGESIMA.
"So run that ye may obtain."

One step more, and the race is ended;
   One word more, and the lesson's done;
One toil more, and a long rest follows
    At set of sun.

5   Who would fail, for one step withholden?
   Who would fail, for one word unsaid?
Who would fail, for a pause too early?
    Sound sleep the dead.

One step more, and the goal receives us;
10   One word more, and life's task is done;
One toil more, and the Cross is carried
    And sets the sun.

SEXAGESIMA.
"Cursed is the ground for thy sake."

Yet earth was very good in days of old,
   And earth is lovely still:
Still for the sacred flock she spreads the fold,
   For Sion rears the hill.

5   Mother she is, and cradle of our race,
   A depth where treasures lie,
The broad foundation of a holy place,
   Man's step to scale the sky.

She spreads the harvest-field which Angels reap,
10   And lo! the crop is white;
She spreads God's Acre where the happy sleep
   All night that is not night.

Earth may not pass till heaven shall pass away,
  Nor heaven may be renewed
15 Except with earth: and once more in that day
  Earth shall be very good.

That Eden of earth's sunrise cannot vie
With Paradise beyond her sunset sky
    Hidden on high.

Four rivers watered Eden in her bliss,
5 But Paradise hath One which perfect is
    In sweetnesses.

Eden had gold, but Paradise hath gold
Like unto glass of splendours manifold
    Tongue hath not told.

10 Eden had sun and moon to make her bright;
But Paradise hath God and Lamb for light,
    And hath no night.

Unspotted innocence was Eden's best;
Great Paradise shows God's fulfilled behest,
15   Triumph and rest.

Hail, Eve and Adam, source of death and shame!
New life has sprung from death, and Jesu's Name
    Clothes you with fame.

Hail Adam, and hail Eve! your children rise
20 And call you blessed, in their glad surmise
    Of Paradise.

QUINQUAGESIMA.

Love is alone the worthy law of love:
  All other laws have presupposed a taint:
  Love is the law from kindled saint to saint,
From lamb to lamb, from dove to answering dove.

5   Love is the motive of all things that move
         Harmonious by free will without constraint:
         Love learns and teaches: love shall man acquaint
      With all he lacks, which all his lack is love.
      Because Love is the fountain, I discern
10   The stream as love: for what but love should flow
            From fountain Love? not bitter from the sweet!
         I ignorant, have I laid claim to know?
            Oh, teach me, Love, such knowledge as is meet
      For one to know who is fain to love and learn.

         Piteous my rhyme is
      What while I muse of love and pain,
      Of love misspent, of love in vain,
      Of love that is not loved again:
5   And is this all then?
            As long as time is,
      Love loveth. Time is but a span,
      The dalliance space of dying man:
      And is this all immortals can?
10   The gain were small then.

         Love loves for ever,
      And finds a sort of joy in pain,
      And gives with nought to take again,
      And loves too well to end in vain:
15   Is the gain small then?
            Love laughs at "never,"
      Outlives our life, exceeds the span
      Appointed to mere mortal man:
      All which love is and does and can
20   Is all in all then.

ASH WEDNESDAY.

My God, my God, have mercy on my sin,
For it is great; and if I should begin

To tell it all, the day would be too small
  To tell it in.

5 My God, Thou wilt have mercy on my sin
For Thy Love's sake: yea, if I should begin
To tell This all, the day would be too small
  To tell it in.

Good Lord, today
I scarce find breath to say:
 Scourge, but receive me.
For stripes are hard to bear, but worse
5 Thy intolerable curse;
 So do not leave me.

Good Lord, lean down
In pity, tho' Thou frown;
 Smite, but retrieve me:
10 For so Thou hold me up to stand
And kiss Thy smiting hand,
 It less will grieve me.

LENT.

It is good to be last not first,
 Pending the present distress;
It is good to hunger and thirst,
 So it be for righteousness.
5 It is good to spend and be spent,
 It is good to watch and to pray:
Life and Death make a goodly Lent
 So it leads us to Easter Day.

EMBERTIDE.

I saw a Saint.—How canst thou tell that he
 Thou sawest was a Saint?—

I saw one like to Christ so luminously
   By patient deeds of love, his mortal taint
5   Seemed made his groundwork for humility.

And when he marked me downcast utterly
   Where foul I sat and faint,
Then more than ever Christ-like kindled he;
   And welcomed me as I had been a saint,
10 Tenderly stooping low to comfort me.

Christ bade him, "Do thou likewise." Wherefore he
   Waxed zealous to acquaint
His soul with sin and sorrow, if so be
   He might retrieve some latent saint:—
15 "Lo, I, with the child God hath given to me!"

MID-LENT.

Is any grieved or tired? Yea, by God's Will:
   Surely God's Will alone is good and best:
   O weary man, in weariness take rest,
O hungry man, by hunger feast thy fill.
5 Discern thy good beneath a mask of ill,
   Or build of loneliness thy secret nest:
   At noon take heart, being mindful of the west,
At night wake hope, for dawn advances still.
At night wake hope. Poor soul, in such sore need
10 Of wakening and of girding up anew,
   Hast thou that hope which fainting doth pursue?
     No saint but hath pursued and hath been faint;
Bid love wake hope, for both thy steps shall speed,
   Still faint yet still pursuing, O thou saint.

PASSIONTIDE.

It is the greatness of Thy love, dear Lord, that we
      would celebrate
   With sevenfold powers.

Our love at best is cold and poor, at best unseemly
    for Thy state,
  This best of ours.
5   Creatures that die, we yet are such as Thine own hands
    deigned to create:
  We frail as flowers,
We bitter bondslaves ransomed at a price incomparably
    great
  To grace Heaven's bowers.

Thou callest: "Come at once"—and still Thou callest
    us: "Come late, tho' late"—
10   (The moments fly)—
"Come, every one that thirsteth, come"—"Come prove
    Me, knocking at My gate"—
  (Some souls draw nigh!)—
"Come thou who waiting seekest Me"—"Come thou for
    whom I seek and wait"—
  (Why will we die?)—
15   "Come and repent: come and amend: come joy the joys
    unsatiate"—
  —(Christ passeth by . . .)—
  Lord, pass not by—I come—and I—and I.
  Amen.

PALM SUNDAY.
"He treadeth the winepress of the fierceness and wrath of Almighty God."

I lift mine eyes, and see
Thee, tender Lord, in pain upon the tree,
Athirst for my sake and athirst for me.

"Yea, look upon Me there,
5   Compassed with thorns and bleeding everywhere,
For thy sake bearing all, and glad to bear."

I lift my heart to pray:
Thou Who didst love me all that darkened day,
Wilt Thou not love me to the end alway?

10   "Yea, thee My wandering sheep,
      Yea, thee My scarlet sinner slow to weep,
      Come to Me, I will love thee and will keep."

      Yet am I racked with fear:
      Behold the unending outer darkness drear,
15   Behold the gulf unbridgeable and near!

      "Nay, fix thy heart, thine eyes,
      Thy hope upon My boundless sacrifice:
      Will I lose lightly one so dear-bought prize?"

      Ah, Lord; it is not Thou,
20   Thou that wilt fail; yet woe is me, for how
      Shall I endure who half am failing now?

      "Nay, weld thy resolute will
      To Mine: glance not aside for good or ill:
      I love thee; trust Me still and love Me still."

25   Yet Thou Thyself hast said,
      When Thou shalt sift the living from the dead
      Some must depart shamed and uncomforted.

      "Judge not before that day:
      Trust Me with all thy heart, even tho' I slay:
30   Trust Me in love, trust on, love on, and pray."

MONDAY IN HOLY WEEK.
"The Voice of my Beloved."

      Once I ached for thy dear sake:
      Wilt thou cause Me now to ache?
      Once I bled for thee in pain:
      Wilt thou rend My Heart again?
5   Crown of thorns and shameful tree,
      Bitter death I bore for thee,
      Bore My Cross to carry thee,
      And wilt thou have nought of Me?

TUESDAY IN HOLY WEEK.

By Thy long-drawn anguish to atone,
Jesus Christ, show mercy on Thine own:
Jesus Christ, show mercy and atone
Not for other sake except Thine own.

5   Thou Who thirsting on the Cross didst see
All mankind and all I love and me,
Still from Heaven look down in love and see
All mankind and all I love and me.

WEDNESDAY IN HOLY WEEK.

Man's life is death. Yet Christ endured to live,
    Preaching and teaching, toiling to and fro,
Few men accepting what He yearned to give,
    Few men with eyes to know
5   His Face, that Face of Love He stooped to show.

Man's death is life. For Christ endured to die
    In slow unuttered weariness of pain,
A curse and an astonishment, passed by,
    Pointed at, mocked again
10   By men for whom He shed His Blood—in vain?

MAUNDY THURSDAY.
"And the Vine said . . . Should I leave my wine, which cheereth God and
man, and go to be promoted over the trees?"

The great Vine left its glory to reign as Forest King.
"Nay," quoth the lofty forest trees, "we will not have this
                    thing;
We will not have this supple one enring us with its ring.
Lo, from immemorial time our might towers shadowing:
5   Not we were born to curve and droop, not we to climb
                    and cling:

We buffet back the buffeting wind, tough to its buffeting:
We screen great beasts, the wild fowl build in our heads
    and sing,
Every bird of every feather from off our tops takes wing:
I a king, and thou a king, and what king shall be our
    king?"

10   Nevertheless the great Vine stooped to be the Forest King,
While the forest swayed and murmured like seas that are
    tempesting:
Stooped and drooped with thousand tendrils in thirsty
    languishing;
Bowed to earth and lay on earth for earth's replenishing;
Put off sweetness, tasted bitterness, endured time's
    fashioning;
15   Put off life and put on death: and lo! it was all to bring
All its fellows down to a death which hath lost the sting,
All its fellows up to a life in endless triumphing,—
I a king, and thou a king, and this King to be our King.

GOOD FRIDAY MORNING.
"Bearing His Cross."

Up Thy Hill of Sorrows
    Thou all alone,
Jesus, man's Redeemer,
    Climbing to a Throne:
5   Thro' the world triumphant,
    Thro' the Church in pain,
Which think to look upon Thee
    No more again.

Upon my hill of sorrows
10   I, Lord, with Thee,
Cheered, upheld, yea, carried,
    If a need should be:
Cheered, upheld, yea, carried,
    Never left alone,
15   Carried in Thy heart of hearts
    To a throne.

GOOD FRIDAY.

Lord Jesus Christ, grown faint upon the Cross,
  A sorrow beyond sorrow in Thy look,
    The unutterable craving for my soul;
    Thy love of me sufficed
5 To load upon Thee and make good my loss
    In face of darkened heaven and earth that shook:—
      In face of earth and heaven, take Thou my whole
    Heart, O Lord Jesus Christ.

GOOD FRIDAY EVENING.
"Bring forth the Spear."

No Cherub's heart or hand for us might ache,
  No Seraph's heart of fire had half sufficed:
Thine own were pierced and broken for our sake,
  O Jesus Christ.

5 Therefore we love Thee with our faint good-will,
  We crave to love Thee not as heretofore,
To love Thee much, to love Thee more, and still
  More and yet more.

"A bundle of myrrh is my Well-beloved unto me."

Thy Cross cruciferous doth flower in all
  And every cross, dear Lord, assigned to us:
Ours lowly-statured crosses; Thine how tall,
  Thy Cross cruciferous.

5 Thy Cross alone life-giving, glorious:
For love of Thine, souls love their own when small,
  Easy and light, or great and ponderous.

Since deep calls deep, Lord, hearken when we call;
  When cross calls Cross racking and emulous:—
10 Remember us with him who shared Thy gall,
  Thy Cross cruciferous.

EASTER EVEN.

The tempest over and gone, the calm begun,
　　Lo, "it is finished" and the Strong Man sleeps:
All stars keep vigil watching for the sun,
　　The moon her vigil keeps.

5　A garden full of silence and of dew
　　Beside a virgin cave and entrance stone:
Surely a garden full of Angels too,
　　Wondering, on watch, alone.

They who cry "Holy, Holy, Holy," still
10　Veiling their faces round God's Throne above,
May well keep vigil on this heavenly hill
　　And cry their cry of love,

Adoring God in His new mystery
　　Of Love more deep than hell, more strong than death;
15　Until the day break and the shadows flee,
　　The Shaking and the Breath.

Our Church Palms are budding willow twigs.

While Christ lay dead the widowed world
　　Wore willow green for hope undone:
Till, when bright Easter dews impearled
　　The chilly burial earth,
5　All north and south, all east and west,
　　Flushed rosy in the arising sun;
Hope laughed, and Faith resumed her rest,
　　And Love remembered mirth.

EASTER DAY.

Words cannot utter
　　Christ His returning:
Mankind, keep jubilee,
　　Strip off your mourning,

5   Crown you with garlands,
          Set your lamps burning.

       Speech is left speechless;
          Set you to singing,
       Fling your hearts open wide,
10   Set your bells ringing:
       Christ the Chief Reaper
          Comes, His sheaf bringing.

       Earth wakes her song-birds,
          Puts on her flowers,
15   Leads out her lambkins,
          Builds up her bowers:
       This is man's spousal day,
          Christ's day and ours.

EASTER MONDAY.

       Out in the rain a world is growing green,
          On half the trees quick buds are seen
             Where glued-up buds have been.
       Out in the rain God's Acre stretches green,
5   Its harvest quick tho' still unseen:
             For there the Life hath been.

       If Christ hath died His brethren well may die,
          Sing in the gate of death, lay by
             This life without a sigh:
10   For Christ hath died and good it is to die;
          To sleep whenso He lays us by,
             Then wake without a sigh.

       Yea, Christ hath died, yea, Christ is risen again:
          Wherefore both life and death grow plain
15   To us who wax and wane;
       For Christ Who rose shall die no more again:
          Amen: till He makes all things plain
             Let us wax on and wane.

EASTER TUESDAY.

"Together with my dead body shall they arise."
   Shall my dead body arise? then amen and yea
On track of a home beyond the uttermost skies
   Together with my dead body shall they.
5   We know the way: thank God Who hath showed us the
        way!
   Jesus Christ our Way to beautiful Paradise,
Jesus Christ the Same for ever, the Same today.

Five Virgins replenish with oil their lamps, being wise,
   Five Virgins awaiting the Bridegroom watch and pray:
10   And if I one day spring from my grave to the prize,
   Together with my dead body shall they.

ROGATIONTIDE.

Who scatters tares shall reap no wheat,
But go hungry while others eat.

Who sows the wind shall not reap grain;
The sown wind whirleth back again.

5   What God opens must open be,
Tho' man pile the sand of the sea.

What God shuts is opened no more,
Tho' man weary himself to find the door.

ASCENSION EVE.

O Lord Almighty, Who hast formed us weak,
   With us whom Thou hast formed deal fatherly;
Be found of us whom Thou hast deigned to seek,
   Be found that we the more may seek for Thee;
5   Lord, speak and grant us ears to hear Thee speak;
   Lord, come to us and grant us eyes to see;

Lord, make us meek, for Thou Thyself art meek;
Lord, Thou art Love, fill us with charity.
O Thou the Life of living and of dead,
10   Who givest more the more Thyself hast given,
    Suffice us as Thy saints Thou hast sufficed;
That beautified, replenished, comforted,
    Still gazing off from earth and up at heaven
    We may pursue Thy steps, Lord Jesus Christ.

ASCENSION DAY.
"A Cloud received Him out of their sight."

When Christ went up to Heaven the Apostles stayed
    Gazing at Heaven with souls and wills on fire,
Their hearts on flight along the track He made,
    Winged by desire.

5   Their silence spake: "Lord, why not follow Thee?
    Home is not home without Thy Blessed Face,
Life is not life. Remember, Lord, and see,
    Look back, embrace.

"Earth is one desert waste of banishment,
10   Life is one long-drawn anguish of decay.
Where Thou wert wont to go we also went:
    Why not today?"

Nevertheless a cloud cut off their gaze:
    They tarry to build up Jerusalem,
15   Watching for Him, while thro' the appointed days
    He watches them.

They do His Will, and doing it rejoice,
    Patiently glad to spend and to be spent:
Still He speaks to them, still they hear His Voice
20   And are content.

For as a cloud received Him from their sight,
    So with a cloud will He return ere long:
Therefore they stand on guard by day, by night,
    Strenuous and strong.

25 They do, they dare, they beyond seven times seven
  Forgive, they cry God's mighty word aloud:
Yet sometimes haply lift tired eyes to Heaven—
  "Is that His cloud?"

WHITSUN EVE.

"As many as I love."—Ah, Lord, Who lovest all,
  If thus it is with Thee why sit remote above,
Beholding from afar, stumbling and marred and small,
  So many Thou dost love?
5 Whom sin and sorrow make their worn reluctant thrall;
  Who fain would flee away but lack the wings of dove;
Who long for love and rest; who look to Thee, and call
  To Thee for rest and love.

WHITSUN DAY.
"When the Day of Pentecost was fully come."

At sound as of rushing wind, and sight as of fire,
  Lo! flesh and blood made spirit and fiery flame,
  Ambassadors in Christ's and the Father's Name,
    To woo back a world's desire.
5 These men chose death for their life and shame for their
      boast,
  For fear courage, for doubt intuition of faith,
  Chose love that is strong as death and stronger than
      death
    In the power of the Holy Ghost.

WHITSUN MONDAY.
"A pure River of Water of Life."

We know not a voice of that River,
  If vocal or silent it be,
Where for ever and ever and ever
  It flows to no sea.

5   More deep than the seas is that River,
           More full than their manifold tides,
       Where for ever and ever and ever
           It flows and abides.

       Pure gold is the bed of that River
10   (The gold of that land is the best),
       Where for ever and ever and ever
           It flows on at rest.

       Oh goodly the banks of that River,
           Oh goodly the fruits that they bear,
15   Where for ever and ever and ever
           It flows and is fair.

       For lo! on each bank of that River
           The Tree of Life life-giving grows,
       Where for ever and ever and ever
20   The Pure River flows.

WHITSUN TUESDAY.

       Lord Jesus Christ, our Wisdom and our Rest,
           Who wisely dost reveal and wisely hide,
           Grant us such grace in wisdom to abide
       According to Thy Will whose Will is best.
5   Contented with Thine uttermost behest,
           Too sweet for envy and too high for pride;
           All simple-souled, dove-hearted and dove-eyed,
       Soft-voiced, and satisfied in humble nest.
       Wondering at the bounty of Thy Love
10   Which gives us wings of silver and of gold;
           Wings folded close, yet ready to unfold
               When Thou shalt say, "Winter is past and gone:"
       When Thou shalt say, "Spouse, sister, love and dove,
           Come hither, sit with Me upon My Throne."

TRINITY SUNDAY.

My God, Thyself being Love Thy heart is love,
 And love Thy Will and love Thy Word to us,
 Whether Thou show us depths calamitous
Or heights and flights of rapturous peace above.
5 O Christ the Lamb, O Holy Ghost the Dove,
 Reveal the Almighty Father unto us;
 That we may tread Thy courts felicitous,
Loving Who loves us, for our God is Love.
Lo, if our God be Love thro' heaven's long day,
10 Love is He thro' our mortal pilgrimage,
  Love was He thro' all aeons that are told.
 We change, but Thou remainest; for Thine age
  Is, Was, and Is to come, nor new nor old;
We change, but Thou remainest; yea and yea!

CONVERSION OF ST. PAUL.

O blessed Paul elect to grace,
 Arise and wash away thy sin,
Anoint thy head and wash thy face,
 Thy gracious course begin.
5 To start thee on thy outrunning race
Christ shows the splendour of His Face:
What will that Face of splendour be
When at the goal He welcomes thee?

In weariness and painfulness St. Paul
 Served God and pleased Him: after-saints no less
Can wait on and can please Him, one and all
 In weariness and painfulness,

5 By faith and hope triumphant thro' distress:
Not with the rankling service of a thrall;
 But even as loving children trust and bless,

Weep and rejoice, answering their Father's call,
  Work with tired hands, and forward upward press
10 On sore tired feet still rising when they fall,
    In weariness and painfulness.

VIGIL OF THE PRESENTATION.

Long and dark the nights, dim and short the days,
Mounting weary heights on our weary ways,
  Thee our God we praise.
Scaling heavenly heights by unearthly ways,
5 Thee our God we praise all our nights and days,
    Thee our God we praise.

FEAST OF THE PRESENTATION.

O Firstfruits of our grain,
Infant and Lamb appointed to be slain,
A Virgin and two doves were all Thy train,
  With one old man for state,
5 When Thou didst enter first Thy Father's gate.

Since then Thy train hath been
Freeman and bondman, bishop, king and queen,
With flaming candles and with garlands green:
  Oh happy all who wait
10 One day or thousand days around Thy gate.

And these have offered Thee,
Beside their hearts, great stores for charity,
Gold, frankincense and myrrh; if such may be
  For savour or for state
15 Within the threshold of Thy golden gate.

Then snowdrops and my heart
I'll bring, to find those blacker than Thou art:
Yet, loving Lord, accept us in good part;
  And give me grace to wait
20 A bruised reed bowed low before Thy gate.

THE PURIFICATION OF ST. MARY THE VIRGIN.

Purity born of a Maid:
Was such a Virgin defiled?
Nay, by no shade of a shade.
She offered her gift of pure love,
5   A dove with a fair fellow-dove.
She offered her Innocent Child
The Essence and Author of Love;
The Lamb that indwelt by the Dove
Was spotless and holy and mild;
10   More pure than all other,
More pure than His Mother,
Her God and Redeemer and Child.

VIGIL OF THE ANNUNCIATION.

All weareth, all wasteth,
All flitteth, all hasteth,
All of flesh and time:—
Sound, sweet heavenly chime,
5   Ring in the unutterable eternal prime.

Man hopeth, man feareth,
Man droopeth:—Christ cheereth,
Compassing release,
Comforting with peace,
10   Promising rest where strife and anguish cease.

Saints waking, saints sleeping,
Rest well in safe keeping;
Well they rest today
While they watch and pray,—
15   But their tomorrow's rest what tongue shall say?

FEAST OF THE ANNUNCIATION.

Whereto shall we liken this Blessed Mary Virgin,
Fruitful shoot from Jesse's root graciously emerging?
Lily we might call her, but Christ alone is white;
Rose delicious, but that Jesus is the one Delight;
5   Flower of women, but her Firstborn is mankind's one
        flower:
He the Sun lights up all moons thro' their radiant hour.
"Blessed among women, highly favoured," thus
Glorious Gabriel hailed her, teaching words to us:
Whom devoutly copying we too cry "All hail!"
10   Echoing on the music of glorious Gabriel.

Herself a rose, who bore the Rose,
   She bore the Rose and felt its thorn.
   All Loveliness new-born
Took on her bosom its repose,
5   And slept and woke there night and morn.

Lily herself, she bore the one
   Fair Lily; sweeter, whiter, far
   Than she or others are:
The Sun of Righteousness her Son,
10   She was His morning star.

She gracious, He essential Grace,
   He was the Fountain, she the rill:
   Her goodness to fulfil
And gladness, with proportioned pace
15   He led her steps thro' good and ill.

Christ's mirror she of grace and love,
   Of beauty and of life and death:
   By hope and love and faith
Transfigured to His Likeness, "Dove,
20   Spouse, Sister, Mother," Jesus saith.

ST. MARK.

Once like a broken bow Mark sprang aside:
Yet grace recalled him to a worthier course,
To feeble hands and knees increasing force,
   Till God was magnified.

5   And now a strong Evangelist, St. Mark
Hath for his sign a Lion in his strength;
And thro' the stormy water's breadth and length
   He helps to steer God's Ark.

Thus calls he sinners to be penitents,
10 He kindles penitents to high desire,
He mounts before them to the sphere of saints,
   And bids them come up higher.

ST. BARNABAS.

"Now when we had discovered Cyprus, we left it on the left hand."—
Acts xxi. 3.
"We sailed under Cyprus, because the winds were contrary."—*Acts* xxvii. 4.

St. Barnabas, with John his sister's son,
   Set sail for Cyprus; leaving in their wake
   That chosen Vessel, who for Jesus' sake
Proclaimed the Gentiles and the Jews at one.
5 Divided while united, each must run
   His mighty course not hell should overtake;
   And pressing toward the mark must own the ache
Of love, and sigh for heaven not yet begun.
For saints in life-long exile yearn to touch
10 Warm human hands, and commune face to face;
    But these we know not ever met again:
Yet once St. Paul at distance overmuch
    Just sighted Cyprus; and once more in vain
Neared it and passed;—not there his landing-place.

VIGIL OF ST. PETER.

O Jesu, gone so far apart
  Only my heart can follow Thee,
That look which pierced St. Peter's heart
  Turn now on me.

5 Thou Who dost search me thro' and thro'
  And mark the crooked ways I went,
Look on me, Lord, and make me too
  Thy penitent.

ST. PETER.

"Launch out into the deep," Christ spake of old
  To Peter: and he launched into the deep;
  Strengthened should tempest wake which lay asleep,
Strengthened to suffer heat or suffer cold.
5 Thus, in Christ's Prescience: patient to behold
  A fall, a rise, a scaling Heaven's high steep;
  Prescience of Love, which deigned to overleap
The mire of human errors manifold.
Lord, Lover of Thy Peter, and of him
10 Beloved with craving of a humbled heart
  Which eighteen hundred years have satisfied;
Hath he his throne among Thy Seraphim
  Who love? or sits he on a throne apart,
  Unique, near Thee, to love Thee human-eyed?

St. Peter once: "Lord, dost Thou wash my feet?"—
  Much more I say: Lord, dost Thou stand and knock
  At my closed heart more rugged than a rock,
Bolted and barred, for Thy soft touch unmeet,
5 Nor garnished nor in any wise made sweet?
  Owls roost within and dancing satyrs mock.
  Lord, I have heard the crowing of the cock

And have not wept: ah, Lord, Thou knowest it.
Yet still I hear Thee knocking, still I hear:
10   "Open to Me, look on Me eye to eye,
          That I may wring thy heart and make it whole;
And teach thee love because I hold thee dear,
          And sup with thee in gladness soul with soul,
And sup with thee in glory by and by."

I followed Thee, my God, I followed Thee
          To see the end:
I turned back flying from Gethsemane,
Turned back on flying steps to see
5   Thy Face, my God, my Friend.

Even fleeing from Thee my heart clave to Thee:
          I turned perforce
Constrained, yea chained by love which maketh free;
I turned perforce, and silently
10   Followed along Thy course.

Lord, didst Thou know that I was following Thee?
          I weak and small
Yet Thy true lover, mean tho' I must be,
Sinning and sorrowing—didst Thou see?
15   O Lord, Thou sawest all.

I thought I had been strong to die for Thee;
          I disbelieved
Thy word of warning spoken patiently:
My heart cried, "That be far from me,"
20   Till Thy bruised heart I grieved.

Once I had urged: "Lord, this be far from Thee:"—
          Rebel to light,
It needed first that Thou shouldst die for me
Or ever I could plumb and see
25   Love's lovely depth and height.

Alas that I should trust myself, not Thee;
          Not trust Thy word:
I faithless slumberer in Gethsemane,

Blinded and rash; who instantly
30   Put trust, but in a sword.

Ah Lord, if even at the last in Thee
       I had put faith,
I might even at the last have counselled me,
And not have heaped up cruelty
35   To sting Thee in Thy death.

Alas for me, who bore to think on Thee
       And yet to lie:
While Thou, O Lord, didst bear to look on me
Goaded by fear to blasphemy,
40   And break my heart and die.

No balm I find in Gilead, yet in Thee
       Nailed to Thy palm
I find a balm that wrings and comforts me:
Balm wrung from Thee by agony,
45   My balm, mine only balm.

Oh blessed John who standeth close to Thee,
       With Magdalene,
And Thine own Mother praying silently,
Yea, blessed above women she,
50   Now blessed even as then.

And blessed the scorned thief who hangs by Thee,
       Whose thirsting mouth
Thirsts for Thee more than water, whose eyes see,
Whose lips confess in ecstasy
55   Nor feel their parching drouth.

Like as the hart the water-brooks I Thee
       Desire, my hands
I stretch to Thee; O kind Lord, pity me:
Lord, I have wept, wept bitterly,
60   I driest of dry lands.

Lord, I am standing far far off from Thee;
       Yet is my heart
Hanging with Thee upon the accursed tree;
The nails, the thorns, pierce Thee and me:
65   My God, I claim my part

Scarce in Thy throne and kingdom; yet with Thee
  In shame, in loss,
In Thy forsaking, in Thine agony:
Love crucified, behold even me,
70   Me also bear Thy cross.

VIGIL OF ST. BARTHOLOMEW.

Lord, to Thine own grant watchful hearts and eyes;
  Hearts strung to prayer, awake while eyelids sleep;
  Eyes patient till the end to watch and weep.
So will sleep nourish power to wake and rise
5   With Virgins who keep vigil and are wise,
  To sow among all sowers who shall reap,
  From out man's deep to call Thy vaster deep,
And tread the uphill track to Paradise.
Sweet souls! so patient that they make no moan,
10   So calm on journey that they seem at rest,
    So rapt in prayer that half they dwell in heaven
    Thankful for all withheld and all things given;
  So lit by love that Christ shines manifest
Transfiguring their aspects to His own.

ST. BARTHOLOMEW.

He bore an agony whereof the name
  Hath turned his fellows pale:
But what if God should call us to the same,
  Should call, and we should fail?
5   Nor earth nor sea could swallow up our shame,
  Nor darkness draw a veil:
For he endured that agony whose name
  Hath made his fellows quail.

ST. MICHAEL AND ALL ANGELS.
"Ye that excel in strength."

Service and strength, God's Angels and Archangels;
  His Seraphs fires, and lamps His Cherubim:
Glory to God from highest and from lowest,
  Glory to God in everlasting hymn
5   From all His creatures.

Princes that serve, and Powers that work His pleasure,
  Heights that soar to'ard Him, Depths that sink to'ard
      Him;
Flames fire out-flaming, chill beside His Essence;
  Insight all-probing, save where scant and dim
10   To'ard its Creator.

Sacred and free exultant in God's pleasure,
  His Will their solace, thus they wait on Him;
And shout their shout of ecstasy eternal,
  And trim their splendours that they burn not dim
15   To'ard their Creator.

Wherefore with Angels, wherefore with Archangels,
  With lofty Cherubs, loftier Seraphim,
We laud and magnify our God Almighty,
  And veil our faces rendering love to Him
20   With all His creatures.

VIGIL OF ALL SAINTS.

Up, my drowsing eyes!
  Up, my sinking heart!
Up to Jesus Christ arise!
  Claim your part
5   In all raptures of the skies.

Yet a little while,
  Yet a little way,
Saints shall reap and rest and smile
  All the day.
10 Up! let's trudge another mile.

ALL SAINTS.

As grains of sand, as stars, as drops of dew,
   Numbered and treasured by the Almighty Hand,
   The Saints triumphant throng that holy land
Where all things and Jerusalem are new.
5 We know not half they sing or half they do,
   But this we know, they rest and understand;
   While like a conflagration freshly fanned
Their love glows upward, outward, thro' and thro'.
Lo! like a stream of incense launched on flame
10 Fresh Saints stream up from death to life above,
   To shine among those others and rejoice:
What matters tribulation whence they came?
   All love and only love can find a voice
Where God makes glad His Saints, for God is Love.

ALL SAINTS: MARTYRS.

Once slain for Him Who first was slain for them,
   Now made alive in Him for evermore,
   All luminous and lovely in their gore
With no more buffeting winds or tides to stem
5 The Martyrs look for New Jerusalem;
   And cry "How long?" remembering all they bore,
   "How long?" with heart and eyes sent on before
Toward consummated throne and diadem.
"How long?" White robes are given to their desire;
10 "How long?" deep rest that is and is to be;
   With a great promise of the oncoming host,
Loves to their love and fires to flank their fire:
   So rest they, worshipping incessantly
     One God, the Father, Son, and Holy Ghost.

"I gave a sweet smell."

Saints are like roses when they flush rarest,
Saints are like lilies when they bloom fairest,
    Saints are like violets sweetest of their kind:
        Bear in mind
5   This today. Then tomorrow:
All like roses rarer than the rarest,
All like lilies fairer than the fairest,
    All like violets sweeter than we know.
        Be it so.
10   Tomorrow blots out sorrow.

Hark! the Alleluias of the great salvation
    Still beginning, never ending, still begin,
The thunder of an endless adoration:
Open ye the gates, that the righteous nation
5   Which have kept the truth may enter in.

Roll ye back, ye pearls, on your twelvefold station:
    No more deaths to die, no more fights to win!
Lift your heads, ye gates, that the righteous nation
Led by the Great Captain of their sole salvation,
10   Having kept the truth, may enter in.

A SONG FOR THE LEAST OF ALL SAINTS.

Love is the key of life and death,
    Of hidden heavenly mystery:
Of all Christ is, of all He saith,
    Love is the key.

5   As three times to His Saint He saith,
    He saith to me, He saith to thee,
Breathing His Grace-conferring Breath:
    "Lovest thou Me?"

Ah, Lord, I have such feeble faith,
10   Such feeble hope to comfort me:
But love it is, is strong as death,
        And I love Thee.

SUNDAY BEFORE ADVENT.

The end of all things is at hand. We all
    Stand in the balance trembling as we stand;
Or if not trembling, tottering to a fall.
    The end of all things is at hand.
5   O hearts of men, covet the unending land!
O hearts of men, covet the musical,
    Sweet, never-ending waters of that strand!
While Earth shows poor, a slippery rolling ball,
    And Hell looms vast, a gulf unplumbed, unspanned,
10   And Heaven flings wide its gates to great and small,
    The end of all things is at hand.

GIFTS AND GRACES.

Love loveth Thee, and wisdom loveth Thee:
    The love that loveth Thee sits satisfied;
    Wisdom that loveth Thee grows million-eyed,
Learning what was, and is, and is to be.
5   Wisdom and love are glad of all they see;
    Their heart is deep, their hope is not denied;
    They rock at rest on time's unresting tide,
And wait to rest thro' long eternity.
Wisdom and love and rest, each holy soul
10   Hath these today while day is only night:
    What shall souls have when morning brings to light
        Love, wisdom, rest, God's treasure stored above?
Palm shall they have, and harp and aureole,
    Wisdom, rest, love—and lo! the whole is love.

Lord, give me love that I may love Thee much,
   Yea, give me love that I may love Thee more,
   And all for love may worship and adore
And touch Thee with love's consecrated touch.
5   I halt today; be love my cheerful crutch,
   My feet to plod, some day my wings to soar:
   Some day; but, Lord, not any day before
Thou call me perfect, having made me such.
This is a day of love, a day of sorrow,
10   Love tempering sorrow to a sort of bliss;
    A day that shortens while we call it long:
A longer day of love will dawn tomorrow,
   A longer, brighter, lovelier day than this,
    Endless, all love, no sorrow, but a song.

"As a king, ... unto the King."

Love doth so grace and dignify
   That beggars treat as king with king
Before the Throne of God most High:
Love recognises love's own cry,
5   And stoops to take love's offering.

A loving heart, tho' soiled and bruised;
   A kindling heart, tho' cold before;
Who ever came and was refused
By Love? Do, Lord, as Thou art used
10   To do, and make me love Thee more.

O ye who love today,
Turn away
From Patience with her silver ray:
   For Patience shows a twilight face,
5   Like a half-lighted moon
   When daylight dies apace.

But ye who love tomorrow
Beg or borrow

Today some bitterness of sorrow:
10   For Patience shows a lustrous face,
       In depth of night her noon;
    Then to her sun gives place.

Life that was born today
Must make no stay,
    But tend to end
As blossom-bloom of May.
5   O Lord, confirm my root,
Train up my shoot,
    To live and give
Harvest of wholesome fruit.

Life that was born to die
10   Sets heart on high,
       And counts and mounts
Steep stages of the sky.
Two things, Lord, I desire
And I require;
15   Love's name, and flame
To wrap my soul in fire.

Life that was born to love
Sends heart above
    Both cloud and shroud,
20   And broods a peaceful dove.
Two things I ask of Thee;
Deny not me;
    Eyesight and light
Thy Blessed Face to see.

"Perfect Love casteth out Fear."

Lord, give me blessed fear,
    And much more blessed love
That fearing I may love Thee here
    And be Thy harmless dove:

5   Until Thou cast out fear,
          Until Thou perfect love,
       Until Thou end mine exile here
          And fetch Thee home Thy dove.

       Hope is the counterpoise of fear
       While night enthralls us here.

       Fear hath a startled eye that holds a tear:
       Hope hath an upward glance, for dawn draws near
5   With sunshine and with cheer.
       Fear gazing earthwards spies a bier;
       And sets herself to rear
       A lamentable tomb where leaves drop sere,
       Bleaching to congruous skeletons austere:
10   Hope chants a funeral hymn most sweet and clear,
       And seems true chanticleer
       Of resurrection and of all things dear
       In the oncoming endless year.

       Fear ballasts hope, hope buoys up fear,
15   And both befit us here.

"Subject to like Passions as we are."

       Whoso hath anguish is not dead in sin,
          Whoso hath pangs of utterless desire.
             Like as in smouldering flax which harbours fire,—
       Red heat of conflagration may begin,
5   Melt that hard heart, burn out the dross within,
          Permeate with glory the new man entire,
             Crown him with fire, mould for his hands a lyre
       Of fiery strings to sound with those who win.
       Anguish is anguish, yet potential bliss,
10   Pangs of desire are birth-throes of delight;
             Those citizens felt such who walk in white,
       And meet, but no more sunder, with a kiss;

Who fathom still unfathomed mysteries,
   And love, adore, rejoice, with all their might.

Experience bows a sweet contented face,
   Still setting to her seal that God is true:
   Beneath the sun, she knows, is nothing new;
All things that go return with measured pace,
5   Winds, rivers, man's still recommencing race:—
   While Hope beyond earth's circle strains her view,
   Past sun and moon, and rain and rainbow too,
Enamoured of unseen eternal grace.
Experience saith, "My God doth all things well:"
10   And for the morrow taketh little care,
    Such peace and patience garrison her soul:—
    While Hope, who never yet hath eyed the goal,
With arms flung forth, and backward floating hair,
Touches, embraces, hugs the invisible.

"Charity never Faileth."

Such is Love, it comforts in extremity,
   Tho' a tempest rage around and rage above,
Tempest beyond tempest, far as eye can see:
   Such is Love,

5   That it simply heeds its mourning inward Dove;
Dove which craves contented for a home to be
   Set amid the myrtles or an olive grove.

Dove-eyed Love contemplates the Twelve-fruited Tree,
   Marks the bowing palms which worship as they move;
10   Simply sayeth, simply prayeth, "All for me!"
   Such is Love.

"The Greatest of these is Charity."

A moon impoverished amid stars curtailed,
   A sun of its exuberant lustre shorn,
   A transient morning that is scarcely morn,
A lingering night in double dimness veiled.—
5 Our hands are slackened and our strength has failed:
   We born to darkness, wherefore were we born?
   No ripening more for olive, grape, or corn:
Faith faints, hope faints, even love himself has paled.
Nay! love lifts up a face like any rose
10 Flushing and sweet above a thorny stem,
Softly protesting that the way he knows;
   And as for faith and hope, will carry them
   Safe to the gate of New Jerusalem,
Where light shines full and where the palm-tree blows.

All beneath the sun hasteth,
All that hath begun wasteth;
Earth-notes change in tune
With the changeful moon,
5 Which waneth
While earth's chant complaineth.

Plumbs the deep, Fear descending;
Scales the steep, Hope ascending;
Faith betwixt the twain
10 Plies both goad and rein,
Half fearing,
All hopeful, day is nearing.

If thou be dead, forgive and thou shalt live;
   If thou hast sinned, forgive and be forgiven;
God waiteth to be gracious and forgive,
     And open heaven.

5 Set not thy will to die and not to live;
   Set not thy face as flint refusing heaven;

Thou fool, set not thy heart on hell: forgive
    And be forgiven.

"Let Patience have her perfect work."

Can man rejoice who lives in hourly fear?
    Can man make haste who toils beneath a load?
    Can man feel rest who has no fixed abode?
All he lays hold of, or can see or hear,
5   Is passing by, is prompt to disappear,
    Is doomed, foredoomed, continueth in no stay:
    This day he breathes in is his latter day,
This year of time is this world's latter year.
Thus in himself is he most miserable:
10   Out of himself, Lord, lift him up to Thee,
    Out of himself and all these worlds that flee;
    Hold him in patience underneath the rod,
Anchor his hope beyond life's ebb and swell,
    Perfect his patience in the love of God.

Patience must dwell with Love, for Love and Sorrow
    Have pitched their tent together here:
Love all alone will build a house tomorrow,
    And sorrow not be near.
5   Today for Love's sake hope, still hope, in sorrow,
    Rest in her shade and hold her dear:
Today she nurses thee; and lo! tomorrow
    Love only will be near.

"Let everything that hath breath praise the Lord."

All that we see rejoices in the sunshine,
    All that we hear makes merry in the Spring:
God grant us such a mind to be glad after our kind,
    And to sing
5   His praises evermore for everything.

Much that we see must vanish with the sunshine,
  Sweet Spring must fail, and fail the choir of Spring:
But Wisdom shall burn on when the lesser lights
    are gone,
    And shall sing
10   God's praises evermore for everything.

What is the beginning? Love. What the course? Love still.
What the goal? The goal is Love on the happy hill.
Is there nothing then but Love, search we sky or earth?
There is nothing out of Love hath perpetual worth:
5   All things flag but only Love, all things fail or flee;
There is nothing left but Love worthy you and me.

    Lord, make me pure:
Only the pure shall see Thee as Thou art
    And shall endure.
    Lord, bring me low;
5 For Thou wert lowly in Thy blessed heart:
    Lord, keep me so.

Love, to be love, must walk Thy way
    And work Thy Will;
      Or if Thou say, "Lie still,"
Lie still and pray.

5 Love, Thine own Bride, with all her might
    Will follow Thee,
      And till the shadows flee
Keep Thee in sight.

Love will not mar her peaceful face
10   With cares undue,
      Faithless and hopeless too
And out of place.

Love, knowing Thou much more art Love,
    Will sun her grief,

15   And pluck her myrtle-leaf,
And be Thy dove.

Love here hath vast beatitude:
    What shall be hers
    Where there is no more curse,
20 But all is good?

Lord, I am feeble and of mean account:
Thou Who dost condescend as well as mount,
    Stoop Thou Thyself to me
    And grant me grace to hear and grace to see.
5   Lord, if Thou grant me grace to hear and see
Thy very Self Who stoopest thus to me,
    I make but slight account
    Of aught beside wherein to sink or mount.

Tune me, O Lord, into one harmony
    With Thee, one full responsive vibrant chord;
Unto Thy praise all love and melody,
    Tune me, O Lord.
5   Thus need I flee nor death, nor fire, nor sword:
A little while these be, then cease to be,
    And sent by Thee not these should be abhorred.

Devil and world, gird me with strength to flee,
    To flee the flesh, and arm me with Thy word:
10 As Thy Heart is to my heart, unto Thee
    Tune me, O Lord.

"They shall be as white as snow."

Whiteness most white. Ah, to be clean again
    In mine own sight and God's most holy sight!
To reach thro' any flood or fire of pain
    Whiteness most white:

5   To learn to hate the wrong and love the right
       Even while I walk thro' shadows that are vain,
          Descending thro' vain shadows into night.

       Lord, not today: yet some day bliss for bane
          Give me, for mortal frailty give me might,
10   Give innocence for guilt, and for my stain
          Whiteness most white.

          Thy lilies drink the dew,
       Thy lambs the rill, and I will drink them too;
          For those in purity
       And innocence are types, dear Lord, of Thee.
5   The fragrant lily flower
       Bows and fulfils Thy Will its lifelong hour;
          The lamb at rest and play
       Fulfils Thy Will in gladness all the day;
          They leave tomorrow's cares
10   Until the morrow, what it brings it bears.
          And I, Lord, would be such;
       Not high or great or anxious overmuch,
          But pure and temperate,
       Earnest to do Thy Will betimes and late,
15   Fragrant with love and praise
       And innocence thro' all my appointed days;
          Thy lily I would be,
       Spotless and sweet, Thy lamb to follow Thee.

"When I was in trouble I called upon the Lord."

       A burdened heart that bleeds and bears
          And hopes and waits in pain,
       And faints beneath its fears and cares,
          Yet hopes again:
5   Wilt Thou accept the heart I bring,
          O gracious Lord and kind,

To ease it of a torturing sting,
    And staunch and bind?

Alas, if Thou wilt none of this,
10   None else have I to give:
Look Thou upon it as it is,
    Accept, relieve.

Or if Thou wilt not yet relieve,
    Be not extreme to sift:
15   Accept a faltering will to give,
    Itself Thy gift.

Grant us such grace that we may work Thy Will
    And speak Thy words and walk before Thy Face,
Profound and calm, like waters deep and still:
    Grant us such grace.

5   Not hastening and not loitering in our pace
For gloomiest valley or for sultriest hill,
    Content and fearless on our downward race.

As rivers seek a sea they cannot fill
    But are themselves filled full in its embrace,
10   Absorbed, at rest, each river and each rill:
    Grant us such grace.

"Who hath despised the day of small things?"

As violets so be I recluse and sweet,
    Cheerful as daisies unaccounted rare,
Still sunward-gazing from a lowly seat,
    Still sweetening wintry air.

5   While half-awakened Spring lags incomplete,
    While lofty forest trees tower bleak and bare,
Daisies and violets own remotest heat
    And bloom and make them fair.

"Do this, and he doeth it."

Content to come, content to go,
   Content to wrestle or to race,
Content to know or not to know,
   Each in his place;

5   Lord, grant us grace to love Thee so
   That glad of heart and glad of face
At last we may sit, high or low,
   Each in his place;

Where pleasures flow as rivers flow,
10   And loss has left no barren trace,
And all that are, are perfect so,
   Each in his place.

"That no man take thy Crown."

Be faithful unto death. Christ proffers thee
   Crown of a life that draws immortal breath:
To thee He saith, yea, and He saith to me,
   "Be faithful unto death."

5   To every living soul that same He saith,
"Be faithful":—whatsoever else we be,
   Let us be faithful, challenging His faith.

Tho' trouble storm around us like the sea,
   Tho' hell surge up to scare us and to scathe,
10   Tho' heaven and earth betake themselves to flee,
   "Be faithful unto death."

"Ye are come unto Mount Sion."

Fear, Faith, and Hope have sent their hearts above:
   Prudence, Obedience, and Humility
   Climb at their call, all scaling heaven toward Love.

Fear hath least grace but great expediency;
5   Faith and Humility show grave and strong;
    Prudence and Hope mount balanced equally.
Obedience marches marshalling their throng,
    Goes first, goes last, to left hand or to right;
    And all the six uplift a pilgrim's song.
10   By day they rest not, nor they rest by night:
    While Love within them, with them, over them,
    Weans them and woos them from the dark to light.
Each plies for staff not reed with broken stem,
    But olive branch in pledge of patient peace;
15   Till Love being theirs in New Jerusalem,
Transfigure them to Love, and so they cease.
    Love is the sole beatitude above:
    All other graces, to their vast increase
Of glory, look on Love and mirror Love.

"Sit down in the lowest room."

Lord, give me grace
To take the lowest place;
Nor even desire,
Unless it be Thy Will, to go up higher.

5   Except by grace,
I fail of lowest place;
Except desire
Sit low, it aims awry to go up higher.

"Lord, it is good for us to be here."

Grant us, O Lord, that patience and that faith:
    Faith's patience imperturbable in Thee,
    Hope's patience till the long-drawn shadows flee,
Love's patience unresentful of all scathe.
5   Verily we need patience breath by breath;
    Patience while faith holds up her glass to see,
    While hope toils yoked in fear's copartnery,

And love goes softly on the way to death.
How gracious and how perfecting a grace
10   Must patience be on which those others wait:
Faith with suspended rapture in her face,
    Hope pale and careful hand in hand with fear,
Love—ah, good love who would not antedate
    God's Will, but saith, Good is it to be here.

Lord, grant us grace to rest upon Thy word,
    To rest in hope until we see Thy Face;
To rest thro' toil unruffled and unstirred,
    Lord, grant us grace.
5   This burden and this heat wear on apace:
Night comes, when sweeter than night's singing bird
    Will swell the silence of our ended race.

Ah, songs which flesh and blood have never heard
    And cannot hear, songs of the silent place
10   Where rest remains! Lord, slake our hope deferred,
    Lord, grant us grace.

THE WORLD.
SELF-DESTRUCTION.

"A vain Shadow."

The world,—what a world, ah me!
    Mouldy, worm-eaten, grey:
Vain as a leaf from a tree,
    As a fading day,
5   As veriest vanity,
    As the froth and the spray
Of the hollow-billowed sea,
As what was and shall not be,
    As what is and passes away.

"Lord, save us, we perish."

O Lord, seek us, O Lord, find us
  In Thy patient care;
Be Thy Love before, behind us,
  Round us, everywhere:
5 Lest the god of this world blind us,
  Lest he speak us fair,
Lest he forge a chain to bind us,
  Lest he bait a snare.
Turn not from us, call to mind us,
10 Find, embrace us, bear;
Be Thy Love before, behind us,
  Round us, everywhere.

What is this above thy head,
  O Man?—
The World, all overspread
With pearls and golden rays
5 And gems ablaze;
A sight which day and night
  Fills an eye's span.

What is this beneath thy feet,
  O Saint?—
10 The World, a nauseous sweet
Puffed up and perishing;
A hollow thing,
A lie, a vanity,
  Tinsel and paint.

15 What is she while time is time,
  O Man?—
In a perpetual prime
Beauty and youth she hath;
And her footpath
20 Breeds flowers thro' dancing hours
  Since time began.

> While time lengthens what is she,
>   O Saint?—
> Nought: yea, all men shall see
25 How she is nought at all,
> When her death-pall
> Of fire ends their desire
>   And brands her taint.

> Ah, poor Man, befooled and slow
30   And faint!
> Ah, poorest Man, if so
> Thou turn thy back on bliss
> And choose amiss!
> For thou art choosing now:
35   Sinner,—or Saint.

Babylon the Great.

> Foul is she and ill-favoured, set askew:
>   Gaze not upon her till thou dream her fair,
>   Lest she should mesh thee in her wanton hair,
> Adept in arts grown old yet ever new.
5   Her heart lusts not for love, but thro' and thro'
>   For blood, as spotted panther lusts in lair;
>   No wine is in her cup, but filth is there
> Unutterable, with plagues hid out of view.
> Gaze not upon her, for her dancing whirl
10   Turns giddy the fixed gazer presently:
>   Gaze not upon her, lest thou be as she
>   When, at the far end of her long desire,
> Her scarlet vest and gold and gem and pearl
>   And she amid her pomp are set on fire.

"Standing afar off for the fear of her torment."

Is this the end? is there no end but this?
   Yea, none beside:
   No other end for pride
And foulness and besottedness.

5   Hath she no friend? hath she no clinging friend?
   Nay, none at all;
   Who stare upon her fall
Quake for themselves with hair on end.

Will she be done away? vanish away?
10   Yea, like a dream;
   Yea, like the shades that seem
Somewhat, and lo! are nought by day.

Alas for her amid man's helpless moan,
   Alas for her!
15   She hath no comforter:
In solitude of fire she sits alone.

"O Lucifer, Son of the Morning!"

Oh fallen star! a darkened light,
   A glory hurtled from its car,
Self-blasted from the holy height:
   Oh fallen star!

5   Fallen beyond earth's utmost bar,
Beyond return, beyond far sight
   Of outmost glimmering nebular.

Now blackness, which once walked in white;
   Now death, whose life once glowed afar;
10 Oh son of dawn that loved the night,
   Oh fallen star!

Alas, alas! for the self-destroyed
  Vanish as images from a glass,
Sink down and die down by hope unbuoyed:—
  Alas, alas!

5   Who shall stay their ruinous mass?
Besotted, reckless, possessed, decoyed,
  They hurry to the dolorous pass.

Saints fall a-weeping who would have joyed,
  Sore they weep for a glory that was,
10 For a fulness emptied into the void,
  Alas, alas!

As froth on the face of the deep,
  As foam on the crest of the sea,
As dreams at the waking of sleep,
  As gourd of a day and a night,
5 As harvest that no man shall reap,
  As vintage that never shall be,
Is hope if it cling not aright,
  O my God, unto Thee.

"Where their worm dieth not, and the fire is not quenched."

In tempest and storm blackness of darkness for ever,
  A fire unextinguished, a worm's indestructible swarm;
Where no hope shall ever be more, and love shall be
      never,
    In tempest and storm;
5   Where the form of all things is fashionless, void of all
      form;
Where from death that severeth all, the soul cannot sever
  In tempest and storm.

Toll, bell, toll. For hope is flying
   Sighing from the earthbound soul:
Life is sighing, life is dying:
   Toll, bell, toll.
5   Gropes in its own grave the mole
Wedding darkness, undescrying,
   Tending to no different goal.

Self-slain soul, in vain thy sighing:
   Self-slain, who should make thee whole?
10 Vain the clamour of thy crying:
   Toll, bell, toll.

DIVERS WORLDS. TIME AND ETERNITY.

Earth has clear call of daily bells,
   A chancel-vault of gloom and star,
   A rapture where the anthems are,
A thunder when the organ swells:
5   Alas, man's daily life—what else?—
Is out of tune with daily bells.

While Paradise accords the chimes
   Of Earth and Heaven, its patient pause
   Is rest fulfilling music's laws.
10 Saints sit and gaze, where oftentimes
Precursive flush of morning climbs
And air vibrates with coming chimes.

"Escape to the Mountain."

I peered within, and saw a world of sin;
   Upward, and saw a world of righteousness;
Downward, and saw darkness and flame begin
     Which no man can express.

5   I girt me up, I gat me up to flee
        From face of darkness and devouring flame:
     And fled I had, but guilt is loading me
        With dust of death and shame.

     Yet still the light of righteousness beams pure,
10   Beams to me from the world of far-off day:—
     Lord, Who hast called them happy that endure,
        Lord, make me such as they.

     I lift mine eyes to see: earth vanisheth.
        I lift up wistful eyes and bend my knee:
     Trembling, bowed down, and face to face with Death,
        I lift mine eyes to see.

5   Lo, what I see is Death that shadows me:
     Yet whilst I, seeing, draw a shuddering breath,
        Death like a mist grows rare perceptibly.

     Beyond the darkness light, beyond the scathe
        Healing, beyond the Cross a palm-branch tree,
10   Beyond Death Life, on evidence of faith:
        I lift mine eyes to see.

"Yet a little while."

     Heaven is not far, tho' far the sky
        Overarching earth and main.
     It takes not long to live and die,
        Die, revive, and rise again.
5   Not long: how long? Oh, long re-echoing song!
     O Lord, how long?

"Behold, it was very good."

     All things are fair, if we had eyes to see
        How first God made them goodly everywhere:

And goodly still in Paradise they be,—
  All things are fair.

5 O Lord, the solemn heavens Thy praise declare;
The multi-fashioned saints bring praise to Thee,
  As doves fly home and cast away their care.

As doves on divers branches of their tree,
  Perched high or low, sit all contented there
10 Not mourning any more; in each degree
  All things are fair.

"Whatsoever is right, that shall ye receive."

When all the overwork of life
  Is finished once, and fallen asleep
We shrink no more beneath the knife,
  But having sown prepare to reap;
5 Delivered from the crossway rough,
    Delivered from the thorny scourge,
    Delivered from the tossing surge,
  Then shall we find—(please God!)—it is enough?

Not in this world of hope deferred,
10   This world of perishable stuff;
Eye hath not seen, nor ear hath heard,
    Nor heart conceived that full "enough":
Here moans the separating sea,
    Here harvests fail, here breaks the heart;
15   There God shall join and no man part,
All one in Christ, so one—(please God!)—with me.

This near-at-hand land breeds pain by measure:
That far-away land overflows with treasure
    Of heaped-up good pleasure.

Our land that we see is befouled by evil:
5 The land that we see not makes mirth and revel,
    Far from death and devil.

This land hath for music sobbing and sighing:
That land hath soft speech and sweet soft replying
    Of all loves undying.

10 This land hath for pastime errors and follies:
That land hath unending unflagging solace
    Of full-chanted "Holies."

Up and away, call the Angels to us;
Come to our home where no foes pursue us,
15   And no tears bedew us;

Where that which riseth sets again never,
Where that which springeth flows in a river
    For ever and ever;

Where harvest justifies labour of sowing,
20 Where that which budded comes to the blowing
    Sweet beyond your knowing.

Come and laugh with us, sing in our singing;
Come, yearn no more, but rest in your clinging.
    See what we are bringing;

25 Crowns like our own crowns, robes for your wearing;
For love of you we kiss them in bearing,
    All good with you sharing:

Over you gladdening, in you delighting;
Come from your famine, your failure, your fighting;
30   Come to full wrong-righting.

Come, where all balm is garnered to ease you;
Come, where all beauty is spread out to please you;
    Come, gaze upon Jesu.

"Was Thy Wrath against the Sea?"

The sea laments with unappeasable
    Hankering wail of loss,
        Lifting its hands on high and passing by
        Out of the lovely light:

5   No foambow any more may crest that swell
        Of clamorous waves which toss;
           Lifting its hands on high it passes by
            From light into the night.
    Peace, peace, thou sea! God's wisdom worketh well,
10   Assigns it crown or cross:
           Lift we all hands on high, and passing by
            Attest: God doeth right.

"And there was no more Sea."

Voices from above and from beneath,
    Voices of creation near and far,
Voices out of life and out of death,
      Out of measureless space,
5   Sun, moon, star,
        In oneness of contentment offering praise.

Heaven and earth and sea jubilant,
    Jubilant all things that dwell therein;
Filled to fullest overflow they chant,
10   Still roll onward, swell,
    Still begin,
        Never flagging praise interminable.

Thou who must fall silent in a while,
    Chant thy sweetest, gladdest, best, at once;
15   Sun thyself today, keep peace and smile;
      By love upward send
      Orisons,
        Accounting love thy lot and love thine end.

Roses on a brier,
    Pearls from out the bitter sea,
Such is earth's desire
    However pure it be.

5   Neither bud nor brier,
    Neither pearl nor brine for me:
Be stilled, my long desire;
    There shall be no more sea.

Be stilled, my passionate heart;
10   Old earth shall end, new earth shall be:
Be still, and earn thy part
    Where shall be no more sea.

We are of those who tremble at Thy word;
    Who faltering walk in darkness toward our close
Of mortal life, by terrors curbed and spurred:
    We are of those.

5   We journey to that land which no man knows
Who any more can make his voice be heard
    Above the clamour of our wants and woes.

Not ours the hearts Thy loftiest love hath stirred,
    Not such as we Thy lily and Thy rose:—
10 Yet, Hope of those who hope with hope deferred,
    We are of those.

"Awake, thou that sleepest."

The night is far spent, the day is at hand:
    Let us therefore cast off the works of darkness,
        And let us put on the armour of light.
    Night for the dead in their stiffness and starkness!
5   Day for the living who mount in their might
Out of their graves to the beautiful land.

Far, far away lies the beautiful land:
    Mount on wide wings of exceeding desire,
        Mount, look not back, mount to life and to light,
10   Mount by the gleam of your lamps all on fire
        Up from the dead men and up from the night.
The night is far spent, the day is at hand.

We know not when, we know not where,
  We know not what that world will be;
But this we know: it will be fair
    To see.

5   With heart athirst and thirsty face
  We know and know not what shall be:
Christ Jesus bring us of His grace
    To see.

Christ Jesus bring us of His grace,
10   Beyond all prayers our hope can pray,
One day to see Him face to Face,
    One day.

"I will lift up mine eyes unto the Hills."

When sick of life and all the world—
How sick of all desire but Thee!—
I lift mine eyes up to the hills,
  Eyes of my heart that see,
5   I see beyond all death and ills
Refreshing green for heart and eyes,
The golden streets and gateways pearled,
  The trees of Paradise.

"There is a time for all things," saith
10   The Word of Truth, Thyself the Word;
And many things Thou reasonest of:
  A time for hope deferred,
But time is now for grief and fears;
A time for life, but now is death;
15   Oh, when shall be the time of love
  When Thou shalt wipe our tears?

Then the new Heavens and Earth shall be
Where righteousness shall dwell indeed;
There shall be no more blight, nor need,
20   Nor barrier of the sea;

No sun and moon alternating,
For God shall be the Light thereof;
No sorrow more, no death, no sting,
    For God Who reigns is Love.

"Then whose shall those things be?"

Oh what is earth, that we should build
Our houses here, and seek concealed
Poor treasure, and add field to field,
And heap to heap, and store to store,
5   Still grasping more and seeking more,
While step by step Death nears the door?

"His Banner over me was Love."

In that world we weary to attain,
    Love's furled banner floats at large unfurled:
There is no more doubt and no more pain
    In that world.

5   There are gems and gold and inlets pearled;
There the verdure fadeth not again;
    There no clinging tendrils droop uncurled.

Here incessant tides stir up the main,
    Stormy miry depths aloft are hurled:
10   There is no more sea, or storm, or stain,
    In that world.

Beloved, yield thy time to God, for He
    Will make eternity thy recompense;
Give all thy substance for His Love, and be
    Beatified past earth's experience.
5   Serve Him in bonds, until He set thee free;
    Serve Him in dust, until He lift thee thence;

Till death be swallowed up in victory
  When the great trumpet sounds to bid thee hence.
Shall setting day win day that will not set?
10   Poor price wert thou to spend thyself for Christ,
  Had not His wealth thy poverty sufficed:
    Yet since He makes His garden of thy clod,
Water thy lily, rose, or violet,
    And offer up thy sweetness unto God.

Time seems not short:
  If so I call to mind
  Its vast prerogative to loose or bind,
And bear and strike amort
5   All humankind.

Time seems not long:
  If I peer out and see
  Sphere within sphere, time in eternity,
And hear the alternate song
10   Cry endlessly.

Time greatly short,
  O time so briefly long,
  Yea, time sole battle-ground of right and wrong:
Art thou a time for sport
15   And for a song?

The half moon shows a face of plaintive sweetness
  Ready and poised to wax or wane;
A fire of pale desire in incompleteness,
  Tending to pleasure or to pain:—
5 Lo, while we gaze she rolleth on in fleetness
  To perfect loss or perfect gain.

Half bitterness we know, we know half sweetness;
  This world is all on wax, on wane:
When shall completeness round time's incompleteness,
10   Fulfilling joy, fulfilling pain?—

Lo, while we ask, life rolleth on in fleetness
   To finished loss or finished gain.

"As the Doves to their windows."

They throng from the east and the west,
   The north and the south, with a song;
To golden abodes of their rest
   They throng.

5   Eternity stretches out long:
Time, brief at its worst or its best,
   Will quit them of ruin and wrong.

A rainbow aloft for their crest,
   A palm for their weakness made strong!
10   As doves breast all winds to their nest,
   They throng.

Oh knell of a passing time,
Will it never cease to chime?
Oh stir of the tedious sea,
Will it never cease to be?
5   Yea, when night and when day,
Moon and sun, pass away.

Surely the sun burns low,
The moon makes ready to go,
Broad ocean ripples to waste,
10   Time is running in haste,
Night is numbered, and day
Numbered to pass away.

Time passeth away with its pleasure and pain,
   Its garlands of cypress and bay,
With wealth and with want, with a balm and a bane,
   Time passeth away.

5   Eternity cometh to stay,
    Eternity stayeth to go not again;
       Eternity barring the way,

    Arresting all courses of planet or main,
       Arresting who plan or who pray,
10   Arresting creation: while grand in its wane
       Time passeth away.

"The Earth shall tremble at the Look of Him."

Tremble, thou earth, at the Presence of the Lord
    Whose Will conceived thee and brought thee to the birth,
Always, everywhere, thy Lord to be adored:
    Tremble, thou earth.

5   Wilt thou laugh time away in music and mirth?
Time hath days of pestilence, hath days of a sword,
    Hath days of hunger and thirst in desolate dearth.

Till eternity wake up the multicord
    Thrilled harp of heaven, and breathe full its organ's
        girth
10 For joy of heaven and infinite reward,
    Tremble, thou earth.

Time lengthening, in the lengthening seemeth long:
    But ended Time will seem a little space,
    A little while from morn to evensong,
A little while that ran a rapid race;
5   A little while, when once Eternity
    Denies proportion to the other's pace.
Eternity to be and be and be,
    Ever beginning, never ending still,
    Still undiminished far as thought can see;
10 Farther than thought can see, by dint of will
    Strung up and strained and shooting like a star
    Past utmost bound of everlasting hill:

Eternity unswaddled, without bar,
   Finishing sequence in its awful sum;
15   Eternity still rolling forth its car,
Eternity still here and still to come.

"All Flesh is Grass."

So brief a life, and then an endless life
   Or endless death;
So brief a life, then endless peace or strife:
   Whoso considereth
5   How man but like a flower
    Or shoot of grass
Blooms an hour,
   Well may sigh "Alas!"

So brief a life, and then an endless grief
10   Or endless joy;
So brief a life, then ruin or relief:
   What solace, what annoy
Of Time needs dwelling on?
   It is, it was,
15 It is done,
   While we sigh "Alas!"

Yet saints are singing in a happy hope
   Forecasting pleasure,
Bright eyes of faith enlarging all their scope;
20   Saints love beyond Time's measure:
Where love is, there is bliss
   That will not pass;
Where love is,
   Dies away "Alas!"

Heaven's chimes are slow, but sure to strike at last:
   Earth's sands are slow, but surely dropping thro':
   And much we have to suffer, much to do,
    Before the time be past.

5   Chimes that keep time are neither slow nor fast:
      Not many are the numbered sands nor few:
      A time to suffer, and a time to do,
        And then the time is past.

"There remaineth therefore a Rest to the People of God."

Rest remains when all is done,
   Work and vigil, prayer and fast,
   All fulfilled from first to last,
   All the length of time gone past
5 And eternity begun!

Fear and hope and chastening rod
   Urge us on the narrow way:
   Bear we now as best we may
   Heat and burden of today,
10 Struggling, panting up to God.

Parting after parting,
   Sore loss and gnawing pain:
Meeting grows half a sorrow
   Because of parting again.
5 When shall the day break
   That these things shall not be?
When shall new earth be ours
   Without a sea,
And time that is not time
10 But eternity?

To meet, worth living for;
   Worth dying for, to meet;
To meet, worth parting for,
   Bitter forgot in sweet:
15 To meet, worth parting before
   Never to part more.

"They put their trust in Thee, and were not confounded."

I.

Together once, but never more
   While Time and Death run out their runs:
Tho' sundered now as shore from shore,
   Together once.

5   Nor rising suns, nor setting suns,
Nor life renewed which springtide bore,
   Make one again Death's sundered ones.

Eternity holds rest in store,
   Holds hope of long reunions:
10   But holds it what they hungered for
   Together once?

II.

Whatso it be, howso it be, Amen.
   Blessed it is, believing, not to see.
Now God knows all that is; and we shall, then,
   Whatso it be.

5   God's Will is best for man whose will is free.
God's Will is better to us, yea, than ten
   Desires whereof He holds and weighs the key.

Amid her household cares He guides the wren,
   He guards the shifty mouse from poverty;
10   He knows all wants, allots each where and when,
   Whatso it be.

Short is time, and only time is bleak;
   Gauge the exceeding height thou hast to climb:
Long eternity is nigh to seek:
   Short is time.

5   Time is shortening with the wintry rime:
    Pray and watch and pray, girt up and meek;
      Praying, watching, praying, chime by chime.

    Pray by silence if thou canst not speak:
    Time is shortening; pray on till the prime:
10   Time is shortening; soul, fulfil thy week:
      Short is time.

For Each.

My harvest is done, its promise is ended,
  Weak and watery sets the sun,
Day and night in one mist are blended,
  My harvest is done.

5   Long while running, how short when run,
Time to eternity has descended,
   Timeless eternity has begun.

Was it the narrow way that I wended?
  Snares and pits was it mine to shun?
10 The scythe has fallen, so long suspended,
  My harvest is done.

For All.

Man's harvest is past, his summer is ended,
  Hope and fear are finished at last,
Day hath descended, night hath ascended,
  Man's harvest is past.

5   Time is fled that fleeted so fast:
All the unmended remains unmended,
   The perfect, perfect: all lots are cast.

Waiting till earth and ocean be rended,
  Waiting for call of the trumpet blast,
10 Each soul at goal of that way it wended,—
  Man's harvest is past.

NEW JERUSALEM AND
ITS CITIZENS.

"The Holy City, New Jerusalem."

Jerusalem is built of gold,
   Of crystal, pearl, and gem:
Oh fair thy lustres manifold,
   Thou fair Jerusalem!
5   Thy citizens who walk in white
Have nought to do with day or night,
And drink the river of delight.

Jerusalem makes melody
   For simple joy of heart;
10   An organ of full compass she,
   One-tuned thro' every part:
While not to day or night belong
Her matins and her evensong,
The one thanksgiving of her throng.

15   Jerusalem a garden is,
   A garden of delight;
Leaf, flower, and fruit make fair her trees,
   Which see not day or night:
Beside her River clear and calm
20   The Tree of Life grows with the Palm,
For triumph and for food and balm.

Jerusalem, where song nor gem
   Nor fruit nor waters cease,
God bring us to Jerusalem,
25   God bring us home in peace;
The strong who stand, the weak who fall,
The first and last, the great and small,
Home one by one, home one and all.

When wickedness is broken as a tree
   Paradise comes to light, ah holy land!

Whence death has vanished like a shifting sand,
And barrenness is banished with the sea.
5   Its bulwarks are salvation fully manned,
    All gems it hath for glad variety,
    And pearls for pureness radiant glimmeringly,
And gold for grandeur where all good is grand.
An inner ring of saints meets linked above,
10   And linked of angels is an outer ring;
      For voice of waters or for thunders' voice
      Lo! harps and songs wherewith all saints rejoice,
    And all the trembling there of any string
Is but a trembling of enraptured love.

Jerusalem of fire
    And gold and pearl and gem,
Saints flock to fill thy choir,
    Jerusalem.

5   Lo, thrones thou hast for them;
Desirous they desire
    Thy harp, thy diadem,

Thy bridal white attire,
    A palm-branch from thy stem:
10   Thy holiness their hire,
    Jerusalem.

"She shall be brought unto the King."

The King's Daughter is all glorious within,
    Her clothing of wrought gold sets forth her bliss;
Where the endless choruses of heaven begin
    The King's Daughter is;

5   Perfect her notes in the perfect harmonies;
With tears wiped away, no conscience of sin,
    Loss forgotten and sorrowful memories;

Alight with Cherubin, afire with Seraphin,
   Lily for pureness, rose for charities,
10 With joy won and with joy evermore to win,
   The King's Daughter is.

Who is this that cometh up not alone
   From the fiery-flying-serpent wilderness,
Leaning upon her own Beloved One:
   Who is this?
5 Lo, the King of kings' daughter, a high princess,
Going home as bride to her Husband's Throne,
   Virgin queen in perfected loveliness.

Her eyes a dove's eyes and her voice a dove's moan,
   She shows like a full moon for heavenliness:
10 Eager saints and angels ask in heaven's zone,
   Who is this?

Who sits with the King in His Throne? Not a slave but a
   Bride,
   With this King of all Greatness and Grace Who reigns
     not alone;
His Glory her glory, where glorious she glows at His side
   Who sits with the King in His Throne.
5 She came from dim uttermost depths which no Angel
   hath known,
Leviathan's whirlpool and Dragon's dominion worldwide,
   From the frost or the fire to Paradisiacal zone.

Lo, she is fair as a dove, silvery, golden, dove-eyed:
   Lo, Dragon laments and Death laments, for their prey
     is flown:
10 She dwells in the Vision of Peace, and her peace shall
   abide
   Who sits with the King in His Throne.

Antipas.

Hidden from the darkness of our mortal sight,
Hidden in the Paradise of lovely light,
Hidden in God's Presence, worshipped face to face,
Hidden in the sanctuary of Christ's embrace.
5   Up, O Wills! to track him home among the bless'd;
Up, O Hearts! to know him in the joy of rest;
Where no darkness more shall hide him from our sight,
Where we shall be love with love, and light with light,
Worshipping our God together face to face,
10 Wishless in the sanctuary of Christ's embrace.

"Beautiful for situation."

A lovely city in a lovely land,
  Whose citizens are lovely, and whose King
  Is Very Love; to Whom all Angels sing;
To Whom all saints sing crowned, their sacred band
5 Saluting Love with palm-branch in their hand:
  Thither all doves on gold or silver wing
  Flock home thro' agate windows glistering
Set wide, and where pearl gates wide open stand.
A bower of roses is not half so sweet,
10 A cave of diamonds doth not glitter so,
   Nor Lebanon is fruitful set thereby:
   And thither thou, beloved, and thither I
  May set our heart and set our face and go,
Faint yet pursuing, home on tireless feet.

Lord, by what inconceivable dim road
  Thou leadest man on footsore pilgrimage!
  Weariness is his rest from stage to stage,
Brief halting-places are his sole abode.

5   Onward he fares thro' rivers overflowed,
         Thro' deserts where all doleful creatures rage;
         Onward from year to year, from age to age,
       He groans and totters onward with his load.
       Behold how inconceivable his way;
10   How tenfold inconceivable the goal,
           His goal of hope deferred, his promised peace:
           Yea, but behold him sitting down at ease,
         Refreshed in body and refreshed in soul,
       At rest from labour on the Sabbath Day.

"As cold waters to a thirsty soul, so is good news from a far country."

       "Golden haired, lily white,
         Will you pluck me lilies?
       Or will you show me where they grow,
         Show where the limpid rill is?
5   But is your hair of gold or light,
         And is your foot of flake or fire,
       And have you wings rolled up from sight
         And songs to slake desire?"

       "I pluck fresh flowers of Paradise,
10   Lilies and roses red,
       A bending sceptre for my hand,
         A crown to crown my head.
       I sing my songs, I pluck my flowers
         Sweet-scented from their fragrant trees;
15   I sing, we sing, amid the bowers
         And gather palm-branches."

       "Is there a path to Heaven
         My stumbling foot may tread?
       And will you show that way to go,
20   That bower and blossom bed?"
       "The path to Heaven is steep and straight
         And scorched, but ends in shade of trees,

Where yet a while we sing and wait
   And gather palm-branches."

Cast down but not destroyed, chastened not slain:
   Thy Saints have lived that life, but how can I?
   I, who thro' dread of death do daily die
By daily foretaste of an unfelt pain.
5   Lo, I depart who shall not come again;
   Lo, as a shadow I am flitting by;
   As a leaf trembling, as a wheel I fly,
While death flies faster and my flight is vain.
Chastened not slain, cast down but not destroyed:—
10   If thus Thy Saints have struggled home to peace,
      Why should not I take heart to be as they?
     They too pent passions in a house of clay,
   Fear and desire, and pangs and ecstasies;
Yea, thus they joyed who now are overjoyed.

Lift up thine eyes to seek the invisible:
   Stir up thy heart to choose the still unseen:
   Strain up thy hope in glad perpetual green
To scale the exceeding height where all saints dwell.
5   —Saints, it is well with you?—Yea, it is well.—
   Where they have reaped, by faith kneel thou to glean:
   Because they stooped so low to reap, they lean
Now over golden harps unspeakable.
   —But thou purblind and deafened, knowest thou
10   Those glorious beauties unexperienced
      By ear or eye or by heart hitherto?—
I know Whom I have trusted: wherefore now
   All amiable, accessible tho' fenced,
     Golden Jerusalem floats full in view.

"Love is strong as Death."

As flames that consume the mountains, as winds that
    coerce the sea,
  Thy men of renown show forth Thy might in the clutch
    of death:
Down they go into silence, yet the Trump of the Jubilee
  Swells not Thy praise as swells it the breathless pause of
    their breath.

5   What is the flame of their fire, if so I may catch the flame;
  What the strength of their strength, if also I may wax
    strong?
The flaming fire of their strength is the love of Jesu's
  Name,
  In Whom their death is life, their silence utters a song.

"Let them rejoice in their beds."

Crimson as the rubies, crimson as the roses,
  Crimson as the sinking sun,
Singing on his crimsoned bed each saint reposes,
  Fought his fight, his battle won;
5   Till the rosy east the day of days discloses,
  All his work, save waiting, done.

Far above the stars, while underneath the daisies,
  Resting, for his race is run,
Unto Thee his heart each quiet saint upraises,
10   God the Father, Spirit, Son;
Unto Thee his heart, unto Thee his praises,
  O Lord God, the Three in One.

Slain in their high places: fallen on rest
  Where the eternal peace lights up their faces,
In God's sacred acre breast to breast:—
  Slain in their high places.

5   From all tribes, all families, all races,
       Gathered home together; east or west
          Sending home its tale of gifts and graces.

       Twine, oh twine, heaven's amaranth for their crest,
          Raise their praise while home their triumph paces;
10   Kings by their own King of kings confessed,
          Slain in their high places.

"What hath God wrought!"

       The shout of a King is among them. One day may I be
       Of that perfect communion of lovers contented and free
       In the land that is very far off, and far off from the sea.

       The shout of the King is among them. One King and one
                    song,
5   One thunder of manifold voices harmonious and strong,
       One King and one love, and one shout of one worshipping
                    throng.

"Before the Throne, and before the Lamb."

       As the voice of many waters all saints sing as one,
          As the voice of an unclouded thundering;
       Unswayed by the changing moon and unswayed by the sun,
          As the voice of many waters all saints sing.

5   Circling round the rainbow of their perfect ring,
       Twelve thousand times twelve thousand voices in unison
          Swell the triumph, swell the praise of Christ the King.

       Where raiment is white of blood-steeped linen slowly spun,
          Where crowns are golden of Love's own largessing,
10   Where eternally the ecstasy is but begun,
          As the voice of many waters all saints sing.

"He shall go no more out."

Once within, within for evermore:
  There the long beatitudes begin:
Overflows the still unwasting store,
  Once within.

5   Left without are death and doubt and sin;
All man wrestled with and all he bore,
  Man who saved his life, skin after skin.

Blow the trumpet-blast unheard before,
  Shout the unheard-of shout for these who win,
10   These, who cast their crowns on Heaven's high floor
  Once within.

Yea, blessed and holy is he that hath part in the First
      Resurrection!
  We mark well his bulwarks, we set up his tokens, we
      gaze, even we,
On this lustre of God and of Christ, this creature of
      flawless perfection:
  Yea, blessed and holy is he.

5   But what? an offscouring of earth, a wreck from the
      turbulent sea,
A bloodstone unflinchingly hewn for the Temple's eternal
      erection,
    One scattered and peeled, one sifted and chastened
      and scourged and set free?

Yea, this is that worshipful stone of the Wise Master
      Builder's election,
  Yea, this is that King and that Priest where all Hallows
      bow down the knee,
10   Yea, this man set nigh to the Throne is Jonathan of David's
      delection,
  Yea, blessed and holy is he.

The joy of Saints, like incense turned to fire
   In golden censers, soars acceptable;
   And high their heavenly hallelujahs swell
Desirous still with still-fulfilled desire.
5   Sweet thrill the harpstrings of the heavenly choir,
   Most sweet their voice while love is all they tell;
   Where love is all in all, and all is well
Because their work is love and love their hire.
All robed in white and all with palm in hand,
10   Crowns too they have of gold and thrones of gold;
   The street is golden which their feet have trod,
Or on a sea of glass and fire they stand:
   And none of them is young, and none is old,
   Except as perfect by the Will of God.

What are these lovely ones, yea, what are these?
   Lo, these are they who for pure love of Christ
Stripped off the trammels of soft silken ease,
   Beggaring themselves betimes, to be sufficed
5   Throughout heaven's one eternal day of peace:
   By golden streets, thro' gates of pearl unpriced,
They entered on the joys that will not cease,
   And found again all firstfruits sacrificed.
And wherefore have you harps, and wherefore palms,
10   And wherefore crowns, O ye who walk in white?
Because our happy hearts are chanting psalms,
   Endless Te Deum for the ended fight;
While thro' the everlasting lapse of calms
   We cast our crowns before the Lamb our Might.

"The General Assembly and Church of the Firstborn."

Bring me to see, Lord, bring me yet to see
   Those nations of Thy glory and Thy grace
   Who splendid in Thy splendour worship Thee.

Light in all eyes, content in every face,
5   Raptures and voices one while manifold,
      Love and are well-beloved the ransomed race:—
Great mitred priests, great kings in crowns of gold,
      Patriarchs who head the army of their sons,
      Matrons and mothers by their own extolled,
10   Wise and most harmless holy little ones,
      Virgins who, making merry, lead the dance,
      Full-breathed victorious racers from all runs,
Home-comers out of every change and chance,
      Hermits restored to social neighbourhood,
15   Aspects which reproduce One Countenance,
Life-losers with their losses all made good,
      All blessed hungry and athirst sufficed,
      All who bore crosses round the Holy Rood,
Friends, brethren, sisters, of Lord Jesus Christ.

"Every one that is perfect shall be as his master."

How can one man, how can all men,
      How can we be like St. Paul,
Like St. John, or like St. Peter,
      Like the least of all
5   Blessed Saints? for we are small.

Love can make us like St. Peter,
      Love can make us like St. Paul,
Love can make us like the blessed
      Bosom friend of all,
10   Great St. John, tho' we are small.

Love which clings and trusts and worships,
      Love which rises from a fall,
Love which, prompting glad obedience,
      Labours most of all,
15   Love makes great the great and small.

"As dying, and behold we live!"
  So live the Saints while time is flying;
Make all they make, give all they give,
  As dying;
5   Bear all they bear without replying;
They grieve as tho' they did not grieve,
  Uplifting praise with prayer and sighing.

Patient thro' life's long-drawn reprieve,
  Aloof from strife, at peace from crying,
10 The morrow to its day they leave,
  As dying.

"So great a cloud of Witnesses."

I think of the saints I have known, and lift up mine eyes
To the far-away home of beautiful Paradise,
Where the song of saints gives voice to an undividing sea
On whose plain their feet stand firm while they keep their
      jubilee.
5   As the sound of waters their voice, as the sound of
      thunderings,
While they all at once rejoice, while all sing and while
      each one sings;
Where more saints flock in, and more, and yet more, and
      again yet more,
And not one turns back to depart thro' the open
      entrance-door.

O sights of our lovely earth, O sound of our earthly sea,
10 Speak to me of Paradise, of all blessed saints to me:
Or keep silence touching them, and speak to my heart
      alone
Of the Saint of saints, the King of kings, the Lamb on the
      Throne.

Our Mothers, lovely women pitiful;
   Our Sisters, gracious in their life and death;
   To us each unforgotten memory saith:
"Learn as we learned in life's sufficient school,
5   Work as we worked in patience of our rule,
    Walk as we walked, much less by sight than faith,
    Hope as we hoped, despite our slips and scathe,
Fearful in joy and confident in dule."
I know not if they see us or can see;
10   But if they see us in our painful day,
    How looking back to earth from Paradise
    Do tears not gather in those loving eyes?—
Ah, happy eyes! whose tears are wiped away
Whether or not you bear to look on me.

Safe where I cannot lie yet,
   Safe where I hope to lie too,
Safe from the fume and the fret;
   You, and you,
5   Whom I never forget.

Safe from the frost and the snow,
   Safe from the storm and the sun,
Safe where the seeds wait to grow
   One by one
10   And to come back in blow.

"Is it well with the child?"

Lying a-dying.
Have done with vain sighing:
Life not lost but treasured,
God Almighty pleasured,
5   God's daughter fetched and carried,
Christ's bride betrothed and married.
Our tender little dove
Meek-eyed and simple,

Our love goes home to Love:
10   There shall she walk in white,
Where God shall be the Light,
And God the Temple.

Dear Angels and dear disembodied Saints
   Unseen around us, worshipping in rest,
May wonder that man's heart so often faints
   And his steps lag along the heavenly quest,
5 What while his foolish fancy moulds and paints
   A fonder hope than all they prove for best;
A lying hope which undermines and taints
   His soul, as sin and sloth make manifest.
Sloth, and a lie, and sin: shall these suffice
10   The unfathomable heart of craving man,
     That heart which being a deep calls to the deep?
Behold how many like us rose and ran
     When Christ, life-giver, roused them from their sleep
To rise and run and rest in Paradise!

"To every seed his own body."

Bone to his bone, grain to his grain of dust:
   A numberless reunion shall make whole
   Each blessed body for its blessed soul,
Refashioning the aspects of the just.
5 Each saint who died must live afresh, and must
   Ascend resplendent in the aureole
   Of his own proper glory to his goal,
As seeds their proper bodies all upthrust.
Each with his own not with another's grace,
10   Each with his own not with another's heart,
Each with his own not with another's face,
Each dove-like soul mounts to his proper place:—
   O faces unforgotten! if to part
Wrung sore, what will it be to re-embrace?

"What good shall my life do me?"

Have dead men long to wait?—

There is a certain term
For their bodies to the worm
And their souls at heaven gate.
5   Dust to dust, clod to clod,
These precious things of God,
Trampled underfoot by man
And beast the appointed years.—

Their longest life was but a span
10   For change and smiles and tears.
Is it worth while to live,
Rejoice and grieve,
Hope, fear, and die?
Man with man, truth with lie,
15   The slow show dwindles by:
At last what shall we have
Besides a grave?—

Lies and shows no more,
No fear, no pain,
20   But after hope and sleep
Dear joys again.
Those who sowed shall reap:
Those who bore
The Cross shall wear the Crown:
25   Those who clomb the steep
There shall sit down.
The Shepherd of the sheep
Feeds His flock there,
In watered pastures fair
30   They rest and leap.
"Is it worth while to live?"
Be of good cheer:
Love casts out fear:
Rise up, achieve.

SONGS FOR STRANGERS
AND PILGRIMS.

"Her Seed; It shall bruise thy head."

Astonished Heaven looked on when man was made,
  When fallen man reproved seemed half forgiven;
Surely that oracle of hope first said,
  Astonished Heaven.

5   Even so while one by one lost souls are shriven,
A mighty multitude of quickened dead;
  Christ's love outnumbering ten times sevenfold seven.

Even so while man still tosses high his head,
  While still the All-Holy Spirit's strife is striven;—
10 Till one last trump shake earth, and undismayed
  Astonished Heaven.

"Judge nothing before the time."

Love understands the mystery, whereof
  We can but spell a surface history:
Love knows, remembers: let us trust in Love:
  Love understands the mystery.

5   Love weighs the event, the long pre-history,
Measures the depth beneath, the height above,
  The mystery, with the ante-mystery.

To love and to be grieved befits a dove
  Silently telling her bead-history:
10 Trust all to Love, be patient and approve:
  Love understands the mystery.

How great is little man!
  Sun, moon, and stars respond to him,
  Shine or grow dim
Harmonious with his span.

5   How little is great man!
        More changeable than changeful moon,
        Nor half in tune
    With Heaven's harmonious plan.

    Ah, rich man! ah, poor man!
10   Make ready for the testing day
        When wastes away
    What bears not fire or fan.

    Thou heir of all things, man,
        Pursue the saints by heavenward track:
15   They looked not back;
    Run thou, as erst they ran.

    Little and great is man:
        Great if he will, or if he will
        A pigmy still;
20 For what he will he can.

    Man's life is but a working day
        Whose tasks are set aright:
    A time to work, a time to pray,
        And then a quiet night.
5   And then, please God, a quiet night
    Where palms are green and robes are white;
    A long-drawn breath, a balm for sorrow,
    And all things lovely on the morrow.

    If not with hope of life,
        Begin with fear of death:
    Strive the tremendous life-long strife
        Breath after breath.

5   Bleed on beneath the rod;
        Weep on until thou see;
    Turn fear and hope to love of God
        Who loveth thee.

Turn all to love, poor soul;
10   Be love thy watch and ward;
Be love thy starting-point, thy goal,
    And thy reward.

"The day is at hand."

Watch yet a while,
Weep till that day shall dawn when thou shalt smile:
Watch till the day
When all save only Love shall pass away.
5   Then Love rejoicing shall forget to weep,
Shall hope or fear no more, or watch or sleep,
But only love and stint not, deep beyond deep.
Now we sow love in tears, but then shall reap.
Have patience as True Love's own flock of sheep:
10   Have patience with His Love
Who served for us, Who reigns for us above.

"Endure hardness."

A cold wind stirs the blackthorn
    To burgeon and to blow,
Besprinkling half-green hedges
    With flakes and sprays of snow.
5   Thro' coldness and thro' keenness,
    Dear hearts, take comfort so:
Somewhere or other doubtless
    These make the blackthorn blow.

"Whither the Tribes go up, even the Tribes of the Lord."

Light is our sorrow for it ends tomorrow,
   Light is our death which cannot hold us fast;
So brief a sorrow can be scarcely sorrow,
   Or death be death so quickly past.

5   One night, no more, of pain that turns to pleasure,
   One night, no more, of weeping weeping sore;
And then the heaped-up measure beyond measure,
   In quietness for evermore.

Our face is set like flint against our trouble,
10   Yet many things there are which comfort us;
This bubble is a rainbow-coloured bubble,
   This bubble-life tumultuous.

Our sails are set to cross the tossing river,
   Our face is set to reach Jerusalem;
15   We toil awhile, but then we rest for ever,
   Sing with all Saints and rest with them.

Where never tempest heaveth,
Nor sorrow grieveth,
Nor death bereaveth,
Nor hope deceiveth,
5   Sleep.

Where never shame bewaileth,
Nor serpent traileth,
Nor death prevaileth,
Nor harvest faileth,
10   Reap.

Marvel of marvels, if I myself shall behold
With mine own eyes my King in His city of gold;
Where the least of lambs is spotless white in the fold,
Where the least and last of saints in spotless white is stoled,

5 Where the dimmest head beyond a moon is aureoled.
 O saints, my beloved, now mouldering to mould in the
    mould,
 Shall I see you lift your heads, see your cerements unrolled,
 See with these very eyes? who now in darkness and cold
 Tremble for the midnight cry, the rapture, the tale untold,
10 "The Bridegroom cometh, cometh, His Bride to enfold."

 Cold it is, my beloved, since your funeral bell was tolled:
 Cold it is, O my King, how cold alone on the wold.

"What is that to thee? follow thou me."

 Lie still, my restive heart, lie still:
 God's Word to thee saith, "Wait and bear."
 The good which He appoints is good,
 The good which He denies were ill:
5 Yea, subtle comfort is thy care,
 Thy hurt a help not understood.

 "Friend, go up higher," to one: to one,
 "Friend, enter thou My joy," He saith:
 To one, "Be faithful unto death."
10 For some a wilderness doth flower,
 Or day's work in one hour is done:—
 "But thou, could'st thou not watch one hour?"

 Lord, I had chosen another lot,
 But then I had not chosen well;
15 Thy choice and only Thine is good:
 No different lot, search heaven or hell,
 Had blessed me fully understood;
 None other, which Thou orderest not.

"Worship God."

 Lord, if Thy word had been "Worship Me not,
  For I than thou am holier: draw not near:"

We had besieged Thy Face with prayer and tear
And manifold abasement in our lot,
5   Our crooked ground, our thorned and thistled plot;
        Envious of flawless Angels in their sphere,
        Envious of brutes, and envious of the mere
Unliving and undying unbegot.
But now Thou hast said, "Worship Me, and give
10   Thy heart to Me, My child:" now therefore we
    Think twice before we stoop to worship Thee:
        We proffer half a heart while life is strong
And strung with hope; so sweet it is to live!
        Wilt Thou not wait? Yea, Thou hast waited long.

"Afterward he repented, and went."

Lord, when my heart was whole I kept it back
    And grudged to give it Thee.
Now then that it is broken, must I lack
    Thy kind word "Give it Me"?
5   Silence would be but just, and Thou art just.
Yet since I lie here shattered in the dust,
        With still an eye to lift to Thee,
    A broken heart to give,
    I think that Thou wilt bid me live,
10   And answer "Give it Me."

"Are they not all Ministering Spirits?"

Lord, whomsoever Thou shalt send to me,
Let that same be
        Mine Angel predilect:
Veiled or unveiled, benignant or austere,
5   Aloof or near;
        Thine, therefore mine, elect.

So may my soul nurse patience day by day,
Watch on and pray
        Obedient and at peace;

10   Living a lonely life in hope, in faith;
    Loving till death,
        When life, not love, shall cease.

    . . . . Lo, thou mine Angel with transfigured face
    Brimful of grace,
15   Brimful of love for me!
    Did I misdoubt thee all that weary while,
    Thee with a smile
        For me as I for thee?

    Our life is long. Not so, wise Angels say
    Who watch us waste it, trembling while they weigh
    Against eternity one squandered day.

    Our life is long. Not so, the Saints protest,
5   Filled full of consolation and of rest:
    "Short ill, long good, one long unending best."

    Our life is long. Christ's word sounds different:
    "Night cometh: no more work when day is spent.
    Repent and work today, work and repent."

10   Lord, make us like Thy Host who day nor night
    Rest not from adoration, their delight,
    Crying "Holy, Holy, Holy," in the height.

    Lord, make us like Thy Saints who wait and long
    Contented: bound in hope and freed from wrong
15   They speed (may be) their vigil with a song.

    Lord, make us like Thyself: for thirty-three
    Slow years of toil seemed not too long to Thee,
    That where Thou art, there Thy Beloved might be.

    Lord, what have I to offer? sickening fear
       And a heart-breaking loss.
    Are these the cross Thou givest me? then dear
       I will account this cross.

5   If this is all I have, accept even this
       Poor priceless offering,

A quaking heart with all that therein is,
    O Thou my thorn-crowned King.

Accept the whole, my God, accept my heart
10   And its own love within:
Wilt Thou accept us and not sift apart?
    —Only sift out my sin.

        Joy is but sorrow,
            While we know
        It ends tomorrow:—
            Even so!
5   Joy with lifted veil
        Shows a face as pale
As the fair changing moon so fair and frail.

        Pain is but pleasure,
            If we know
10   It heaps up treasure:—
            Even so!
        Turn, transfigured Pain,
        Sweetheart, turn again,
For fair thou art as moonrise after rain.

Can I know it?—Nay.—
Shall I know it?—Yea,
When all mists have cleared away
For ever and aye.—
5   Why not then today?—
Who hath said thee nay?
Lift a hopeful heart and pray
In a humble way.—

Other hearts are gay.—
10 Ask not joy today:
Toil today along thy way
Keeping grudge at bay.—

On a past May-day
Flowers pranked all the way;

15   Nightingales sang out their say
       On a night of May.—

       Dost thou covet May
       On an Autumn day?
       Foolish memory saith its say
20   Of sweets past away.—

       Gone the bloom of May,
       Autumn beareth bay:
       Flowerless wreath for head grown grey
       Seemly were today.—

25   Dost thou covet bay?
       Ask it not today:
       Rather for a palm-branch pray;
       None will say thee nay.

"When my heart is vexed I will complain."

       "The fields are white to harvest, look and see,
       Are white abundantly.
       The full-orbed harvest moon shines clear,
       The harvest time draws near,
5   Be of good cheer."

       "Ah, woe is me!
       I have no heart for harvest time,
       Grown sick with hope deferred from chime to chime."

       "But Christ can give thee heart Who loveth thee:
10   Can set thee in the eternal ecstasy
       Of His great jubilee:
       Can give thee dancing heart and shining face,
       And lips filled full of grace,
       And pleasures as the rivers and the sea.
15   Who knocketh at His door
       He welcomes evermore:

Kneel down before
That ever-open door
(The time is short) and smite
20   Thy breast, and pray with all thy might."

"What shall I say?"
                         "Nay, pray.
Tho' one but say 'Thy Will be done,'
He hath not lost his day
25   At set of sun."

"Praying always."

After midnight, in the dark
    The clock strikes one,
    New day has begun.
Look up and hark!
5   With singing heart forestall the carolling lark.

After mid-day, in the light
    The clock strikes one,
    Day-fall has begun.
Cast up, set right
10 The day's account against the on-coming night.

After noon and night, one day
    For ever one
    Ends not, once begun.
Whither away,
15 O brothers and O sisters? Pause and pray.

"As thy days, so shall thy strength be."

Day that hath no tinge of night,
    Night that hath no tinge of day,
These at last will come to sight
    Not to fade away.
5   This is twilight that we know,
    Scarcely night and scarcely day;

This hath been from long ago
    Shed around man's way:

Step by step to utter night,
10   Step by step to perfect day,
To the Left Hand or the Right
    Leading all away.

This is twilight: be it so;
    Suited to our strength our day:
15 Let us follow on to know,
    Patient by the way.

A heavy heart, if ever heart was heavy,
    I offer Thee this heavy heart of me.
Are such as this the hearts Thou art fain to levy
    To do and dare for Thee, to bleed for Thee?
5   Ah, blessed heaviness, if such they be!

Time was I bloomed with blossom and stood leafy
    How long before the fruit, if fruit there be:
Lord, if by bearing fruit my heart grows heavy,
    Leafless and bloomless yet accept of me
10   The stripped fruit-bearing heart I offer Thee.

Lifted to Thee my heart weighs not so heavy,
    It leaps and lightens lifted up to Thee;
It sings, it hopes to sing amid the bevy
    Of thousand thousand choirs that sing, and see
15   Thy Face, me loving, for Thou lovest me.

If love is not worth loving, then life is not worth living,
    Nor aught is worth remembering but well forgot;
For store is not worth storing and gifts are not worth
        giving,
    If love is not;

5   And idly cold is death-cold, and life-heat idly hot,
And vain is any offering and vainer our receiving,
    And vanity of vanities is all our lot.

Better than life's heaving heart is death's heart
    unheaving,
Better than the opening leaves are the leaves that rot,
10 For there is nothing left worth achieving or retrieving,
    If love is not.

What is it Jesus saith unto the soul?
    "Take up the Cross, and come and follow Me."
    One word He saith to all men: none may be
Without a cross yet hope to touch the goal.
5 Then heave it bravely up, and brace thy whole
    Body to bear; it will not weigh on thee
    Past strength; or if it crush thee to thy knee
Take heart of grace, for grace shall be thy dole.
Give thanks today, and let tomorrow take
10 Heed to itself; today imports thee more,
    Tomorrow may not dawn like yesterday:
    Until that unknown morrow go thy way,
Suffer and work and strive for Jesus' sake:—
    Who tells thee what tomorrow keeps in store?

They lie at rest, our blessed dead;
The dews drop cool above their head,
They knew not when fleet summer fled.

Together all, yet each alone;
5 Each laid at rest beneath his own
Smooth turf or white allotted stone.

When shall our slumber sink so deep,
And eyes that wept and eyes that weep
Weep not in the sufficient sleep?

10 God be with you, our great and small,
Our loves, our best beloved of all,
Our own beyond the salt sea-wall.

"Ye that fear Him, both small and great."

Great or small below,
   Great or small above;
Be we Thine, whom Thou dost know
    And love:
5 First or last on earth,
   First or last in Heaven;
Only weighted with Thy worth,
    And shriven.

Wise or ignorant,
10   Strong or weak; Amen;
Sifted now, cast down, in want:—
    But then?

Then,—when sun nor moon,
   Time nor death, finds place,
15 Seeing in the eternal noon
    Thy Face:

Then,—when tears and sighing,
   Changes, sorrows, cease;
Living by Thy Life undying
20   In peace:

Then,—when all creation
   Keeps its jubilee,
Crowned amid Thy holy nation;
Crowned, discrowned, in adoration
25   Of Thee.

"Called to be Saints."

The lowest place. Ah, Lord, how steep and high
   That lowest place whereon a saint shall sit!
Which of us halting, trembling, pressing nigh,
    Shall quite attain to it?

5 Yet, Lord, Thou pressest nigh to hail and grace
       Some happy soul, it may be still unfit
   For Right Hand or for Left Hand, but whose place
       Waits there prepared for it.

   The sinner's own fault? So it was.
       If every own fault found us out,
       Dogged us and hedged us round about,
   What comfort should we take because
5   Not half our due we thus wrung out?

   Clearly his own fault. Yet I think
       My fault in part, who did not pray
       But lagged and would not lead the way.
   I, haply, proved his missing link.
10   God help us both to mend and pray.

   Who cares for earthly bread tho' white?
       Nay, heavenly sheaf of harvest corn!
   Who cares for earthly crown tonight?
       Nay, heavenly crown tomorrow morn!
5 I will not wander left or right,
       The straightest road is shortest too;
       And since we hold all hope in view
   And triumph where is no more pain,
       Tonight I bid good night to you
10 And bid you meet me there again.

   Laughing Life cries at the feast,—
       Craving Death cries at the door,—
   "Fish, or fowl, or fatted beast?"
       "Come with me, thy feast is o'er."—
5 "Wreathe the violets."—"Watch them fade."—
   "I am sunshine."—"I am shade:
   I am the sun-burying west."—
   "I am pleasure."—"I am rest:
   Come with me, for I am best."

"The end is not yet."

Home by different ways. Yet all
    Homeward bound thro' prayer and praise,
Young with old, and great with small,
    Home by different ways.
5   Many nights and many days
Wind must bluster, rain must fall,
    Quake the quicksand, shift the haze.

Life hath called and death will call
    Saints who praying kneel at gaze,
10   Ford the flood or leap the wall,
    Home by different ways.

Who would wish back the Saints upon our rough
    Wearisome road?
        Wish back a breathless soul
        Just at the goal?
5   My soul, praise God
For all dear souls which have enough.

I would not fetch one back to hope with me
    A hope deferred,
        To taste a cup that slips
10   From thirsting lips:—
    Hath he not heard
And seen what was to hear and see?

How could I stand to answer the rebuke
    If one should say:
15   "O friend of little faith,
        Good was my death,
        And good my day
Of rest, and good the sleep I took"?

"That which hath been is named already, and it is known that it is Man."

"Eye hath not seen:"—yet man hath known and weighed
    A hundred thousand marvels that have been:
What is it which (the Word of Truth hath said)
    Eye hath not seen?

5   "Ear hath not heard:"—yet harpings of delight,
    Trumpets of triumph, song and spoken word,
Man knows them all: what lovelier, loftier might
    Hath ear not heard?

"Nor heart conceived:"—yet man hath now desired
10   Beyond all reach, beyond his hope believed,
Loved beyond death: what fire shall yet be fired
    No heart conceived?

"Deep calls to deep:"—man's depth would be despair
    But for God's deeper depth: we sow to reap,
15 Have patience, wait, betake ourselves to prayer:
    Deep answereth deep.

Of each sad word which is more sorrowful,
    "Sorrow" or "Disappointment"? I have heard
Subtle inflections baffling subtlest rule,
    Of each sad word.

5   Sorrow can mourn: and lo! a mourning bird
Sings sweetly to sweet echoes of its dule,
    While silent disappointment broods unstirred.

Yet both nurse hope, where Penitence keeps school
    Who makes fools wise and saints of them that erred:
10 Wise men shape stepping stone, or curb, or tool,
    Of each sad word.

"I see that all things come to an end."

I.

No more! while sun and planets fly,
  And wind and storm and seasons four,
And while we live and while we die,—
  No more.

5   Nevertheless old ocean's roar,
And wide earth's multitudinous cry,
  And echo's pent reverberant store

Shall hush to silence by and bye:
  Ah, rosy world gone cold and hoar!
10 Man opes no more a mortal eye,
  No more.

"But Thy Commandment is exceeding broad."

II.

Once again to wake, nor wish to sleep;
  Once again to feel, nor feel a pain!
Rouse thy soul to watch and pray and weep
  Once again.

5   Hope afresh, for hope shall not be vain:
Start afresh along the exceeding steep
  Road to glory, long and rough and plain.

Sow and reap: for while these moments creep,
  Time and earth and life are on the wane:
10 Now, in tears; tomorrow, laugh and reap
  Once again.

Sursum Corda.

"Lift up your hearts." "We lift them up." Ah me!
I cannot, Lord, lift up my heart to Thee:
Stoop, lift it up, that where Thou art I too may be.

"Give Me thy heart." I would not say Thee nay,
5   But have no power to keep or give away
My heart: stoop, Lord, and take it to Thyself today.

Stoop, Lord, as once before, now once anew
Stoop, Lord, and hearken, hearken, Lord, and do,
And take my will, and take my heart, and take me too.

O ye, who are not dead and fit
Like blasted tree beside the pit
But for the axe that levels it,

Living show life of love, whereof
5   The force wields earth and heaven above:
Who knows not love begetteth love?

Love poises earth in space, Love rolls
Wide worlds rejoicing on their poles,
And girds them round with aureoles.

10   Love lights the sun, Love thro' the dark
Lights the moon's evanescent arc,
Lights up the star, lights up the spark.

O ye who taste that love is sweet,
Set waymarks for all doubtful feet
15   That stumble on in search of it.

Sing notes of love: that some who hear
Far off inert may lend an ear,
Rise up and wonder and draw near.

Lead life of love: that others who
20   Behold your life, may kindle too
With love, and cast their lot with you.

Where shall I find a white rose blowing?—
    Out in the garden where all sweets be.—
But out in my garden the snow was snowing
    And never a white rose opened for me.
5   Nought but snow and a wind were blowing
        And snowing.

Where shall I find a blush rose blushing?—
   On the garden wall or the garden bed.—
But out in my garden the rain was rushing
10   And never a blush rose raised its head.
Nothing glowing, flushing or blushing:
     Rain rushing.

Where shall I find a red rose budding?—
   Out in the garden where all things grow.—
15 But out in my garden a flood was flooding
   And never a red rose began to blow.
Out in a flooding what should be budding?
     All flooding!

Now is winter and now is sorrow,
20 No roses but only thorns today:
Thorns will put on roses tomorrow,
   Winter and sorrow scudding away.
No more winter and no more sorrow
     Tomorrow.

"Redeeming the Time."

A life of hope deferred too often is
A life of wasted opportunities;
A life of perished hope too often is
A life of all-lost opportunities:
5 Yet hope is but the flower and not the root,
And hope is still the flower and not the fruit;—
Arise and sow and weed: a day shall come
When also thou shalt keep thy harvest home.

"Now they desire a Better Country."

Love said nay, while Hope kept saying
   All his sweetest say,
Hope so keen to start a-maying!—
   Love said nay.

5   Love was bent to watch and pray;
Long the watching, long the praying;
   Hope grew drowsy, pale and grey.

Hope in dreams set off a-straying,
   All his dream-world flushed by May;
10 While unslumbering, praying, weighing,
   Love said nay.

A CASTLE-BUILDER'S WORLD.
"The line of confusion, and the stones of emptiness."

Unripe harvest there hath none to reap it
   From the misty gusty place,
Unripe vineyard there hath none to keep it
   In unprofitable space.
5 Living men and women are not found there,
   Only masks in flocks and shoals;
Flesh-and-bloodless hazy masks surround there,
   Ever wavering orbs and poles;
Flesh-and-bloodless vapid masks abound there,
10   Shades of bodies without souls.

"These all wait upon Thee."

   Innocent eyes not ours
   Are made to look on flowers,
Eyes of small birds and insects small:
   Morn after summer morn
5   The sweet rose on her thorn
Opens her bosom to them all.
   The least and last of things
   That soar on quivering wings,
Or crawl among the grass blades out of sight,
10   Have just as clear a right
To their appointed portion of delight
   As Queens or Kings.

"Doeth well . . . doeth better."

My love whose heart is tender said to me,
  "A moon lacks light except her sun befriend her.
Let us keep tryst in heaven, dear Friend," said she,
  My love whose heart is tender.

5   From such a loftiness no words could bend her:
Yet still she spoke of "us" and spoke as "we,"
  Her hope substantial, while my hope grew slender.

Now keeps she tryst beyond earth's utmost sea,
  Wholly at rest, tho' storms should toss and rend her;
10   And still she keeps my heart and keeps its key,
  My love whose heart is tender.

Our heaven must be within ourselves,
  Our home and heaven the work of faith
All thro' this race of life which shelves
      Downward to death.

5   So faith shall build the boundary wall,
  And hope shall plant the secret bower,
That both may show magnifical
      With gem and flower.

While over all a dome must spread,
10   And love shall be that dome above;
And deep foundations must be laid,
      And these are love.

"Vanity of Vanities."

Of all the downfalls in the world,
  The flutter of an Autumn leaf
  Grows grievous by suggesting grief:
Who thought, when Spring was first unfurled,
5   Of this? The wide world lay empearled;
Who thought of frost that nips the world?
           Sigh on, my ditty.

There lurk a hundred subtle stings
　To prick us in our daily walk:
10　An apple cankered on its stalk,
A robin snared for all his wings,
A voice that sang but never sings;
Yea, sight or sound or silence stings.
　　　　　　Kind Lord, show pity.

The hills are tipped with sunshine, while I walk
　In shadows dim and cold:
The unawakened rose sleeps on her stalk
　In a bud's fold,
5　Until the sun flood all the world with gold.

The hills are crowned with glory, and the glow
　Flows widening down apace:
Unto the sunny hill-tops I, set low,
　Lift a tired face,—
10　Ah, happy rose, content to wait for grace!

How tired a face, how tired a brain, how tired
　A heart I lift, who long
For something never felt but still desired;
　Sunshine and song,
15　Song where the choirs of sunny heaven stand choired.

Scarce tolerable life, which all life long
　Is dominated by one dread of death;
　Is such life, life? if so, who pondereth
May call salt sweetness or call discord song.
5　Ah me, this solitude where swarms a throng!
　　Life slowly grows and dwindles breath by breath:
　　Death slowly grows on us; no word it saith,
Its cords all lengthened and its pillars strong.
Life dies apace, a life that but deceives:
10　　Death reigns as tho' it lived, and yet is dead:
Where is the life that dies not but that lives?
　　The sweet long life, immortal, ever young,

True life that wooes us with a silver tongue
Of hope, much said and much more left unsaid.

All heaven is blazing yet
   With the meridian sun:
Make haste, unshadowing sun, make haste to set;
   O lifeless life, have done.
5   I choose what once I chose;
   What once I willed, I will:
Only the heart its own bereavement knows;
   O clamorous heart, lie still.

That which I chose, I choose;
10   That which I willed, I will;
That which I once refused, I still refuse:
   O hope deferred, be still.
That which I chose and choose
   And will is Jesus' Will:
15   He hath not lost his life who seems to lose:
   O hope deferred, hope still.

"Balm in Gilead."

Heartsease I found, where Love-lies-bleeding
   Empurpled all the ground:
Whatever flowers I missed unheeding,
   Heartsease I found.

5   Yet still my garden mound
Stood sore in need of watering, weeding,
   And binding growths unbound.

Ah, when shades fell to light succeeding
   I scarcely dared look round:
10   "Love-lies-bleeding" was all my pleading,
   Heartsease I found.

"In the day of his Espousals."

That Song of Songs which is Solomon's
   Sinks and rises, and loves and longs,
Thro' temperate zones and torrid zones,
   That Song of Songs.

5   Fair its floating moon with her prongs:
Love is laid for its paving stones:
   Right it sings without thought of wrongs.

Doves it hath with music of moans,
   Queens in throngs and damsels in throngs,
10   High tones and mysterious undertones,
   That Song of Songs.

"She came from the uttermost part of the earth."

"The half was not told me," said Sheba's Queen,
   Weighing that wealth of wisdom and of gold:
"Thy fame falls short of this that I have seen:
   The half was not told.

5   "Happy thy servants who stand to behold,
Stand to drink in thy gracious speech and mien;
   Happy, thrice happy, the flock of thy fold.

"As the darkened moon while a shadow between
   Her face and her kindling sun is rolled,
10   I depart; but my heart keeps memory green:
   The half was not told."

Alleluia! or Alas! my heart is crying:
So yours is sighing;
Or replying with content undying,
    Alleluia!

5   Alas! grieves overmuch for pain that is ending,
Hurt that is mending,
Life descending soon to be ascending,
    Alleluia!

The Passion Flower hath sprung up tall,
  Hath east and west its arms outspread;
  The heliotrope shoots up its head
To clear the shadow of the wall:
5 Down looks the Passion Flower,
  The heliotrope looks upward still,
    Hour by hour
  On the heavenward hill.

The Passion Flower blooms red or white,
10 A shadowed white, a cloudless red;
  Caressingly it droops its head,
Its leaves, its tendrils, from the light:
Because that lowlier flower
  Looks up, but mounts not half so high,
15   Hour by hour
  Tending toward the sky.

God's Acre.

Hail, garden of confident hope!
  Where sweet seeds are quickening in darkness and cold;
    For how sweet and how young will they be
  When they pierce thro' the mould.
5 Balm, myrtle, and heliotrope
  There watch and there wait out of sight for their Sun:
    While the Sun, which they see not, doth see
  Each and all one by one.

"The Flowers appear on the Earth."

Young girls wear flowers,
  Young brides a flowery wreath,
But next we plant them
  In garden plots of death.
5 Whose lot is best:

The maiden's curtained rest,
　Or bride's whose hoped-for sweet
　May yet outstrip her feet?
Ah! what are such as these
10　To death's sufficing ease?
He sleeps indeed who sleeps in peace
　Where night and morning meet.

Dear are the blossoms
　For bride's or maiden's head,
15　But dearer planted
　Around our blessed dead.
Those mind us of decay
And joys that fade away,
　These preach to us perfection,
20　Long love and resurrection.
We make our graveyards fair,
For spirit-like birds of air,
For Angels may be finding there
　Lost Eden's own delection.

"Thou knewest . . . thou oughtest therefore."

Behold in heaven a floating dazzling cloud,
　So dazzling that I could but cry Alas!
　Alas, because I felt how low I was;
Alas, within my spirit if not aloud,
5　Foreviewing my last breathless bed and shroud:
　Thus pondering, I glanced downward on the grass;
　And the grass bowed when airs of heaven would pass,
Lifting itself again when it had bowed.
That grass spake comfort; weak it was and low,
10　Yet strong enough and high enough to bend
　In homage at a message from the sky:
　As the grass did and prospered, so will I;
Tho' knowing little, doing what I know,
　And strong in patient weakness till the end.

"Go in Peace."

Can peach renew lost bloom,
Or violet lost perfume,
Or sullied snow turn white as overnight?
Man cannot compass it, yet never fear:
5   The leper Naaman
Shows what God will and can;
God Who worked there is working here;
Wherefore let shame, not gloom, betinge thy brow,
God Who worked then is working now.

"Half dead."

O Christ the Life, look on me where I lie
    Ready to die:
O Good Samaritan, nay, pass not by.

O Christ, my Life, pour in Thine oil and wine
5   To keep me Thine;
Me ever Thine, and Thee for ever mine.

Watch by Thy saints and sinners, watch by all
    Thy great and small:
Once Thou didst call us all,—O Lord, recall.

10 Think how Thy saints love sinners, how they pray
    And hope alway,
And thereby grow more like Thee day by day.

O Saint of saints, if those with prayer and vow
    Succour us now. . . .
15 It was not they died for us, it was Thou.

"One of the Soldiers with a Spear pierced His Side."

Ah, Lord, we all have pierced Thee: wilt Thou be
    Wroth with us all to slay us all?
Nay, Lord, be this thing far from Thee and me:
    By whom should we arise, for we are small,
5   By whom if not by Thee?

Lord, if of us who pierced Thee Thou spare one,
    Spare yet one more to love Thy Face,
And yet another of poor souls undone,
    Another, and another—God of grace,
10   Let mercy overrun.

Where love is, there comes sorrow
Today or else tomorrow:
    Endure the mood,
    Love only means our good.

5   Where love is, there comes pleasure
With or withouten measure,
    Early or late
    Cheering the sorriest state.

Where love is, all perfection
10   Is stored for heart's delection;
    For where love is
    Dwells every sort of bliss.

Who would not choose a sorrow
Love's self will cheer tomorrow?
15   One day of sorrow,
    Then such a long tomorrow!

Bury Hope out of sight,
    No book for it and no bell;
It never could bear the light
    Even while growing and well:
5   Think if now it could bear

The light on its face of care
And grey scattered hair.

No grave for Hope in the earth,
  But deep in that silent soul
10 Which rang no bell for its birth
  And rings no funeral toll.
Cover its once bright head;
Nor odours nor tears be shed:
It lived once, it is dead.

15 Brief was the day of its power,
  The day of its grace how brief:
As the fading of a flower,
  As the falling of a leaf,
So brief its day and its hour;
20 No bud more and no bower
Or hint of a flower.

Shall many wail it? not so:
  Shall one bewail it? not one:
Thus it hath been from long ago,
25   Thus it shall be beneath the sun.
O fleet sun, make haste to flee;
O rivers, fill up the sea;
O Death, set the dying free.

The sun nor loiters nor speeds,
30   The rivers run as they ran,
Thro' clouds or thro' windy reeds
  All run as when all began.
Only Death turns at our cries:—
Lo, the Hope we buried with sighs
35 Alive in Death's eyes!

A Churchyard Song of Patient Hope.

All tears done away with the bitter unquiet sea,
  Death done away from among the living at last,
Man shall say of sorrow—Love grant it to thee and me!—
  At last, "It is past."

324 The Complete Poems of Christina Rossetti

5   Shall I say of pain, "It is past," nor say it with thee,
           Thou heart of my heart, thou soul of my soul, my Friend?
       Shalt thou say of pain, "It is past," nor say it with me
           Beloved to the end?

       One woe is past. Come what come will
           Thus much is ended and made fast:
       Two woes may overhang us still;
           One woe is past.

5   As flowers when winter puffs its last
       Wake in the vale, trail up the hill,
           Nor wait for skies to overcast;

       So meek souls rally from the chill
           Of pain and fear and poisonous blast,
10   To lift their heads: come good, come ill,
           One woe is past.

"Take no thought for the morrow."

       Who knows? God knows: and what He knows
           Is well and best.
       The darkness hideth not from Him, but glows
       Clear as the morning or the evening rose
5   Of east or west.

       Wherefore man's strength is to sit still:
           Not wasting care
       To antedate tomorrow's good or ill;
       Yet watching meekly, watching with good will,
10   Watching to prayer.

       Some rising or some setting ray
           From east or west,
       If not today, why then another day
       Will light each dove upon the homeward way
15   Safe to her nest.

"Consider the Lilies of the field."

Solomon most glorious in array
    Put not on his glories without care:—
Clothe us as Thy lilies of a day,
    As the lilies Thou accountest fair,
5   Lilies of Thy making,
        Of Thy love partaking,
    Filling with free fragrance earth and air:
Thou Who gatherest lilies, gather us and wear.

"Son, remember."

I laid beside thy gate, am Lazarus;
    See me or see me not I still am there,
    Hungry and thirsty, sore and sick and bare,
Dog-comforted and crumbs-solicitous:
5 While thou in all thy ways art sumptuous,
    Daintily clothed, with dainties for thy fare:
    Thus a world's wonder thou art quit of care,
And be I seen or not seen I am thus.
One day a worm for thee, a worm for me:
10   With my worm angel songs and trumpet burst
    And plenitude an end of all desire:
But what for thee, alas! but what for thee?
    Fire and an unextinguishable thirst,
    Thirst in an unextinguishable fire.

"Heaviness may endure for a night, but Joy cometh in the morning."

No thing is great on this side of the grave,
    Nor any thing of any stable worth:
    Whatso is born from earth returns to earth:
No thing we grasp proves half the thing we crave:

5   The tidal wave shrinks to the ebbing wave:
         Laughter is folly, madness lurks in mirth:
         Mankind sets off a-dying from the birth:
     Life is a losing game, with what to save?
     Thus I sat mourning like a mournful owl,
10   And like a doleful dragon made ado,
             Companion of all monsters of the dark:
     When lo! the light cast off its nightly cowl,
         And up to heaven flashed a carolling lark,
         And all creation sang its hymn anew.

15   While all creation sang its hymn anew
         What could I do but sing a stave in tune?
         Spectral on high hung pale the vanishing moon
     Where a last gleam of stars hung paling too.
     Lark's lay—a cockcrow—with a scattered few
20   Soft early chirpings—with a tender croon
         Of doves—a hundred thousand calls, and soon
     A hundred thousand answers sweet and true.
     These set me singing too at unawares:
         One note for all delights and charities,
25   One note for hope reviving with the light,
         One note for every lovely thing that is;
     Till while I sang my heart shook off its cares
             And revelled in the land of no more night.

"The Will of the Lord be done."

     O Lord, fulfil Thy Will
     Be the days few or many, good or ill:
     Prolong them, to suffice
     For offering up ourselves Thy sacrifice;
5   Shorten them if Thou wilt,
         To make in righteousness an end of guilt.
     Yea, they will not be long
     To souls who learn to sing a patient song;
     Yea, short they will not be

10　To souls on tiptoe to flee home to Thee.
　　O Lord, fulfil Thy Will:
　　Make Thy Will ours, and keep us patient still
　　Be the days few or many, good or ill.

"Lay up for yourselves treasures in Heaven."

　　Treasure plies a feather,
　　　　Pleasure spreadeth wings,
　　Taking flight together,—
　　　　Ah! my cherished things.
5　Fly away, poor pleasure,
　　　　That art so brief a thing:
　　Fly away, poor treasure,
　　　　That hast so swift a wing.

　　Pleasure, to be pleasure,
10　　　Must come without a wing:
　　Treasure, to be treasure,
　　　　Must be a stable thing.

　　Treasure without feather,
　　　　Pleasure without wings,
15　Elsewhere dwell together
　　　　And are heavenly things.

"Whom the Lord loveth He chasteneth."

　　"One sorrow more? I thought the tale complete."—
　　　　He bore amiss who grudges what he bore:
　　Stretch out thy hands and urge thy feet to meet
　　　　One sorrow more.
5　　Yea, make thy count for two or three or four:
　　The kind Physician will not slack to treat
　　　　His patient while there's rankling in the sore.

Bear up in anguish, ease will yet be sweet;
  Bear up all day, for night has rest in store:
10 Christ bears thy burden with thee, rise and greet
  One sorrow more.

"Then shall ye shout."

It seems an easy thing
Mayhap one day to sing
Yet the next day
We cannot sing or say.

5 Keep silence with good heart,
While silence fits our part:
Another day
We shall both sing and say.

Keep silence, counting time
10 To strike in at the chime:
Prepare to sound,—
Our part is coming round.

Can we not sing or say?
In silence let us pray,
15 And meditate
Our love-song while we wait.

Everything that is born must die;
  Everything that can sigh may sing;
Rocks in equal balance, low or high,
  Everything.

5   Honeycomb is weighed against a sting;
Hope and fear take turns to touch the sky;
  Height and depth respond alternating.

O my soul, spread wings of love to fly,
  Wings of dove that soars on home-bound wing:
10 Love trusts Love, till Love shall justify
  Everything.

Lord, grant us calm, if calm can set forth Thee;
  Or tempest, if a tempest set Thee forth;
  Wind from the east or west or south or north,
Or congelation of a silent sea,
5 With stillness of each tremulous aspen tree.

Still let fruit fall, or hang upon the tree;
  Still let the east and west, the south and north,
Curb in their winds, or plough a thundering sea;
  Still let the earth abide to set Thee forth,
10 Or vanish like a smoke to set forth Thee.

Changing Chimes.

It was not warning that our fathers lacked,
  It is not warning that we lack today.
The Voice that cried still cries: "Rise up and act:
  Watch alway,—watch and pray,—watch alway,—
        All men."

Alas, if aught was lacked goodwill was lacked;
  Alas, goodwill is what we lack today.
O gracious Voice, grant grace that all may act,
  Watch and act,—watch and pray,—watch alway.—
10   Amen.

"Thy Servant will go and fight with this Philistine."

Sorrow of saints is sorrow of a day,
  Gladness of saints is gladness evermore:
  Send on thy hope, send on thy will before
To chant God's praise along the narrow way.
5 Stir up His praises if the flesh would sway,
  Exalt His praises if the world press sore,
  Peal out His praises if black Satan roar
A hundred thousand lies to say them nay.

Devil and Death and Hades, threefold cord
10   Not quickly broken, front thee to thy face;
            Front thou them with a face of tenfold flint:
            Shout for the battle, David! never stint
        Body or breath or blood, but proof in grace
        Die for thy Lord, as once for thee thy Lord.

Thro' burden and heat of the day
    How weary the hands and the feet
That labour with scarcely a stay,
    Thro' burden and heat!

5   Tired toiler whose sleep shall be sweet,
    Kneel down, it will rest thee to pray:
        Then forward, for daylight is fleet.

Cool shadows show lengthening and grey,
    Cool twilight will soon be complete:
10 What matters this wearisome way
        Thro' burden and heat?

"Then I commended Mirth."

"A merry heart is a continual feast."
    Then take we life and all things in good part:
To fast grows festive while we keep at least
    A merry heart

5   Well pleased with nature and well pleased with art;
    A merry heart makes cheer for man and beast,
        And fancies music in a creaking cart.

Some day, a restful heart whose toils have ceased,
    A heavenly heart gone home from earthly mart:
10 Today, blow wind from west or wind from east,
        A merry heart.

Sorrow hath a double voice,
    Sharp today but sweet tomorrow:
Wait in patience, hope, rejoice,
    Tried friends of sorrow.

5   Pleasure hath a double taste,
    Sweet today but sharp tomorrow:
Friends of pleasure, rise in haste,
    Make friends with sorrow.

Pleasure set aside today
10   Comes again to rule tomorrow:
Welcomed sorrow will not stay,
    Farewell to sorrow!

Shadows today, while shadows show God's Will.
    Light were not good except He sent us light.
    Shadows today, because this day is night
Whose marvels and whose mysteries fulfil
5   Their course and deep in darkness serve Him still.
    Thou dim aurora, on the extremest height
    Of airy summits wax not over-bright;
Refrain thy rose, refrain thy daffodil.
Until God's Word go forth to kindle thee
10   And garland thee and bid thee stoop to us,
    Blush in the heavenly choirs and glance not down:
    Today we race in darkness for a crown,
In darkness for beatitude to be,
    In darkness for the city luminous.

"Truly the Light is sweet."

Light colourless doth colour all things else:
Where light dwells pleasure dwells
And peace excels.
    Then rise and shine,
5   Thou shadowed soul of mine,
    And let a cheerful rainbow make thee fine.

Light, fountain of all beauty and delight,
Leads day forth from the night,
Turns blackness white.
10   Light waits for thee
Where all have eyes to see:
Oh, well is thee, and happy shalt thou be!

"Are ye not much better than they?"

The twig sprouteth,
The moth outeth,
The plant springeth,
The bird singeth:
5   Tho' little we sing today
Yet are we better than they;
Tho' growing with scarce a showing,
Yet, please God, we are growing.

The twig teacheth,
10   The moth preacheth,
The plant vaunteth,
The bird chanteth,
God's mercy overflowing
Merciful past man's knowing.
15   Please God to keep us growing
Till the awful day of mowing.

"Yea, the sparrow hath found her an house."

Wisest of sparrows that sparrow which sitteth alone
     Perched on the housetop, its own upper chamber, for
          nest;
Wisest of swallows that swallow which timely has flown
     Over the turbulent sea to the land of its rest:
5   Wisest of sparrows and swallows, if I were as wise!

Wisest of spirits that spirit which dwelleth apart
    Hid in the Presence of God for a chapel and nest,
Sending a wish and a will and a passionate heart
    Over the eddy of life to that Presence in rest:
10   Seated alone and in peace till God bids it arise.

"I am small and of no reputation."

The least, if so I am;
    If so, less than the least,
May I reach heaven to glorify the Lamb
    And sit down at the Feast.

5   I fear and I am small,
      Whence am I of good cheer;
For I who hear Thy call, have heard Thee call
    To Thee the small who fear.

O Christ my God Who seest the unseen,
    O Christ my God Who knowest the unknown,
    Thy mighty Blood was poured forth to atone
For every sin that can be or hath been.

5   O Thou Who seest what I cannot see,
      Thou Who didst love us all so long ago,
      O Thou Who knowest what I must not know,
Remember all my hope, remember me.

Yea, if Thou wilt, Thou canst put up Thy sword;
    But what if Thou shouldst sheathe it to the hilt
Within the heart that sues to Thee, O Lord?
    Yea, if Thou wilt.

5   For if Thou wilt Thou canst purge out the guilt
Of all, of any, even the most abhorred:
    Thou canst pluck down, rebuild, build up the unbuilt.

Who wanders, canst Thou gather by love's cord?
    Who sinks, uplift from the under-sucking silt

10   To set him on Thy rock within Thy ward?
       Yea, if Thou wilt.

      Sweetness of rest when Thou sheddest rest,
        Sweetness of patience till then;
      Only the Will of our God is best
        For all the millions of men.

5   For all the millions on earth today,
        On earth and under the earth;
      Waiting for earth to vanish away,
        Waiting to come to the birth.

      O foolish Soul! to make thy count
        For languid falls and much forgiven,
      When like a flame thou mightest mount
        To storm and carry heaven.

5   A life so faint,—is this to live?
        A goal so mean,—is this a goal?
      Christ love thee, remedy, forgive,
        Save thee, O foolish Soul.

      Before the beginning Thou hast foreknown the end,
        Before the birthday the death-bed was seen of Thee:
      Cleanse what I cannot cleanse, mend what I cannot mend,
        O Lord All-Merciful, be merciful to me.

5   While the end is drawing near I know not mine end;
        Birth I recall not, my death I cannot foresee:
      O God, arise to defend, arise to befriend,
        O Lord All-Merciful, be merciful to me.

      The goal in sight! Look up and sing,
        Set faces full against the light,
      Welcome with rapturous welcoming
        The goal in sight.

5   Let be the left, let be the right:
         Straight forward make your footsteps ring
            A loud alarum thro' the night.

       Death hunts you, yea, but reft of sting;
         Your bed is green, your shroud is white:
10   Hail! Life and Death and all that bring
            The goal in sight.

       Looking back along life's trodden way
         Gleams and greenness linger on the track;
       Distance melts and mellows all today,
            Looking back.

5   Rose and purple and a silvery grey,
         Is that cloud the cloud we called so black?
       Evening harmonizes all today,
            Looking back.

       Foolish feet so prone to halt or stray,
10   Foolish heart so restive on the rack!
       Yesterday we sighed, but not today
            Looking back.

Introduction to Textual Notes

The variant readings given in the textual notes are taken from three sources: the extant manuscripts of Christina's poems, the private printing or publication of individual poems before they were incorporated into her published collections, and all of the English and American editions of her poems through William Michael Rossetti's *The Poetical Works of Christina Georgina Rossetti* (1904). I have not recorded the textual variants from publications of individual poems after they were included in one of her collections, because these texts were usually copied directly from the texts in the published collections.

William Michael Rossetti's 1896 and 1904 editions are to some extent unreliable. Many of his spelling, paragraphing, and punctuation variants are not in Christina's extant manuscripts or in editions published during her lifetime; moreover, he rarely explains the sources of his texts. Nevertheless, I have included his readings in the textual notes because, as her brother, he had access to materials no longer available.

The American texts likewise contain some nonauthorial editing of spelling and punctuation, but they also reflect many of the changes Christina made in the collections after they were published. In one case she added new poems to the Roberts Brothers edition before adding them to the Macmillan edition.[1] Her evident interest in the American texts warrants their inclusion in the variant notes.

At the beginning of the textual notes for each poem is a headnote listing the manuscripts and editions in which the poem occurs

---

1. *Poems* (2 vols.; Boston: Roberts Brothers, 1888), II, contains seventeen new poems not seen earlier in Christina's collections; the new poems are at the end of the section entitled "A Pageant and Other Poems." Two years later they were added to the English edition of *Poems* (London: Macmillan, 1890) in the section entitled "The Second Series."

and any separate publications of the poem before it became part of the collection. The basic text (or copy-text), taken from the first English edition that includes the poem, appears in italics. Reprints are not listed in the headnotes or cited in the variant notes unless they show a new variant. Editions and reprints are identified by date of publication rather than by title; the titles are given in the listing of editions and reprints herein. An *a* after the date of publication indicates an American edition, and parentheses enclose the dates of reprints. The variants designated 1896s (s = special edition) are recorded only if they differ from the first edition published in that year.

In the textual notes, Am. eds. refers to all the American editions in which the poem appears. Matter in roman type within square brackets [thus] is supplied by the editor. Italic print within square brackets [*thus*] indicates words or letters deleted, erased, or written over in the manuscripts. Angle brackets <thus> enclose words or letters written in the manuscripts as additions or as replacements for deletions and erasures. Words added in the manuscripts and then deleted are in italic print enclosed in angle brackets and square brackets [<*thus*>]. A solidus represents a line break. The abbreviation for *manuscript* is MS.

A variant within the line is preceded by a pickup word and is followed by a drop word and any punctuation immediately after the drop word.[2] A capitalized variant with no pickup word indicates the beginning of a line.[3] A variant at the end of the line is accompanied by a pickup word and the end-of-line punctuation.[4] If the variation is in the end line punctuation itself, a pickup word precedes it.[5] When a capitalized pickup word occurs within the line, it is accompanied by the preceding word.[6] When a pickup word appears more than once in the line, it is accompanied by the preceding word.[7] If a text contains several variants within the same line, they are presented together in one reading; where the variants are

2. For example, see the manuscript variant for line 2 of "Why did baby die."
3. For example, see the manuscript variant for line 7 of "January cold desolate."
4. For example, see the manuscript variant for line 4 of "Eight o'clock."
5. For example, see the manuscript variant for line 2 of "Love me,—I love you."
6. For example, see the manuscript variant for line 3 of "If I were a Queen."
7. For example, see the manuscript variant for line 3 of "What is pink? a rose is pink."

separated by more than two words in the line, empty angle brackets represent the word or words omitted between the variants.[8]

All of the manuscripts and manuscript revisions cited are in ink and in Christina's handwriting unless otherwise indicated. Christina's later pencil changes, her brothers' markings in her manuscripts, and the manuscripts not in her own hand are noted as such.

The following kinds of variants are not registered because they do not seem to perceptibly affect the sound or sense of the poem. I have not recorded the false starts and obvious slips of the pen, which were immediately corrected in the manuscripts. In some of her manuscripts Christina preceded every line of a quotation with quotation marks, but I have followed the practice in her later manuscripts and in all her editions of inserting only the opening and closing sets of quotation marks. In the manuscript titles only the first letter of a word is capitalized, but in the printed titles and in this edition all of the letters are capitals.[9] Titles are centered in Christina's manuscripts and editions, but they are aligned at the left margin in this edition. I have eliminated the house practices (noted earlier) imposed upon Christina's paragraphing, namely, of setting the first word of the poem in capital letters and indenting the first line of each new paragraph in the longer narrative poems. Sometimes Christina used an ampersand in her manuscripts, but I have followed the practice in all her editions of using the spelling *and*. In Christina's editions, quotation marks are not always counted in the paragraphing, but in this edition they are. In cases where the printed spelling consistently differs from that in the manuscripts, I have emended the text to the manuscript spelling; thus I have changed the house spellings *though, through, to-day, to-night*, and *to-morrow* to the manuscript spellings *tho', thro', today, tonight*, and *tomorrow* and ignored such American spellings as *neighbor*. The American texts leave a space before the apostrophe in contractions and sometimes place the punctuation outside the quotation marks, but I have followed the practice in the manuscripts and English edi-

---

8. For example, see the manuscript variant for line 1 of "My baby has a father and a mother."

9. In *Verses* (1893) the titles and opening quotations are in Gothic print; and in a number of cases, usually where the title itself consists of a quotation, only the first letter of a word is capitalized. I have followed the *Verses* capitalization.

tions of eliminating the space before the apostrophe and placing the punctuation inside the quotation marks. Christina's editions leave a double space after the colon, but this edition does not. The 1896 and 1904 editions omit the period after the title, but I have retained it because it is in the manuscripts and all her editions. The 1904 edition uses single rather than double quotation marks, but since almost all the manuscripts and all her editions use double quotation marks, I have followed her usual practice. I have not recorded the occurrence of partially printed or missing end-of-line punctuation due to faulty inking, which I found in collating copies of the editions and reprints.[10] All variants in words, paragraphing, spelling, and punctuation other than the kinds described above are recorded in the textual notes.

SING-SONG

[Date of composition unknown. Editions: *1872*, 1872a, 1893, 1904. The notebook MS is in the British Library.]

Title. MS: Sing Song: a < > Book
  1872, 1872a: Sing-Song. / A < >
  Book.
Dedication. MS: Rhymes / dedicated /

without permission / to the / Baby /
who / suggested them.
1872, 1872a: THEM.

ANGELS AT THE FOOT

[Date of composition unknown. Editions: *1872*, 1872a, 1893, 1904. The notebook MS is in the British Library.]

1. MS: 1. / Angels

LOVE ME,—I LOVE YOU

[Date of composition unknown. Editions: *1872*, 1872a, 1893, 1904. The notebook MS is in the British Library.]

1. MS: 2. / Love me, I
2. MS: baby,
6. MS: you,
    1872, 1872a: you

8. MS: me, I

10. For exact copies, see the listing of editions and reprints herein.

MY BABY HAS A FATHER AND A MOTHER

[Date of composition unknown. Editions: *1872*, 1872a, 1893, 1904. The notebook MS is in the British Library. In the MS, lines 2, 4, and 5 are indented two spaces.]

1. MS: 3. / My < > father
   [, *has*] and
2. MS: baby!—

4. MS: be
5. MS: baby.

OUR LITTLE BABY FELL ASLEEP

[Date of composition unknown. Editions: *1872*, 1872a, 1893, 1904. The notebook MS is in the British Library.]

1. MS: 4 / Our
2. MS: And [*will*] <may> not
3. MS: For days and days and weeks
   and weeks:

5. MS: look

"KOOKOOROOKOO! KOOKOOROOKOO!"

[Date of composition unknown. Editions: *1872*, 1872a, 1893, 1904. The notebook MS is in the British Library.]

1. MS: 5 / "Kookoorookoo,
   kookoorookoo"
2. MS: morn,
3. MS: "Kikirikee, kikirikee,"
4. MS: born,

5. MS: "Kookoorookoo,
   kookoorookoo,"
6. MS: singing,
7. MS: "Kikirikee, kikirikee,"
8. 1872a: springing

BABY CRY

[Date of composition unknown. Editions: *1872*, 1872a, 1893, 1904. The notebook MS is in the British Library.]

1. MS: 6. / Baby

EIGHT O'CLOCK

[Date of composition unknown. Editions: *1872*, 1872a, 1893, 1904. The notebook MS is in the British Library. In the MS, lines 2 and 5 are indented one space, lines 3 and 6 are indented two spaces, and lines 1 and 4 are not indented.]

1. MS: 7. / Eight o'clock—

4. MS: for [*Sue*,] Lou,

BREAD AND MILK FOR BREAKFAST

[Date of composition unknown. Editions: *1872*, 1872a, 1893, 1904. The notebook MS is in the British Library.]

1. MS: 8. / Bread <> breakfast   2. MS: wear

THERE'S SNOW ON THE FIELDS

[Date of composition unknown. Editions: *1872*, 1872a, 1893, 1904. The notebook MS is in the British Library.]

1. MS: 9. / There's <> fields,   5. MS: warm

DEAD IN THE COLD, A SONG-SINGING THRUSH

[Date of composition unknown. Editions: *1872*, 1872a, 1893, 1904. The notebook MS is in the British Library. In the MS, lines 3, 4, and 5 are indented one space.]

1. MS: 10. / Dead <> a song
    singing thrush,

I DUG AND DUG AMONGST THE SNOW

[Date of composition unknown. Editions: *1872*, 1872a, 1893, 1904. The notebook MS is in the British Library.]

1. MS: 11. / I <> snow   6. MS: snow:
3. MS: sand   7. MS: from every-land

A CITY PLUM IS NOT A PLUM

[Date of composition unknown. Editions: *1872*, 1872a, 1893, 1904. The notebook MS (MS1) is in the British Library. The copy of *Sing-Song* owned by Mrs. Geoffrey Dennis (MS2) contains Christina's holograph revision of line 3.]

1. MS1: 12. / A <> not a plum,   MS2: A [*statesman's*] <party> rat
2. MS1: A dumb bell is <> bell   1872, 1872a: A statesman's rat
    though dumb,   4. MS1: not a cat,
3. MS1: A statesman's rat <> not   5. MS1: not a frog,
    a rat,

YOUR BROTHER HAS A FALCON

[Date of composition unknown. Editions: *1872*, 1872a, 1893, 1904. The notebook MS is in the British Library.]

1. MS: 13. / Your   3. MS: mannikin
2. MS: flower,   5. MS: I'll [*perch*] <nurse> you

HEAR WHAT THE MOURNFUL LINNETS SAY

[Date of composition unknown. Editions: *1872*, 1872a, 1893, 1904. The notebook MS (MS1) and the MS in the handwriting of Christina's sister, Maria Francesca Rossetti, (MS2) are both in the British Library.]

1. MS1: 14. / Hear <> mournful
    sparrows say:
    MS2: 14 / Hear
2. MS1, MS2: We

5. MS1, MS2: They
6. MS1, MS2: wing
8. MS1, MS2: sing.

A BABY'S CRADLE WITH NO BABY IN IT

[Date of composition unknown. Editions: *1872*, 1872a, 1893, 1904. The notebook MS is in the British Library. In the MS, line 4 is indented four spaces.]

1. MS: 15. / A
3. MS: home [*from*] [<*to*>] <to>
    Paradise,

HOP-O'-MY-THUMB AND LITTLE JACK HORNER

[Date of composition unknown. Editions: *1872*, 1872a, 1893, 1904. The notebook MS is in the British Library.]

1. MS: 16 / Hopo'mythumb and
    Little Jack Horner
4. MS: [*He'd be ashamed of barking*

and biting.] <I never caught him
growling and biting.>

HOPE IS LIKE A HAREBELL TREMBLING FROM ITS BIRTH

[Date of composition unknown. Editions: *1872*, 1872a, 1893, 1904. The notebook MS is in the British Library.]

1. MS: 17. / Hope
6. MS: all [illegible erasure] <its>
    thorns

O WIND, WHY DO YOU NEVER REST

[Date of composition unknown. Editions: *1872*, 1872a, 1893, 1904. The notebook MS is in the British Library.]

1. MS: 18. / O wind why <> rest

2. MS: Wandering whistling

CRYING, MY LITTLE ONE, FOOTSORE AND WEARY?

[Date of composition unknown. Editions: *1872*, 1872a, 1893, 1904. The notebook MS is in the British Library.]

1. MS: 19. / Crying,

GROWING IN THE VALE

[Date of composition unknown. Editions: *1872*, 1872a, 1893, 1904. The notebook MS is in the British Library.]

   1. MS: 20 / Growing   5. MS: crown

A LINNET IN A GILDED CAGE

[Date of composition unknown. Editions: *1872*, 1872a, 1893, 1904. The notebook MS is in the British Library.]

   1. MS: 21. / A   6. 1904: bough,—
   5. MS: leaf   7. MS: bird

WRENS AND ROBINS IN THE HEDGE

[Date of composition unknown. Editions: *1872*, 1872a, 1893, 1904. The notebook MS is in the British Library.]

   1. MS: 22 / Wrens   4. MS: Everywhere.
   2. MS: there,

MY BABY HAS A MOTTLED FIST

[Date of composition unknown. Editions: *1872*, 1872a, 1893, 1904. The notebook MS is in the British Library.]

   1. MS: 23. / My   3. MS: is kiss'd
   2. MS: creases,

WHY DID BABY DIE

[Date of composition unknown. Editions: *1872*, 1872a, 1893, 1904. The notebook MS is in the British Library.]

   1. MS: 24. / Why <> die   4. MS: Flowers that <> die
   2. MS: Making [ʃ]<F>ather sigh,   6. MS: Of "why["?]<?">

IF ALL WERE RAIN AND NEVER SUN

[Date of composition unknown. Editions: *1872*, 1872a, 1893, 1904. The notebook MS is in the British Library.]

   1. MS: 25. / If

O WIND, WHERE HAVE YOU BEEN

[Date of composition unknown. Editions: *1872*, 1872a, 1893, 1904. The notebook MS is in the British Library.]

1. MS: 26 / O wind where < > been
2. MS: you [*smell*] <blow> so sweet?—
6. MS: For [*s*]<S>ummer and < > heat,

1872a: heat,
1904: heat;

ON THE GRASSY BANKS

[Date of composition unknown. Editions: *1872*, 1872a, 1893, 1904. The notebook MS is in the British Library.]

1. MS: 27 / On
2. MS: pranks:
3. MS, 1872a: brothers,
4. MS, 1872a: feet;

RUSHES IN A WATERY PLACE

[Date of composition unknown. Editions: *1872*, 1872a, 1893, 1904. The notebook MS is in the British Library.]

1. MS: 28 / Rushes
2. MS: hollow,
3. MS: A [*singing*] <soaring> skylark
4. MS: swallow,
5. MS: to [*blow*] <hang>

MINNIE AND MATTIE

[Date of composition unknown. Editions: *1872*, 1872a, 1893, 1904. The notebook MS is in the British Library.]

1. MS: 29. / Minnie
2. MS: little May
3. MS: country
5. MS: day
6. MS: glowing
7. MS: leaf
13. MS: Cluck, cluck, the
    1872: Cluck! cluck? the
14. MS: folk,
15. 1904: soft,
17. MS: Cluck, cluck, the
22. MS: posies
23. MS: violets
25. MS: enough
31. MS: O Minnie, Mattie

HEARTSEASE IN MY GARDEN BED

[Date of composition unknown. Editions: *1872*, 1872a, 1893, 1904. The notebook MS is in the British Library. In the MS, lines 3, 5, and 7 are indented two spaces; lines 1, 2, 4, and 6 are not indented.]

1. MS: 30. / Heartsease
2. MS: With sweet-William white
5. 1904: call;
6. MS: part
7. 1872a: fall

IF I WERE A QUEEN

[Date of composition unknown. Editions: *1872*, 1872a, 1893, 1904. The notebook MS is in the British Library.]

1. MS: 31. / If < > a Queen
    1904: 'If
3. MS: you King
4. MS: you.—
    1872a: you
    1904: you.'

5. MS: a King
    1904: 'If
7. MS: you Queen
8. 1904: you.'

WHAT ARE HEAVY? SEA-SAND AND SORROW

[Date of composition unknown. Editions: *1872*, 1872a, 1893, 1904. The notebook MS is in the British Library.]

1. MS: 32 / What < > heavy? sea sand and
3. MS: [*What are deep? the ocean and*

truth:] What are frail? spring blossoms and youth:

THERE IS BUT ONE MAY IN THE YEAR

[Date of composition unknown. Editions: *1872*, 1872a, 1893, 1904. The notebook MS is in the British Library. In the MS, lines 4 and 8 are indented four spaces.]

1. MS: 33 / There

5. MS: chilliest May

THE SUMMER NIGHTS ARE SHORT

[Date of composition unknown. Editions: *1872*, 1872a, 1893, 1904. The notebook MS is in the British Library. In the MS, lines 4 and 8 are indented four spaces.]

1. MS: 34 / The

THE DAYS ARE CLEAR

[Date of composition unknown. Editions: *1872*, 1872a, 1893, 1904. The notebook MS is in the British Library. In the MS, no lines are indented.]

1. MS: 35 / The
3. MS: here

7. MS: —Stay, < > stay—

TWIST ME A CROWN OF WIND-FLOWERS

[Date of composition unknown. Editions: *1872*, 1872a, 1893, 1904. The notebook MS is in the British Library.]

1. MS: 36 / Twist <> of
    windflowers;
    1904: 'Twist
4. MS: [*F*]<A>nd players <>
    play.—
    1872a: play
    1904: play.'
5. MS: of windflowers;
    1904: 'Put

6. MS: go?—
    1904: go?'
7. 1904: 'Beyond
8. MS: blow.—
    1904: blow.'
9. MS: Alas, your <> of
    windflowers
    1904: 'Alas!
12. 1904: die.'

BROWN AND FURRY

[Date of composition unknown. Editions: *1872*, 1872a, 1893, 1904. The notebook MS is in the British Library. In the MS, lines 1, 3, 5, 7, and 9 are indented two spaces.]

1. MS: 37 / Brown
2. 1904: hurry

8. MS: Hovering bird[*s*] of

A TOADSTOOL COMES UP IN A NIGHT

[Date of composition unknown. Editions: *1872*, 1872a, 1893, 1904. The notebook MS is in the British Library. In the MS, line 4 is indented four spaces.]

1. MS: 38 / A

A POCKET HANDKERCHIEF TO HEM

[Date of composition unknown. Editions: *1872*, 1872a, 1893, 1904. The notebook MS is in the British Library.]

1. MS: 39 / A pockethandkerchief
    to
4. MS: done I

5. MS: Yet [*take*] <set> a <> then a
    stitch.

IF A PIG WORE A WIG

[Date of composition unknown. Editions: *1872*, 1872a, 1893, 1904. The notebook MS is in the British Library.]

1. MS: 40 / If
2. MS: say?—
3. MS: gentleman

4. MS: day".
    1904: say 'Good-day.'
5. MS: fail

SELDOM "CAN'T"

[Date of composition unknown. Editions: *1872*, 1872a, 1893, 1904. The notebook MS is in the British Library. In the first three lines of the MS, the end-of-line punctuation is directly under the quotation marks.]

1. MS: 41. / Seldom
2. 1893, 1904: "don't";

4. MS: "won't".

1 AND 1 ARE 2

[Date of composition unknown. Editions: *1872*, 1872a, 1893, 1904. The notebook MS is in the British Library.]

1. MS: 42 / 1
6. MS: Barleysugar sticks.
8. 1872a: gate
10. 1893: men

16. MS: the Doctor's mixing.
20. MS: Roses—[*what a*] <pleasant> plenty!

HOW MANY SECONDS IN A MINUTE?

[Date of composition unknown. Editions: *1872*, 1872a, 1893, 1904. The notebook MS is in the British Library.]

1. MS: 43 / How
2. MS: 60 and
4. MS: 60 for
6. MS: 24 for

8. MS: 7 both
10. MS: 4 as
12. MS: 12 the
14. MS: 100 says

WHAT WILL YOU GIVE ME FOR MY POUND?

[Date of composition unknown. Editions: *1872*, 1872a, 1893, 1904. The notebook MS is in the British Library. In the MS, lines 2, 4, and 6 are indented two spaces.]

1. MS: 44. / What

JANUARY COLD DESOLATE

[Date of composition unknown. Editions: *1872*, 1872a, 1893, 1904. The notebook MS is in the British Library. In the MS, no lines are indented.]

1. MS: 45 / January
7. MS, 1872, 1872a: Till sunny
10. MS: The

storm-[*winds*]<clouds> fly
11. 1893, 1904: Lightning-torn;

WHAT IS PINK? A ROSE IS PINK

[Date of composition unknown. Editions: *1872*, 1872a, 1893, 1904. The notebook MS is in the British Library. In the MS, lines 2, 4, 6, 8, 10, 12, 14, and 16 are indented two spaces.]

1. MS: 46 / What is pink? A rose
3. MS: is red? A poppy's
5. MS: What is blue? The sky
6. MS: [illegible deletion] [<*Which th*>] Where the clouds [*sail*] <float> thro'.
7. MS: What is white? A swan
9. MS: is yellow? Pears are
11. MS: What is green? [*t*]<T>he grass <> green
13. MS: is violet? Clouds are
14. 1872, 1872a: twilight
15. MS: is orange? Why, an 1872a: an orange

MOTHER SHAKE THE CHERRY-TREE

[Date of composition unknown. Editions: *1872*, 1872a, 1893, 1904. The notebook MS is in the British Library.]

1. MS: 47. / Mother <> the cherrytree,
2. MS: [*Baby*] <Susan> catch
7. MS: father hot <> tired

A PIN HAS A HEAD, BUT HAS NO HAIR

[Date of composition unknown. Editions: *1872*, 1872a, 1893, 1904. The notebook MS is in the British Library.]

1. MS: 48 / A
6. MS: A cornfield dimples
8. MS: A wineglass a
13. MS: lock;—

HOPPING FROG, HOP HERE AND BE SEEN

[Date of composition unknown. Editions: *1872*, 1872a, 1893, 1904. The notebook MS is in the British Library.]

1. MS: 49 / Hopping frog hop
4. MS: Goodbye, we'll
   1904: Good-bye, we'll
5. MS: toad plod
7. MS: [*But though you're lumpish you're harmless too*;] <But though you're lumpish you're harmless too;>
8. MS: [*You won't h*[a]<u>*rt me, and I won't hurt you.*] <You won't h[a]<u>rt me, and I won't hurt you.>

WHERE INNOCENT BRIGHT-EYED DAISIES ARE

[Date of composition unknown. Editions: *1872*, 1872a, 1893, 1904. The notebook MS is in the British Library.]

1. MS: 50 / Where innocent bright eyed daisies are

THE CITY MOUSE LIVES IN A HOUSE

[Date of composition unknown. Editions: *1872*, 1872a, 1893, 1904. The notebook MS is in the British Library.]

1. MS: 51 / The   3. MS: toads

WHAT DOES THE DONKEY BRAY ABOUT?

[Date of composition unknown. Editions: *1872*, 1872a, 1893, 1904. The notebook MS is in the British Library.]

1. MS: 52 / What   7. MS: do?",
4. MS: O Nurse if you will tell < >   8. MS: away",
    this

THREE PLUM BUNS

[Date of composition unknown. Editions: *1872*, 1872a, 1893, 1904. The notebook MS is in the British Library.]

1. MS: 53 / Three   8. MS: scare [*birds*] <sheep> from

A MOTHERLESS SOFT LAMBKIN

[Date of composition unknown. Editions: *1872*, 1872a, 1893, 1904. The notebook MS is in the British Library. In the MS, lines 2 and 6 are indented two spaces.]

1. MS: 54 / A   6. MS: will,
2. MS: hill,

DANCING ON THE HILL-TOPS

[Date of composition unknown. Editions: *1872*, 1872a, 1893, 1904. The notebook MS is in the British Library.]

1. MS: 55 / Dancing < > the   10. MS: palace
    hilltops,   11. MS: the hilltops

WHEN FISHES SET UMBRELLAS UP

[Date of composition unknown. Editions: *1872*, 1872a, 1893, 1904. The notebook MS is in the British Library.]

1. MS: 56. / [*If*] <When> fishes
2. MS: For when the raindrops
    run,

THE PEACOCK HAS A SCORE OF EYES

[Date of composition unknown. Editions: *1872*, 1872a, 1893, 1904. The notebook MS is in the British Library.]

1. MS: 57 / The <> eyes
2. MS: see,
3. MS: The codfish has <> sound

5. MS: time
6. MS: clocks,
8. 1872: fox

PUSSY HAS A WHISKERED FACE

[Date of composition unknown. Editions: *1872*, 1872a, 1893, 1904. The notebook MS is in the British Library.]

1. MS: 58 / Pussy
2. MS: ways,

3. MS: scampers [*if*] when <> call

THE DOG LIES IN HIS KENNEL

[Date of composition unknown. Editions: *1872*, 1872a, 1893, 1904. The notebook MS is in the British Library.]

1. MS: 59 / The <> in [*the ke*] his kennel
2. MS: And puss purrs

3. MS: baby [*sits up*] <perches> on
5. MS: cat

IF HOPE GREW ON A BUSH

[Date of composition unknown. Editions: *1872*, 1872a, 1893, 1904. The notebook MS is in the British Library.]

1. MS: 60 / If <> bush
2. MS: And [*love*] <joy> grew
5. MS: But oh in <> autumn
    1904: oh in

6. MS: wither
7. MS: and [*love*] <joy>

I PLANTED A HAND

[Date of composition unknown. Editions: *1872*, 1872a, 1893, 1904. The notebook MS is in the British Library.]

1. MS: 61 / I

6. MS: thorn

UNDER THE IVY BUSH

[Date of composition unknown. Editions: *1872*, 1872a, 1893, 1904. The notebook MS is in the British Library.]

1. MS: 62 / Under
4. MS: crying[;]<:>—

7. MS: [*And*] But under

THERE IS ONE THAT HAS A HEAD WITHOUT AN EYE

[Date of composition unknown. Editions: *1872*, 1872a, 1893, 1904. The notebook MS is in the British Library. In the MS, lines 4 and 5 are indented four spaces.]

1. MS: 63 / There   4. MS: said
2. MS: head:—   5. 1904: thread.

IF A MOUSE COULD FLY

[Date of composition unknown. Editions: *1872*, 1872a, 1893, 1904. The notebook MS is in the British Library. In the 1893 and 1904 texts, line 10 is not indented.]

1. MS: 64 / If   7. MS: swim
5. MS: fly   8. MS: grey,
6. MS: away,   9. MS: talk

SING ME A SONG

[Date of composition unknown. Editions: *1872*, 1872a, 1893, 1904. The notebook MS is in the British Library.]

1. MS: 65 / Sing   9. MS: sisters
    1904: song.—   11. MS: dong
7. 1904: tale.—

THE LILY HAS AN AIR

[Date of composition unknown. Editions: *1872*, 1872a, 1893, 1904. The notebook MS is in the British Library. In the MS, line 6 is indented two spaces.]

1. MS: 66 / The

MARGARET HAS A MILKING-PAIL

[Date of composition unknown. Editions: *1872*, 1872a, 1893, 1904. The notebook MS is in the British Library.]

1. MS: 67 / Margaret < >   6. MS: [*While*] <Where> the
    milking-pail   7. MS: say "good morrow"
2. MS: early,   1904: say 'Good-morrow' as
3. MS: a thrashing-flail   8. MS: [*Near*] <By> the [*honeyed*]
4. MS: betimes: <leafy> limes.

IN THE MEADOW—WHAT IN THE MEADOW?

[Date of composition unknown. Editions: *1872*, 1872a, 1893, 1904. The notebook MS is in the British Library. In the MS, no lines are indented.]

1. MS: 68 / In
2. MS, 1872a: Daisies, buttercups,
7. MS, 1872, 1872a: And

Love-lies-bleeding with none to heal

A FRISKY LAMB

[Date of composition unknown. Editions: *1872*, 1872a, 1893, 1904. The notebook MS is in the British Library. In the MS, lines 2 and 6 are indented two spaces.]

1. MS: 69 / A

MIX A PANCAKE

[Date of composition unknown. Editions: *1872*, 1872a, 1893, 1904. The notebook MS is in the British Library.]

1. MS: 70 / Mix

THE WIND HAS SUCH A RAINY SOUND

[Date of composition unknown. Editions: *1872*, 1872a, 1893, 1904. The notebook MS is in the British Library.]

1. MS: 71 / The
6. MS: from the<ir> tree,—

7. 1872, 1872a, 1893: Oh, will

THREE LITTLE CHILDREN

[Date of composition unknown. Editions: *1872*, 1872a, 1893, 1904. The notebook MS is in the British Library.]

1. MS: 72 / Three
2. 1872: earth
5. 1872, 1872a, 1893, 1904: tender angels.

7. MS: sea
10. 1872, 1872a, 1893, 1904: guardian angels.

FLY AWAY, FLY AWAY OVER THE SEA

[Date of composition unknown. Editions: *1872*, 1872a, 1893, 1904. The notebook MS is in the British Library.]

1. MS: 73. / Fly

2. MS: swallow for <> done—

MINNIE BAKES OATEN CAKES

[Date of composition unknown. Editions: *1872*, 1872a, 1893, 1904. The notebook MS is in the British Library. In the 1904 text, line 4 is indented two spaces.]

1. MS: 74 / Minnie   5. MS: rose

A WHITE HEN SITTING

[Date of composition unknown. Editions: *1872*, 1872a, 1893, 1904. The notebook MS is in the British Library.]

1. MS: 75 / A   5. MS, 1904: owl and < > hawk
2. MS: three;   6. 1904: see;

CURRANTS ON A BUSH

[Date of composition unknown. Editions: *1872*, 1872a, 1893, 1904. The notebook MS is in the British Library.]

1. MS: 76 / Currants   4. MS: them
3. MS: bough

I HAVE BUT ONE ROSE IN THE WORLD

[Date of composition unknown. Editions: *1872*, 1872a, 1893, 1904. The notebook MS is in the British Library.]

1. MS: 77 / I   3. 1872, 1872a, 1893: Oh, when
2. MS: a-drooping:—   4. 1872: stooping

ROSY MAIDEN WINIFRED

[Date of composition unknown. Editions: *1872*, 1872a, 1893, 1904. The notebook MS is in the British Library. In the MS, lines 3, 5, 7, 8, 11, and 12 are indented two spaces; lines 1, 2, 4, 6, 9, and 10 are not indented. In the 1904 text, line 5 is not indented.]

1. MS: 78 / Rosy maiden Winifred   2. MS: head

WHEN THE COWS COME HOME THE MILK IS COMING

[Date of composition unknown. Editions: *1872*, 1872a, 1893, 1904. The notebook MS is in the British Library.]

1. MS: 79 / When   5. MS: funny, pert little bunny
    1872: coming   1904: bunny
    1872a: coming;

ROSES BLUSHING RED AND WHITE

[Date of composition unknown. Editions: *1872*, 1872a, 1893, 1904. The notebook MS is in the British Library. In the MS, lines 2, 4, 6, 8, 10, and 12 are indented two spaces.]

1. MS: 80 / Roses   11. MS: of fra[*rg*]<gr>ant breath,

"DING A DING"

[Date of composition unknown. Editions: *1872*, 1872a, 1893, 1904. The notebook MS is in the British Library.]

1. MS: 81 / "Ding a ding"   6. MS: a dong"
3. 1904: say,   8. 1904: call,
4. MS: "Come all <> gay,"   9. MS, 1904: all,"
    1904: gay,'   10. MS: a funeral[*l*].

A RING UPON HER FINGER

[Date of composition unknown. Editions: *1872*, 1872a, 1893, 1904. The notebook MS is in the British Library.]

1. MS: 83 / A <> finger   10. MS: bride,
5. MS: forehead

"FERRY ME ACROSS THE WATER"

[Date of composition unknown. Editions: *1872*, 1872a, 1893, 1904. The notebook MS is in the British Library.]

1. MS: 82 / Ferry   5. MS: I <> purse
2. MS: boatman, do.—   8. MS: boatman, do.—
3. MS: If   9. MS: Step <> my ferry boat
4. MS: you.—   12. MS: you.

WHEN A MOUNTING SKYLARK SINGS

[Date of composition unknown. Editions: *1872*, 1872a, 1893, 1904. The notebook MS is in the British Library.]

1. MS: 84 / When   7. MS: merely earth
3. MS: high

WHO HAS SEEN THE WIND?

[Date of composition unknown. Editions: *1872*, 1872a, 1893, 1904. The notebook MS is in the British Library.]

1. MS: 85 / Who
3. MS: leaves [*are*] <hang>
    trembling

THE HORSES OF THE SEA

[Date of composition unknown. Editions: *1872*, 1872a, 1893, 1904. The notebook MS is in the British Library.]

1. MS: 86 / The   7. MS: foaming sea horses

O SAILOR, COME ASHORE

[Date of composition unknown. Editions: *1872*, 1872a, 1893, 1904. The notebook MS is in the British Library.]

1. MS: 87 / O sailor come   5. MS: ground
2. MS: me?—   6. MS: it off a
4. 1872: sea

A DIAMOND OR A COAL?

[Date of composition unknown. Editions: *1872*, 1872a, 1893, 1904. The notebook MS is in the British Library.]

1. MS: 88 / A <> coal?—   5. MS: coal?—
4. MS: trees?—

AN EMERALD IS AS GREEN AS GRASS

[Date of composition unknown. Editions: *1872*, 1872a, 1893, 1904. The notebook MS is in the British Library.]

1. MS: 89 / An <> grass,   5. MS: stone
2. MS: blood,   6. MS: desire,
3. MS: sapphire is as <>   7. MS: spark,—
    heaven,—

BOATS SAIL ON THE RIVERS

[Date of composition unknown. Editions: *1872*, 1872a, 1893, 1904. The notebook MS is in the British Library.]

1. MS: 90 / Boats <> rivers   7. MS: heaven
2. MS: seas,   8. MS: trees
5. MS: rivers   9. MS: sky
6. MS: please,

THE LILY HAS A SMOOTH STALK

[Date of composition unknown. Editions: *1872*, 1872a, 1893, 1904. The notebook
MS is in the British Library.]

1. MS: 91 / The <> stalk
2. MS: hand,
5. MS: an appletree
6. MS: corn,

10. MS: briar
11. MS: And yields a glimpse of her
    deep heart,

HURT NO LIVING THING

[Date of composition unknown. Editions: *1872*, 1872a, 1893, 1904. The notebook
MS is in the British Library.]

1. MS: 92 / Hurt

I CAUGHT A LITTLE LADYBIRD

[Date of composition unknown. Editions: *1872*, 1872a, 1893, 1904. The notebook
MS (MS1) is in the British Library. The copy of *Sing-Song* owned by Mrs. Roderic
O'Conor (MS2) contains Christina's holograph addition of lines 5–12. The copy of
Sing-Song owned by Mrs. Geoffrey Dennis (MS3) also contains Christina's holograph
addition of lines 5–12.]

1. MS1: 93 / I
2. MS1: away,
4. MS1: both [*good*] <staid> and
5. MS1, 1872, 1872a: [Lines 5–12
   are not in the text.]

6. MS2: away:
8. MS2: [illegible deletion]
   <p>lay.
11. MS2: cold,

ALL THE BELLS WERE RINGING

[Date of composition unknown. Editions: *1872*, 1872a, 1893, 1904. The notebook
MS is in the British Library.]

1. MS: 94 / All
   1872a: ringing,
2. MS: singing
4. MS: doll—

8. MS, 1904: ringing
9. MS: singing.—

WEE WEE HUSBAND

[Date of composition unknown. Editions: *1872*, 1872a, 1893, 1904. The notebook
MS is in the British Library.]

1. MS: 95 / Wee <> husband
3. MS: comfits
4. MS: honey.—

5. MS: wifie
7. MS: Milk nor meat nor
8. MS: Comfits nor

I HAVE A LITTLE HUSBAND

[Date of composition unknown. Editions: *1872*, 1872a, 1893, 1904. The notebook MS (MS1) is in the British Library. The copy of *Sing-Song* owned by Mrs. Roderic O'Conor (MS2) contains Christina's holograph addition of lines 5–8. The copy of *Sing-Song* owned by Mrs. Geoffrey Dennis (MS3) also contains Christina's holograph addition of lines 5–8.]

1. MS1: 96 / I   6. MS2: him:
2. 1904: sea;
5. MS1, 1872, 1872a: [Lines 5–8
    are not in the text.]

THE DEAR OLD WOMAN IN THE LANE

[Date of composition unknown. Editions: *1872*, 1872a, 1893, 1904. The notebook MS (MS1) is in the British Library. The copy of *Sing-Song* owned by Mrs. Roderic O'Conor (MS2) contains Christina's holograph addition of lines 5–8. The copy of *Sing-Song* owned by Mrs. Geoffrey Dennis (MS3) also contains Christina's holograph addition of lines 5–8.]

1. MS1: 97 / The   5. MS1, 1872, 1872a: [Lines 5–8
3. MS1: afternoon   are not in the text.]

SWIFT AND SURE THE SWALLOW

[Date of composition unknown. Editions: *1872*, 1872a, 1893, 1904. The notebook MS is in the British Library.]

1. MS: 98 / Swift

"I DREAMT I CAUGHT A LITTLE OWL"

[Date of composition unknown. Editions: *1872*, 1872a, 1893, 1904. The notebook MS is in the British Library. In the MS, lines 4 and 8 are indented two spaces, and there are no stanza breaks. In the 1904 text, no lines are indented.]

1. MS: 99 / "I   5. MS: sunflower
2. MS: blue"—   6. MS: it [*bl*]<gr>ew"—
4. MS: one"—   8. MS: sun"—.

WHAT DOES THE BEE DO?

[Date of composition unknown. Editions: *1872*, 1872a, 1893, 1904. The notebook MS is in the British Library.]

1. MS: 100 / What

I HAVE A POLL PARROT

[Date of composition unknown. Editions: *1872*, 1872a, 1893, 1904. The notebook MS (MS1) is in the British Library. The copy of *Sing-Song* owned by Mrs. Roderic O'Conor (MS2) contains Christina's holograph addition of lines 5–8. The copy of *Sing-Song* owned by Mrs. Geoffrey Dennis (MS3) also contains Christina's holograph addition of lines 5–8.]

1. MS1: 101 / I <> a [*p*]
   <P>oll parrot,
5. MS1, 1872, 1872a: [Lines 5–8 are not in the text.]

6. MS2: tear Polly"—
7. 1893, 1904: While soft-hearted Poll

A HOUSE OF CARDS

[Date of composition unknown. Editions: *1872*, 1872a, 1893, 1904. The notebook MS is in the British Library. In the MS, lines 2, 4, and 6 are not indented.]

1. MS: 102 / A

5. MS: the courtcards

THE ROSE WITH SUCH A BONNY BLUSH

[Date of composition unknown. Editions: *1872*, 1872a, 1893, 1904. The notebook MS is in the British Library.]

1. MS: 103 / The

THE ROSE THAT BLUSHES ROSY RED

[Date of composition unknown. Editions: *1872*, 1872a, 1893, 1904. The notebook MS is in the British Library.]

1. MS: 104 / The

OH FAIR TO SEE

[Date of composition unknown. Editions: *1872*, 1872a, 1893, 1904. The notebook MS is in the British Library.]

1. MS: 106 / Oh
   1872, 1872a, 1893: Oh, fair
2. MS: Bloom laden cherry
3. MS: white
   1904: white,
4. MS: delight
   1904: delight;

5. 1872, 1872a, 1893: Oh, fair
6. 1872, 1872a, 1893: Oh fair
7. MS: Fruit laden cherry
9. MS: head
   1904: head;
10. 1872, 1872a, 1893: Oh, fair

CLEVER LITTLE WILLIE WEE

[Date of composition unknown. Editions: *1872*, 1872a, 1893, 1904. The notebook MS (MS1) is in the British Library. The copy of *Sing-Song* owned by Mrs. Roderic O'Conor (MS2) contains Christina's holograph addition of lines 5–8. The copy of *Sing-Song* owned by Mrs. Geoffrey Dennis (MS3) also contains Christina's holograph addition of lines 5–8. In MS1, no lines are indented.]

1. MS1: 105 / Clever little Willie Wee
2. MS1: Bright eyed blue eyed little fellow,
   1893, 1904: Bright-eyed, blue-eyed little

5. MS1, 1872, 1872a: [Lines 5–8 are not in the text.]
7. MS2: a [illegible deletion] <ch>art
8. MS2: With merry Margery.

THE PEACH TREE ON THE SOUTHERN WALL

[Date of composition unknown. Editions: *1872*, 1872a, 1893, 1904. The notebook MS (MS1) is in the British Library. The copy of *Sing-Song* owned by Mrs. Roderic O'Conor (MS2) contains Christina's holograph addition of lines 1–4, written at the top of the page above lines 5–8, which are printed on the lower half of the page. The copy of *Sing-Song* owned by Mrs. Geoffrey Dennis (MS3) also contains Christina's holograph addition of lines 1–4, written at the bottom of the page, with a *2* beside lines 5–8, a *1* beside lines 1–4, and the letters *tr* written in the left margin.]

1. MS1, 1872, 1872a: [Lines 1–4 are not in the text.]
2. MS2, MS3: sun
4. MS2: Are rosy every
   MS3: rosy every

5. MS1: 107 / A
6. MS1: me,
7. MS1: biggest rosiest downiest
8. MS1: For [g]<G>randmamma with

A ROSE HAS THORNS AS WELL AS HONEY

[Date of composition unknown. Editions: *1872*, 1872a, 1893, 1904. The notebook MS is in the British Library.]

1. MS: 108 / A
3. MS: iris [*is*] <grows> so <>
   fine
   1904: fine

9. MS: convolvolus but
12. MS: And poppy juice would

IS THE MOON TIRED? SHE LOOKS SO PALE

[Date of composition unknown. Editions: *1872*, 1872a, 1893, 1904. The notebook MS is in the British Library. In the MS, lines 2, 4, 6, and 8 are indented two spaces.]

1. MS: 109 / Is

3. MS: scales the[y] sky <> west

IF STARS DROPPED OUT OF HEAVEN

[Date of composition unknown. Editions: *1872*, 1872a, 1893, 1904. The notebook
MS is in the British Library.]

1. MS: 110 / If star[*d*]<s>
   dropped
3. MS: fair
5. MS: Winged [*a*]<A>ngels

might [*come*] fly down
1872, 1872a, 1893, 1904:
Winged angels might

"GOODBYE IN FEAR, GOODBYE IN SORROW"

[Date of composition unknown. Editions: *1872*, 1872a, 1893, 1904. The notebook
MS is in the British Library.]

1. MS: 111 / "Goodbye <> fear,
   Goodbye in
   1904: 'Good-bye in fear,
   good-bye in
2. MS: Goodbye and
3. MS: dear,"—
   1904: dear'—

4. MS: to [*mee*]<par>t again."—
5. 1904: 'Good-bye to-day,
   good-bye to-morrow,
6. 1904: Good-bye till
7. MS: dear,—"
   1904: dear'—
8. MS: to [*mee*]<par>t again."—

IF THE SUN COULD TELL US HALF

[Date of composition unknown. Editions: *1872*, 1872a, 1893, 1904. The notebook
MS is in the British Library.]

1. MS: 112 / If
3. MS: He would make us laugh
   and laugh,

4. MS: He would make

IF THE MOON CAME FROM HEAVEN

[Date of composition unknown. Editions: *1872*, 1872a, 1893, 1904. The notebook
MS is in the British Library.]

1. MS: 113 / If <> heaven
3. MS: us
4. MS: say?—
5. MS: things

7. MS: think: I [*look*] <peep> by
8. MS: "And [*never look*] <do not
   peep> by

O LADY MOON, YOUR HORNS POINT TOWARD THE EAST

[Date of composition unknown. Editions: *1872*, 1872a, 1893, 1904. The notebook MS is in the British Library. In the MS, lines 2 and 4 are indented two spaces.]

1. MS: 114 / O Lady Moon your < > the East; 1904: east;
2. MS: increased:— 1904: increased:
3. MS: O Lady Moon your < > the West; 1904: west;

WHAT DO THE STARS DO

[Date of composition unknown. Editions: *1872*, 1872a, 1893, 1904. The notebook MS is in the British Library.]

1. MS: 115 / What
2. MS: sky
3. MS: blow
6. MS: Circles circles still
7. MS: set
8. MS: its Maker's [w]<W>ill. 1872, 1872a, 1893, 1904: its Maker's will.

MOTHERLESS BABY AND BABYLESS MOTHER

[Date of composition unknown. Editions: *1872*, 1872a, 1893, 1904. The notebook MS is in the British Library.]

1. MS: 116 / Motherless

CRIMSON CURTAINS ROUND MY MOTHER'S BED

[Date of composition unknown. Editions: *1872*, 1872a, 1893, 1904. The notebook MS is in the British Library.]

1. MS: 117 / Crimson < > bed

BABY LIES SO FAST ASLEEP

[Date of composition unknown. Editions: *1872*, 1872a, 1893, 1904. The notebook MS is in the British Library.]

1. MS: 118 / Baby

I KNOW A BABY, SUCH A BABY

[Date of composition unknown. Editions: *1872*, 1872a, 1893, 1904. The notebook MS is in the British Library.]

1. MS: 119 / I
5. 1893, 1904: "Cuddle and love me, cuddle and love me,"
7. 1872, 1872a, 1893; Oh, the < > and oh the
8. 1872, 1872a, 1893: And, oh, the

LULLABY, OH LULLABY!

[Date of composition unknown. Editions: *1872*, 1872a, 1893, 1904. The notebook MS is in the British Library. In the MS, lines 2, 4, 6, and 8 are indented two spaces; lines 1, 3, 5, 7, and 9 are not indented.]

1. MS: 120 / Lullaby oh
   1872, 1872a, 1893: oh, lullaby!
2. MS: and [*birds*] <lambs> are
   sleeping—
3. MS: Lullaby oh
   1872, 1872a, 1893: oh, lullaby!
4. MS: peeping—
5. MS: Lullaby oh
   1872, 1872a, 1893: oh, lullaby!

6. MS: the [*world is*] <birds are>
   silence keeping
7. MS: (Lullaby oh
   1872, 1872a, 1893: oh, lullaby!)
8. MS: Sleep my <> fall asleeping.
9. MS: Lullaby oh lullaby.
   1872, 1872a, 1893: oh, lullaby!

LIE A-BED

[Date of composition unknown. Editions: *1872*, 1872a, 1893, 1904. The notebook MS is in the British Library.]

1. MS: 121. / Lie abed,
3. MS: eyes, bopeep;

4. MS: Till day break
   1904: Till day-break

BROWNIE, BROWNIE, LET DOWN YOUR MILK

[Date of composition unknown. Editions: *1893*, 1904. The copy of *Sing-Song* owned by Mrs. Roderic O'Conor (MS1) contains Christina's holograph MS of the poem, written at the front of the book. The copy of *Sing-Song* owned by Mrs. Geoffrey Dennis (MS2) also contains Christina's holograph MS of the poem, attached to p. 26 of the book.]

1. 1904: milk,

STROKE A FLINT, AND THERE IS NOTHING TO ADMIRE

[Date of composition unknown. Editions: *1893*, 1904. The copy of *Sing-Song* owned by Mrs. Roderic O'Conor (MS1) contains Christina's holograph MS of the poem, written at the back of the book. The copy of *Sing-Song* owned by Mrs. Geoffrey Dennis (MS2) also contains Christina's holograph MS of the poem, attached to p. 34 of the book.]

I AM A KING

[Date of composition unknown. Editions: *1893*, 1904. The copy of *Sing-Song* owned by Mrs. Roderic O'Conor (MS1) contains Christina's holograph MS of the poem, written at the back of the book. The copy of *Sing-Song* owned by Mrs. Geoffrey Dennis (MS2) also contains Christina's holograph MS of the poem, attached to p. 66 of the book. In MS1, there is no stanza break.]

2. MS1: rather:
7. 1893, 1904: purple flag-flower

12. MS1: age:
13. MS2: Lord's-&-ladies in

PLAYING AT BOB CHERRY

[Date of composition unknown. Editions: *1893*, 1904. The copy of *Sing-Song* owned by Mrs. Roderic O'Conor (MS1) contains Christina's holograph MS of the poem, written at the front of the book. The copy of *Sing-Song* owned by Mrs. Geoffrey Dennis (MS2) also contains Christina's holograph MS of the poem, attached to p. 84 of the book. In MS1, there are no stanza breaks.]

7. MS1: While curly pated Nelly   11. MS1: wind plays at bob cherry
10. MS1: Oh w[a]<h>at a

BLIND FROM MY BIRTH

[Date of composition unknown. Editions: *1893*, 1904. The copy of *Sing-Song* owned by Mrs. Geoffrey Dennis contains Christina's holograph MS of the poem, attached to p. 86 of the book.]

12. 1904: all joy-bells are

SONNETS ARE FULL OF LOVE, AND THIS MY TOME

[Date of composition unknown. Editions: *1881*, 1881a, 1890, 1904. An undated letter from Christina to her brother Dante Gabriel Rossetti, containing lines 3–7 of the poem, (MS1) is in the library of the University of British Columbia. A fair copy (MS2) is owned by Harold F. Rossetti. The notebook MS (MS3) is in the University of Texas Humanities Research Center.]

Title. 1904: DEDICATORY SONNET
1. MS2: this our tome
2. MS2: Is full of sonnets:
3. MS1: A sonnet & a love sonnet from
   MS2: A sonnet & a love-sonnet from
   MS3: [A] <One> sonnet
6. MS1: troublesome,

7. MS1: Whose service — &c.
   MS2: dignity
8. 1904: my lodestar while
10. MS2, MS3: you Mother,
14. MS3: [On the back of the page is written and heavily deleted:] [*To / my Mother / I offer / love / reverence / and / this little volume.*]

THE KEY-NOTE.

[Date of composition unknown. Editions: *1881*, 1881a, 1890, 1896, 1904. The notebook MS (MS1) is in the University of Texas Humanities Research Center. A partial MS of lines 1–8 (MS2) is in the Rossetti Collection of Janet Camp Troxell, Princeton University Library; Christina wrote the lines first in pencil and then wrote over the same text in ink. The lines were then deleted. In MS1, lines 2, 5, 10, and 13 are indented two spaces; lines 3, 7, 11, and 15 are indented four spaces; lines 6, 8, 14, and 16 are indented six spaces; and lines 1, 4, 9, and 12 are not indented. In MS2, no lines are indented, and the last word is missing from lines 1, 2, 5, 6, 7, and 8. In the 1896 text, only the first stanza is printed.]

Title. MS1: The Key-note. / [*An Autumn Song.*]
MS2: [untitled]
1896: LINES
1. 1896: to sing,
2. 1896: to know?
4. MS1: long [*g*] ago:
MS2: ago:
1896: ago.
6. MS1, 1896, 1904: sere

7. MS1: [*I*] [indented eight spaces and then deleted] <I> [indented four spaces] scarcely
9. MS1: Yet [*r*]<R>obin sings <> rest
11. MS1: don
12. MS1: breast:
14. 1881a: lie
1904: lie;
16. MS1: pause,—&

THE MONTHS: / A PAGEANT.

[Date of composition unknown. Editions: *1881*, 1881a, 1890, 1904. The rough draft of lines 181–221 (MS1) is in the Iowa State Department of History and Archives. The notebook MS (MS2) is in the University of Texas Humanities Research Center. An undated letter from Christina to her brother William Michael Rossetti, containing lines 274–76, (MS3) is in the library of the University of British Columbia. In the 1904 text, lines 132, 138, and 144 are not indented. In MS2, the speakers' names are in the left margin, and the stage directions begin at the left margin of the page. In the variant notes, the large brackets represent brackets in the text of the poem.]

Title. MS2: The Months: / a / Pageant.
Personifications. MS2: Person[*ages represented*]<ifications>: / *Boys*: / January / March / July / August / October / December [In a column opposite *Boys*:] *Girls*: / February / April / May / June / September / November [Below Personifications:] Robin Redbreasts — Lambs & Sheep — Nightingale <&> nestlings — / Various Flowers, Fruits, &c.
Stage direction. MS2: *Scene*: a Cottage with its Grounds. / <> cottage: a <> hearth; a [*breakfast*] table [*ready laid*] <on which <the> breakfast things have been left standing.> January
1. MS2: *January*. Cold
2. Stage direction. MS2: fire.]
3. MS2: embers, glow:
1881a: sparkle, fagot; embers
8. MS2: crumb
11. MS2: bread
12. MS2: crumb,

13. MS2: the hearth rug,
22. Stage direction. 1904: meal when <> hand.] / Good-morrow,
23. MS2: *January*. Good morrow, Sister.
24. MS2: *February*. Brother,
25. MS2: snowdrops, only
28. Stage direction. MS2: on the windowsill, a
Stage direction. 1904: her.] / O
29. MS2: *February*. O <> wonder, come, come
35. Stage direction. MS2: [[*Febr*] / [February
37. MS2: wear,
40. MS2: lamb a <> pair
43. Stage direction. MS2: windows: branches
44. MS2: rattle &
46. MS2: that [*whistle*] <eddy> &
1881a: sing.
Stage direction. MS2: open & <> violets & anemones.]
Stage direction. 1904: anemones.] / Come,

47.   MS2: *February.* Come, < >
      bring:
49.   Stage direction. MS2: *March,*
      stopping short on the threshold:—
51.   MS2: house,
56.   MS2: frown
57.   MS2: down,
63.   MS2: quake
      1881, 1881a, 1890, 1904: Frail
      wind-flowers quake,
69.   MS2: tall
80.   MS2: *April, outside*:—Pretty
97.   MS2: bird!
98.   MS2: herd!—
99.   MS2: play
100. 1904: to-day. / [Appearing
      Stage direction. MS2: *April,*
      appear[*s*]<*ing*> *at the open*
      door:—
101. MS2: Good morrow & good
      bye: if
103. MS2: *March.* You're
104. MS2: *April.*   Birth
105. MS2: [*And I, I soon shall die*;]
      <As wings & wind mean
      flying / So you & I & all things
      fly or die>
107. MS2: [*So*] <And> sometimes
      < > sit [illegible deletion]
      <si>ghing [*&*] <to> think
109. MS2: a lapfull of
111. MS2: sitting [;]<,>
      1904: sitting;
113. Stage direction. MS2: her
      apronfull of < > & nestfull of
      < > grounds. April without < >
      cottage hangs
      Stage direction. 1904: them.] /
      What
114. MS2: *April.* What
115. MS2: weak:
117. MS2: [A stanza break follows
      the line.]
118. MS2: day
119. 1881a: the country-side,
121. Stage direction. 1890: kiss /
      April
      Stage direction. 1904: round.] /
      Ah
122. MS2: *April.* Ah May, good
      morrow May, < > so good bye.
      1904: good-morrow, May,

123. MS2: *May.* That's
129. MS2: shower,
      Stage direction. MS2: an armfull
      of
      Stage direction. 1904: garden.] /
      And
130. MS2: *May.* And
131. 1881, 1881a: [No stanza break
      follows the line.]
133. MS2: care:
136. MS2, 1904: is
139. MS2: may,
      1881a: my namesake-blossom,
      may;
141. MS2: here forgetmenot,
149. Stage direction. MS2: towards
      May; who seeing
      Stage direction. 1904: exclaims] /
      Surely
150. MS2: *May.* Surely
151. MS2: *June.* Indeed
157. MS2: roses &
      Stage direction. MS2: [May
      eating strawberries withdraws
      Stage direction. 1904: beds.] /
      The
158. MS2: *June.* The
159. MS2: everything:
161. Stage direction. MS2: a [*deodara*]
      <laburnum>.]
      Stage direction. 1904:
      laburnum.]
165. Stage direction. MS2: asleep: &
      < > of July who < > singing
      half calling]
166. MS2: *July, behind the scenes.* Blue
169. Stage direction. MS2: peaches
      <balanced> [illegible deletion]
      <upon> the
170. MS2: *June.* What,
171. MS2: *July.* Nay, < > kept:
173. Stage direction. MS2, 1904:
      plate.]
174. MS2: peaches; gathered
      1881a: flowers, but
177. MS2: in: a < > heels,
179. MS2: Lightning flash[illegible
      deletion]<es> &
180. Stage direction. MS2: a [*thickly*
      woven] <thickly-woven>
      arbour.]

Stage direction. 1904:
arbour.] / The

181. MS1: *July.* Song. / The [*shout*]
<roar> of
MS2: *July.* The

183. MS1: The <darkening> sky
like a [*hollowed*] cup
MS2: sky like <> cup

184. MS1: brink:

187. MS1, MS2: earth parched <>
desire

194. MS1: [*All h*] <H>er [*fainting*]
<famish[*ed*]ing> life <> up,
MS2: up,

195. MS1, MS2: first

198. MS1, MS2: crest:

200. Stage direction. MS1: Enter
August carrying <>
grain.] / Hail,
Stage direction. 1904:
grain. / Hail

201. MS2: *July.* Hail,

202. MS1: storm;

204. MS1: be[,]<:>

205. MS2: smell as [*w*]<s>weet as

206. MS1: calm;

207. Stage direction. MS1: [July
[*retreats*] [<*disappears*>]
<retires> in[*to*]<to> a

208. MS1: *August.* Song. / Wheat
[*waves*] <sways> heavy,
MS2: *August.* Wheat

209. MS1: Barley droops a
MS2: Barley [*droops*] <bows> a

212. MS1, MS2: man, or

213. MS1: [*Or*] [indented eight
spaces] <Or> [indented six
spaces] at [*least*] very least

216. MS1, MS2: food:

217. MS1, MS2: of younger brother
1904: of foster-brother

218. MS1, 1904: litter or <> brood

219. MS1, MS2, 1904: feather

220. MS1: Who with [illegible
deletion] <men> together
MS2: Who with <> together

221. MS1: Brewe the
Stage direction. 1904: lawn.] /
My

222. MS2: *August.* My <> ended: &

227. MS2: *September.* Unload

228. MS2: Plums, &

232. Stage direction, MS2: speaking
August
Stage direction. 1904: goes] / My

233. MS2: *September.* My [*S*]<s>ong
is

235. MS2: dying:

242. MS2: fall

251. MS2: vale:

255. Stage direction. MS2: other. [*J*]
<A dahlia is stuck in his
buttonhole.]>

256. MS2: *October.* Nay, <> over
1881a: up, sister.

258. MS2: leaves: besides, <> true

259. MS2, 1904: too

261. Stage direction. MS2, 1890,
1904: to September.]

263. Stage direction. MS2: wreaths
the hop bine about <> gives
[*her*] <her> the
Stage direction. 1904:
roast.] / Crack

264. MS2: *October.* Crack

266. 1881a: higher;

270. MS2: flowers:

272. 1904: showers:

273. Stage direction. MS2, 1890:
approaching.]
Stage direction. 1904:
approaching.] / Here

274. MS2: *October.* Here
MS3: "Here <> sister looking
grim

275. MS2: grim
MS3: "And dim

276. MS3: ways"!!!

277. Stage direction. MS2: *November,
entering & shutting the door:*

278. 1881a, 1904: bring,

280. MS2: these pine cones for

283. MS2: a hoarfrost here

286. Stage direction. MS2:
background; while
Stage direction. 1890: her
pine-cones on
Stage direction. 1904: her
pine-cones on <>
listlessly.] / The

287. MS2: *November.* The

288. MS2: deep:

294. Stage direction. MS2: window,
December <> running past &

leaping along in <> / *November*
calls out, without rising:—
Stage direction. 1904: knocks.] /
Ah,
295.   MS2: last.
       1890: November. / Ah, <>
       last: / [Calls out without rising.]
       1904: last: / [Calls out without
       rising.]
296.   Stage direction. MS2: berry[.*]*]
       <, &c.]>
       Stage direction. 1904:
       etc.] / Come,
297.   MS2: *November.* Come, <> door
298.   MS2: fast,
299.   MS2: snows &
301.   MS2: aglow: how
302.   MS2: [No stanza break follows
       the line.]

303.   MS2: *December.* Nay,
307.   MS2: begin:
309.   MS2, 1904: sings.]
       Stage direction. 1890: sings.]
       [No stanza break precedes or
       follows the stage direction.]
310.   MS2: night
315.   MS2: pale:—
318.   MS2: bird
320.   MS2: a Carol which some
       Shepherds heard
321.   Stage direction. MS2: song all
       the <other> Months <>
       garden or <> background[,] <.
       The[*t*]<T>welve> join <>
       as the curtain falls.] / _____ /
       [*The End.*]

PASTIME.

[Date of composition unknown. Editions: *1881*, 1881a, 1890, 1904. The notebook
MS is in the University of Texas Humanities Research Center. In the 1904 text, lines
2, 6, and 10 are not indented.]

1.   MS: the eddies drifting,
     1904: rocking;
2.   MS: aim,—
3.   1904: ominous West there
5.   1904: A hay-cock in a hay-field,
     backing, lapping;

6.   MS: about,—
     1904: pillowed round- / about;
7.   1904: ominous West across
10. MS, 1904: soft:
11. 1904: ominous West glooms

"ITALIA, IO TI SALUTO!"

[Date of composition unknown. Editions: *1881*, 1881a, 1890, 1904. The MS is miss-
ing from the notebook in the University of Texas Humanities Center.]

Title.   1904: ITALIA, <> SALUTO

MIRRORS OF LIFE AND DEATH.

[Date of composition unknown. Editions: *1881*, 1881a, 1890, 1904. The notebook
MS is in the British Library. Lines 6–135 of the poem were published in *Athenaeum*,
No. 2577 (March 17, 1877), 350.]

3.   MS: glass:
6.   MS, 1877: a Morning Sky,—
7.   MS, 1877: colourless,—
9.   MS, 1877: dry,

34. MS, 1877: waters clear
36. MS, 1877: One new-dead, and
38. MS: pale [*f*]<F>lower
     1877: pale Flower

39.   MS, 1877: dower
40.   MS: Each [illegible deletion]
      <h>our of <> dead,
      1877: dead,
44.   MS: an [e]<E>agle half
      1877: an Eagle half
46.   MS: light,
      1877: the glory of light,
48.   MS, 1877: sight:
49.   1904: rest
61.   MS, 1877: crevice
62.   MS: two [illegible deletion of
      punctuation] <:>
64.   MS, 1877: boughs;
67.   MS: Scarlet or golden or
      1877: Scarlet or golden or blue
79.   MS: mend:
      1877: mend;
80.   MS, 1877: drop,—
81.   MS, 1877: Stop,—
86.   MS, 1877: rise
91.   MS, 1877: fire;

93.   MS, 1877: wings,
97.   MS, 1877: As Wind, with
100. MS: river:
101. MS: a [*sorrowful*] <desolate>
      moan
      1877: a sorrowful moan
105. MS, 1904: solace or dwelling or
107. MS: lion [illegible deletion]
      <&> vulture,
108. MS: To [*ot*] ostrich & jackal &
      1877: To ostrich and jackal and
      1904: ostrich and jackal and
111. MS, 1877, 1904: balm
113. MS, 1877: the Sea
114. MS, 1877: swaying,
116. MS: slaying:
120. MS, 1877: deep,—
121. MS, 1877: brawl,—
128. MS: While [*pe*] breaths
129. MS, 1877: desire,—
130. MS, 1877: fire,—
131. MS, 1877: glow,—

A BALLAD OF BODING.

[Date of composition unknown. Editions: *1881*, 1881a, 1890, 1904. The notebook
MS is in the Houghton Library, Harvard University.]

1.   MS: dreams:
4.   MS: barges [*went sailing toward
      the East*:] <of manifold
      adorning / Went sailing toward
      the East:>
10.   MS: flutes
11.   MS: guitars:
15.   MS: trumpeters,—
24.   MS: sceptre &
25.   MS: of [*dus*] earth
29.   MS: crew
35.   MS: sighing sweet <> low
40.   MS: sank I <> whither in <>
      plight
47.   MS: counter-tacking;
50.   MS: helm or sail or shroud;
52.   MS: [*Feasting th*] <Hoarding>
      to
53.   MS: <Feasting to their fill,>
57.   MS: pleasure:
58.   MS: [*A*] <The> sword [*went*]
      <flashed> cleaving
59.   MS: Sceptre[*s*] & crown[*s*]
      changed

61.   MS: different:
62.   MS: contrary
68.   MS: splashing
69.   MS: dashing
70.   MS: Down on them & up on
      them more
77.   MS: sight:
82.   MS: and [illegible deletion]
      <h>arpers round
84.   MS: shout:
86.   MS: eat &
90.   MS: man [*leap*] <plunge>
      overboard,
94.   MS: interchangeable:
95.   1904: another,—
96.   MS: Changed openly or
      changed by stealth
      1904: Like
97.   MS: (Like bloodless spectres
      some, some flushed by health),
98.   MS: To scale a <> side & scale
      it
102. MS: boat:

104.	MS: mount; &
106.	MS: companions
109.	1881a: the water-bed,
111.	MS: out
113.	1904: dim
115.	MS: ship:
127.	MS: waves:
129.	1904: deep open graves
134.	MS: deep,
136.	MS: third [*barge*] <bark> held
137.	MS: hoof;
138.	MS: [*Till I saw him take a flying leap onto its deck. / Then full of awe*] <Despite his urgent beck,>

142.	MS: awe
145.	MS: babe's new-born,
151.	MS: monotone[,]
157.	MS, 1881a: sore
178.	MS: abhorred
179.	MS: desire
180.	MS: worm [*up the*] infirm
183.	MS: gnashed:
191.	1904: threw;
197.	MS: sea;
198.	MS: voices
202.	MS: dying,—
203.	1904: me
209.	MS: strand
216.	MS: are

YET A LITTLE WHILE.

[Date of composition unknown. Editions: *1881*, 1881a, 1890, 1904. The MS is missing from the notebook in the University of Texas Humanities Research Center. The poem was published in *Dublin University Magazine,* NSI (January, 1878), 104. In the 1878 text, lines 5, 10, and 15 are indented four spaces.]

6.	1904: work,	12.	1878: side:

HE AND SHE.

[Date of composition unknown. Editions: *1881*, 1881a, 1890, 1904. The MS is in the British Library.]

3.	MS: do:—	7.	MS: do:—
	1904: do,	9.	MS: yet.

MONNA INNOMINATA. / A SONNET OF SONNETS.

[Date of composition unknown. Editions: *1881*, 1881a, 1890, 1904. The notebook MS is in the University of Texas Humanities Research Center.]

Title. MS: Monna Innominata / a
    Sonnet
Preface. MS: Beatrice immortalized
    <> cotanto "amante," Laura
    celebrated <> bard, have <>
    honour & <> charms but <>
    least to <> poets: & in <>
    both yet <> portrait <left us>
    might <> tender if less

[illegible deletion] <di>gnified
than <> us, in li[illegible
deletion]<eu> of the <>
feeling &
1881a: cotanto amante;" Laura,
1890: Beatrice, immortalised by
1904: ladies, 'donne
innominate,' sung

MONNA INNOMINATA. / 1.

[Date of composition unknown. Editions: *1881*, 1881a, 1890, 1904. The notebook MS is in the University of Texas Humanities Research Center. In the 1904 text, lines 12 and 14 are indented two spaces.]

Opening quotations. MS: addio.”
Dante. / < > vinci!” Petrarca.
1881a: “Lo di che
1904: addio.’ / DANTE. / < >
vinci!’ / PETRARCÁ.

1. MS: me who
3. MS: again
6. MS, 1904: sweetest “when”:
11. MS: waning waxing like

MONNA INNOMINATA. / 2.

[Date of composition unknown. Editions: *1881*, 1881a, 1890, 1904. The notebook MS is in the University of Texas Humanities Research Center.]

Title. MS: [The number 2 is written below the opening quotations.]
Opening quotations. MS: desio.”
Dante. / < > prima.” Petrarca.
1904: prima.’ / PETRARCA.

3. MS: season; it
4. MS: say:
8. MS: That should not
12. MS: much:

MONNA INNOMINATA. / 3.

[Date of composition unknown. Editions: *1881*, 1881a, 1890, 1904. The notebook MS is in the University of Texas Humanities Research Center.]

Title. MS: [The number 3 is written below the opening quotations.]
Opening quotations. MS:
l’aspetto!” Dante. / < >
conduce.” Petrarca.
1904: l’aspetto!’ / DANTE. / < >
conduce.’ / PETRARCA.

1. 1904: you, to
4. MS: As [s]<S>ummer ended
    1904: As, Summer ended,
    Summer
9. MS: one;
11. MS: give:
13. MS: live

MONNA INNOMINATA. / 4.

[Date of composition unknown. Editions: *1881*, 1881a, 1890, 1904. The notebook MS is in the Unversity of Texas Humanities Research Center.]

Title. MS: [The number 4 is written below the opening quotations.]
Opening quotations. MS:
seconda.” Dante. / “E < >
amore.” Petrarca.
1904: seconda.’ / DANTE. / < >
amore,’ / PETRARCA.

1. 1904: love,
4. 1904: most? My love
7. MS: be:—
9. MS: “thine”;
14. 1881a: Both of us of

MONNA INNOMINATA. / 5.

[Date of composition unknown. Editions: *1881*, 1881a, 1890, 1904. The notebook MS is in the University of Texas Humanities Research Center. In the 1904 text, lines 12 and 13 are not indented.]

Title. MS: [The number 5 is written below the opening quotations.]

Opening quotations. MS: [*"Amor che a nulla amato amar perdona." Dante.*] / <"Amor che a nulla amar perdona." Dante.> / <> spene." Petrarca.
1890: a nullo amato
1904: perdona.' / DANTE. / <> spene.' / PETRARCA.

1. MS: [*O my hearts*] / O my heart's heart &
2. MS: you;
4. MS: To Him Whose noble
    1904: free;
9. MS: you: but
10. 1904: can,
14. MS: woman [*at*] <is> the [*first was*] <helpmet> made

MONNA INNOMINATA. / 6.

[Date of composition unknown. Editions: *1881*, 1881a, 1890, 1904. The notebook MS is in the University of Texas Humanities Research Center.]

Title. MS: [The number 6 is written below the opening quotations.]

Opening quotations. MS: "Comprender [*di*] <de> l'amor <> scalda." Dante. / <> scioglia. Petrarca. 1904: scalda.' / DANTE. / <> scioglia.' / PETRARCA.
1. 1904: rebuke,—

3. MS: lost;
4. 1904: look,
5. MS: forsook:
6. MS: cost;
8. 1890: crook
10. MS: overmuch:
11. MS: too:

MONNA INNOMINATA. / 7.

[Date of composition unknown. Editions: *1881*, 1881a, 1890, 1904. The notebook MS is in the University of Texas Humanities Research Center. In the 1904 text, line 12 is indented two spaces.]

Title. MS: [The number 7 is written below the opening quotations.]

Opening quotations. MS: frutto." Dante / <> lui." Petrarca. 1904: frutto.' / DANTE. / <> lui.' / PETRARCA.
1. MS: me
2. 1904: for I love you': so

6. MS: desperately[,]<:>
7. MS: unmanned[;]<?>
8. 1904: liberty?—
9. MS: brave:—
11. MS: often: there's
12. MS: his book who saith
    1904: his Book who

MONNA INNOMINATA. / 8.

[Date of composition unknown. Editions: *1881*, 1881a, 1890, 1904. The notebook MS is in the University of Texas Humanities Research Center.]

Title. MS: [The number *8* is written
    below the opening quotations.]
Opening quotations. MS: calme."
    Dante. / <> perdono."
    Petrarca.

1904: a Dio, D'altro <>
    calme.' / DANTE. / <>
    perdono.' / PETRARCA.
1. MS: "I if I perish perish"—
12. MS: hand

MONNA INNOMINATA. / 9.

[Date of composition unknown. Editions: *1881*, 1881a, 1890, 1904. The notebook
MS is in the University of Texas Humanities Research Center. In the 1904 text, lines
11 and 14 are not indented, and lines 12 and 13 are indented two spaces.]

Title. MS: [The number *9* is written
    below the opening quotations.]
Opening quotations. MS: "[*Oh*] <O>
    dignitosa <> netta!"
    Dante. / <> ardenti." Petrarca.
    1904: ardenti.' / PETRARCA.

3. MS: excellence &
5. MS: who am so
7. 1904: (ah woe
10. MS: [illegible deletion]
    <B>ecause not loveless: love

MONNA INNOMINATA. / 10.

[Date of composition unknown. Editions: *1881*, 1881a, 1890, 1904. The notebook
MS is in the University of Texas Humanities Research Center.]

Title. MS: [The number *10* is written
    below the opening quotations.]
Opening quotations. MS: stella."
    Dante. / <> ora." Petrarca.
    1904: stella.' / DANTE. / <>
    ora." / PETRARCA.
1. MS: wing,
2. MS: apace,

5. MS: earth & <> sing,
6. MS: all [*speeds carolling,*]
    <uplifts his praise,>
7. MS: thanks for grace
9. MS: wanes: &
12. MS: while &
13. MS: while &

MONNA INNOMINATA. / 11.

[Date of composition unknown. Editions: *1881*, 1881a, 1890, 1904. The notebook
MS is in the University of Texas Humanities Research Center. In the 1904 text, lines
12 and 14 are not indented.]

Title. MS: [The poem is not
    numbered.]
Opening quotations. MS: genti."
    Dante. / <> nostra." Petrarca.
    1904: genti. / DANTE. / <>
    nostra.' / PETRARCA.

2. MS: her":—while
3. MS: play
5. MS: them speak: who
6. MS: love & parting <> pain;
8. MS: earth &

MONNA INNOMINATA. / 12.

[Date of composition unknown. Editions: *1881*, 1881a, 1890, 1904. The notebook MS is in the University of Texas Humanities Research Center.]

Title. MS: [The number *12* is written below the opening quotations.]
Opening quotations. MS: ragiona." Dante. / < > costei." Petrarca. 1904: 'Amor che < > ragiona.' / DANTE. / 'Amor < > costei.' / PETRARCA.

2. MS: to grieve
5. MS: face:
7. MS: crowned while < > weave
10. MS: delight:
11. MS: own
13. MS: Your honorable freedom

MONNA INNOMINATA. / 13.

[Date of composition unknown. Editions: *1881*, 1881a, 1890, 1904. The notebook MS is in the University of Texas Humanities Research Center. In the 1890 text, line 11 is indented two spaces. In the 1904 text, lines 12 and 13 are not indented.]

Title. MS: [The number *13* is written below the opening quotations.]
Opening quotations. MS: al Primo Amore." Dante. / < > braccia." Petrarca. 1904: al Primo Amore.' / DANTE. / < > braccia.' / PETRARCA.

2. MS: hand?—
3. MS: Without [*w*]<W>hose Will
4. MS: date:
9. MS: you
10. MS: love's good will
12. MS: dim:

MONNA INNOMINATA. / 14.

[Date of composition unknown. Editions: *1881*, 1881a, 1890, 1904. The notebook MS is in the University of Texas Humanities Research Center.]

Title. MS: [The number *14* is written below the opening quotations.]
Opening quotations. MS: pace." Dante. / < > chiome." Petrarca. 1904: pace.' / DANTE. / < > chiome.' / PETRARCA.

2. MS: this,—
4. MS: hair
5. MS: fair,[—]
6. MS: —Leave

"LUSCIOUS AND SORROWFUL."

[Date of composition unknown. Editions: *1881*, 1881a, 1890, 1904. The notebook MS is in the University of Texas Humanities Research Center.]

Title. MS: & [*S*]<s>orrowful"—.
2. MS: today: &
3. MS: tender,—what

6. MS: sea:
8. MS: Salt sea shore.

DE PROFUNDIS.

[Date of composition unknown. Editions: *1881*, 1881a, 1890, 1904. The notebook MS is in the Rossetti Collection of Janet Camp Troxell, Princeton University Library.]

7. MS: Yet [*she no*] even   11. MS: desire

TEMPUS FUGIT.

[Date of composition unknown. Editions: *1881*, 1881a, 1890, 1904. The notebook MS is in the University of Texas Humanities Research Center.]

Title. MS: Tempus fugit.   6. MS: past,—
 1. MS: Lovely Spring   9. 1904: blast.
 2. MS: thing   12. MS: upon:
 3. MS: wing,—   1904: upon.
 4. MS: Gracious Summer   15. 1904: done;
 5. MS: comer

GOLDEN GLORIES.

[Date of composition unknown. Editions: *1881*, 1881a, 1890, 1904. The notebook MS is in the University of Texas Humanities Research Center.]

5. 1904: daffodil;   9. MS: sweet heart of

JOHNNY. / FOUNDED ON AN ANECDOTE OF THE FIRST FRENCH REVOLUTION.

[Date of composition unknown. Editions: *1881*, 1881a, 1890, 1904. The notebook MS is in the University of Texas Humanities Research Center.]

Title. MS: the [*F*]<f>irst French   42. MS: And [*strong*] <apt> at
 2. MS: golden [*dandelion*;] <mop   43. MS: poor;
     in blow;>   44. MS: had [*he*] he
 3. MS: spread,   48. MS: loved yet
 4. MS: [*Dance & glance & stream out   50. MS: advice;
     flying,*] <In a glory & a glow,>   1904: would—he could—not
 7. MS: thick they   52. MS: price,
 8. MS: hung: 53. MS: clipped &
14. MS: he: 54. MS: silver or
28. MS: suffice: 57. MS: could
29. MS: sad   59. MS: locket!
31. MS: Now while he sat thinking,   61. MS: money,—tea
35. 1904: by,   65. MS: shorn
36. 1904: him, why did <> cry.   66. 1904: lamb new-born.
37. 1904: Alas his   69. 1904: oh when

"HOLLOW-SOUNDING AND MYSTERIOUS."

[Date of composition unknown. Editions: *1881*, 1881a, 1890, 1904. The notebook MS is in the University of Texas Humanities Research Center. In the MS, the poem is written in double columns on one page.]

Title. MS: mysterious"—.
2. 1904: sighing;
11. MS: fleeting,—
   1904: fleeting;—
14. MS: the [*w*]<W>ind's sighing.
18. MS: sinking swelling

22. MS: Never ah
23. MS: wiser,—
   1904: wiser.
28. MS: treasure
29. 1904: darkens.
33. 1904: wordless, flying

MAIDEN MAY.

[Date of composition unknown. Editions: *1881*, 1881a, 1890, 1904. The notebook MS is in the University of Texas Humanities Research Center.]

2. MS: flower
7. 1904: thorn,
9. 1904: corn,
10. MS: [*Not so*] <Much less> sweet
   in strength
   1904: Scentless, in
12. 1881a: of the gale,
13. MS: breath?—
14. MS: & perfect-pale,
15. MS: Yet so
17. MS: flower
21. MS: trills:
22. MS: only thrills
   1904: skylark, only,
23. 1904: earth,
27. 1904: delight
30. 1904: throne.
31. MS: sings a<> sing,
32. 1904: flight, below <> wing,

33. MS: flight,
38. MS: throne?—
41. MS: bower:
43. MS: prime
47. MS: along
49. MS: strong,
50. MS: As the shallows
54. MS: Wake & plead &
55. MS: Wisdom part &
59. MS: today &
65. MS: at "Why?"
71. 1904: mysteries;
73. MS: low,—
   1904: low:
74. 1904: vanities;
78. MS: days:
83. MS: Maiden May:
93. 1881a: loss;

TILL TOMORROW.

[Date of composition unknown. Editions: *1881*, 1881a, 1890, 1904. The notebook MS is in the University of Texas Humanities Research Center. In the MS, lines 5, 10, and 15 are indented two spaces.]

2. MS: [*Of*] [indented eight spaces] <Of> [indented four spaces] longing <> desire:
9. MS: [*Dre*] Dreams
10. MS: Glowworms that
   1904: gleaming,—

14. MS: [*Where*] <Thro'> cloud[*s*]<y> [*half*] cover;
   1904: cover;

DEATH-WATCHES.

[Date of composition unknown. Editions: *1881*, 1881a, 1890, 1904. The notebook MS is in the University of Texas Humanities Research Center. In the MS, lines 4, 6, 10, and 12 are indented four spaces, and lines 5 and 11 are indented two spaces.]

Title. MS: Death-watches.
4. MS: recall:

10. MS: dim:

TOUCHING "NEVER."

[Date of composition unknown. Editions: *1881*, 1881a, 1890, 1904. The notebook MS is in the University of Texas Humanities Research Center. In the MS, lines 12 and 14 are indented two spaces, and line 13 is indented four spaces.]

Title. MS: Touching "Never"—.
1. MS: me, Dear,

6. MS: daffodil[?]<;>
13. MS, 1904: me

BRANDONS BOTH.

[Date of composition unknown. Editions: *1881*, 1881a, 1890, 1904. The notebook MS is in the University of Texas Humanities Research Center.]

Title. MS: Brandons both.
5. MS: flowers but
6. MS: her songs but
7. MS: high summer her
8. MS: high summer her
9. MS: maid Milly:
    1904: secret, keep
14. MS: know but not every thing,
15. MS: plumage & <> an [*eaglet*] <egret>
16. MS: music &
17. MS: fair; but
19. MS: Oh but
22. MS: her Mother's eyes:
24. MS: where Love sets
25. MS: no Mother; & <> beyond [*most others*] <another>
26. MS: [*She*] <Is she> whose blessed Mother is
27. 1881a, 1904: a mother
28. MS: with all & <> all &
29. MS: terrace
33. MS: her Father's palace
36. MS: her Father's &
40. MS: the water fowl rise
41. MS: turns composed
42. MS: her Father's house
45. MS: "Good morrow, fair

cousin."—"Good morrow, fairest
46. MS: course & 1904: to-day:
47. MS: dozen;
48. MS: away."—
51. MS: upon the hill top & <> hollow
52. MS: sedge."—
53. MS: hawking
54. 1881a: bait towards the
55. MS: cousin: I
56. MS: of nothing & <> win."—
57. MS: hour
58. MS: sweet?——
60. MS: it."—
64. MS: mine & <> see."—
65. MS: reviving;
66. MS: own:
68. MS: gone."—
69. MS: "Goodbye, Milly Brandon: I <> you
70. MS: be goodbye between <> today:
72. MS: say."—
73. MS: "Goodbye, Walter.
75. MS: rose I
76. MS: thorn."—

A LIFE'S PARALLELS.

[Date of composition unknown. Editions: *1881*, 1881a, 1890, 1904. The notebook MS is in the University of Texas Humanities Research Center.]

 4. 1904: Never.   9. MS, 1881a: fainting, ruing,
 8. 1904: Ever.

AT LAST.

[Date of composition unknown. Editions: *1881*, 1881a, 1890, 1904. No MS known. In the 1904 text, lines 12 and 14 are indented two spaces.]

 12. 1904: change, and

GOLDEN SILENCES.

[Date of composition unknown. Editions: *1881*, 1881a, 1890, 1904. The notebook MS is in the University of Texas Humanities Research Center.]

Title. MS: Golden Silences   7. MS: not but
 1. MS: saith "ah me!"   8. MS: born:
   1904: saith 'Ah   12. MS: silent night:
 4. MS: death: 14. MS: Shall [*ho*] shout < > delight

IN THE WILLOW SHADE.

[Date of composition unknown. Editions: *1881*, 1881a, 1890, 1904. The notebook MS is in the University of Texas Humanities Research Center.]

Title.	MS: In the Willow shade.	26.	MS: above,
1.	MS: tree	27.	MS: words
2.	MS: calls,	34.	MS: by
3.	MS: me:	36.	MS: sky:
6.	1904: pass	38.	MS: air
7.	1881a, 1904: heliotrope,	39.	MS: away
8.	MS: wan lookingglass:	48.	MS: undone:
10.	1904: ill	52.	MS: night:
11.	MS: swim	57.	1881a: The weeping-willow
12.	MS: will:		shook
18.	MS: amain,	58.	MS: long,
19.	MS: sang a < > visible sky high	60.	MS: song,
20.	MS: again:	63.	MS: grieves:
22.	MS: track,	65.	MS: chill
23.	MS: lark	68.	MS: meant:
24.	MS: back:	69.	1881a: silvery weeping-willow
			tree

FLUTTERED WINGS.

[Date of composition unknown. Editions: *1881*, 1881a, 1890, 1904. The notebook MS is in the University of Texas Humanities Research Center.]

3. MS: way
10. MS: veiled &
11. MS, 1881, 1881a: of the awful stars,

15. MS: grief twin
20. MS: [*Are*] <Grow> dim

A FISHER-WIFE.

[Date of composition unknown. Editions: *1881*, 1881a, 1890, 1904. The notebook MS is in the University of Texas Humanities Research Center.]

Title. MS: A Fisher-wife.
2. MS: west:
    1904: west,
4. MS: in my [illegible deletion] breast.
5. 1904: wind, swoop
6. 1904: wind, linger
7. MS: forth

9. MS: For I've [*h*] a <> sea
10. MS: wood:—
11. MS: be:
12. MS: could,
14. MS: heart,
15. MS: harms
    1904: oh the
16. 1904: apart!

WHAT'S IN A NAME?

[Date of composition unknown. Editions: *1881*, 1881a, 1890, 1904. The notebook MS is in the University of Texas Humanities Research Center.]

3. MS: reason
4. MS: guess,—
6. 1904: hope, and
8. 1904: name,
11. MS: Soft-named Summer
12. MS: comer
14. MS: we [*think*] <dream> or
15. MS: sigh:
16. MS: then Summer wends <> way

1881a, 1904: then Summer wends
18. MS: Goodbye!
19. MS: lingers
21. MS: singers:
26. MS: all-lack Winter
34. MS: shine:
    1904: shine,
35. 1904: old.
36. MS: young

MARIANA.

[Date of composition unknown. Editions: *1881*, 1881a, 1890, 1904. The MS is missing from the notebook in the University of Texas Humanities Research Center.]

8. 1904: Ah sweet

MEMENTO MORI.

[Date of composition unknown. Editions: *1881*, 1881a, 1890, 1904. The notebook MS is in the University of Texas Humanities Research Center.]

2. MS: measure
4. MS: leaf:
8. MS: tomorrow,

9. MS: sore
10. MS: for [*ever more*] <evermore>:

"ONE FOOT ON SEA, AND ONE ON SHORE."

[Date of composition unknown. Editions: *1881*, 1881a, 1890, 1904. The notebook MS is in the University of Texas Humanities Research Center.]

Title. MS: "One foot on [*S*]<s>ea & one on shore."
1904: ONE <> SHORE
4. MS: again."—
6. MS: fishes [*dart*] skim
8. MS: again."—
15. MS: of lead

16. MS: again."—
17. MS: be;
19. MS: part
22. MS: plain:
23. MS: roses, let <> be;
1904: roses, let <> be,—
24. MS: again."—

BUDS AND BABIES.

[Date of composition unknown. Editions: *1881*, 1881a, 1890, 1904. The notebook MS is in the University of Texas Humanities Research Center.]

6. MS: One hope, by

BOY JOHNNY.

[Date of composition unknown. Editions: *1881*, 1881a, 1890, 1904. The notebook MS is in the University of Texas Humanities Research Center.]

4. MS: lady."—
8. MS: boy Johnny?"—

12. MS: lady?"—
16. MS: boy Johnny."—

FREAKS OF FASHION.

[Date of composition unknown. Editions: *1881*, 1881a, 1890, 1904. The notebook MS is in the University of Texas Humanities Research Center.]

3. MS: Nestlings guiltless
5. MS: Ask: "And
9. MS: them
10. MS: Gay Papas & grave Mammas
11. MS: nestlings:—
12. MS: gay Papas.
15. MS: Snug &
19. MS, 1904: "Neat grey hoods

20. MS: a Jackdaw: "Glossy grey,
1904: a Jackdaw: 'glossy grey,
21. MS: close yet
23. MS: mornings;
24. 1881a: *A la*
27. MS: Answer: "Hoods
29. MS: head-dresses curved <> crescents
1890, 1904: crescents

31. MS: yes: yet
33. 1881a: lustrous
     1904: the Peacock: 'gemmed
     and
34. MS: too sti[illegible
     deletion]<ff> &
51. MS: a Blackbird justly
52. MS: bill [*arigerous*:]
     <aurigerous:>
57. MS: somehow

58. MS: thick
60. 1904: And snapped-to his
63. MS: that Mammas felt
70. MS: peach:
72. MS: teach
73. MS: texture; elegance;
76. 1881: clime
77. MS: now let's <> ourselves:
78. MS: almost breakfast time."

AN OCTOBER GARDEN.

[Date of composition unknown. Editions: *1881*, 1881a, 1890, 1904. The notebook MS is in the University of Texas Humanities Research Center. The poem was published in *Athenaeum*, No. 2609 (October 27, 1877), 532.]

1. MS, 1877: my autumn garden
2. MS, 1877: roses:
4. MS: To autumn's languid
    1877: To autumn's languid <>
    rain,

9. MS: are [*P*] but
10. 1904: uncloses,

"SUMMER IS ENDED."

[Date of composition unknown. Editions: *1881*, 1881a, 1890, 1904. The notebook MS is in the University of Texas Humanities Research Center. In the 1904 text, lines 4 and 9 are indented eight spaces.]

Title. MS: "Summer is ended."
       1904: SUMMER <> ENDED
3. MS: knows?),

4. MS: bliss
6. 1904: comes the end,

PASSING AND GLASSING.

[Date of composition unknown. Editions: *1881*, 1881a, 1890, 1904. The notebook MS is in the University of Texas Humanities Research Center.]

2. MS: woman's lookingglass:—
6. MS: peach
10. MS: tiring-glass:—
14. 1904: lavender,
18. MS: wisdom's lookingglass

20. MS: Brim full of <> ill
     1904: Brimfull of
21. MS: will:—
22. MS: sun:
24. MS: be, was.

"I WILL ARISE."

[Date of composition unknown. Editions: *1881*, 1881a, 1890, 1904. The notebook MS is in the University of Texas Humanities Research Center.]

Title. MS: "I will arise"—.   18.   1890: Re-energise my
       1904: I < > ARISE   19.   MS: faith:
  1.   MS: weariness: 23.   MS: again:
  7.   MS: rest   24.   MS, 1904: best;
 10.   MS: Of longdrawn straining   27.   MS, 1881, 1881a: and listen to
 11.   MS: me: 30.   MS: prayers [illegible deletion of
 15.   MS: Of self-less love   punctuation] — O
 16.   1904: chill?

A PRODIGAL SON.

[Date of composition unknown. Editions: *1881*, 1881a, 1890, 1904. The notebook
MS is in the University of Texas Humanities Research Center. In the MS, lines 19
and 20 are indented two spaces.]

  1.   MS: my Father's [*H*] house   7.   MS: reap:
       1904: house   12.   MS: spare,
  3.   MS: boughs   13.   MS: purple winefat froths
  4.   MS: ray:

SOEUR LOUISE DE LA MISÉRICORDE. / (1674.)

[Date of composition unknown. Editions: *1881*, 1881a, 1890, 1904. The notebook
MS is in the University of Texas Humanities Research Center.]

Title. MS: la Miséricorde / (1674.).   13.   MS: desire,—
  1.   MS: have desired &   1904: desire:
       1904: been desired: 14.   1904: Alas my < > prickles!
  3.   MS, 1904: fire: 16.   MS: desire[*!*]<;>
  7.   MS: love a   1904: desire!
  9.   MS, 1904: measure: 18.   1904: my garden-plot to
 11.   MS: love's death bed, trickles,   19.   MS: Oh love struck dead, oh
       trickles

AN "IMMURATA" SISTER.

[Lines 1–12 and 17–24 composed in June, 1865. Date of composition of lines 13–
16 and 25–28, and of revision of lines 21–24, unknown. Editions: *1881*,1881a,
1890, 1904. The dated notebook MS (MS1) is in the British Library. The undated
notebook MS (MS2) is in the University of Texas Humanities Research Center. In
MS1, line 4 is indented four spaces. In MS2, lines 4, 16, and 28 are indented four
spaces. In the 1890 and 1904 texts, line 23 is not indented and line 24 is indented
two spaces.]

Title. MS1: En Route.   Wherefore art thou strange, and
       MS2: An "immurata" Sister.   not my mother?
  4.   MS1: [After line 4 are the   Thou hast stolen my heart
       following stanzas:]   and broken it:

Would that I might call thy sons
　　"My brother",
Call thy daughters "Sister
　　sweet";
Lying in thy lap not in another,
　　Dying at thy feet.
Farewell land of love, Italy,
　　Sister-land of Paradise:
With mine own feet I have
　　trodden thee,
　　Have seen with mine own
　　　　eyes;
I remember, thou forgettest me,
　　I remember thee.
Blessed be the land that warms
　　my heart,
　　And the kindly clime that
　　　　cheers,
And the cordial faces clear from
　　art,
　　And the tongue sweet in mine
　　　　ears:
Take my heart, its truest
　　tenderest part,
　　Dear land, take my tears.

5.　MS1, MS2: feel:
7.　1904: die,
13.　MS1: [Lines 13–16 are not in
　　　the text.]
　　　MS2: Hearts & souls by
14.　MS2: Hushed awhile their
　　　praises & their sighs;
20.　MS1: mind.
　　　MS2: mind:

21.　MS1: Our words have been
　　　already said,
　　　MS2: [*For words have been already
　　　said,*] <The world hath sought
　　　& I have sought,—>
22.　MS1: Our deeds have been
　　　already done:
　　　MS2: [*Our deeds have been already
　　　done;*] <Ah empty world &
　　　empty I!>
　　　1904: Ah empty
23.　MS1: [*Yet life runs past though slow
　　　to run,*] <There's nothing new
　　　beneath the sun> [Deletion and
　　　revision are in pencil in
　　　Christina's handwriting.]
　　　MS2: [*There's nothing new beneath
　　　the sun,*] <For we have spent our
　　　strength for nought,>
24.　MS1: [*And*] <But> there is
　　　peace among the dead.
　　　[Deletion and revision are in
　　　pencil in Christina's
　　　handwriting. A short horizontal
　　　line is centered below the line.]
　　　MS2: [*But there is peace among the
　　　dead.*] <And soon it will be time
　　　to die.>
25.　MS1: [Lines 25–28 are not in
　　　the text.]
　　　MS2: [*Hearts*] [s]<S>parks fly
28.　MS2: whole burnt offering!

"IF THOU SAYEST, BEHOLD, WE KNEW IT NOT." / 1.

[Date of composition unknown. Editions: *1881*, 1881a, 1890, 1904. The notebook
MS is in the University of Texas Humanities Research Center.]

Title.　MS: "If thou sayest, Behold, we
　　　　knew it not"—. Proverbs 24.11,
　　　　12.
4.　1904: race I run,
5.　MS: undone:
6.　1904: fly,

7.　1904: by,
8.　1904: sun!
11.　MS: so?—
12.　MS: Lord Jesus Christ my <>
　　　pity Thou:

"IF THOU SAYEST, BEHOLD, WE KNEW IT NOT." / 2.

[Date of composition unknown. Editions: *1881*, 1881a, 1890, 1904. The notebook MS is in the University of Texas Humanities Research Center.]

  7. MS: undo: Lord,
13. MS: forget?—
      1904: yea how

"IF THOU SAYEST, BEHOLD, WE KNEW IT NOT." / 3.

[Date of composition unknown. Editions: *1881*, 1881a, 1890, 1904. The notebook MS is in the University of Texas Humanities Research Center.]

  6. MS: heal:—
13. MS: sake not our's supply
      1904: not ours, supply

14. MS: sake not our's, [*Lord*]
      <Christ>, pity
      1904: not ours, Christ,

THE THREAD OF LIFE. / 1.

[Date of composition unknown. Editions: *1881*, 1881a, 1890, 1904. The notebook MS is in the University of Texas Humanities Research Center.]

  4. 1904: 'Aloof, <> stand aloof; so
  7. MS: free,
  8. MS: thy heart, what
      1904: touch thy heart? what
      hand thy hand?'—

12. MS: cold
13. MS: gold

THE THREAD OF LIFE. / 2.

[Date of composition unknown. Editions: *1881*, 1881a, 1890, 1904. The notebook MS is in the University of Texas Humanities Research Center. In the 1881a text, line 7 is indented four spaces.]

  4. MS: where the [*s*] gay
10. 1904: sigh,

11. 1904: Thinking, Why

THE THREAD OF LIFE. / 3.

[Date of composition unknown. Editions: *1881*, 1881a, 1890, 1904. The notebook MS is in the University of Texas Humanities Research Center.]

  7. MS: his s[*ei*]<ie>ve;
  8. MS: own when Saints break

13. 1904: sing, O Death, where
14. 1904: sing, O

AN OLD-WORLD THICKET.

[Date of composition unknown. Editions: *1881*, 1881a, 1890, 1904. The notebook MS is in the University of Texas Humanities Research Center. In the MS, line 65 is indented two spaces, and lines 5 and 10 are not indented. In the 1881a and 1904 texts, lines 5 and 10 are not indented.]

Title.	MS: An old-world Thicket.	107.	MS: peaceful [*p*] bed < > term:
	Opening quotation. MS: "*Oltre* il	108.	MS: worm,—
	mezzo cammin di nostra vita"—.	109.	MS: grief,—
	Dante.	110.	MS: haply, always;
	1904: 'Una	112.	1881a: feel is passing, passing
7.	MS: or warmer tinted sycomore,		1904: feel, is
	1881a: warmer-tinted sycamore,	123.	MS: I trembling cling
11.	MS: desire:	124.	MS: perpetual Now?——
15.	MS: seemed &	125.	MS: deathless void < >
16.	MS: made, such [*sweetness*]		stop[*?*]<,>
	<warblings> &	129.	MS: From eve to
	1904: chat,	130.	MS: Of promises which had no
17.	MS: a well tuned beak,	131.	MS: The wood & < > of the
21.	MS: [*The shade wherein they*		wood
	revell] / Their	132.	MS: undertone:
23.	MS: dew which	134.	1904: rustling, where
33.	MS: everywhere	135.	MS: compassion on my
35.	1904: Root fathom-deep and	138.	MS: burned
36.	MS, 1904: said	139.	MS: less
38.	MS: one who<m> [illegible	142.	MS: music yet
	deletion] fears	143.	MS: harmony:
	1904: oppress,	147.	MS: sky:
40.	MS: the [*lack*] <dearth> of	148.	MS: high,
	bread:	149.	MS: [*Ho*] <Had> stooped < >
43.	MS: to [*he*] yearning		earth in
62.	MS: which):	151.	1881a: Each water-drop made
69.	MS: [*Adown*] Sheer < > steep,	158.	MS: noon
72.	MS: hear:	162.	MS: west,
79.	MS: In-gathering wrath	163.	MS: mother-bird & mate-bird &
80.	MS: In-gathering wrath	164.	MS: Nestling & < > nest
81.	MS: revolt	167.	MS: them &
82.	MS: hate;	175.	MS: together journeying
85.	MS: shakes &	176.	MS: bleating one
87.	MS: desire:	177.	MS: west:
89.	1904: eyes, that	178.	MS: by face &
90.	MS: depth &	179.	MS: Patient, sunbrightened too,
104.	MS: die		

"ALL THY WORKS PRAISE THEE, O LORD." / A PROCESSIONAL OF CREATION.

[Date of composition unknown. Editions: *1881*, 1881a, 1890, 1904. The notebook MS is in the University of Texas Humanities Research Center. In the MS, the names of the speakers are not centered but begin at the left margin of the line.]

Title. MS: "All Thy Works praise
Thee,
1904: ALL < > LORD
1. MS: *All* / I all-Creation sing
2. MS: days
4. MS: *Seraph* / I,
5. MS: is Love & < > me,
6. MS: The Holy Holy Holy
7. MS: *Cherub* / I,
8. MS: is Wisdom & < > me,
9. MS: The Holy Holy Holy
10. MS: *All Angels* / We
11. MS: pleasure:
1881a: we, brimmed
13. MS: *Heavens* / We
16. MS: *Firmament* / I blue [*a*] <&>
beautiful &
17. MS: fair:
18. MS: His Glory by
19. MS: *Powers* / We < > strong:
22. MS: *Sun* / I
25. MS: *Moon* / I < > do His Will:
27. 1881a: strait, His
28. MS: *Stars* / We
31. MS: *Galaxies & Nebulae* / No < >
near: &
34. MS: *Comets & Meteors* / Our
35. MS: glow,
37. MS: *Showers* / We < > ourselves:
&
40. MS: *Dews* / We
41. MS: grace:
43. MS: *Winds* / We < > earth:
46. MS: *Fire* / My
49. MS: *Heat* / I < >
52. MS: *Winter & Summer* / Our
55. MS: *Spring & Autumn* / I
60. MS: *Frost* / I
63. MS: *Cold* / I
1881a: slothful, apt
66. MS: *Snow* / My
69. MS: *Vapours* / We
70. MS: The good-Will of
72. MS: *Night* / Moon
74. MS, 1904: feet Who
75. MS: *Day* / I < > before Him, in
78. MS: *Light & Darkness* / I am
God's dwelling place,—
82. MS: of God most High.
83. MS: *Lightning & Thunder* / We
86. MS: *Clouds* / Sweet < > store
exhaled

89. MS: *Earth* / I
92. MS: *Mountains* / Our
93. MS: Him Higher than
94. MS: God Higher than
95. MS: *Hills* / We green tops praise
97. MS: We green tops praise
1881a: from out beds.
98. MS: *Green Things* / We all
[*g*]<G>reen Things, we
99. MS: brushwood, [*seeds*] <corn>
&
101. MS: *Rose,—Lily,—Violet* / I
1904:ROSE—LILY—
VIOLET / I
104. MS: *Apple,—Citron,—
Pomegranate* / We
1881a: We, Apple-blossom,
1904: APPLE—CITRON—
POMEGRANATE / We
105. 1881a: We, clothed
107. MS: *Vine,—Cedar,—Palm* / I
1904: VINE—CEDAR—
PALM / I
109. 1904: before His Judgment seat.
110. MS: *Medicinal Herbs* / I
114. MS: pitiful Will, &
115. MS: *Wells* / Clear
116. 1904: still;
118. MS: *Sea* / Today
120. MS: to His [*g*]<G>race.
121. MS: *Floods* / We
123. 1890: We fertilise the
124. MS: *Whales & Sea Mammals* / We
1904: sight,
127. MS: *Fishes* / Our
130. MS: *Birds* / Winged
133. MS: *Eagle & Dove* / I
134. 1881a: the Dove,
136. 1881a: above
137. MS: *Beasts & Cattle* / We
139. MS: border-loving
[*c*]<C>reatures of
141. MS: *Small Animals* / God
144. MS: *Lamb* / I
147. MS: *Lion* / I
150. MS: *All Men* / All
153. MS: *Israel* / Flock
156. MS: *Priests* / We
1881a: sheep, and
159. MS: *Servants of God* / We
162. MS: *Holy & Humble Persons* / All
[*holy*] <humble> souls

163. MS: calls, to
165. MS: *Babes* / He
171. MS: *Women* / God
174. MS: *Men* / God
177. MS: *Spirits & Souls*— / Lo,
      1904: Lo in
180. MS: *of Babes* / With

183. MS: *of Women* / We
186. MS: *of Men* / We praise His Will
      Who [illegible deletion] bore
187. MS: strong
189. MS: *All* / Let every thing that
191. MS: Praise God, praise God,
      praise God, His Creature saith.

LATER LIFE: A DOUBLE SONNET OF SONNETS.

[Date of composition unknown. Editions: *1881*, 1881a, 1890, 1904. The notebook MS is in the Huntington Library.]

Title. MS: Later Life: / a double
        Sonnet of Sonnets.

LATER LIFE. / 1.

[Date of composition unknown. Editions: *1881*, 1881a, 1890, 1904. The notebook MS is in the Huntington Library.]

3. 1904: be God when

7. 1904: evermore,

LATER LIFE. / 2.

[Date of composition unknown. Editions: *1881*, 1881a, 1890, 1904. The notebook MS is in the Huntington Library. In the 1904 text, lines 12 and 14 are indented two spaces.]

4. 1904: won nor < > wins,
6. 1881a: Or left

9. 1881a: to-day, while < > to-day,
10. MS: avail,—

LATER LIFE. / 3.

[Date of composition unknown. Editions: *1881*, 1881a, 1890, 1904. The notebook MS is in the Huntington Library. In the 1904 text, lines 12 and 14 are not indented.]

3. 1904: tearless numbness of
9. 1881a: us Thine, then < > are;

10. 1881a: redemption, we

LATER LIFE. / 4.

[Date of composition unknown. Editions: *1881*, 1881a, 1890, 1904. The notebook MS is in the Huntington Library.]

Title. MS: [*Today*] / [*3*] <4.>
4. MS: way;
7. 1904: Ah always
8. MS: toil & [*strife*] [*strive*] <aim>
    as

14. MS: [Below the poem, written in
     pencil by Christina:] "I would
     tell you more, but I am tired—"

LATER LIFE. / 5.

[Date of composition unknown. Editions: *1881*, 1881a, 1890, 1904. The notebook MS is in the Huntington Library.]

 8. MS: anything but
 9. MS: O Love, accept according
    1904: O Love, accept,
 10. MS: [*O*] [not indented] <O>

    [indented] Love, exhaust
    fulfilling
    1904: O Love, exhaust,
 13. MS: unkindled Fire

LATER LIFE. / 6.

[Date of composition unknown. Editions: *1881*, 1881a, 1890, 1904. The notebook MS is in the Huntington Library.]

LATER LIFE. / 7.

[Date of composition unknown. Editions: *1881*, 1881a, 1890, 1904. The notebook MS is in the Huntington Library.]

 13. 1881a: the heart of
    1904: sufficed

LATER LIFE. / 8.

[Date of composition unknown. Editions: *1881*, 1881a, 1890, 1904. The notebook MS is in the Huntington Library.]

 2. 1904: in Thee,
 7. MS: me:
 13. MS: breath
    1881a: breath;
 14. MS: love Thee & <> see Thee
    eyes. [The second "Thee" is

    underlined in pencil, and there
    is a question mark in pencil in
    the right margin.]
    1881: see Thee eyes.
    1881a: love Thee; and <> see
    Thee, eyes.

LATER LIFE. / 9.

[Date of composition unknown. Editions: *1881*, 1881a, 1890, 1904. The notebook MS is in the Huntington Library.]

Title. MS: [*"One Star differeth from
   another Star."*] / 9. [Above the
   deleted title, written in pencil by
   Christina:] —the stars in Night's
   pale fillet wrought / Gleam
   undividably—".
 2. 1904: strength.
 4. MS: from [*its*] <a> flaming
    Car;

 5. MS: upon [*its*] <a> throne
 7. MS: to [*be*] <reign> the
 9. MS: They [*feel*] <own> no
 12. MS: their [*courses*] <orbits>
    pitched
 13. MS: whose [*breadth*] <depth> &

LATER LIFE. / 10.

[Date of composition unknown. Editions: *1881*, 1881a, 1890, 1904. The notebook MS is in the Huntington Library. In the MS, lines 1, 2, and 3 of the footnote are indented two spaces, four spaces, and six spaces respectively.]

  9. MS: thy Maker's word:
10. 1904: slain.'

14. MS: nest.* / "Quali

LATER LIFE. / 11.

[Date of composition unknown. Editions: *1881*, 1881a, 1890, 1904. The notebook MS is in the Huntington Library.]

  3. MS: witness "God
      1904: good,'

  9. MS: desire,

LATER LIFE. / 12.

[Date of composition unknown. Editions: *1881*, 1881a, 1890, 1904. The notebook MS is in the Huntington Library. In the 1904 text, lines 12 and 14 are indented two spaces.]

11. MS: sweets & < > far
12. MS: relished more & < >
      desired

14. MS: untired &

LATER LIFE. / 13.

[Date of composition unknown. Editions: *1881*, 1881a, 1890, 1904. The notebook MS is in the Huntington Library.]

  2. MS: grace
  6. MS: One [*good thing*] <virtue>
      pent

  7. MS: fight &
12. MS: Nevertheless men

LATER LIFE. / 14.

[Date of composition unknown. Editions: *1881*, 1881a, 1890, 1904. The notebook MS is in the Huntington Library. In the 1904 text, lines 12 and 13 are not indented.]

  1. 1904: left Paradise,

  6. MS: to fulfi[*ll*]<l>

LATER LIFE. / 15.

[Date of composition unknown. Editions: *1881*, 1881a, 1890, 1904. The notebook MS is in the Huntington Library.]

3.   MS: the enquiring snake,   13.   MS: dominant clenched
6.   1881a, 1904: and hers to   embrace
10. MS: so: as < > ill

LATER LIFE. / 16.

[Date of composition unknown. Editions: *1881*, 1881a, 1890, 1904. The notebook MS is in the Huntington Library.]

9.   MS: & wit[*t*]<1>ess, in   13.   MS: fasting &
10. MS: good
12. MS: half this world's long-beaten
     ways,

LATER LIFE. / 17.

[Date of composition unknown. Editions: *1881*, 1881a, 1890, 1904. The notebook MS is in the Huntington Library. In the 1904 text, lines 12 and 14 are indented two spaces.]

Title. MS: [*Befogged.*] / 17.   12.   MS: new,—
6.   MS: Ah, pleasant   14.   MS: [Below the poem is an
11. MS: [*I*] [indented four spaces]   undecipherable line, perhaps in
     <I> [indented two spaces] < >   Italian, written in pencil in
     & all I [*do,*] <see>   Christina's hand.]

LATER LIFE. / 18.

[Date of composition unknown. Editions: *1881*, 1881a, 1890, 1904. The notebook MS is in the Huntington Library. Lines 9–14 originally formed the sestet of a sonnet entitled "Cor Mio," which Christina never published as such. "Cor Mio" is presented in its own right in Volume III of the present edition, but for purposes of comparison it is also included here. Since the location of the MS of "Cor Mio" is unknown, the text given below is that found in William Michael Rossetti (ed.), *New Poems by Christina Rossetti Hitherto Unpublished or Uncollected* (London and New York: Macmillan, 1896), 168.]

COR MIO

Still sometimes in my secret heart of
    hearts
I say "Cor mio" when I remember
    you,
And thus I yield us both one tender
    due
Welding one whole of two divided
    parts.

Ah Friend, too wise or unwise for
    such arts,
Ah noble Friend, silent and strong
    and true,
Would you have given me roses for
    the rue
For which I bartered roses in love's
    marts?

So late in autumn one forgets the
    spring,
Forgets the summer with its
    opulence,
The callow birds that long have found
    a wing,
The swallows that more lately got
    them hence:
Will anything like spring, will
    anything
Like summer, rouse one day the
    slumbering sense?

Title. MS: [*Late*] [<*A Heart's*>]
    [*Autumn.*] / [*19*] <18>.
1. MS: asleep;
2. MS: pale[;]<:>
9. "Cor Mio": in autumn one < >
    the spring,
10. MS: the [*s*]<S>ummer with
    "Cor Mio": the summer with
12. "Cor Mio": lately got them
13. "Cor Mio": like spring, will
14. "Cor Mio": Like summer, rouse

LATER LIFE. / 19.

[Date of composition unknown. Editions: *1881*, 1881a, 1890, 1904. The notebook MS is in the Huntington Library.]

Title. MS: [*Zero.*] / 19.
9. 1904: flowers, and fruit, and
    < > song,
10. MS: Remain: the
    1904: nights,

11. MS: long hang
12. MS: too long:
13. MS: weak, [*but strengthens*]
    <while strengthening> still

LATER LIFE. / 20.

[Date of composition unknown. Editions: *1881*, 1881a, 1890, 1904. The notebook MS is in the Huntington Library.]

6. MS: sing them &
10. 1904: birds;

11. 1904: wise,

LATER LIFE. / 21.

[Date of composition unknown. Editions: *1881*, 1881a, 1890, 1904. The notebook MS is in the Huntington Library.]

1. MS: trust: I take [*the*]
8. 1881a: senses wide-awake.
11. MS: need

14. MS: For May that < > glowed
    opulent as June.

LATER LIFE. / 22.

[Date of composition unknown. Editions: *1881*, 1881a, 1890, 1904. The notebook MS is in the Huntington Library. In the MS, line 8 is not indented, line 9 is indented two spaces, line 10 is indented four spaces, and lines 11 and 12 are indented six spaces.]

3. MS: delight:
6. 1881a: Forever unrenewed
7. MS: night
10. MS: us [*b*] we
    1904: us, we

11. MS: of forgetmenot:
13. MS: went,

LATER LIFE. / 23.

[Date of composition unknown. Editions: *1881*, 1881a, 1890, 1904. The notebook MS is in the Huntington Library. In the MS, line 13 is indented four spaces.]

1. 1881a, 1904: know stretch < >   3.   1904: see stretch
    unknown,   9.   MS: dead [*a*] <&> living
2. 1890: green,   14. MS: we gaze beyond

LATER LIFE. / 24.

[Date of composition unknown. Editions: *1881*, 1881a, 1890, 1904. The notebook MS is in the Huntington Library.]

Title. MS: [*Doubleminded.*] / 24.   14. MS: O fool [Below the poem is
2.   1881a: Dear blessèd Heaven,   an erased line.]
13. MS: Half-choosing,   1904: quest!
     wholly-missing, the

LATER LIFE. / 25.

[Date of composition unknown. Editions: *1881*, 1881a, 1890, 1904. The notebook MS is in the Huntington Library.]

2. MS: not &   11. MS: again[?]<:>
    1881a: not, and is; how   14. MS: part[?]<?>
6. MS, 1881a: treasures mourned

LATER LIFE. / 26.

[Date of composition unknown. Editions: *1881*, 1881a, 1890, 1904. The notebook MS is in the Huntington Library.]

Title. MS: [*Veiled Death.*] [deleted in   3.   MS: unfulfilled, of every thing
        ink and pencil] / 26.   7.   MS: like Spring
        [Above the title is an illegible   10. MS: is set < > pilgrimage
        pencil erasure, over which is   14. MS: not [*d*]<D>eath.
        written in pencil by Christina:]
        <Resurgam>

LATER LIFE. / 27.

[Date of composition unknown. Editions: *1881*, 1881a, 1890, 1904. The notebook MS is in the Huntington Library.]

Title. MS: [*Memento Mori.*] / [illegible   1.   MS: of death:—what
        deletion] 27. [Above the title:]   2.   MS: dream but
        [<*"My flesh & my heart*   1904: truth,
        faileth"—>]   3.   MS: all death's adjuncts

5. MS: last goodbye,
10. MS: slow breaths &
11. 1881a: supine, with
12. 1881a: glaze, with heart-pulse running down,

1904: with heart- / pulse running
14. MS: [Below the poem is an erased ink line.]

LATER LIFE. / 28.

[Date of composition unknown. Editions: *1881*, 1881a, 1890, 1904. The notebook MS is in the Huntington Library.]

11. 1881a: us, with <> heart,
    1890: heart
    1904: heart,

12. MS: Brimfull of
13. MS: Brimfull of
14. MS: Brimfull of

"FOR THINE OWN SAKE, O MY GOD."

[Date of composition unknown. Editions: *1881*, 1881a, 1890, 1904. The notebook MS is in the University of Texas Humanities Research Center. In the MS, lines 6, 12, and 18 are indented two spaces.]

Title. MS: "For Thine own sake, O my God."
       1904: FOR <> GOD

13. 1904: my maker,
16. 1904: infirmity;

UNTIL THE DAY BREAK.

[Date of composition unknown. Editions: *1881*, 1881a, 1890, 1904. The notebook MS is in the University of Texas Humanities Research Center.]

Title. MS: Until the Day break.
7. MS: pale.
9. MS: fail:
11. 1904: glory,
12. 1881a: Tenfold, fifty-fold, hundred-fold;

24. MS: down,—
28. MS: toilers, [*m*]<M>y weary, [*m*]<M>y weepers,

"OF HIM THAT WAS READY TO PERISH."

[Date of composition unknown. Editions: *1881*, 1881a, 1890, 1904. The notebook MS is in the University of Texas Humanities Research Center.]

Title. MS: "Of him that was ready to perish."
3. MS: hath [*nowhere*] <not where> to

7. MS: sun [*has gone*] went down in
15. MS: love [*&*] &
16. 1904: friend,—
17. MS: [*Who hast said "Take on thee*

[*m*]<*M*>*y yoke & learn of*
Me,"] / <Who hast said "Come
to Me & I will give thee rest,">
19. 1881a: come to Thee
20. MS: on Thy Breast,

21. MS: sorrowing
22. MS: own,
23. MS: alone
30. MS: extremity, cry
31. 1904: to Paradise, also me,

"BEHOLD THE MAN!"

[Date of composition unknown. Editions: *1881*, 1881a, 1890, 1904. The notebook MS is in the Huntington Library.]

Title. 1904: BEHOLD <> MAN
2. MS: first
    1881a: earth, and
    1904: earth, and hell, stood

3. MS: counted curs[']<e>d;
11. 1904: cheeks on flame.
14. 1904: tearful night watches.

THE DESCENT FROM THE CROSS.

[Date of composition unknown. Editions: *1881*, 1881a, 1890, 1904. The notebook MS is in the University of Texas Humanities Research Center.]

"IT IS FINISHED."

[Date of composition unknown. Editions: *1881*, 1881a, 1890, 1904. The notebook MS is in the University of Texas Humanities Research Center.]

Title. MS: "It is finished."
    1904: IT <> FINISHED
2. 1881a: things thou hast

31. 1904: always—me
34. 1904: death hell and lay
45. 1881a: me bring back

AN EASTER CAROL.

[Date of composition unknown. Editions: *1881*, 1881a, 1890, 1904. The notebook MS is in the University of Texas Humanities Research Center.]

10. 1904: a thorn.
18. MS: Angels & Men & Birds & Everything.

"BEHOLD A SHAKING." / 1.

[Date of composition unknown. Editions: *1881*, 1881a, 1890, 1904. The notebook MS is in the University of Texas Humanities Research Center.]

Title. MS: "Behold a shaking." / 1.
1. MS: doom [*which*] <that> shall
2. MS: each[*?*]<;>
    1904: dread—the <> each?

11. MS: evermore

"BEHOLD A SHAKING." / 2.

[Date of composition unknown. Editions: *1881*, 1881a, 1890, 1904. The notebook MS is in the University of Texas Humanities Research Center.]

1. 1881a: Blessèd that
2. 1881a: Blessèd this
    1904: ways.

7. MS: solace for,
    1904: for behold it
10. MS: the startingpoint whence

ALL SAINTS.

[Date of composition unknown. Editions: *1881*, 1881a, 1890, 1904. The notebook MS is in the University of Texas Humanities Research Center.]

1. MS: are [*co*]<fl>ocking from
6. 1890: lion.
8. 1904: burning.
15. 1904: [No stanza break follows the line.]
19. MS: counting:
21. MS: Like innumerable[*s*] bees
22. 1904: humming,
24. 1881a, 1904: Many-tinted,
25. 1881a, 1904: Many-scented,

31. MS: the hill tops sunny,—
33. MS: when [*its*] <in> strength
35. MS: [Sets to shore;] It sets to shore;
    1904: shore.
38. MS: shore,
    1904: shore;
39. MS, 1904: Unlike
41. MS, 1904: roar.
44. 1904: and South;

"TAKE CARE OF HIM."

[Date of composition unknown. Editions: *1881*, 1881a, 1890, 1904. The notebook MS is in the University of Texas Humanities Research Center.]

Title. MS: "Take care of him."
2. MS: "Lovest
28. 1881a: sufferer, Thee.

29. MS: last upon
32. MS: to Me."—

A MARTYR. / THE VIGIL OF THE FEAST.

[Date of composition unknown. Editions: *1881*, 1881a, 1890, 1904. The notebook MS is in the University of Texas Humanities Research Center.]

Title. MS: A Martyr: / the Vigil
7. MS: darkened Pillar cast,
    1904: cast
8. MS: gracious Eyes all-seeing
15. MS: day &
18. 1904: followeth.'
26. 1904: dare,—
33. 1881a: stage?
45. MS: own wine settled upon its lees?
47. MS: gone:—
55. MS: now:—

62. MS, 1904: my grey Father
63. MS: me who
65. MS, 1904: day sits
69. MS: fro
70. 1904: helplessness,
75. MS: sea
76. MS: forlorn,
    1904: forlorn.
83. 1881a: to Thy Blessèd Name.
84. 1881a: from thy bliss
85. MS: down upon me, shrinking from the

87.	MS: flame	121.	1881a: Am I, that
89.	MS: a gazingstock,	122.	1881a: ago, a little, little
90.	MS: eyes while	128.	MS: dies;
96.	MS: forth Thy [s]<S>oul for	130.	MS: wakes &
98.	MS: part	131.	MS: lips
103.	1904: sight.	136.	MS: slow Blood [*priceless*]
107.	1904: care.		priceless
110.	MS: Abhorred lest	137.	MS: me &
112.	MS: sweet &	139.	MS: north

WHY?

[Date of composition unknown. Editions: *1881*, 1881a, 1890, 1904. The notebook MS is in the University of Texas Humanities Research Center.]

1.	MS: me	8.	1904: agony?'—
	1904: 'Lord,	9.	MS: lovest Me
2.	MS: days:		1904: 'Bride
	1904: days?	13.	MS: thee
3.	MS: into Heaven, to	14.	1904: satisfied.'
6.	MS: praise:		
	1904: praise?		

"LOVE IS STRONG AS DEATH."

[Date of composition unknown. Editions: *1881*, 1881a, 1890, 1904. The notebook MS is in the University of Texas Humanities Research Center.]

Title.	MS: "Love is strong as Death."	7.	MS: Yea,
	1904: LOVE <> DEATH	10.	MS: thee;—
1.	1890, 1904: I have not sought		

BIRCHINGTON CHURCHYARD.

[Date of composition unknown. Editions: 1888a, *1890*, 1904. No MS known. The poem was published in *Athenaeum*, No. 2844 (April 29, 1882), 538.]

4.	1888a: chalky, weedy	12.	1882: neither fast nor

ONE SEA-SIDE GRAVE.

[Composed February 6, 1853. Editions: 1888a, *1890*, 1904. The dated notebook MS (MS1) is in the Bodleian Library. A fair copy (MS2) is owned by Christopher Erb. The poem was published in *Century Magazine*, XXVIII (May, 1884), 134. The second stanza of MS1 contains a delete sign and a vertical line, both written in pencil in the right margin.]

Title.	MS1: From the Antique.	1.	MS1: [The following stanza
	MS2: One Seaside Grave.		opens the poem:]

I wish that I were dying,
Deep-drowsing without pain:
I wish that I were lying
Below the wind and rain,
Never to rise again.

1. MS1: Forgetful of
2. MS1: Forgetful of < > thorn;

3. MS1: So sleeping, as reposes
4. MS1: a child until the dawn,
   MS2: corn:—
5. MS1: So sleeping without morn.
7. MS1: set;
9. MS1: forget,—
   MS2: forget,

BROTHER BRUIN.

[Date of composition unknown. Editions: 1888a, *1890*, 1904. No MS known.]

5. 1904: wood,
7. 1888a: There, cottage
15. 1888a: gruffest, bluffest
23. 1888a: faster.
24. 1904: Ah could
32. 1904: vain;
33. 1904: pain,
35. 1888a: growled; he
36. 1888a: coaxed,—that
45. 1888a: Friends; but
    1904: Friends, but

46. 1888a: him but
47. 1888a: door, which
48. 1888a: on,—a < > sinner,
    1904: sinner,
49. 1888a: Toothless, and
51. 1888a: (The rate-payers not
52. 1888a: spare;
    1904: spare.
53. 1888a: hungry, gaunt
55. 1888a: Indeed, I < > so, for
56. 1888a: relented,

"A HELPMEET FOR HIM."

[Date of composition unknown. Editions: 1888a, *1890*, 1904. No MS known.]

Title. 1904: A < > HIM
1. 1888a: delight,—
2. 1888a: Charm, O woman!

7. 1904: stays by
9. 1888a: gloom, and

A SONG OF FLIGHT.

[Date of composition unknown. Editions: 1888a, *1890*, 1904. A fair copy is in the British Library.]

1. 1888a: sleep,
2. MS: The Sun leaps
   1888a: deep,—
   1904: deep—
3. 1888a: Daylight < > leap,—
   1904: Daylight
6. 1888a, 1904: play—
7. MS: —Golden hair will turn to
   grey!—
   1888a, 1904: If

8. 1888a: away,
10. 1888a: goal, wherever
12. 1888a: prize;
    1904: prize,—
13. MS: —The Sun flies, the Wind
    flies,—
    1888a: The sun flies, the wind
    flies,
    1904: The Sun

A WINTRY SONNET.

[Date of composition unknown. Editions: 1888a, *1890*, 1904. No MS known. The poem was published in *Macmillan's Magazine*, XLVII (April, 1883), 498.]

1.	1904: said: 'The	6.	1904: wane.'
2.	1904: again.'	7.	1904: said: 'I
3.	1904: said: 'These	8.	1888a: main.
4.	1904: rain.'		1904: main.—'
5.	1883: The round moon	9.	1888a: When springtime came,
	1904: said: 'These	14.	1888a: blue,—yet

RESURGAM.

[Date of composition unknown. Editions: 1888a, *1890*, 1904. No MS known. The poem was published in *Athenaeum*, No. 2831 (January 28, 1882), 124.]

6.	1888a: with Time, and	11.	1882: unbreathable pure air,
8.	1888a: Will, Love,—a	12.	1888a: dead,—
9.	1888a: seek;		

TODAY'S BURDEN.

[Date of composition unknown. Editions: 1888a, *1890*, 1904. No MS known. The poem was published in T. Hall Caine (ed.), *Sonnets of Three Centuries: A Selection, Including Many Examples Hitherto Unpublished* (London: Elliot Stock, 1882), 190.]

1.	1888a: rest."	9.	1888a: Unrest, the
2.	1888a: Oh, burden < >	10.	1882: broadcast on all human
	burdens,—still		kind, on
3.	1904: depart nor		1888a: humankind,—on
4.	1888a: west,	11.	1888a: die.
	1904: thus from East to West,		1904: live—for, living, < > die.
6.	1882, 1888a, 1904: guise.	12.	1888a, 1904: man.
8.	1888a, 1904: manifest		

"THERE IS A BUDDING MORROW IN MIDNIGHT."

[Date of composition unknown. Editions: 1888a, *1890*, 1904. No MS known.]

3.	1888a: bright.	10.	1888a: everything
9.	1888a: own;	11.	1888a: Grown or blown

EXULTATE DEO.

[Date of composition unknown. Editions: 1888a, *1890*, 1904. No MS known.]

4.	1888a: along,—	8.	1888a: desire;
6.	1904: humble peaceful	9.	1888a: praise,

A HOPE CAROL.

[Date of composition unknown. Editions: 1888a, *1890*, 1904. No MS known. The poem was published in *Century Guild Hobby Horse*, No. 10 (April, 1888), 41.]

1.	1888a: day was near; 1904: near;	15.	1888a: sings,—
7.	1888a: sing,— 1904: see the birds	18.	1888a: not to-night;
		19.	1888a, 1904: pray,
10.	1888a, 1904: day,	21.	1888a: fire,
		22.	1888a: light,

CHRISTMAS CAROLS. / 1.

[Date of composition unknown. Editions: 1888a, *1890*, 1896, 1904. No MS known. The poem was published in *Century Guild Hobby Horse*, No. 5 (January, 1887), 1.]

Title.	1887: A CHRISTMAS CAROL. 1896: A CHRISTMAS CAROL	7.	1888a, 1904: replying, 1896: in heaven with < > replying,
1.	1896, 1904: nighest		
3.	1888a, 1896: like palm-boughs waving	8.	1896: good and < > for Christ is best."
4.	1896: [No stanza break follows the line.]		

CHRISTMAS CAROLS. / 2.

[Date of composition unknown. Editions: 1888a, *1890*, 1904. A fair copy is in the Rossetti Collection of Janet Camp Troxell, Princeton University Library. In the MS, the poem is written in double columns on one page.]

Title.	MS: A Christmas Carol.	26.	MS: a [*v*]< V >oice
1.	MS, 1904: holy heavenly	27.	MS: baby-noise?
9.	1888a: praise,—	28.	1888a: might:
12.	1888a: state.	29.	MS: "'Let < > light',—& 1888a: 'Let < > be light' and 1904: "Let
14.	MS: & enfold		
16.	MS: love		
17.	MS: above	33.	MS: of mortal heart?
18.	MS: Beholding God, 1888a: their God look down.	34.	1888a, 1904: smart,
		36.	MS: see, His
19.	MS: a crown	37.	MS: us awhile
21.	MS: weak,	38.	MS: kin:
22.	MS: tender [*c*]< C >heek,	40.	MS: To bring His
23.	MS: small [*h*]< H >and? 1888a: soft, small	42.	MS: salute:— 1888a: salute.
24.	MS: which spanned	43.	1888a: sing;
25.	MS: was planned.		

CHRISTMAS CAROLS. / 3.

[Date of composition unknown. Editions: 1888a, *1890*, 1904. No MS known.]

1.	1888a: newborn Jesus,	26.	1888a: newborn Jesus,
16.	1888a: things,		

A CANDLEMAS DIALOGUE.

[Date of composition unknown. Editions: 1888a, *1890*, 1904. No MS known.]

1.	1888a: down; and	15.	1888a: thou?"
11.	1888a: death; but	18.	1888a: raise, and
14.	1904: My Cross, balm-bearing	28.	1888a: still;

MARY MAGDALENE AND THE OTHER MARY. / A SONG FOR ALL MARIES.

[Date of composition unknown. Editions: 1888a, *1890*, 1904. No MS known.]

1.	1888a: rest;	9.	1888a: reap:
2.	1888a: weep.	10.	1888a: crest;
3.	1888a: west;		

PATIENCE OF HOPE.

[Date of composition unknown. Editions: 1888a, *1890*, 1896, 1904. No MS known. The poem was published in W. Walsham How, Ashton Oxenden, and John Ellerton (eds.), *The Children's Hymn Book for Use in Children's Services, Sunday Schools and Families, Arranged in Order of the Church's Year* (London: Rivington's, [1881]), 212–13. In the 1881 text, the poem is numbered *260* and the stanzas are numbered *1, 2,* and *3*; line 3 is indented four spaces. In the 1904 text, line 2 is indented two spaces and line 3 is indented four spaces.]

Title.	1881: *"Thou art the same, and Thy years shall not fail."*	5.	1881: lovely spring is new
	1896: THOU ART THE SAME AND THY YEARS SHALL NOT FAIL		1888a: lovely spring is
			1896, 1904: new
1.	1881, 1896, 1904: shade,	7.	1881, 1896, 1904: strength,
2.	1881: dew;	10.	1881: shore,
	1896, 1904: dew—	11.	1896, 1904: curled
4.	1881: sing,	14.	1881, 1896, 1904: only Thou,
		16.	1881, 1896, 1904: The same to
		18.	1881, 1896: to Thee. Amen.

"ALONE LORD GOD, IN WHOM OUR TRUST AND PEACE"

[Date of composition unknown. Editions: 1892, *1893*, 1904. In the 1892 text, lines 10 and 14 are not indented, and lines 11 and 12 are indented two spaces.]

11.   1892: pray:

"SEVEN VIALS HOLD THY WRATH: BUT WHAT CAN HOLD"

[Date of composition unknown. Editions: 1892, *1893*, 1904. In the 1892 text, line 12 is indented four spaces, and line 14 is indented two spaces. In the 1904 text, lines 12 and 14 are indented two spaces.]

2.   1904: own Infinitude,

"WHERE NEITHER RUST NOR MOTH DOTH CORRUPT."

[Date of composition unknown. Editions: 1892, *1893*, 1904. In the 1904 text, lines 12 and 14 are indented two spaces.]

Title.   1892: [untitled]
       1904: Where < > corrupt.

"AS THE SPARKS FLY UPWARDS."

[Date of composition unknown. Editions: 1892, *1893*, 1904. In the 1904 text, lines 12 and 14 are indented two spaces.]

Title.   1892: [untitled]
       1904: As < > upwards.
2.   1904: desire
4.   1904: in Thy Name,

7.   1904: nigher,
8.   1904: being, to
10.   1892: nothing: they
11.   1892, 1904: that blessed place

"LORD, MAKE US ALL LOVE ALL: THAT WHEN WE MEET"

[Date of composition unknown. Editions: 1892, *1893*, 1904. In the 1892 text, line 11 is indented two spaces and line 12 is not indented.]

1.   1904: meet,
2.   1904: earth's myriads, at
5.   1892, 1904: around Thy blessed
    Feet,

9.   1904: Oh if
14.   1892: the vision Beatifical.

"O LORD, I AM ASHAMED TO SEEK THY FACE"

[Date of composition unknown. Editions: 1892, *1893*, 1904. In the 1892 text, lines 10 and 13 are not indented, and lines 11 and 12 are indented two spaces.]

"IT IS NOT DEATH, O CHRIST, TO DIE FOR THEE"

[Date of composition unknown. Editions: 1892, *1893*, 1904.]

7.   1892: hand

"LORD, GRANT US EYES TO SEE AND EARS TO HEAR"

[Date of composition unknown. Editions: 1892, *1893*, 1904. In the 1892 text, lines 11 and 14 are indented two spaces, and line 13 is not indented.]

1. 1892: hear
7. 1892: where there chanting [In the list entitled "Errata" that precedes the "Prefatory Note" to the volume, Christina states of line 12: "*for* there *read* their."] (1893): where their chanting

"CRIED OUT WITH TEARS."

[Date of composition unknown. Editions: 1892, *1893*, 1904. In the 1892 text, lines 11 and 12 are indented two spaces, and line 14 is not indented.]

"O LORD ON WHOM WE GAZE AND DARE NOT GAZE"

[Date of composition unknown. Editions: 1892, *1893*, 1904.]

6. 1892: Kind Lord, companion of

"I WILL COME AND HEAL HIM."

[Date of composition unknown. Editions: 1892, *1893*, 1904.]

Title. 1892: [untitled]
5. 1904: goal

"AH LORD, LORD, IF MY HEART WERE RIGHT WITH THINE"

[Date of composition unknown. Editions: 1892, *1893*, 1904. In the 1892 text, line 13 is indented two spaces. In the 1904 text, lines 12 and 14 are indented two spaces.]

"THE GOLD OF THAT LAND IS GOOD."

[Date of composition unknown. Editions: 1892, *1893*, 1904.]

Title. 1892: [untitled]
1904: The < > good.

"WEIGH ALL MY FAULTS AND FOLLIES RIGHTEOUSLY"

[Composed February 26, 1854. Editions: 1885, 1886a, *1893*, 1904. The notebook MS is in the Bodleian Library. In the MS and the 1904 text, lines 12 and 14 are not indented.]

Title. MS: "The blood of Jesus Christ cleanseth from all sin."
3. MS: Make the scale deep, O
4. MS: Yea, let the accuser stand hard by, to
5. MS: All are remembered that belong
6. MS: life my judgement < > begin;
   1885, 1886a: the judgment may
7. MS: And Thou mayest know how
8. MS: My soul that it may rest, O God, with Thee.
9. MS: counterpoise—
10. MS: day!—
11. MS: What shall I < > voice?—
12. MS: But drop < > in that scale one drop alone
13. MS: From Thy pierced Heart, my God, and
14. MS: The world, my sins, my very heart

"LORD, GRANT ME GRACE TO LOVE THEE IN MY PAIN"

[Date of composition unknown. Editions: 1885, 1886a, *1893*, 1904. In the 1885 and 1886a texts, lines 11 and 13 are indented two spaces, and line 14 is not indented.]

5. 1885, 1886a: wane.
6. 1904: perfect Will,
13. 1885, 1886a: hungering, thirsting, longing

"LORD, MAKE ME ONE WITH THINE OWN FAITHFUL ONES"

[Date of composition unknown. Editions: 1892, *1893*, 1904.]

3. 1892: flee
4. 1892: orisons:
5. 1892: runs
9. 1904: Ah my belovèd ones

"LIGHT OF LIGHT."

[Date of composition unknown. Editions: 1892, *1893*, 1904.]

Title. 1892: [untitled]
   1904: Light of Light.
1. 1892: our Light Whom
5. 1892: see;
6. 1904: or be gone

"THE RANSOMED OF THE LORD."

[Date of composition unknown. Editions: 1892, *1893*, 1904.]

Title. 1892: [untitled]
   1904: The < > the Lord.
12. 1892: boundless love of
15. 1892: spark, O Jesus, from

"LORD, WE ARE RIVERS RUNNING TO THY SEA"

[Date of composition unknown. Editions: 1892, *1893*, 1904.]

"AN EXCEEDING BITTER CRY."

[Date of composition unknown, Editions: 1892, *1893*, 1904. In the 1904 text, line 6 is indented two spaces.]

Title. 1892: [untitled]   14.   1892: and God, Lord
        1904: An < > cry.

"O LORD, WHEN THOU DIDST CALL ME, DIDST THOU KNOW"

[Date of composition unknown. Editions: 1892, *1893*, 1904.]

    3.   1892: view,
   16.   1892: Good Lord Who
         1904: know,

"THOU, GOD, SEEST ME."

[Date of composition unknown. Editions: 1892, *1893*, 1904. In the 1892 text, no lines are indented.]

Title. 1904: Thou, < > me.   13.   1892: —Without
    1.   1904: me that   17.   1892: prove My love's excess."—
    7.   1892: —Without   19.   1892: —Without

"LORD JESUS, WHO WOULD THINK THAT I AM THINE?"

[Date of composition unknown. Editions: 1885, 1886a, *1893*, 1904.]

    2.   1904: Ah who < > think,
    5.   1885: fast, tho'
         1886a: fast though

"THE NAME OF JESUS."

[Date of composition unknown. Editions: 1885, 1886a, *1893*, 1904.]

Title. 1885, 1886a: FEAST OF THE   3.   1885, 1886a: plead Thy life with
        NAME OF JESUS.   4.   1885, 1886a: plead Thy death, I
        1904: The < > of Jesus.

"LORD GOD OF HOSTS, MOST HOLY AND MOST HIGH"

[Date of composition unknown. Editions: 1885, 1886a, *1893*, 1904. In the 1885 text, lines 4, 8, 12, and 16 are indented eight spaces. In the 1886a text, lines 4, 8, 12, and 16 are indented twelve spaces. In the 1893 text, line 14 is not indented.]

    1.   1885, 1886a: of Hosts most   high> [The revision is in pencil
   13.   1885, 1886a: thing in the sky   in Christina's handwriting.]
         1885r: thing [*in the sky*] <hid on

"LORD, WHAT HAVE I THAT I MAY OFFER THEE?"

[Date of composition unknown. Editions: 1885, 1886a, *1893*, 1904.]

1.	1886a: offer thee? 1904: 'Lord,	12.	1885, 1886a: Clean-handed, lovely < > uplift. 1904: uplift.'—
2.	1885, 1886a: see. 1904: see.'—	13.	1904: 'Nay,
3.	1904: 'What	14.	1885, 1886a: thee. 1904: thee.'—
7.	1904: small;		
8.	1885, 1886a: all. 1904: all.'—	15.	1904: 'Ah Lord Who
9.	1904: 'I	16.	1904: give I Thee.'

"IF I SHOULD SAY 'MY HEART IS IN MY HOME'"

[Date of composition unknown. Editions: 1885, 1886a, *1893*, 1904.]

3.	1885: Where Jesu sits: for no where else 1886a: Where Jesu sits:	7.	1885, 1886a: from Jesu risen < > save,
		9.	1904: I too deny
4.	1885, 1886a: treasure, dwells	12.	1885, 1886a: art:

"LEAF FROM LEAF CHRIST KNOWS"

[Date of composition unknown. Editions: 1881, *1893*, 1904.]

"LORD, CARRY ME.—NAY, BUT I GRANT THEE STRENGTH"

[Date of composition unknown, Editions: 1892, *1893*, 1904.]

6. 1904: goal who
12. 1892: [No stanza break follows the line.]

"LORD, I AM HERE.—BUT, CHILD, I LOOK FOR THEE"

[Date of composition unknown. Editions: 1892, *1893*, 1904. In the 1892 text, lines 2, 4, 6, 8, 10, 12, and 14 are indented two spaces.]

"NEW CREATURES; THE CREATOR STILL THE SAME"

[Date of composition unknown. Editions: 1892, *1893*, 1904. In the 1892 text, lines 12 and 13 are indented two spaces, and line 14 is not indented. In the 1904 text, lines 13 and 14 are not indented.]

3. 1904: decree
5. 1904: same; and

"KING OF KINGS AND LORD OF LORDS."

[Date of composition unknown. Editions: 1892, *1893*, 1904. In the 1904 text, lines 12 and 14 are indented two spaces.]

Title. 1892: KING <> LORDS.
        1904: King <> lords.
   1.   1904: ointment pourèd forth
   2.   1892: love Thee: King
        1904: love Thee—King

   4.   1892: All Cherubs and all
        wheels which
   7.   1892: fashionings;
  12.   1892: And ever-springing
        ever-singing wave,

"THY NAME, O CHRIST, AS INCENSE STREAMING FORTH"

[Date of composition unknown. Editions: 1892, *1893*, 1904. In the 1892 and 1904 texts, lines 4 and 8 are indented two spaces.]

   1.   1892: as ointment is poured
        forth

   2.   1892: Sweetening our
   5.   1892: and Yea,

"THE GOOD SHEPHERD."

[Date of composition unknown. Editions: 1892, *1893*, 1904.]

Title. 1892: [untitled]
        1904: The Good Shepherd.
   1.   1904: 'O
   8.   1904: nine?'
   9.   1893: stay my bleeding

        1904: 'How <> stay my
        bleeding
  10.   1893, 1904: hush my pleading
  16.   1904: nine.'

"REJOICE WITH ME."

[Date of composition unknown. Editions: 1892, *1893*, 1904.]

Title. 1892: [untitled]
        1904: with Me.
   1.   1904: 'Little <> thee?'—
   2.   1904: 'I <> other.'—
   3.   1904: 'Little <> thee?'—

   4.   1904: 'Jesus,
   6.   1904: desire?'—
   7.   1904: 'Still
   9.   1904: nigher.'

"SHALL NOT THE JUDGE OF ALL THE EARTH DO RIGHT?"

[Date of composition unknown. Editions: 1885, 1886a, *1893*, 1904. In the 1885 text, lines 4 and 8 are indented four spaces.]

   2.   1885, 1886a, 1904: nay.

"ME AND MY GIFT: KIND LORD, BEHOLD"

[Date of composition unknown. Editions: 1892, *1893*, 1904. In the 1892 text, lines 4 and 11 are indented four spaces.]

   1.   1892: gift; kind

   2.   1892: sift:

"HE CANNOT DENY HIMSELF."

[Date of composition unknown. Editions: 1892, *1893*, 1904.]

Title. 1892: [untitled]
  2. 1892: Whether he show < >
      hell,
      1904: hell,

  6. 1904: say 'Depart,'
12. 1892: "Come" on
13. 1892: "Come" unto
19. 1904: still,

"SLAIN FROM THE FOUNDATION OF THE WORLD."

[Date of composition unknown. Editions: 1892, *1893*, 1904.]

Title. 1892: [untitled]
      1904: Slain < > world.

  2. 1892, 1904: end, look
  7. 1892: blasting, thundering

"LORD JESU, THOU ART SWEETNESS TO MY SOUL"

[Date of composition unknown. Editions: 1892, *1893*, 1904.]

"I, LORD, THY FOOLISH SINNER LOW AND SMALL"

[Date of composition unknown. Editions: 1892, *1893*, 1904.]

  1. 1904: 'I,
  9. 1904: Alas what
10. 1892: me! alas!
      1904: Alas alas
11. 1892: yet more.—
      1904: yet more!'—
12. 1904: 'Nay,

22. 1904: do.'—
23. 1904: 'Lord,
27. 1904: grace.'—
28. 1904: 'Not
30. 1904: day.
33. 1904: thou Me.'

"BECAUSE HE FIRST LOVED US."

[Date of composition unknown. Editions: 1892, *1893*, 1904. In the 1892 text, lines 4, 8, 12, and 16 are indented four spaces.]

  1. 1904: 'I
  4. 1904: first?'—
  5. 1904: 'Feed
  8. 1904: thee.'—

  9. 1904: 'Yea,
12. 1904: day.'—
13. 1904: 'Let
16. 1904: thee.'

"LORD, HAST THOU SO LOVED US, AND WILL NOT WE"

[Date of composition unknown. Editions: 1892, *1893*, 1904.]

  1. 1892: us: and
  5. 1892: saints, cry

  7. 1892: many crowns, beyond

"AS THE DOVE WHICH FOUND NO REST"

[Date of composition unknown. Editions: 1892, *1893*, 1904. In the 1892 text, lines 4, 8, 12, and 16 are indented four spaces. In the 1893 text, line 15 is indented two spaces.]

1. 1904: dove, which
2. 1892: For sole of

11. 1892: of love,
12. 1892: save;

"THOU ART FAIRER THAN THE CHILDREN OF MEN."

[Date of composition unknown. Editions: 1885, 1886a, *1893*, 1904.]

Title. 1885, 1886a: [untitled]
1904: Thou < > men.

1. 1904: of Christ,
5. 1886a: the Valley, He,

"AS THE APPLE TREE AMONG THE TREES OF THE WOOD."

[Date of composition unknown. Editions: 1892, *1893*, 1904.]

Title. 1892: [untitled]

"NONE OTHER LAMB, NONE OTHER NAME"

[Date of composition unknown. Editions: 1892, *1893*, 1904. In the 1892 text, lines 4, 8, and 12 are indented four spaces.]

10. 1904: art, however

"THY FRIEND AND THY FATHER'S FRIEND FORGET NOT."

[Lines 1–8 composed August 26, 1859; date of composition of lines 9–16 unknown. Editions: 1885, 1886a, *1893*, 1904. The notebook MS is owned by Mrs. Geoffrey Dennis. The first stanza originally formed part of a poem entitled "'Then they that feared the Lord spake often one to another,'" which Christina never published as such. "'Then they that feared the Lord spake often one to another" is presented in its own right in Volume III of the present edition. In the MS, lines 1, 4, and 7 are indented two spaces, and lines 2, 3, 5, 6, and 8 are not indented. In the 1904 text, lines 3, 5, 9, 11, and 15 are not indented, and lines 4, 10, and 16 are indented two spaces.]

Title. MS: "Then they that feared the Lord spake often one to another."
1885, 1886a: [untitled]
1904: Thy < > not.
1. MS: Friend I < > to thee the
3. MS: the love-feast of < > day
5. MS: This world is old and < > core

6. MS: Here death's heads mock us with a toothless grin
1885, 1886a: hollow death's-heads mock
7. MS: us spent and
8. MS: We heap up treasures for the fretting moth,
9. MS: [Lines 9–16 are not in the

text; the remainder of the MS text is as follows:]

Our children heap our fathers
 heaped before,
 But what shall profit us the
  cumbrous growth?
It cannot journey with us, cannot
 save,
Stripped in that darkness be we lief
 or loth
 Stripped bare to what we are from
  all we have,
Naked we came, naked we must
 return
To one obscure inevitable grave.
 If this the lesson is which we must
  learn

Taught by God's discipline of love or
 wrath
(To brand or purify His fire must
 burn)—
 Friend I commend to thee the
  narrow path
That thou and I, please God, may
 walk therein,
May taste and see how good is God
 Who hath
 Loved us while hating even to
  death our sin.

11. 1885, 1886a: us; not
14. 1885, 1886a: answer "nay" to
15. 1885, 1886a: say "nay" when

"SURELY HE HATH BORNE OUR GRIEFS."

[Lines 1–8 composed probably after March 7, 1853, and before May 9, 1853. Date of composition of lines 9–14 unknown. Editions: 1885, 1886a, *1893*, 1904. The notebook MS is in the Bodleian Library. In the MS the lower portion of the page—containing the remainder of the poem after line 13, and the date of composition—is missing.]

Title. MS: "Like as we are."
 1885, 1886a: [untitled]
 1893: griefs.
 1904: Surely < > griefs.
1. MS: His Heart hath bled for me,
 when mine < > sore;
 1893: mine sore;
2. MS: And when my
3. MS: lay His Head,
4. MS: When I am weary, He was
 weary more.
5. MS: I suffer what He suffered
 long before,
 1904: drink He
6. MS: He dreaded the same
 anguish that I

9. MS: [The remainder of the
 extant portion of the MS reads
 as follows:]

 Lord Thou hast wept for me, so
  teach mine eyes;
  Break my heart, Lord, Who
   wouldst not spare Thine
   Own;
 Lead me the thorny road to Paradise,
  Thou Who didst wear the mocking
   <thorns> for me:—
 Flesh of Thy Flesh, O Lord, bone
  of Thy Bone,

12. 1885, 1886a: fret, or faint, or

"THEY TOIL NOT, NEITHER DO THEY SPIN."

[Date of composition unknown. Editions: 1892, *1893*, 1904.]

Title. 1892: [untitled]
 1904: They < > spin.

5. 1904: a ploughed-up field
8. 1892: to Thy word. Amen.

"DARKNESS AND LIGHT ARE BOTH ALIKE TO THEE"

[Date of composition unknown. Editions: 1885, 1886a, *1893*, 1904. In the 1885 and 1886a texts, line 14 is not indented. In the 1885r text, a line is drawn to indicate that line 14 should be indented two spaces.]

7.	1904: to breath so	12.	1885, 1886a: finding, seek
11.	1904: Yea Thou	13.	1904: oh that

"AND NOW WHY TARRIEST THOU?"

[Date of composition unknown. Editions: 1892, *1893*, 1904.]

Title.	1892: [untitled]	4.	1892: sorrow,
2.	1892: my God, to Thee:	14.	1892: far:
3.	1892: to-morrow		

"HAVE I NOT STRIVEN, MY GOD, AND WATCHED AND PRAYED?"

[Composed September 30, 1863. Editions: 1885, 1886a, *1893*, 1904. The notebook MS is in the British Library. In the MS and in the 1885, 1886a, and 1904 texts, lines 12 and 14 are indented two spaces.]

Title.	MS: Have I not striven?—	8.	MS: When in the dark at last my
1.	MS: my God, have I not prayed,		1885, 1886a: reach, my
3.	MS: Why is Thy face still turned away from	9.	MS: [illegible deletion] <And> piteous
	1885, 1886a: Wherefore dost Thou still turn Thy Face from		1885, 1886a, 1904: blame,
4.	MS: Is Thine arm shortened that Thou [illegible deletion] <c>anst not	10.	MS: [*Whis*] [out to left margin] <Whis>pering [indented two spaces] together of <> loss,—
5.	MS: Or is the load of one more sinner laid	11.	MS: for me one time didst <> the cross,
6.	MS: On Thee, too heavy a load for even Thee?	12.	MS: Lord wilt [*t*]<T>hou turn
7.	MS: not, look but	13.	MS: in Thy glory hide away my shame
			1885, 1886a: in Thy glory bring

"GOD IS OUR HOPE AND STRENGTH."

[Date of composition unknown. Editions: 1892, *1893*, 1904. In the 1904 text, lines 7 and 9 are indented two spaces, and lines 8 and 10 are not indented.]

Title.	1892: [untitled]	6.	1904: [No stanza break follows the line.]
	1904: God <> and Strength.		
1.	1892: below: but	7.	1892: ground:

"DAY AND NIGHT THE ACCUSER MAKES NO PAUSE"

[Date of composition unknown. Editions: 1892, *1893*, 1904. In the 1892 text, lines 6 and 12 are not indented.]

3. 1892: flaws: 7.   1892: our Jesu makes

"O MINE ENEMY"

[Date of composition unknown. Editions: *1893*, 1904.]

14. 1904: Thy Love, in

"LORD, DOST THOU LOOK ON ME, AND WILL NOT I"

[Date of composition unknown. Editions: 1892, *1893*, 1904. In the 1893 text, line 7 is not indented.]

2. 1892: on Thee?—   10.   1893: Thy heart is

"PEACE I LEAVE WITH YOU."

[Date of composition unknown. Editions: 1892, *1893*, 1904. In the 1904 text, lines 4 and 8 are indented two spaces.]

Title. 1892: [untitled]
˜   1904: Peace < > you.

"O CHRIST OUR ALL IN EACH, OUR ALL IN ALL!"

[Composed September 28, 1862. Editions: 1885, 1886a, *1893*, 1904. The notebook MS is in the British Library. In the MS no lines are indented.]

Title. MS: Hold Thou me up.
1. MS: O Christ mine All in all, mine All
3. MS: An honoured teacher, a long-worked-for end: 1885, 1886a: teacher, a long-worked-for end:
4. MS: or were Paul,
5. MS: Or name, or fame, or
6. MS: Thee only will < > love, Thee only seek,
7. MS: Tread in Thy Footsteps, hearken
8. MS: in all my
9. MS: A craving trembling traitor

<trembling fawning tyrant> unto [The added words are above the line in pencil in Christina's handwriting.]
11. MS: Tho' outer darkness clutch me as its thrall,
12. MS: Tho' I be <sink> flooded with the utmost sea, [The added word is above the line in pencil in Christina's handwriting.]
13. MS: rise, Thou h[o]<e>lping, when
14. MS: fast yet

"BECAUSE THY LOVE HATH SOUGHT ME"

[Date of composition unknown. Editions: 1892, *1893*, 1904.]

   1. 1892: (Because   8. 1892: for Thine?)

"THY FAINTING SPOUSE, YET STILL THY SPOUSE"

[Date of composition unknown. Editions: 1892, *1893*, 1904.]

   6. 1892: Recall Thy love, if

"LIKE AS THE HART DESIRETH THE WATER BROOKS."

[Date of composition unknown. Editions: 1892, *1893*, 1904. In the 1893 text, line 20 is not indented.]

Title. 1892: [untitled]   3. 1892: And stoop low
       1904: Like < > brooks.   19. 1892: unknown untold,
   2. 1892: heart;

"THAT WHERE I AM, THERE YE MAY BE ALSO."

[Date of composition unknown. Editions: 1892, *1893*, 1904.]

Title. 1892: [untitled]   9. 1892: know: for < > so:
       1904: That < > also.   11. 1892: O Lord Christ Whom
   2. 1892: morning-glories and   12. 1892: O Lord Christ Who
      heartease and   13. 1892: fair:
   4. 1892: know: but < > so: 14. 1892: so:
   7. 1892: eyes;

"JUDGE NOT ACCORDING TO THE APPEARANCE."

[Date of composition unknown. Editions: 1892, *1893*, 1904.]

Title. 1892: [untitled]   4. 1892: [No stanza break follows
       1904: Judge < > appearance.   the line.]
   1. 1892: Lord, grant us eyes   7. 1892: word

"MY GOD, WILT THOU ACCEPT, AND WILL NOT WE"

[Date of composition unknown. Editions: 1892, *1893*, 1904.]

   7. 1893: lost for Thee, Whose   1904: lost for Thee Whose
      love is   love is

"A CHILL BLANK WORLD. YET OVER THE UTMOST SEA"

[Date of composition unknown. Editions: 1892, *1893*, 1904.]

   5.   1904: [No stanza break follows
       the line.]

"THE CHIEFEST AMONG TEN THOUSAND."

[Date of composition unknown. Editions: 1892, *1893*, 1904.]

Title. 1892: [untitled]   3.   1892: Palm-branch its
       1904: The < > thousand.

ADVENT SUNDAY.

[Date of composition unknown. Editions: 1885, 1886a, *1893*, 1904.]

   1.   1885: cometh:—go   11.   1885, 1886a: Veiled she
   4.   1885, 1886a: midnight black   13.   1885, 1886a: the presence of
      < > pitch   18.   1885: cometh:—go

ADVENT.

[Date of composition unknown. Editions: 1885, 1886a, *1893*, 1904. In the 1885 and 1886a texts, lines 2, 4, 5, 7, 9, and 11 are indented two spaces.]

Title. 1885, 1886a: [untitled]   3.   1885, 1886a: unseen,—
   1.   1885, 1886a: old yet

"SOONER OR LATER: YET AT LAST"

[Date of composition unknown. Editions: 1881, *1893*, 1904.]

  21.   1904: earth wrapt in   26.   1881: name

CHRISTMAS EVE.

[Date of composition unknown. Editions: 1885, 1886a, *1893*, 1904. The MS readings are taken from the facsimile in *Books Manuscripts Bindings and Autograph Letters Remarkable for Their Interest & Rarity Being the Five Hundred and Fiftyfifth Catalogue Issued by Maggs Bros* (London: Maggs Bros, 1931), p. 183. The facsimile is of the undated *Verses* notebook MS. In the MS, lines 8 and 16 are indented six spaces.]

   6.   MS, 1885, 1886a: show,   12.   1885, 1886a: sing;
   7.   MS, 1885, 1886a: bringeth Jesus   14.   MS, 1885, 1886a: snow,
  11.   1885, 1886a: music,   15.   MS, 1885, 1886a: bringeth Jesus

CHRISTMAS DAY.

[Date of composition unknown. Editions: 1885, 1886a, *1893*, 1904.]

1.	1885, 1886a: thing,	14.	1904: Upon his Mother's
3.	1885, 1886a: of babies was their	15.	1885: be,
	King	19.	1885, 1886a: stirred
10.	1885, 1886a: sod,	22.	1885, 1886a: melody,—
11.	1885, 1886a: And Jesus Christ		
	the		

CHRISTMASTIDE.

[Date of composition unknown. Editions: 1885, 1886a, *1893*, 1904.]

Title.	1885, 1886a: [untitled]	7.	1885, 1886a: our Jesus,—
2.	1885, 1886a: lovely, Love	12.	1885, 1886a: Love the universal
	Divine,		sign.
6.	1885, 1886a: Love Incarnate,		
	Love Divine,		

ST. JOHN, APOSTLE.

[Date of composition unknown. Editions: 1892, *1893*, 1904.]

Title.   1892: [untitled]

"'BELOVED, LET US LOVE ONE ANOTHER,' SAYS ST. JOHN"

[Date of composition unknown. Editions: 1885, 1886a, *1893*, 1904.]

Title.	1885, 1886a: FEAST OF	7.	1904: lo it
	ST. JOHN, APOSTLE AND		
	EVANGELIST.		

HOLY INNOCENTS.

[Date of composition unknown. Editions: 1881, *1893*, 1904.]

Title.   1881: [The poem is untitled, but
it appears in the chapter entitled
"Holy Innocents."]

"UNSPOTTED LAMBS TO FOLLOW THE ONE LAMB"

[Date of composition unknown. Editions: 1892, *1893*, 1904.]

4.   1904: lo their

EPIPHANY.

[Date of composition unknown. Editions: 1885, 1886a, *1893*, 1904. In the 1904 text, line 2 is indented two spaces.]

Title. 1885, 1886a: FEAST OF THE
EPIPHANY.
8. 1885, 1886a: began."—
10. 1885, 1886a: kings King."
15. 1885, 1886a: Low lying
desolate?"—
20. 1885, 1886a: Thou Sole
Omnipotence."
28. 1885, 1886a: this same is
29. 1904: alas, yea woe

30. 1885, 1886a: befitteth Thee."
31. 1885, 1886a: frankincense and
32. 1904: lo from
33. 1885, 1886a: Good will doth
36. 1904: lo the < > a Dove,
37. 1885: and cooes above:
39. 1885, 1886a: Come, all
mankind, come, all creation,
hither,

EPIPHANYTIDE.

[Date of composition unknown. Editions: 1892, *1893*, 1904. In the 1892 text, line 10 is not indented.]

Title. 1892: [untitled]
5. 1892: [No stanza break follows
the line.]
8. 1892: O Faithful Lord and true!
stand

1904: faithful Lord and true!
stand
9. 1892: free,
10. 1892: spirit to

SEPTUAGESIMA.

[Date of composition unknown. Editions: 1885, 1886a, *1893*, 1904. In the 1885 and 1886a texts, lines 4, 8, and 12 are indented two spaces.]

Title. 1885, 1886a: [untitled]
Opening quotation. 1885,
1886a: [There is no opening
quotation.]

1. 1885, 1886a: ended,
2. 1885, 1886a: done,
9. 1885, 1886a: us,
10. 1885, 1886a: done,

SEXAGESIMA.

[Date of composition unknown. Editions: 1892, *1893*, 1904.]

Title. 1892: [untitled]
Opening quotation. 1892:
[There is no opening quotation.]

5. 1892, 1904: is and
10. 1904: lo the

"THAT EDEN OF EARTH'S SUNRISE CANNOT VIE"

[Date of composition unknown. Editions: 1892, *1893*, 1904. In the 1892 text, lines 3, 6, 9, 12, 15, 18, and 21 are indented four spaces.]

19. 1892: Hail Adam and

21. 1904: Of Paradise

QUINQUAGESIMA.

[Date of composition unknown. Editions: 1892, *1893*, 1904.]

Title. 1892: [untitled]   13.   1892, 1904: Oh teach
  2.   1892: have pre-supposed a
  4.   1892: From lamb to lamb, from
       tended dove to dove.

"PITEOUS MY RHYME IS"

[Date of composition unknown. Editions: 1885, 1886a, *1893*, 1904.]

  1.   1885, 1886a: is,   19.   1885, 1886a: That which < >
  3.   1904: Of love mis-spent, of   can,
  6.   1885, 1886a: is

ASH WEDNESDAY.

[Date of composition unknown. Editions: 1885, 1886a, *1893*, 1904. In the 1885 and
1886a texts, lines 3 and 7 are indented two spaces, and lines 4 and 8 are indented
four spaces.]

  1.   1885, 1886a: sin   7.   1885, 1886a: tell this all,
⁴ 6.   1885, 1886a: sake; yea,

"GOOD LORD, TODAY"

[Date of composition unknown. Editions: 1892, *1893*, 1904.]

  8.   1892: pity tho'

LENT.

[Date of composition unknown. Editions: 1885, 1886a, *1893*, 1904.]

Title. 1885, 1886a: [untitled]   3.   1885, 1886a: thirst
  1.   1885, 1886a: first   6.   1885, 1886a: pray,
  2.   1885, 1886a: distress,

EMBERTIDE.

[Date of composition unknown. Editions: 1892, *1893*, 1904.]

Title. 1892: [untitled]

MID-LENT.

[Date of composition unknown. Editions: 1885, 1886a, *1893*, 1904.]

Title. 1885, 1886a: [untitled]
6. 1885, 1886a: nest;
7. 1885, 1886a: heart being
1904: west;

8. 1885, 1886a: hope for
12. 1885, 1886a: faint:
13. 1885, 1886a: speed

PASSIONTIDE.

[Date of composition unknown. Editions: *1893*, 1904.]

11. 1904: thirsteth, come—Come
13. 1904: seekest Me—Come

17. 1904: come—and I—and
I. Amen.

PALM SUNDAY.

[Date of composition unknown. Editions: 1892, *1893*, 1904.]

Title. 1892: [The opening quotation is the title.]
2. 1892: the Tree,
4. 1892: there
6. 1892: all and
17. 1892: boundless Sacrifice:

19. 1904: Ah Lord, it
28. 1892: day,
29. 1892: Trust me with < > heart even
30. 1893: pray.'

MONDAY IN HOLY WEEK.

[Date of composition unknown. Editions: 1885, 1886a, *1893*, 1904. The notebook MS is in the Bodleian Library. In the MS notebook, the poem is the first in a group of ten poems entitled "Odds and Ends." At the end of the group is written, "Copied, September 1853."]

Title. MS: (For under a Crucifix) Opening quotation. MS: [There is no opening quotation.]
1. MS: sake,
3. MS: pain,
4. MS: thou pierce My

7. MS: Gave up glory, broke [*m*]<M>y will,
1885, 1886a: Bore My cross to
8. MS: And canst thou reject Me still?—

TUESDAY IN HOLY WEEK.

[Date of composition unknown. Editions: 1885, 1886a, *1893*, 1904. In the 1886a text, lines 2, 4, 6, and 8 are indented two spaces.]

1. 1885: By Thy long drawn anguish

3. 1885, 1886a: atone,
5. 1885, 1886a: the cross didst

WEDNESDAY IN HOLY WEEK.

[Date of composition unknown. Editions: 1885, 1886a, *1893*, 1904.]

Title. 1885, 1886a: [untitled]
  6. 1885, 1886a: die,
  9. 1885, 1886a: again,

10. 1885, 1886a: shed His
  blood—in

MAUNDY THURSDAY.

[Date of composition unknown. Editions: 1885, 1886a, *1893*, 1904.]

Title. 1885, 1886a: Thursday in Holy
  Week.
  Opening quotation. 1885,
  1886a: said, . . . Should < >
  trees?"—(JUDGES ix. 13.)
  1904: wine which
  1. 1885, 1886a: as Forest King:—
  2. 1885, 1886a: trees, "We will
  3. 1885, 1886a: ring;
  4. 1885, 1886a: shadowing;
  1904: Lo from

  5. 1885, 1886a: cling;
  6. 1885, 1886a: buffeting.
  7. 1885, 1886a: the wild-fowl build
  9. 1886a: [No stanza break follows
  the line.]
  13. 1885, 1886a: on earth, for
  15. 1904: death:—and lo it
  18. 1885, 1886a: our king.

GOOD FRIDAY MORNING.

[Date of composition unknown. Editions: *1893*, 1904.]

  11. 1904: yea carried

  13. 1904: yea carried,

GOOD FRIDAY.

[Date of composition unknown. Editions: 1885, 1886a, *1893*, 1904. In the 1885 and 1886a texts, lines 4 and 8 are indented fourteen spaces.]

  1. 1885, 1886a: Lord Jesus Christ
  grown

  3. 1885, 1886a: soul,

GOOD FRIDAY EVENING.

[Date of composition unknown. Editions: 1892, *1893*, 1904. In the 1892 text, lines 4 and 8 are indented four spaces.]

Title. 1892: "OUT OF THE ANGEL'S
  HAND."
  Opening quotation. 1892:

  [There is no opening quotation.]
  5. 1892: faint good will,

"A BUNDLE OF MYRRH IS MY WELL-BELOVED UNTO ME."

[Date of composition unknown. Editions: 1892, *1893*, 1904.]

Title. 1892: [untitled]
3. 1892: crosses; Thine, how

6. 1892: For Love of < > small
10. 1892: us, with

EASTER EVEN.

[Date of composition unknown. Editions: 1885, 1886a, *1893*, 1904.]

1. 1885, 1886a: begun.
2. 1885, 1886a: finished," and

5. 1885, 1886a: dew,

OUR CHURCH PALMS ARE BUDDING WILLOW TWIGS.

[Date of composition unknown. Editions: 1892, *1893*, 1904. In the 1892 text, lines 4 and 8 are indented two spaces. In the textual notes, the larger brackets denote brackets in the text.]

Title. 1892: [Our < > twigs.]
1904: (Our < > twigs.)
2. 1892: undone;

7. 1892: and faith resumed
8. 1892: And love remembered

EASTER DAY.

[Date of composition unknown. Editions: 1885, 1886a, *1893*, 1904.]

2. 1885, 1886a: returning:—
7. 1885, 1886a: speechless;—

13. 1885, 1886a: her song birds,

EASTER MONDAY.

[Composed April 4, 1864. Editions: 1885, 1886a, *1893*, 1904. The notebook MS is in the British Library. In the MS, no lines are indented.]

Title. MS: Easter.
1885, 1886a: Easter Tuesday.
1. MS: rain this world < > green;
3. MS: Where lifeless knobs have [A stanza break follows the line.]
4. MS: rain our heaped-up graves are green;
5. MS: Preparing where the Lord hath been
6. MS: A harvest not yet seen. [A stanza break follows the line.]
7. MS: died, then we will gladly die;

8. MS: Make up this life's account, lay
9. MS: Poor life < > sigh. [A stanza break follows the line.]
10. MS: If Christ < > died, how good
11. MS: To die, to sleep till by and by,
1904: sleep when so He
12. MS: [A stanza break follows the line.]
13. MS: If Christ < > died, yea rather rose again,

14.   MS: We yet shall wax who now   16.   MS: If Christ <> again,
      must wane,   17.   MS: Then good it is to wax, to
15.   MS: Life's riddle is made   wane,
      <read> plain. [The added   18.   MS: Till Death makes all things
      word is in pencil in Christina's   plain.
      handwriting. A stanza break
      follows the line.]
      1885, 1886a: wane,

EASTER TUESDAY.

[Date of composition unknown. Editions: 1892, *1893*, 1904.]

Title. 1892: [untitled]   3.   1892: In quest of
  1.   1892: Together <> arise.   8.   1892: lamps being

ROGATIONTIDE.

[Date of composition unknown. Editions: 1885, 1886a, *1893*, 1904.]

Title. 1885, 1886a: [untitled]   5.   1885, 1886a: be
  1.   1885, 1886a: wheat   7.   1885, 1886a: more
  3.   1885, 1886a: grain,

ASCENSION EVE.

[Date of composition unknown. Editions: 1892, *1893*, 1904. In the 1892 text, lines 11 and 13 are not indented, and lines 12 and 14 are indented two spaces.]

Title. 1892: [untitled]   13.   1892, 1904: heaven,
  1.   1904: O Lord Almighty Who

ASCENSION DAY.

[Date of composition unknown. Editions: 1885, 1886a, *1893*, 1904. In the 1904 text, lines 4, 8, 12, 16, 20, 24, and 28 are indented four spaces.]

  9.   1885: Earth   1885r: [Lines 27 and 28 are
 10.   1885: one long drawn anguish   bracketed in the left margin,
 13.   1885, 1886a: Nevertheless, a   and below the poem is added in
 21.   1885, 1886a: sight   pencil in Christina's handwrit-
 22.   1885, 1886a: cloud He will   ing:] An idea picked up I cannot
       return   recollect where.
 27.   1885, 1886a: to Heaven,—

WHITSUN EVE.

[Date of composition unknown. Editions: 1892, *1893*, 1904. In the 1892 and 1904 texts, lines 4 and 8 are indented four spaces.]

Title. 1892: [untitled]
1. 1904: love.'—Ah Lord,

3. 1892: afar stumbling < > small

WHITSUN DAY.

[Date of composition unknown. Editions: 1885, 1886a, *1893*, 1904. In the 1885 and 1886a texts, lines 2, 3, 6, and 7 are not indented, and lines 4 and 8 are indented two spaces. In the 1904 text, lines 4 and 8 are indented four spaces.]

1. 1885, 1886a: wind and
2. 1904: Lo flesh

5. 1885, 1886a: life, and

WHITSUN MONDAY.

[Date of composition unknown. Editions: 1892, *1893*, 1904.]

Title. 1892: [untitled]
Opening quotation. 1892:
[There is no opening quotation.]

13. 1892: that River.
17. 1904: lo on
18. 1892: of Life, life-giving

WHITSUN TUESDAY.

[Date of composition unknown. Editions: 1885, 1886a, *1893*, 1904. In the 1885, 1886a, and 1904 texts, lines 12 and 14 are indented two spaces.]

1. 1885, 1886a: Lord Jesus Christ our < > and our Rest
4. 1885, 1886a: to Thy Will Whose Will
6. 1885, 1886a: pride,

7. 1885, 1886a: dove-hearted, and
12. 1885, 1886a: say,—"Winter
13. 1885, 1886a: say,—"Spouse, < > love, and

TRINITY SUNDAY.

[Date of composition unknown. Editions: 1892, *1893*, 1904. In the 1892 text, line 1 is indented four spaces, lines 11 and 13 are indented two spaces, and line 12 is not indented.]

Title. 1892: [untitled]
14. 1892: remainest: yea, and

CONVERSION OF ST. PAUL.

[Date of composition unknown. Editions: 1885, 1886a, *1893*, 1904. In the 1885 and 1886a texts, lines 2 and 4 are indented two spaces.]

Title. 1885, 1886a: FEAST OF THE   4. 1885, 1886a: [A stanza break
CONVERSION OF ST. PAUL   follows the line.]
IN THE YEAR 35.   7. 1885, 1886a: What shall that

"IN WEARINESS AND PAINFULNESS ST. PAUL"

[Date of composition unknown. Editions: 1885, 1886a, *1893*, 1904. In the 1885, 1886a, and 1904 texts, line 4 and 11 are indented two spaces.]

9. 1886a: forward, upward   10. 1885, 1886a: feet, still

VIGIL OF THE PRESENTATION.

[Date of composition unknown. Editions: 1892, *1893*, 1904.]

Title. 1892: [untitled]

FEAST OF THE PRESENTATION.

[Date of composition unknown. Editions: 1881, *1893*, 1904.]

Title. 1881: [The poem is untitled, but   10. 1904: gate!
it appears in the chapter entitled   11. 1881: offered Thee
"The Presentation of Christ in   13. 1904: frankincense, and
the Temple, and Purification of   16. 1881: Then Snowdrops and
St. Mary the Virgin."]   19. 1904: wait,
1. 1904: O firstfruits of   20. 1904: A bruisèd reed
7. 1881: king, and

THE PURIFICATION OF ST. MARY THE VIRGIN.

[Date of composition unknown. Editions: 1885, 1886a, *1893*, 1904.]

Title. 1885, 1886a: FEAST OF THE   5. 1885: fair fellow dove.
PRESENTATION OF CHRIST IN   6. 1885, 1886a: her Innocent
THE TEMPLE, COMMONLY   Child,
CALLED, THE PURIFICATION   8. 1885, 1886a: that (conceived by
OF ST. MARY THE VIRGIN.]   The Dove)
1. 1885, 1886a: a Maid,—   9. 1885, 1886a: spotless, and holy,
3. 1885, 1886a: a shade.—   and

VIGIL OF THE ANNUNCIATION.

[Date of composition unknown. Editions: 1892, *1893*, 1904.]

Title. 1892: [untitled]
5. 1892: unutterable, eternal

FEAST OF THE ANNUNCIATION.

[Date of composition unknown. Editions: 1885, 1886a, *1893*, 1904.]

Title. 1885, 1886a: FEAST OF THE
NATIVITY OF THE BLESSED
VIRGIN MARY.

4. 1885, 1886a: one delight;
5. 1885, 1886a: flower;

"HERSELF A ROSE, WHO BORE THE ROSE"

[Date of composition unknown. Editions: 1881, *1893*, 1904. In the 1881 text, lines 5, 10, 15, and 20 are indented two spaces.]

ST. MARK.

[Date of composition unknown. Editions: 1881, *1893*, 1904. In the 1881 text, lines 1, 5, and 9 are not indented, and lines 4, 8, and 12 are indented four spaces. In the 1904 text, lines 1, 5, and 9 are not indented.]

Title. 1881: [The poem is untitled, but
it appears in the chapter entitled
"St. Mark, Evangelist."]

ST. BARNABAS.

[Date of composition unknown. Editions: 1881, *1893*, 1904. In the 1881 text, lines 11 and 13 are indented two spaces.]

Title. 1881: [The poem is untitled, but
it appears in the chapter entitled
"St. Barnabas, Apostle."]
Opening quotations. 1881: Now
< > hand.—*Acts* < > / We < >
contrary.—*Acts*

3. 1881: That Chosen Vessel,
1904: That Chosen Vessel who
9. 1881: in lifelong exile
14. 1881: his resting-place.
1893: his landing-/ place.

VIGIL OF ST. PETER.

[Date of composition unknown. Editions: 1892, *1893*, 1904. In the 1904 text, lines 4 and 8 are indented six spaces.]

Title. 1892: [untitled]
5. 1893, 1904: Thou who dost

ST. PETER.

[Date of composition unknown. Editions: 1892, *1893*, 1904.]

Title. 1892: [untitled]
7. 1892: of Love which

"ST. PETER ONCE: 'LORD, DOST THOU WASH MY FEET?'"

[Date of composition unknown. Editions: 1892, *1893*, 1904.]

  7. 1892: cock,   10. 1892: on Me eye to eye
  9. 1892: knocking. Still I

"I FOLLOWED THEE, MY GOD, I FOLLOWED THEE"

[Date of composition unknown. Editions: 1881, *1893*, 1904.]

13.	1881: be	54. 1881: in extasy
21.	1904: from Thee':—	56. 1881: hart the water brooks I
37.	1904: lie!	65. 1881: part.
46.	1881: O blessed	1904: part—
48.	1881: own mother praying silently:	

VIGIL OF ST. BARTHOLOMEW.

[Date of composition unknown. Editions: 1892, *1893*, 1904.]

Title. 1892: [untitled]
  11. 1904: heaven,

ST. BARTHOLOMEW.

[Date of composition unknown. Editions: 1885, 1886a, *1893*, 1904.]

Title. 1885: FEAST OF ST. BARTHOLOMEW, APOSTLE. Tradition assigns to this / Saint, martyrdom in one of its most appalling forms 1886a: FEAST OF ST. BARTHOLOMEW, APOSTLE. Tradition / assigns to this Saint, martyrdom in one of its most ap- / palling forms.

  2. 1885, 1886a: pale:—

ST. MICHAEL AND ALL ANGELS.

[Date of composition unknown. Editions: 1881, *1893*, 1904.]

Title. 1881: [The poem is untitled, but it appears in the chapter entitled "St. Michael and All Angels."] Opening quotation. 1881:

[There is no opening quotation.]
  8. 1881: Flames fire-out-flaming, chill

VIGIL OF ALL SAINTS.

[Date of composition unknown. Editions: 1885, 1886a, *1893*, 1904.]

Title. 1885, 1886a: [untitled]   9. 1885, 1886a: day:—
  3. 1885: to Jesus Christ! arise

ALL SAINTS.

[Date of composition unknown. Editions: 1885, 1886a, *1893*, 1904. In the 1885 and 1886a texts, line 11 is indented four spaces. In the 1904 text, lines 11 and 13 are indented four spaces, and line 14 is indented two spaces.]

Title. 1885, 1886a: FEAST OF ALL SAINTS.
7. 1885, 1886a: fanned,
8. 1893: and thro'
9. 1904: Lo like
11. 1885, 1886a: rejoice.
13. 1885, 1886a: All love, and only love, can

ALL SAINTS: MARTYRS.

[Date of composition unknown. Editions: 1892, *1893*, 1904.]

Title. 1892: [untitled]
1. 1893, 1904: Once slain for Him who first
3. 1904: gore,
4. 1892, 1904: stem,
13. 1904: they, worshiping incessantly

"I GAVE A SWEET SMELL."

[Date of composition unknown. Editions: 1885, 1886a, *1893*, 1904. In the 1885 and 1886a texts, lines 3 and 8 are not indented; lines 4 and 9 are indented eight spaces; and lines 5 and 10 are indented two spaces. In the 1904 text, line 3 is indented two spaces.]

3. 1885, 1886a: kind.
5. 1885, 1886a: to-morrow:—

"HARK! THE ALLELUIAS OF THE GREAT SALVATION"

[Date of composition unknown. Editions: 1892, *1893*, 1904.]

1. 1904: salvation,
8. 1904: nation,
9. 1892: salvation
10. 1892: truth may

A SONG FOR THE LEAST OF ALL SAINTS.

[Date of composition unknown. Editions: 1892, *1893*, 1904. In the 1892 text, lines 4, 8, and 12 are indented four spaces.]

Title. 1892: THE FEAST OF

SUNDAY BEFORE ADVENT.

[Date of composition unknown. Editions: 1892, *1893*, 1904.]

Title. 1892: [untitled]

"LOVE LOVETH THEE, AND WISDOM LOVETH THEE"

[Date of composition unknown. Editions: 1892, *1893*, 1904. In the 1892 text, line 13 is indented two spaces. In the 1904 text, lines 12 and 14 are indented two spaces.]

1. 1892: wisdom loveth Thee.
   1904: wisdom loveth Thee;
2. 1892: satisfied.

4. 1892: was and is and
13. 1892: have and

"LORD, GIVE ME LOVE THAT I MAY LOVE THEE MUCH"

[Date of composition unknown. Editions: 1892, *1893*, 1904.]

8. 1892: perfect having

"AS A KING, ... UNTO THE KING."

[Composed January 13, 1863. Editions: 1885, 1886a, *1893*, 1904. The notebook MS is in the British Library. The poem originally formed part of a poem entitled "For a Mercy received," which Christina never published as such. "For a Mercy received" is presented in its own right in Volume III of the present edition.]

Title. MS: For a Mercy received.
    1885, 1886a: [untitled]
    1904: a king, . . . unto
1. MS: [Line 1 is preceded by the following stanzas:]

Thank God Who spared me what I feared!
Once more I gird myself to run.
Thy promise stands, [O] <Thou> Faithful One. [The deletion and addition are in pencil in Christina's handwriting.]
Horror of darkness disappeared
At length; once more I see the sun,
And dare to wait in hope for Spring,
To face and b[a]<e>ar the Winter's cold:
The dead cocoon shall yet unfold
And give to light the living wing;
There's hidden sap beneath the mould.

My god, how could my courage flag
So long as Thou art still the same?
For what were [illegible erasure] <labour>, failure, shame,
Whilst Thy sure promise doth not lag
And Thou dost shield me with Thy Name?

Yet am I weak, my faith is weak,
My heart is weak that pleads with Thee:

O Thou *t*]<T>hat art not far to seek
Turn to me, hearken when I speak,
Stretch forth Thy Hand to succour me.
Thro' many perils have I pass'd,
Deaths, plagues, and wonders, have I seen:
Till now Thy Hand hath held me fast:
Lord help me, hold me, to the last;
Still be what Thou hast always been.

Open Thy Heart of Love to me,
Give me Thyself, keep nothing back
Even as I give myself to Thee.
Love paid by Love doth nothing lack,
And Love to pay Love is not slack.

1. 1885, 1886a: dignify,
2. MS: beggars sue as [*k*]<K>ing with King
3. MS: of Grace on high:
   1885: cry
4. MS: My God, be gracious to my cry;
   1886a: Love recognizes love's <> cry
   1904: Love recognizes love's

5. MS: My God, accept what gift I bring:
   1885, 1886a: offering,
6. MS: A heart that loves; tho' < > bruised,
   1885, 1886a: heart though < > bruised,
7. MS: Yet chosen by Thee in time of yore:
   1885, 1886a: heart though < > before:—
8. MS: [*Whoever*] <Who ever> [separated with a solidus written in pencil] came
   1885, 1886a: Whoever came
9. MS: By Thee? Do,

"O YE WHO LOVE TODAY"

[Date of composition unknown. Editions: 1892, *1893*, 1904. In the 1892 text, no lines are indented.]

1. 1892: O, ye
7. 1892, 1904: to-morrow,
10. 1892: face

"LIFE THAT WAS BORN TODAY"

[Date of composition unknown. Editions: 1892, *1893*, 1904. In the 1892 text, the first stanza of the poem is repeated later in the book, and variants therein are designated "1892-b."]

1. 1904: stay,
4. 1892-b: Like bloom of
8. 1892-b: A wholesome

"PERFECT LOVE CASTETH OUT FEAR."

[Date of composition unknown. Editions: 1892, *1893*, 1904.]

Title. 1904: Perfect < > out Fear.
1. 1892: fear
2. 1892, 1904: love,

"HOPE IS THE COUNTERPOISE OF FEAR"

[Date of composition unknown. Editions: 1892, *1893*, 1904.]

8. 1892: tomb, where < > sere
10. 1892: hymn so sweet < > clear
11. 1892: He seems

"SUBJECT TO LIKE PASSIONS AS WE ARE."

[Date of composition unknown. Editions: 1892, *1893*, 1904. In the 1904 text, line 3 is not indented.]

Title. 1892: [untitled]
   1904: Subject < > are.
10. 1892: delight:
12. 1892: meet but < > sunder with
13. 1904: fathom still-unfathomed mysteries,

"EXPERIENCE BOWS A SWEET CONTENTED FACE"

[Date of composition unknown. Editions: 1892, *1893*, 1904.]

2.   1904: Still setting-to her
7.   1892: moon and
9.   1892: well";
      1904: well':

12.   1892: While Hope who
13.   1892: forth and < > hair
       1904: and backward-floating
       hair,

"CHARITY NEVER FAILETH."

[Date of composition unknown. Editions: 1892, *1893*, 1904.]

Title.   1904: Charity never faileth.
   1.   1892: extremity;
   3.   1892: beyond tempest far
   4.   1904: is Love

5.   1892: inward Dove,
7.   1904: myrtles of an
11.   1904: is Love

"THE GREATEST OF THESE IS CHARITY."

[Date of composition unknown. Editions: 1892, *1893*, 1904.]

Title.   1892: [untitled]
      1904: The < > is Charity.
   4.   1892: veiled,—

9.   1892: Nay!—love
13.   1892: of New Jerusalem,
14.   1892: the palm tree blows.

"ALL BENEATH THE SUN HASTETH"

[Date of composition unknown. Editions: 1892, *1893*, 1904. In the 1892 text, the poem is printed in double columns.]

1.   1892: All that hath begun
      wasteth,
2.   1892: All beneath the sun
      hasteth;

11.   1892: Half-fearing,

"IF THOU BE DEAD, FORGIVE AND THOU SHALT LIVE"

[Date of composition unknown. Editions: 1892, *1893*, 1904. In the 1892 and 1904 texts, lines 4 and 8 are indented four spaces.]

"LET PATIENCE HAVE HER PERFECT WORK."

[Date of composition unknown. Editions: 1892, *1893*, 1904. In the 1904 text, lines 12 and 14 are indented two spaces.]

Title.   1892: [untitled]
      1904: Let < > work.

4.   1892: of or < > hear
9.   1892: miserable:—

"PATIENCE MUST DWELL WITH LOVE, FOR LOVE AND SORROW"

[Date of composition unknown. Editions: 1892, *1893*, 1904. In the 1892 and 1904 texts, lines 4 and 8 are indented two spaces.]

4.   1904: And Sorrow not
5.   1904: sake hope; still hope in
       Sorrow,

6.   1904: dear.
7.   1904: lo tomorrow

"LET EVERYTHING THAT HATH BREATH PRAISE THE LORD."

[Date of composition unknown. Editions: 1892, *1893*, 1904. In the 1892 text, lines 4 and 9 are indented two spaces. In the 1904 text, lines 4 and 9 are indented six spaces.]

Title.   1892: [untitled]
          1904: Let < > the Lord.

7.   1892: must fail and

"WHAT IS THE BEGINNING? LOVE. WHAT THE COURSE? LOVE STILL"

[Date of composition unknown. Editions: 1892, *1893*, 1904.]

"LORD, MAKE ME PURE"

[Date of composition unknown. Editions: 1892, *1893*, 1904.]

2.   1892, 1904: art,

"LOVE, TO BE LOVE, MUST WALK THY WAY"

[Date of composition unknown. Editions: 1892, *1893*, 1904. In the 1892 text, lines 2, 3, 6, 7, 10, 11, 14, 15, 18, and 19 are indented two spaces.]

15.   1892: her myrtle leaf,

"LORD, I AM FEEBLE AND OF MEAN ACCOUNT"

[Date of composition unknown. Editions: 1892, *1893*, 1904. In the 1892 text, lines 4 and 8 are not indented.]

1.   1892: account;

8.   1904: mount

"TUNE ME, O LORD, INTO ONE HARMONY"

[Date of composition unknown. Editions: 1892, *1893*, 1904. In the 1892 text, lines 4 and 11 are indented four spaces.]

3.   1904: praise, all
5.   1904: death nor fire nor
6.   1904: to be;

8.   1892: flee;
      1904: world gird

"THEY SHALL BE AS WHITE AS SNOW."

[Date of composition unknown. Editions: 1892, *1893*, 1904. In the 1892 text, lines 4 and 11 are indented four spaces.]

Title. 1892: [untitled]
        1904: They < > snow.

1.   1904: white. Ah to
5.   1892: right,

"THY LILIES DRINK THE DEW"

[Date of composition unknown. Editions: 1885, 1886a, *1893*, 1904. In the 1885 and 1886a texts, lines 1, 3, 5, 7, 9, 11, 13, 15, and 17 are indented two spaces. In the 1904 text, line 1 is not indented and lines 2, 3, 5, 7, 9, 11, 13, 15, and 17 are indented two spaces.]

12.   1885, 1886a: high, or great, or

17.   1885, 1886a: be

"WHEN I WAS IN TROUBLE I CALLED UPON THE LORD."

[Date of composition unknown. Editions: 1885, 1886a, *1893*, 1904. In the 1904 text, line 2 is indented four spaces.]

Title. 1885, 1886a: [untitled]
        1904: When < > the Lord.
1.   1885, 1886a: bears,
4.   1885, 1886a: again.

8.   1886a: And stanch and
14.   1904: sift;
15.   1885, 1886a: give,—

"GRANT US SUCH GRACE THAT WE MAY WORK THY WILL"

[Date of composition unknown. Editions: 1892, *1893*, 1904. In the 1892 text, lines 4 and 11 are indented four spaces.]

1.   1892: work Thy Will,

3.   1892: calm like

"WHO HATH DESPISED THE DAY OF SMALL THINGS?"

[Date of composition unknown. Editions: 1892, *1893*, 1904. In the 1892 and 1904 texts, lines 4 and 8 are indented two spaces.]

Title. 1892: [untitled]
        1904: Who < > things?

6.   1892: lofty forest-trees tower

"DO THIS, AND HE DOETH IT."

[Date of composition unknown. Editions: 1892, *1893*, 1904.]

Title. 1892: [untitled]
7.   1892: sit high < > low
8.   1892: place:

11.   1892: so
      1904: that are are

"THAT NO MAN TAKE THY CROWN."

[Date of composition unknown. Editions: 1892, *1893*, 1904.]

Title. 1892: [untitled]
3. 1904: yea and

6. 1892: faithful:"—whatsoever
7. 1892: faithful challenging

"YE ARE COME UNTO MOUNT SION."

[Date of composition unknown. Editions: 1892, *1893*, 1904.]

Title. 1892: [untitled]
     1904: Ye <> unto Mount Sion.
1. 1904: and Hope, have

2. 1904: and Humility,
15. 1904: in New Jerusalem

"SIT DOWN IN THE LOWEST ROOM."

[Date of composition unknown. Editions: 1892, *1893*, 1904.]

Title. 1892: [untitled]
     1904: Sit <> room.

4. 1893: [Line 4 is the last line on the page.]
     1904: [No stanza break follows the line.]

"LORD, IT IS GOOD FOR US TO BE HERE."

[Date of composition unknown. Editions: 1892, *1893*, 1904.]

Title. 1892: [untitled]
     1904: Lord, <> here.
6. 1904: while Faith holds
7. 1904: While Hope toils <> in Fear's copartnery,

8. 1904: And Love goes
10. 1904: Must Patience be
12. 1904: with Fear,
13. 1892: good love, who
     1904: ah good Love who

"LORD, GRANT US GRACE TO REST UPON THY WORD"

[Date of composition unknown. Editions: 1892, *1893*, 1904. In the 1892 text, lines 4, 7, and 11 are indented four spaces.]

8. 1904: Ah songs

11. 1904: grace!

"A VAIN SHADOW."

[Date of composition unknown. Editions: 1892, *1893*, 1904.]

Title. 1892: [untitled]
     1904: A vain Shadow.

2. 1892: Mouldy, wormeaten, grey:

"LORD, SAVE US, WE PERISH."

[Date of composition unknown. Editions: 1892, *1893*, 1904.]

Title. 1892: [untitled]
        1904: Lord, < > perish.

"WHAT IS THIS ABOVE THY HEAD"

[Date of composition unknown. Editions: 1892, *1893*, 1904. In the 1892 text, the first four stanzas are printed in double columns and the fifth stanza is centered below them. In the 1904 text, lines 19 and 20 intrude two spaces into the left margin, and line 21 is not indented.]

26. 1892: her death pall   31. 1904: Ah poorest
29. 1904: Ah poor

BABYLON THE GREAT.

[Date of composition unknown. Editions: 1892, *1893*, 1904. In the 1904 text, lines 12 and 14 are indented two spaces.]

Title. 1892: [untitled]   12. 1892: desire
    9. 1892: upon her; for

"STANDING AFAR OFF FOR THE FEAR OF HER TORMENT."

[Date of composition unknown. Editions: 1892, *1893*, 1904.]

Title. 1892: STANDING < >   6. 1892: all:
        TORMENT.   7. 1892: fall,
        1904: Standing < > torment. 12. 1904: lo are

"O LUCIFER, SON OF THE MORNING!"

[Date of composition unknown. Editions: 1892, *1893*, 1904. In the 1893 text, line 11 is indented two spaces. In the 1904 text, lines 4 and 11 are indented two spaces.]

Title. 1892: [untitled]   7. 1892: nebular:
        1904: O < > the Morning!   10. 1904: O son
    1. 1904: O fallen   11. 1904: O fallen
    4. 1904: O fallen

"ALAS, ALAS! FOR THE SELF-DESTROYED"

[Date of composition unknown. Editions: 1892, *1893*, 1904.]

"AS FROTH ON THE FACE OF THE DEEP"

[Date of composition unknown. Editions: 1892, *1893*, 1904.]

"WHERE THEIR WORM DIETH NOT, AND THE FIRE IS NOT QUENCHED."

[Date of composition unknown. Editions: 1892, *1893*, 1904. In the 1892 text, lines 4 and 7 are indented two spaces.]

Title. 1904: Where <> quenched.
  1. 1904: storm, blackness

"TOLL, BELL, TOLL. FOR HOPE IS FLYING"

[Date of composition unknown. Editions: 1892, *1893*, 1904. In the 1892 text, lines 4 and 11 are indented four spaces.]

  5. 1904: mole,   11. 1892: bell, toll,

"EARTH HAS CLEAR CALL OF DAILY BELLS"

[Composed August 6, 1858. Editions: 1885, 1886a, *1893*, 1904. The notebook MS is in the British Library. The poem originally formed part of a poem entitled "'Yet a little while,'" which Christina never published as such. "'Yet a little while'" is presented in its own right in Volume III of the present edition. In the MS, a vertical pencil line is drawn through both stanzas, and in the right margin the word "stet" is added in pencil in Christina's handwriting. The third and fourth stanzas of the MS are printed in *Verses* as a separate poem entitled "'Vanity of Vanities.'"]

Title. MS: "Yet a little while."
  1. MS: [Preceding line 1 are the following stanzas:]

These days are long before I die:
[*T*] [not indented] <T>o [indented
            two spaces] sit alone upon a
            thorn
  Is what the nightingale forlorn
Does night by night continually;
She swells her heart to extasy
Until it bursts and she can die.

These days are long that wane and
            wax:
  Waxeth and wanes the ghostly
            moon
  Achill and pale in cordial June;
What is it that she wandering lacks?
She seems as one that aches and
            aches
Most sick to wane most sick to wax.

Of all the sad sights in the world
  The downfall of an [*a*]<A>utumn
            leaf
  Is grievous and suggesteth grief:
Who thought when Spring was fresh
            unfurled
Of this? when Spring twigs gleamed
            impearled
Who thought of frost that nips the
            world?

There are a hundred subtle stings
  To prick us in our daily walk:
  A young fruit cankered on its
            stalk,
A strong bird snared for all his
            wings,
A nest that sang but never sings;
Yea sight and sound and silence
            stings.

There is a lack in solitude,
  There is a load in throng of life;
  One with another genders strife,
To be alone yet is not good:
I know but of one neighbourhood
At peace and full; death's solitude.
Sleep soundly, dears, who lulled at
    last
  Forget the bird and all her pains,
  Forget the moon that waxes,
    wanes,
The leaf, the sting, the frostful blast;
Forget the troublous years that past
In strife or ache did end at last.

1. MS: We have clear
2. MS: A dimness where the
   anthems are,
   1885, 1886a: A rapture where
   the anthems are,
3. MS: A chancel vault of sky and
   star,
   1885, 1886a: A chancel-vault of
   gloom and star,
4. MS: thunder if the
5. MS: Alas our daily
6. MS: Is not in tune
7. MS: You have deep pause
   betwixt the
8. MS: Of earth and heaven, a
   patient
   1885, 1886a: and Heaven: its
9. MS: Yet glad with rest by certain
   laws:
10. MS: You look and long; while
    oftentimes

"ESCAPE TO THE MOUNTAIN."

[Date of composition unknown. Editions: 1892, *1893*, 1904. In the 1892 and 1904
texts, lines 4, 8, and 12 are indented four spaces.]

Title. 1892: [untitled]
       1904: Escape < > the Mountain.

1. 1892: sin:
2. 1892: righteousness:

"I LIFT MINE EYES TO SEE: EARTH VANISHETH"

[Date of composition unknown. Editions: 1892, *1893*, 1904.]

2. 1892: and bow my

5. 1904: Lo what

"YET A LITTLE WHILE."

[Date of composition unknown. Editions: 1892, *1893*, 1904.]

Title. 1892: [untitled]
       1904: Yet < > while.

5. 1892, 1904: how long? Oh long

"BEHOLD, IT WAS VERY GOOD."

[Date of composition unknown. Editions: 1892, *1893*, 1904.]

Title. 1892: [untitled]
       1904: Behold < > good.
5. 1892: declare;

8. 1892: tree
9. 1904: there,

"WHATSOEVER IS RIGHT, THAT SHALL YE RECEIVE."

[Composed August 27, 1857. Editions: 1885, 1886a, *1893*, 1904. The notebook MS is in the British Library. The poem originally formed part of a poem entitled "'The heart knoweth its own bitterness,'" which Christina never published as such. "'The heart knoweth its own bitterness'" is presented in its own right in Volume III of the present edition.]

Title.   MS: "The heart knoweth its own
     bitterness."
     1885, 1886a: [untitled]
     1904: Whatsoever < > receive.
1.   MS: the over-work of
2.   MS: and fast asleep
3.   MS: We swerve no < > knife
4.   MS: But taste that silence cool
    and deep;
    1885, 1886a: reap,
5.   MS: Forgetful of the highways
    rough,
6.   MS: Forgetful of the
7.   MS: Forgetful of the
8.   MS: find it < > enough?—
    [After line 8 are the following
    stanzas:]

    How can we say 'enough' on earth;
      'Enough' with such a craving
        heart:
    I have not found it since my birth
      But still have bartered part for
        part.
    I have not held and hugged the
      whole,
      But paid the old to gain the new;
    Much have I paid, yet much is due,
    Till I am beggared sense and soul.

    I used to labour, used to strive
      For pleasure with a restless will:
    Now if I save my soul alive
    All else what matters, good or ill?
    I used to dream alone, to plan
      Unspoken hopes and days to
        come:—
    Of all my past this is the sum:
    I will not lean on child of man.

    To give, to give, not to receive,
      I long to pour myself, my soul,

Not to keep back or count or leave
    But king with king to give the
      whole:
I long for one to stir my deep—
    I have had enough of help and
      gift—
    I long for one to search and sift
Myself, to take myself and keep.

You scratch my surface with your
      pin,
    You stroke me smooth with
      hushing breath;—
Nay pierce, nay probe, nay dig
      within,
    Probe my quick core and sound
      my depth.
You call me with a puny call,
    You talk, you smile, you nothing
      do;
    How should I spend my heart on
      you,
My heart that so outweighs you all?

Your vessels are by much too strait;
    Were I to pour you could not hold,
Bear with me: I must bear to wait
    A fountain sealed thro' heat and
      cold.
Bear with me days or months or
      years;
    Deep must call deep until the end
When friend shall no more envy
      friend
Nor vex his friend at unawares.

10.   MS: stuff;—
12.   MS: full 'enough':
    1885, 1886a: "enough:"
    1904: 'enough';
16.   MS: I full of Christ and Christ
    of me.

"THIS NEAR-AT-HAND LAND BREEDS PAIN BY MEASURE"

[Date of composition unknown. Editions: 1881, *1893*, 1904. In the 1881 text, the last line of each stanza is indented two spaces.]

11.	1881: unending, unflagging	22.	1904: 'Come
13.	1904: 'Up <> away,' call	24.	1881: bringing:
14.	1904: 'Come	25.	1904: 'Crowns
16.	1904: 'Where	28.	1904: 'Over
19.	1904: 'Where	31.	1904: 'Come,
20.	1881, 1904: blowing,	33.	1904: upon Jesu.'

"WAS THY WRATH AGAINST THE SEA?"

[Date of composition unknown. Editions: 1892, *1893*, 1904. In the 1904 text, line 2 is indented four spaces.]

Title.	1892: [untitled]	10.	1892: Assigns It crown
9.	1892: sea! God's Wisdom	12.	1904: Attest—God

"AND THERE WAS NO MORE SEA."

[Date of composition unknown. Editions: 1892, *1893*, 1904.]

Title.	1892: [untitled]	11.	1904: begin
	1904: And <> more Sea.	14.	1892: gladdest best at

"ROSES ON A BRIER"

[Date of composition unknown. Editions: 1885, 1886a, *1893*, 1904.]

10.   1885, 1886a: be;

"WE ARE OF THOSE WHO TREMBLE AT THY WORD"

[Date of composition unknown. Editions: 1892, *1893*, 1904. In the 1892 text, lines 4 and 11 are indented four spaces, lines 5 and 7 are not indented, and line 6 is indented two spaces.]

5.   1892: knows,

"AWAKE, THOU THAT SLEEPEST."

[Date of composition unknown. Editions: 1892, *1893*, 1904.]

Title.	1892: [untitled]	7.	1892: Far far
	1904: Awake thou <> sleepest.	10.	1892: the glow of <> fire,

"WE KNOW NOT WHEN, WE KNOW NOT WHERE"

[Date of composition unknown. Editions: 1885, 1886a, *1893*, 1904. In the 1885 and 1886a texts, lines 4, 8, and 12 are indented two spaces.]

2. 1885, 1886a: be,
3. 1904: know—it
6. 1885, 1886a: be:—

11. 1885, 1886a: see Him face to face,—

"I WILL LIFT UP MINE EYES UNTO THE HILLS."

[Composed June 26, 1856. Editions: 1885, 1886a, *1893*, 1904. The notebook MS is in the British Library. The poem originally formed part of a poem entitled "The Chiefest among ten thousand," which Christina never published as such. "The Chiefest among ten thousand" is presented in its own right in Volume III of the present edition. In the MS, no lines are indented. The second, third, sixth, seventh, eighth, ninth, tenth, eleventh, twelfth, and fourteenth stanzas of the MS are deleted with a vertical pencil line, and below the title is added in pencil in Dante Gabriel Rossetti's handwriting: "might be shortened."]

Title. MS: The Chiefest among ten thousand.
1885, 1886a: [untitled]
1904: I < > the Hills.
1. MS: world,
2. MS: all the earth but Thee,
1885, 1886a: all the earth but
4. MS: that truly see:
6. MS: eyes;
8. MS: The living trees of paradise. [After line 8 are the following stanzas:]

[*Thyself the Vine with living Fruit,*
The twelvefold fruited Tree of Life,
The Balm in Gilead after strife,
The valley Lily and the Rose:
Stronger than Lebanon, [t]<T>hou Root,
Sweeter than clustered grapes, Thou Vine;
Oh best, Thou Vineyard of new Wine
Keeping Thy best Wine till the close.]

[*Pearl of great price Thyself alone*
And ruddier than the ruby Thou,
Most precious lightening Jasper Stone,
Head of the corner spurned before;
Fair Gate of pearl, Thyself the Door,
Clear golden Street, Thyself the Way,
By Thee we journey toward Thee now
Thro' Thee shall reach Thee in that day.]

Oh that a dove's white wings I had
To flee away from this distress
For Thou art in the wilderness
Drawing and leading Thine Own love:
Wherefore it blossoms like a rose,
The solitary place is glad;

There sounds the soft voice of the dove
And there the spicy south wind blows.

Draw us, we will run after Thee;
Call us by name, the name we know;
Call her beloved who was not so,
Beulah and blessed Hepzibah:
That where Thou art I too may be
Bride of the Bridegroom heart to heart;
Thou God, my Love, the Fairest art
Where all things fair and lovely are.

[*I thirst for Thee, full Fount and Flood,*
My heart calls Thine as deep to deep:
Dost Thou forget Thy sweat and pain,
Thy provocation on the Cross?
Heart pierced for me, vouchsafe to keep
The purchase of Thy lavished Blood;
The gain is Thine Lord if I gain,
Or if I lose Thine Own the loss.]

[*The sparrow findeth her a house,*
The swallow for her young a nest,
But Thou art far away my Rest,
Thyself my Rest and Thou alone:
No home on earth sufficeth me,
Not Thine Own house most fair to see,
Tho' rich with gold and costly stone,
Painted and ceiled with cedar boughs.]

9–16. MS: [The stanza is deleted with a vertical pencil line.]
9. MS: There < > things, saith
10. 1885, 1886a: of Truth, Thyself the Word,
1904: of Truth, Thyself the Word:

11. MS: things [t]<T>hou
     reasonest
12. MS: hope so long deferred,
13. MS: But this is time for [illegible
     deletion] <g>rief and
     [t]<f>ears;
14. MS: but this is
15. MS, 1904: Oh when
     1885, 1886a: Oh! when < >
     love,
16. MS: When Thou Thyself shalt
     [After line 16 are the following
     stanzas:]

     [*At midnight, saith the parable,*
     A cry was made, the Bridegroom came:
     Those who were ready entered in;
     The rest shut out in death and shame
     Strove all too late that feast to win
     Their die was cast and fixed their lot,
     A gulph divided heaven from hell,
     The Bridegroom said, 'I know you not.']

     [*But Who is This That shuts the door*
     And saith 'I know you not' to them?
     I see the wounded Hands and Side,
     The Brow thorn-tortured long [before:]
     <*ago:*> [The deletion and
     revision are in pencil in
     Christina's handwriting.]
     Yes, This Who grieved and bled and died,
     This Same is He Who must condemn;
     He called, but they refused to know,
     So now He hears their cry no more.]

     [*When shall Thy coming be, my Lord?*
     At midnight? at the cockcrow? when?
     Thou Whom the people once abhorred
     Art of all nations the Desire:
     Thou art as a Refiner's Fire,
     As Fuller's Sope to purge and bless;
     For Thou shalt judge the sons of men,

Shalt judge the world in righteousness.]

[*But when Thou comest, King of kings,*
Who shall abide Thy triumph day?
Shalt Thou find faith upon the earth,
Loins girt, lamps burning for Thy Sake?
Then will be dreams of frantic mirth
Tho' now it is high time to wake
Or ever earth and earthly things
With a great noise shall pass away.]

From north and south from east and
     west
Thy sons and daughters all shall
     flock
Who built their house upon the Rock
And eagle-like renew their strength:
How glad and glorious is their rest
Whom Thou hast purged from
     fleshly scum,—
The long-desired is come at length,
The fulness of the time is come.

[*Cast in my lot with theirs, cast in*
The lot of those I love with theirs,
Make those I love not follow he[a]<i>rs
Heirs of Thy throne Thy love and life:
Teach us to love both foes and friends
With love like Thine which never ends,
For loving and made pure from sin
Must be the Lamb's blood-purchased
     wife.]

17. MS: new heavens and earth shall
18. MS: indeed:
19. MS: blight nor need
20. MS: the tossing sea;
21. MS: alternating
22. MS: thereof,
23. MS: more no death no sting
24. MS: For God shall reign and
     God is

"THEN WHOSE SHALL THOSE THINGS BE?"

[Composed July 16, 1858. Editions, 1885, 1886a, *1893*, 1904. The notebook MS
(MS1) is in the British Library. A fair copy MS (MS2), signed "Christina G. Ros-
setti," is in the Open Collection, Princeton University Library. The poem originally
formed part of a poem entitled "A Burthen," which Christina never published as
such. "A Burthen" is presented in its own right in Volume III of the present edition.
The first, fifth, sixth, and twenty-second stanzas of MS1 are printed in *Verses* as
"'They lie at rest, our blessed dead.'"]

Title. MS1: A Burthen.
MS2: My old Friends.
1885, 1886a: [untitled]
1904: Then < > be?

1. MS1: [Preceding line 1 are the
following stanzas:]

They lie at rest asleep and dead,
The dew is cool above their head,
They knew not when past summer
fled—
Amen.

They lie at rest and quite forget
The hopes and fears that wring us
yet;
Their eyes are set, their heart is set—
Amen.

They lie with us, yet gone away
Hear nothing that we sob or say
Beneath the thorn of wintry may—
Miserere.

They lie asleep with us, and take
Sweet rest altho' our heart should
ache,
Rest on altho' our heart should
break—
Miserere.

Together all yet each alone,
Each laid at rest beneath his own
Smooth turf or white appointed
stone—
Amen.

When shall our slumbers be so deep,
And bleeding heart and eyes that
weep
Lie lapped in the sufficient sleep?—
Miserere.

We dream of them: and who shall say
They never dream while far away
Of us between the night and day?—
Sursum corda.

Gone far away: or it may be
They lean toward us and hear and
see
Yea and remember more than we—
Amen.

For wherefore should we think them
far
Who know not where those spirits
are
That shall be glorious as a star?—
Hallelujah.

Where chill or change can never rise
Deep in the depth of Paradise

They rest world-wearied heart and
eyes—
Jubilate.

Safe as a hidden brooding dove,
With perfect peace within, above,
They love and look for perfect
love—
Hallelujah.

We hope and love with throbbing
breast,
They hope and love and are at rest;
And yet we question which is best—
Miserere.

1. MS2: [Preceding line 1 are the
following stanzas:]

They lie at rest asleep and dead,
The dew drops cool above their
head,
They knew not when past summer
fled—
Amen.

They lie at rest and quite forget
The hopes and fears that wring us
yet;
Their eyes are set, their heart is set—
Amen.

They lie with us, yet gone away
Hear nothing that we sob or say
Beneath the thorn of wintry [M]
may—
Miserere.

Together all yet each alone,
Each laid at rest beneath his own
Smooth turf or white appointed
stone—
Amen.

When shall our slumbers be so deep,
And bleeding heart and eyes that
weep
Lie lapped in the sufficient sleep?—
Miserere.

We dream of them: and who shall say
They never dream while far away
Of us between the night and day?—
Sursum corda.

Gone far away: or it may be
They lean toward us and hear and
see
Yea and remember more than we—
Amen.

For wherefore should we deem them
far
Who know not where those spirits
are

That shall outshine both moon and
    star?—
            Hallelujah.
Where check or change can never
    rise
Deep in recovered Paradise
They rest world-wearied heart and
    eyes—
            Jubilate.
We hope and love with throbbing
    breast,
They hope and love and are at rest:
And yet we question which is best—
            Miserere.

1. 1885, 1886a: Oh! what
2. MS2: Brief houses
3. MS1, MS2: to field [A stanza
    break follows the line.]
4. MS1, MS2, 1904: And heap to
    heap and
5. MS1: seeking more
    MS2: grasping, ever grasping
    more,
    1885, 1886a: grasping more,
    and
6. MS1: While death stands
    knocking at the door?— / *Cui
    bono?* [indented thirty spaces]
    MS2: While death stands
    knocking at our door?— / *Cui
    bono?* [indented thirty spaces]
6. MS1: [After line 6 are the
    following stanzas:]

    But one will answer: Changed and
        pale
    And sick at heart, I thirst I fail
    For love, I thirst without avail—
            Miserrima.
    Sweet love, a fountain sealed to me:
    Sweet love, the one sufficiency
    For all the longings that can be—
            Amen.
    Oh happy they alone whose lot
    Is love: I search from spot to spot;
    In life, in death, I find it not—
            Miserrima.
    Not found in life; nay, verily.
    I too have sought: come sit with me
    And grief for grief shall answer
        thee—
            Miserrima.
    Sit with me where the sapless leaves
    Are heaped and sere: to him who
        grieves

What cheer have last year's harvest
    sheaves?—
            Cui bono?
Not found in life: yet found in death.
Hush throbbing heart and sobbing
    breath:
There is a nest of love beneath
The sod, a home prepared before;
Our brethren whom one mother
    bore
Live there, and toil and ache no
    more—
            Hallelujah
Our friends, our kinsfolk, great and
    small,
Our loved, our best beloved of all:
They watch across the parting wall
(Do they not watch?) and count the
    creep
Of time, and sound the shallowing
    deep,
Till we in port shall also sleep—
            Hallelujah, Amen.

6. MS2: [After line 6 are the
    following stanzas:]

    But one will answer: Changed and
        pale
    And starved at heart, I thirst I fail
    For love, I thirst without avail—
            Miserrima.
    Sweet love, a fountain sealed to me:
    Mere love, the sole sufficiency
    For every longing that can be—
            Amen.
    Oh happy those alone whose lot
    Is love: I search from spot to spot;
    In life, in death, I find it not—
            Miserrima.
    Not found in life: nay, verily.
    I too have sought: come sit with me
    And grief for grief shall answer
        thee—
            Miserrima.
    Sit with me where the sapless leaves
    Are fallen and sere: to one who
        grieves
    What cheer have last year's harvest
        sheaves?—
            Cui bono?
    Not found in life: yet found in death.
    Hush painful heart and labouring
        breath: <I sought life as but
        a breath> [The addition is
        in pencil in Christina's
        handwriting.]

There is a nest of love beneath
The sod, a home prepared before;
Our brethren whom one mother
     bore
Live there, and toil and ache no
     more—
          Hallelujah.
Dear friends and kinsfolk great and
     small;

Not lost but saved both one and all:
They w[illegible deletion]<a>tch
     across the parting wall
(Do they not watch?) and count the
     creep
Of time, and sound the shallowing
     deep,
Till we in port shall also sleep—
          Hallelujah, Amen.

"HIS BANNER OVER ME WAS LOVE."

[Date of composition unknown. Editions: 1885, 1886a, *1893*, 1904.]

Title. 1885, 1886a: [untitled]
        1904: His < > was Love.
2.   1886a: unfurled
        1904: unfurled;

3.   1885, 1886a: pain,
6.   1885, 1886a: the greenness
        fadeth
9.   1885, 1886a: hurled:—

"BELOVED, YIELD THY TIME TO GOD, FOR HE"

[Date of composition unknown. Editions: 1892, *1893*, 1904. In the 1904 text, lines 12 and 14 are indented two spaces.]

7.   1892: victory,

"TIME SEEMS NOT SHORT"

[Date of composition unknown. Editions: 1892, *1893*, 1904.]

13.   1892: sole battleground of < >
        wrong;

"THE HALF MOON SHOWS A FACE OF PLAINTIVE SWEETNESS"

[Date of composition unknown. Editions: 1892, *1893*, 1904.]

5.   1904: Lo while
9.   1892: incompleteness

10.   1904: pain?

"AS THE DOVES TO THEIR WINDOWS."

[Date of composition unknown. Editions: 1892, *1893*, 1904. In the 1892 text, lines 4 and 11 are indented four spaces.]

Title. 1892: [untitled]
        1904: As

2.   1892: south with
9.   1904: strong:

"OH KNELL OF A PASSING TIME"

[Date of composition unknown. Editions: 1892, *1893*, 1904.]

   6.   1892: sun pass

"TIME PASSETH AWAY WITH ITS PLEASURE AND PAIN"

[Date of composition unknown. Editions: 1892, *1893*, 1904. In the 1892 text, lines 4 and 11 are indented four spaces.]

   6.   1892: again: 10.   1892: creation,—while

"THE EARTH SHALL TREMBLE AT THE LOOK OF HIM."

[Date of composition unknown. Editions: 1892, *1893*, 1904.]

Title. 1892: [untitled]   8.   1904: the multichord
        1904: The <> of Him.   9.   1892: heaven and
   3. 1892: Always everywhere thy   10.   1892: of harvest and

"TIME LENGTHENING, IN THE LENGTHENING SEEMETH LONG"

[Date of composition unknown. Editions: 1892, *1893*, 1904. In the 1892 and 1904 texts, lines 3, 5, 9, 11 and 15 are not indented, and lines 4, 10, and 16 are indented two spaces.]

"ALL FLESH IS GRASS."

[Date of composition unknown. Editions: 1892, *1893*, 1904.]

Title. 1892: [untitled]   3.   1892: strife.
        1904: All <> is Grass.   9.   1904: life and
   1. 1892: brief al ife, and   10.   1892: joy:
        (1893): brief a life, and   11.   1892: relief.
   2. 1892: death: 19.   1892: scope.

"HEAVEN'S CHIMES ARE SLOW, BUT SURE TO STRIKE AT LAST"

[Lines 1–4 composed July 25, 1854. Date of composition of lines 5–8 unknown. Editions: 1885, 1886a, *1893*, 1904. The notebook MS is in the Bodleian Library. Lines 1–4 originally formed one stanza of a poem entitled "Three Stages. / 3." which Christina never published as such. "Three Stages. / 3." is presented in its own right in Volume III of the present edition. In the MS, the second, fourth, fifth, sixth, and ninth stanzas are deleted in pencil.]

Title. MS: Three Stages. / [*3*.]   addition are in pencil in William
       <Restive.> [The deletion and   Michael Rossetti's handwriting.]

1. MS: [Preceding line 1 are the
   following stanzas:]

   I thought to deal the death-stroke at
       a blow,
     To give all, once for all, but
       nevermore;—
     Then sit to hear the low waves fret
       the shore,
       [*And*] <Or> watch the silent
         snow. [The deletion and
         addition are in pencil in
         Christina's handwriting.]

   [*Once and for ever: lapsing without end,*
     Lapsing and yet perpetually the same,
     Wave after wave, a current without
       aim—
     Where should such current tend?—]

   "Oh rest," I thought, "in silence and
       the dark;
     Oh rest, if nothing else, from head
       to feet:
     Though I may see no more the
       poppied wheat,
       Or sunny soaring lark.

   [*Rest out of sight, forgotten, and how cold*
     To hope and dear delights of buried
       youth;
     Rest in the darkness, which indeed is
       truth
       Until the earth wax old.]

   [*Night came upon the noontide of my day,*
     Frost killed my buds fresh opening to
       the sun;—
     Now I will leap no more, nor p
       [illegible erasure] <*a*>*nt,*
       nor run,
     But toil <*plod*> *along the way.*]
       [The addition is in pencil in
       Christina's handwriting.]

   [*My joys are hidden from my sight—*
       amen,
     If mine eyes weep not, who should weep
       for these?—
     Yet when the axe shall smite all
       pleasant trees,
       What will it matter then?—]

1. MS: "The<se> <> but surely
   strike <> last; [The addition is
   in pencil in Christina's
   handwriting.]
2. MS: Th[*e*]<is> sand is slow,
   <> surely droppeth thro'; [The
   addition is in pencil in
   Christina's handwriting.]
3. MS: much there is to

4. MS: [After line 4 are the
   following stanzas:]

   "So will I labour, but will not rejoice:
     Will do and bear, but will not
       hope again;
     [*Grown dull*] <Gone dead> alike
       to pulses of quick pain,
       [The deletion and addition
       are in pencil in Christina's
       handwriting.]
       And pleasure's counterpoise:"

   [*So will I close mine ears and seal mine*
       eyes,
     Grown cold to songs of mirth and
       summer light;—
     For all is vanity, both depth and height,
       Vanity of vanities.—]

   I said so in my heart; and so I
       thought
     My life would lapse, a tedious
       monotone:
     I thought to shut myself, and dwell
       alone
       Unseeking and unsought.

   But first I tired, and then my care
       grew slack;
     Till my heart [*dreamed, and*]
       <slumbered> may-be
       wandered too:—[The
       deletion and addition are in
       pencil in Christina's
       handwriting.]
     I felt the sunshine glow again, and
       knew
       The swallow on its track;

   All birds awoke to bui[*e*]<l>ding in
       the leaves,
     All buds awoke to fulness and
       sweet scent;
     Ah, too, my heart woke unawares,
       intent
       On fruitful harvest sheaves.

   Full pulse of life, that I had deemed
       was dead,
     Full [illegible erasure] <throb> of
       youth, that I had deemed at
       rest,—
     Alas, I cannot build myself a nest,
       I cannot crown my head

   With royal purple blossoms for the
       feast,
     Nor flush with laughter, nor exult
       in song;—
     These joys may drift, as time now
       drifts along;
       And cease, as once they ceased.

Content

> I may pursue, and yet may not attain,
> Athirst and panting all the days I
> live:

> Or seem to hold, yet nerve myself
> to give
> What once I gave, again.

"THERE REMAINETH THEREFORE A REST TO THE PEOPLE OF GOD."

[Composed February 17, 1854. Editions: 1885, 1886a, *1893*, 1904. The notebook MS is in the Bodleian Library. The poem comprises the last two stanzas of a poem entitled "'There remaineth therefore a rest,'" which Christina never published as such. "'There remaineth therefore a rest'" is presented in its own right in Volume III of the present edition. The second and fifth stanzas of the MS text are printed in *The Prince's Progress and Other Poems* (1866) as "The Bourne," and a vertical pencil line is written in the right margin of those two stanzas.]

Title. MS: "There remaineth therefore a rest." [Above the title is added in pencil in Dante Gabriel Rossetti's handwriting:] Take 2 stanzas
1885, 1886a: [untitled]
1904: There < > of God.

1. MS: [Preceding line 1 are the following stanzas:]

Very cool that bed must be
  Where our last sleep shall be slept:
  There for weary vigils kept,
  There for tears that we have wept,
Is our guerdon certainly.

<(1)> [in pencil in Dante
  Gabriel Rossetti's hand]
Underneath the growing grass,
Underneath the living flowers,
Deeper than the sound of
    showers;—
There we shall not count the hours
By the shadows as they pass.

No more struggling then at length,
  Only slumber everywhere;
  Nothing more to do or bear:
We shall rest, and resting there
Eagle-like renew our strength.

In the grave will be no space
  For the purple of the proud,
  They must mingle with the crowd;
  In the wrappings of a shroud
Jewels would be out of place. [In the
    right margin of the stanza is
    added in pencil in William
    Michael Rossetti's
    handwriting:] <a>

<(2)> [in pencil in Dante
  Gabriel Rossetti's hand]

Youth and health will be but vain,
  Courage reckoned of no worth;
  There a very little girth
  Shall hold round what once the
    earth
Seemed too narrow to contain.

High and low and rich and poor,
  All will fare alike at last:
  The old promise standeth fast:
  None shall care then if the past
Held more joys for him or fewer.

There no laughter shall be heard,
  Nor the heavy sound of sighs;
  Sleep shall seal the aching eyes;
  All the ancient and the wise
There shall utter not a word. [In the
    right margin of the stanza is
    added in pencil in William
    Michael Rossetti's
    handwriting:] <b>

Yet it may be we shall hear
  How the mounting skylark sings
  And the bell for matins rings;
  Or perhaps the whisperings
Of white Angels sweet and clear. [In
    the right margin of the
    stanza is added in pencil in
    William Michael Rossetti's
    handwriting:] <c>

Sun or moon hath never shone
  In that hidden depth of night;
  But the souls there washed and
    white
  Are more fair than fairest light
Mortal eye hath looked upon.

The die cast whose throw is life—
  Rest complete; not one in seven—
  Souls love-perfected and shriven
  Waiting at the door of heaven,

Perfected from fear of strife.

1. MS: What a calm when [Above the line is added in pencil in Christina's handwriting:] <1.> [In the right margin of the stanza is added in pencil in William Michael Rossetti's handwriting:] <d> 1885, 1886a: remains, when
2. MS: Wearing vigil, <> fast:—
3. MS: All [*is full*] <fulfilled> from <> last: [The deletion and revision are in pencil in Christina's handwriting.]
4. MS: time [*is*] <gone> past [The deletion and revision are in pencil in Christina's handwriting.]
5. MS, 1885, 1886a, 1904: begun.
6. MS: [*Bitter cup*] <Fear & hope> and [The deletion and revision are in pencil in Christina's handwriting. In the right margin of the stanza is added in pencil in William Michael Rossetti's handwriting:] <e>
8. MS: we still as
9. MS: of the day,
10. MS: Struggling panting

"PARTING AFTER PARTING."

[Lines 1–10 composed June 15, 1858; lines 11–16 composed June 11, 1864. Editions: 1885, 1886a, *1893*, 1904. The notebook MS of lines 1–10 (MS1) and the notebook MS of lines 11–16 (MS2) are in the British Library. Lines 11–16 form the last stanza of a poem entitled "Meeting," which Christina never published as such. "Meeting" is presented in its own right in Volume III of the present edition. In MS2, line 16 is not indented. In the 1885 and 1886a texts, the poem is presented as two separate poems, the first comprising lines 1–10, the second, lines 11–16; and lines 2, 4, 6, 8, 10, and 16 are not indented.]

Title. MS1: Goodbye.
    MS2: Meeting.
1. MS1: [Preceding line 1 is the following stanza:]

    Parting after parting
      All one's life long:
    It's a bitter pang, parting,
      While love and life are strong.

2. MS1: Sore fear and sore sore pain
3. MS1: Till one dreads the pang of meeting
    1885, 1886a: sorrow,
4. MS1: More than of [A stanza break follows the line.]
5. 1885, 1886a: break,
6. MS1: When this thing shall <> be:
7. MS1: When shall the earth be born
8. MS1: That hath no more sea:
9. MS1: The time
    1885, 1886a: not time,
10. MS1: But all eternity?— [Below the line is written:] (In the train from Newcastle.)
11. MS2: [Preceding line 11 are the following stanzas:]

If we shall live, we live;
  If we shall die, we die;
If we live, we shall meet again;
  But tonight, good bye.
One word, let but one be heard—
What, not one word?

If we sleep, we Shall wake again
  And see tomorrow's light;
If we wake, we shall meet again;
  But tonight, good night.
Good night, my lost and found—
Still not a sound?

If we live, we must part;
  If we die, we part in pain;
If we die, we shall part
  Only to meet again.

By those tears on either cheek,
Tomorrow you will speak.

13. MS2: for;

14. MS2: sweet.
15. MS2: parting [*f*]<b>efore
     1904: before,

"THEY PUT THEIR TRUST IN THEE, AND WERE NOT CONFOUNDED." / I.

[Date of composition unknown. Editions: 1885, 1886a, *1893*, 1904.]

Title. 1885, 1886a: I.
        1904: They < > confounded.
   6.   1885, 1886a: which Springtide
        bore,

9. 1886a: reunions.

"THEY PUT THEIR TRUST IN THEE, AND WERE NOT CONFOUNDED." / II.

[Date of composition unknown. Editions: 1885, 1886a, *1893*, 1904.]

Title. 1885, 1886a: 2.
   4.   1904: be.

9. 1885, 1886a: poverty,

"SHORT IS TIME, AND ONLY TIME IS BLEAK"

[Date of composition unknown. Editions: 1892, *1893*, 1904. In the 1892 text, lines 4 and 11 are indented four spaces.]

FOR EACH.

[Date of composition unknown. Editions: 1892, *1893*, 1904. In the 1892 text, lines 4 and 11 are indented four spaces.]

   10.   1892: fallen so

FOR ALL.

[Date of composition unknown. Editions: 1892, *1893*, 1904. In the 1892 text, lines 4 and 11 are indented four spaces.]

   3.   1904: ascended

9. 1892: the trumpet-blast,

"THE HOLY CITY, NEW JERUSALEM."

[Date of composition unknown. Editions: 1881, *1893*, 1904.]

Title. 1881: [The poem is untitled but is preceded by the following opening quotation:] "He shewed me the holy Jerusalem."— *Revelation* xxi. 10.
1904: The Holy City, New Jerusalem.

2. 1881: pearl and
7. 1881: delight:
17. 1881: trees
1904: fruit, make
20. 1881: with the Palm
22. 1881: Jerusalem where

"WHEN WICKEDNESS IS BROKEN AS A TREE"

[Date of composition unknown. Editions: 1892, *1893*, 1904.]

3. 1892: sand
10. 1892: ring:

12. 1904: Lo harps

"JERUSALEM OF FIRE"

[Date of composition unknown. Editions: 1892, *1893*, 1904.]

9. 1892: A palm branch from

"SHE SHALL BE BROUGHT UNTO THE KING."

[Date of composition unknown. Editions: 1892, *1893*, 1904. In the 1892 text, lines 4 and 11 are indented four spaces.]

Title. 1892: [untitled]
1904: She < > the King.

4. 1892: is:

"WHO IS THIS THAT COMETH UP NOT ALONE"

[Date of composition unknown. Editions: 1885, 1886a, *1893*, 1904. In the 1885 and 1886a texts, line 5 is not indented.]

2. 1886a: the fiery-flying serpent wilderness,
3. 1885, 1886a: own Beloved One, 1904: own Beloved One?
5. 1885, 1886a: of King's daughter,
9. 1885, 1886a: heavenliness,
10. 1885, 1886a: zone:

11. 1885r: [In the left margin, in pencil in Christina's handwriting:] These lines were suggested by a sermon I heard from the Rev.–Marshall Turner in Christ Church, Woburn Square.

"WHO SITS WITH THE KING IN HIS THRONE? NOT A SLAVE BUT A BRIDE"

[Date of composition unknown. Editions: 1892, *1893*, 1904.]

10.   1892: of Peace and

ANTIPAS.

[Date of composition unknown. Editions: 1892, *1893*, 1904.]

Title. 1892: [untitled]   5. 1904: the blest;
  3. 1892: in God's Presence   8. 1892: be love with love and
    worshipped   9. 1904: Worshiping our

"BEAUTIFUL FOR SITUATION."

[Date of composition unknown. Editions: 1892, *1893*, 1904.]

Title. 1892: [untitled]   13. 1892: face, and go
  3. 1892: all angels sing;   14. 1892: pursuing home

"LORD, BY WHAT INCONCEIVABLE DIM ROAD"

[Date of composition unknown. Editions: 1892, *1893*, 1904. In the 1892 text, lines 5 and 8 are indented two spaces, and lines 6 and 7 are indented four spaces.]

11.   1892: peace:—   14. 1892: the Sabbath-day.
12.   1892: Yea but

"AS COLD WATERS TO A THIRSTY SOUL, SO IS GOOD NEWS FROM A FAR COUNTRY."

[Composed November 11, 1858. Editions: 1885, 1886a, 1893, 1904. The notebook MS (MS1) is in the British Library. A fair copy MS (MS2), signed "Christina G. Rossetti," is in the Open Collection, Princeton University Library. The poem originally formed part of a poem entitled "A shadow of Dorothea," which Christina never published as such. "A shadow of Dorothea" is presented in its own right in Volume III of the present edition. In MS1, line 16 is not indented, and the quotation marks are written in pencil. In MS2, line 16 is not indented, and every line of the poem is preceded by quotation marks. In the 1904 text, line 14 is not indented.]

Title. MS1: A shadow of Dorothea.   MS2: "Rivals." / A Shadow of
    [Added in the left margin in   Saint Dorothea.
    pencil:] <P.>   1904: As <> country.

1. MS1: <">Golden-haired,
   lily-white,
   1904: 'Golden-haired, lily-white,
2. MS1, MS2: lilies;
4. MS1, MS2: the summer rill
5. MS1: is you<r> hair
7. MS1, MS2, 1885, 1886a:
   sight,
8. MS1: And joy to <>
   desire?—<">
   MS2: And joy <> desire?"—
9. MS1: <">I pluck young flowers
   MS2: pluck young flowers
10. MS1, MS2: red;
11. MS1, MS2: A sceptre
12. MS1, MS2: my golden head.
13. MS1, MS2: Love makes me wise:
14. MS1, MS2: [The line is not in
    the text. The stanza contains
    only seven lines.]
    1885, 1886a: trees:
15. MS1, MS2: I sing, I stand,
    1885, 1886a: we sing amid <>
    bowers,
    1904: bowers,
16. MS1: I pluck palm-branches in
    the sheltered land.<">
    MS2: I pluck palm-branches in
    the sheltered land."—
    1885, 1886a: gather palm
    branches."
17. MS1: <">Is
18. MS1, MS2: My heavy foot <>
    tread;
20. MS1, MS2: That rose and lily
    bed?
21. MS1, MS2: Which day of all
    these seven
22. MS1, MS2: Will lighten my
    heart of lead,
23. MS1, MS2: Will purge mine eyes
    and make me wise
    1885, 1886a: yet awhile we <>
    wait,
24. MS1: Alive or dead?—<">
    MS2: "Alive or dead?"—

1885, 1886a: gather palm
branches."
24. MS1: [After line 24 are the
    following stanzas:]
    <">There is a Heavenward stair—
    Mount, strain upwards, strain and
    strain—
    Each step will crumble to your foot
    That never shall descend again.
    There grows a tree from ancient
    root
    [Illegible erasure] <With healing
    le>aves and twelvefold fruit
    In musical Heaven air:
    Feast with me there.—<">
    <">I have a home on earth I cannot
    leave,
    I have a friend on earth I cannot
    grieve:
    Come down to me, I cannot
    mount to you.—<">
    <">Nay, choose between us both,
    Choose as you are lief or lo[illegible
    erasure]<th:>
    You cannot keep these things and
    have me too.—<">
24. MS2: [After line 24 are the
    following stanzas:]
    "There is a Heavenward stair—
    "Mount, strain upwards, strain
    and strain—
    "Each step will crumble to your foot
    "That never shall descend again.
    "There grows a tree from ancient
    root,
    "With healing leaves and twelvefold
    fruit,
    "In [M] musical Heaven air:
    "Feast with me there."—
    "I have a home on earth I cannot
    leave,
    "I have a friend on earth I cannot
    grieve:
    "Come down to me, I cannot
    mount to you."—
    "Nay choose between us both,
    "Choose as you are lief or loath:
    "You cannot keep these things and
    have me too."—

CAST DOWN BUT NOT DESTROYED, CHASTENED NOT SLAIN"

[Date of composition unknown. Editions: 1892, *1893*, 1904. In the 1892 text, lines 11 and 12 are indented two spaces, and line 13 is not indented.]

1. 1892: slain:—   6.   1904: Lo as
3. 1892: I who   13. 1892: desire and
5. 1904: Lo I   14. 1892: Yea, then they

"LIFT UP THINE EYES TO SEEK THE INVISIBLE"

[Date of composition unknown. Editions: 1892, *1893*, 1904.]

5. 1904: Saints,   9.   1904: But
8. 1904: unspeakable.—

"LOVE IS STRONG AS DEATH."

[Date of composition unknown. Editions: *1893*, 1904.]

Title. 1904: Love < > as Death.

"LET THEM REJOICE IN THEIR BEDS."

[Date of composition unknown. Editions: 1892, *1893*, 1904.]

Title. 1892: [untitled]   7.   1892: stars while
        1904: Let < > beds.   8.   1892: Resting for
5. 1892: discloses   12. 1892: O Lord God the
6. 1892: work save waiting done.

"SLAIN IN THEIR HIGH PLACES: FALLEN ON REST"

[Date of composition unknown. Editions: 1892, *1893*, 1904.]

1. 1892: places:—fallen

"WHAT HATH GOD WROUGHT!"

[Date of composition unknown. Editions: 1892, *1893*, 1904.]

Title. 1892: [untitled]   6.   1892: love and
        1904: wrought!   1904: of one worshiping throng.
3. 1892: [No stanza break follows
    the line.]

"BEFORE THE THRONE, AND BEFORE THE LAMB."

[Date of composition unknown. Editions: 1892, *1893*, 1904.]

Title. 1892: [untitled]   5.   1892: ring
      1904: Before < > the Lamb.

"HE SHALL GO NO MORE OUT."

[Date of composition unknown. Editions: 1892, *1893*, 1904. In the 1892 text, lines 5 and 7 are not indented, and line 6 is indented two spaces.]

Title. 1892: [untitled]   7.   1892: life skin
      1904: He < > out.

"YEA, BLESSED AND HOLY IS HE THAT HATH PART IN THE FIRST
RESURRECTION!"

[Date of composition unknown. Editions: 1892, *1893*, 1904.]

  2.   1892: gaze even we

"THE JOY OF SAINTS, LIKE INCENSE TURNED TO FIRE"

[Date of composition unknown. Editions: 1892, *1893*, 1904.]

  6.   1892: tell,   9.   1892: All clad in
  7.   1892: well;   14.   1892: the will of

"WHAT ARE THESE LOVELY ONES, YEA, WHAT ARE THESE?"

[Date of composition unknown. Editions: 1892, *1893*, 1904.]

  2.   1904: Lo these   4.   1892: themselves bytimes, to
  3.   1892: Cast off < > ease

"THE GENERAL ASSEMBLY AND CHURCH OF THE FIRSTBORN."

[Date of composition unknown. Editions: 1892, *1893*, 1904. In the 1904 text, lines 3, 5, 9, 11, 15, and 17 are not indented, and lines 4, 10, and 16 are indented two spaces.]

Title. 1892: [untitled]
       1904: The < > of the Firstborn.

11. 1892: who making merry lead
15. reproduce One countenance,

"EVERY ONE THAT IS PERFECT SHALL BE AS HIS MASTER."

[Date of composition unknown. Editions: 1885, 1886a, *1893*, 1904.]

Title. 1885, 1886a: [untitled]
      1904: Every < > his Master.
9. 1885: all
10. 1885, 1886a: Great St. John,—
     though

13. 1885, 1886a: which teaching
     glad obedience

"'AS DYING, AND BEHOLD WE LIVE!'"

[Date of composition unknown. Editions: 1892, *1893*, 1904. In the 1892 text, lines 4 and 11 are indented four spaces, lines 5 and 7 are not indented, and line 6 is indented two spaces.]

"SO GREAT A CLOUD OF WITNESSES."

[Date of composition unknown. Editions: 1892, *1893*, 1904.]

Title. 1892: [untitled]
      1904: So < > of Witnesses.
4. 1893. [Line 4 is the last
     line on the page.]

8. 1892: open entrance door. [No
     stanza break follows the line.]
10. 1892: saints to me;

"OUR MOTHERS, LOVELY WOMEN PITIFUL"

[Date of composition unknown. Editions: 1892, *1893*, 1904.]

6. 1892: walked much
7. 1892: hoped despite

9. 1892: can see:
13. 1904: Ah happy

"SAFE WHERE I CANNOT LIE YET"

[Date of composition unknown. Editions: 1892, *1893*, 1904.]

7. 1892: sun;

"IS IT WELL WITH THE CHILD?"

[Composed November 3, 1865. Editions: 1885, 1886a, *1893*, 1904. The notebook MS is in the British Library. The poem originally formed part of a poem entitled "Young Death," which Christina never published as such. "Young Death" is presented in its own right in Volume III of the present edition. In the MS, a vertical pencil line is written in the right margin of lines 1–6 and lines 7–12.]

Title. MS: Young Death.
1885, 1886a: 2.

1. MS: [Preceding line 1 is the following stanza:]

Lying adying—
Such sweet things untasted,
Such rare beauties wasted:
Her hair a hidden treasure,
Her voice a lost pleasure;
Her soul made void of passion;
Her body going to nothing
Though long it took to fashion,
Soon to be a loathing:
Her road hath no turning,
Her light is burning burning
With last feeble flashes;
Dying from the birth:
Dust to dust, earth to earth,
Ashes to ashes.

1. MS: Lying adying—
1885, 1886a: a-dying,—

6. MS: [After line 6 are the following lines:]

Lo, in the Room, the Upper,
She shall sit down to supper,
New bathed from head to feet
And on Christ gazing:
Her mouth kept clean and sweet
Shall laugh and sing, God praising:
Then shall be no more weeping,
Or fear, or sorrow,
Or waking more, or sleeping,
Or night, or morrow,
Or cadence in the song
Of songs, or thirst, or hunger;
The strong shall rise more strong
And the young younger.

7. 1885, 1886a: dove,
9. MS: to Love;
10. MS: white
11. MS: the Light

"DEAR ANGELS AND DEAR DISEMBODIED SAINTS"

[Date of composition unknown. Editions: 1892, *1893*, 1904.]

2. 1904: us, worshiping in
3. 1904: faints,
11. 1892: heart that being
13. 1892: When Christ life-Giver
roused

1904: When Christ, Life-giver,
roused

"TO EVERY SEED HIS OWN BODY."

[Date of composition unknown. Editions: 1892, *1893*, 1904.]

Title. 1892: [untitled]
1904: To

7. 1892: goal;
12. 1892: Each dovelike soul

"WHAT GOOD SHALL MY LIFE DO ME?"

[Composed probably after August 6, 1858, and before October 15, 1858. Editions: 1885, 1886a, *1893*, 1904. The notebook MS is in the British Library. The poem originally formed part of a poem entitled "'Only believe,'" which Christina never published as such. "'Only believe'" is presented in its own right in Volume III of the present edition. In the MS, the lines following line 28, and the date of composition, are missing from the notebook; and the added quotation marks are written in pencil.]

Title. MS: "Only believe."
1885, 1886a: [untitled]
1904: What < > me?

1. MS: [Preceding line 1 are the following stanzas:]

I stood by weeping
Yet a sorrowful silence keeping
While an Angel smote my love
As she lay sleeping.—
<">Is there a bed above
More fragrant than these violets
That are white like death?<">
<">White like a dove
Flowers in the blessed islets
Breathe sweeter breath
All fair morns and twilights.<">
<">Is the gold there
More golden than these tresses?<">
<">There heads are aureoled
And crowned like gold
With light most rare.<">
<">Are the bowers of Heaven
More choice than these?<">
<">To them are given
All odorous shady trees.
Earth's bowers are wildernesses
Compared with the recesses
Made soft there now
Nest-like twixt bough and
bough.<">
<">Who shall live in such a
nest?<">
<">Heart with heart at rest:
All they whose troubles cease
In peace:
Souls that wrestled
Now are nestled
There at ease:
Throng from east and west
From north and south

To plenty from the land of
drouth.<">

1. MS: <">How long must they
wait?<">
1885, 1886a: [No stanza break
follows the line.]
2. MS: <">There
3. MS: at Heaven-gate.
4. 1885, 1886a: at Heaven gate.
1904: gate:
5. MS: Dust to dust, clod to
[*g*]<*c*>lod
6. MS: of God;
8. MS: years.<">
1886a: [No stanza break follows
the line.]
9. MS: <">Their
10. MS: For birth, death, laughter,
tears:
1885, 1886a, 1904: tears:
13. MS: fear and
14. MS: Man with man, lie with
17. MS: grave?<">
1885, 1886a: grave?
18. MS: <">Lies
24. MS: The cross shall wear the
crown:
1904: wear the Crown;
26. MS: down.<"> 1893. [Line 26 is
the last line on the page.]
1904. [A stanza break follows
the line.]
27. MS: [*The Shepherd of the sheep*]
[The deletion is in pencil.]
28. MS: [*Feeds His flock there*;] [The
deletion is in pencil.]
1904: there;

"HER SEED; IT SHALL BRUISE THY HEAD."

[Date of composition unknown. Editions: 1892, *1893*, 1904. In the 1892 text, lines 5 and 7 are not indented, and line 6 is indented two spaces.]

Title. 1892: [untitled]   1904: hope, first
  3. 1892: said   9. 1892: the All-holy Spirit's

"JUDGE NOTHING BEFORE THE TIME."

[Date of composition unknown. Editions: 1885, 1886a, *1893*, 1904.]

Title. 1885, 1886a: [untitled]
       1904: Judge < > time.

"HOW GREAT IS LITTLE MAN!"

[Date of composition unknown. Editions: 1892, *1893*, 1904.]

  2. 1892: moon and   10. 1892: day,
  9. 1892, 1904: Ah rich man! ah   13. 1892: things man,
     poor

"MAN'S LIFE IS BUT A WORKING DAY"

[Composed March 19, 1864. Editions: 1885, 1886a, *1893*, 1904. The notebook MS is in the British Library. The poem originally formed the final stanza of a poem entitled "In Patience," which Christina never published as such. "In Patience" is presented in its own right in Volume III of the present edition. In the 1885 text, lines 2 and 4 are not indented. In the 1886a text, line 4 is not indented.]

Title. MS: In Patience.   1. MS: My life
  1. MS: [Preceding line 1 is the   3. MS: a while to work, a while to
    following stanza:]   6. MS: Where Saints and Angels
    I will not faint, but trust in God   walk in white:
    Who [*all*] <this> my lot hath   1885, 1886a: white,
      given; [The deletion and   7. MS: One dreamless sleep from
      addition are in pencil in   work and sorrow,
      Christina's handwriting.]   1885, 1886a: sorrow,—
    He leads me by the thorny road   8. MS: But re-awakening on the
      Which is the road to heaven.   morrow.
    Tho' sad my day that lasts so long,
    At evening I shall have a song;
    Tho' dim my day until the night,
    At evening time there shall be light.

"IF NOT WITH HOPE OF LIFE"

[Date of composition unknown. Editions: 1892, *1893*, 1904. In the 1892 text, the first two stanzas are printed in double columns and the third stanza is centered below them.]

    3.   1892: tremendous lifelong strife

"THE DAY IS AT HAND."

[Date of composition of lines 1–4 unknown; lines 5–11 composed December 23, 1852. Editions: 1885, 1886a, *1893*, 1904. The notebook MS is in the Bodleian Library. The poem originally formed part of a poem entitled "'The heart knoweth its own bitterness,'" which Christina never published as such. "'The heart knoweth its own bitterness'" is presented in its own right in Volume III of the present edition. In the MS, the first stanza is deleted with horizontal pencil lines, and lines 1–4 are added below the poem in pencil in Christina's handwriting; lines 1–4 are also added in pencil in William Michael Rossetti's handwriting between the lines of the first stanza. In the final stanza of the MS, the first, third, fifth, seventh, ninth, tenth, and eleventh lines are not indented, and the second, fourth, sixth, and eighth lines are indented two spaces.]

Title. MS: "The heart knoweth its own bitterness."
    1885, 1886a: [untitled]
    1904: The < > hand.

    1. MS: [The following stanza opens the poem:]

> [*Weep, for none shall know*
>   *Why sick at heart thou weepest;*
> *Wake and weep, for none shall guess*
> *In thy loneliness*
>   *Why thou thy vigil keepest.*
> *Weep yet a while;*
> *Weep till the day shall dawn when thou*
>   *shalt smile.*]

[Below the poem is added:]

Weep yet a while
Weep till that day shall dawn when
    thou shalt smile
Watch till the day
When all save only Love shall pass
    away.>

    1. MS: Weep < > while
    2. MS: smile
    4. MS: [After the first stanza are the following stanzas:]

Weep, sick and lonely,
  Bow thy heart to tears,
For none shall guess the secret
  Of thy griefs and fears.

Weep, till the day dawn,
Refreshing dew:
Weep till the spring;
For genial showers
Bring up the flowers,
And thou shalt sing
In summer time of blossoming.

Heart sick and silent,
  Weep and watch in pain.
Weep for hope perished,
  Not to live again;
Weep for love's hope and fear
  And passion vain.
Watch till the day
When all save only love shall pass
    away.

    5. MS: Then love rejoicing / Shall forget < > weep;
        1885, 1886a: Then love rejoicing
    6. MS: more, / Or watch, or
    7. MS: and cease not, / Deep beyond
        1885, 1886a: not deep
    8. MS: tears, / But then < > reap:
    9. MS: as the Lord's Own flock
  10. MS: with His Love,
       1885, 1886a: with His love
  11. MS: Who died below, Who lives for thee above.

"ENDURE HARDNESS."

[Date of composition unknown. Editions: 1885, 1886a, *1893*, 1904.]

Title. 1885, 1886a: [untitled]
       1904: Endure hardness.
4. 1885, 1886a: With vegetable
      snow.

7. 1885, 1886a: doubtless,

"WHITHER THE TRIBES GO UP, EVEN THE TRIBES OF THE LORD."

[Date of composition unknown. Editions: 1881, *1893*, 1904. In the 1881 text, the last line of each stanza is indented four spaces.]

Title. 1881: [The poem is untitled, but
      it appears in the chapter entitled
      "All Saints."]

10. 1881: us,

"WHERE NEVER TEMPEST HEAVETH"

[Date of composition unknown. Editions: 1892, *1893*, 1904. In the 1892 text, the two stanzas are printed in double columns, and lines 5 and 10 are indented four spaces.]

"MARVEL OF MARVELS, IF I MYSELF SHALL BEHOLD"

[Date of composition unknown. Editions: 1892, *1893*, 1904.]

6. 1892: saints my

11. 1892: tolled,

"WHAT IS THAT TO THEE? FOLLOW THOU ME."

[Lines 1–12 composed May 6, 1864; lines 13–18 composed March 1, 1864. Editions: 1885, 1886a, *1893*, 1904. The notebook MS of lines 1–12 (MS1) and the notebook MS of lines 13–18 (MS2) are in the British Library. The first eight stanzas of MS2 are printed in *Goblin Market, the Prince's Progress, and Other Poems* (1875) as "Who Shall Deliver Me?" In MS2, lines 13 and 16 are indented two spaces. In the 1885 and 1886a texts, the poem is presented as two separate poems, the first comprising lines 1–12, the second, lines 13–18.]

Title. MS1: The Audience Chamber.
      MS2: Who shall deliver me?
      1885, 1886a: [untitled]
      1904: What < > thou Me.
1. MS1: Lie still my troubled heart,
     < > still,
2. MS1: Because God wills that
     thou shouldst bear:
4. MS1: denies is ill;
5. MS1: subtle ease is this thy

6. MS1: hurt is help
7. MS1: higher," to one; to one
8. MS1: thou," He wills and saith;
9. MS1: death:"
10. MS1: For these the wilderness
      shall flower
11. MS1: When harvest's past and
      summer gone.
      1885, 1886a: done,—

12.   MS1: hour? [After line 12 is the
       following stanza:]

"Where is thy faith?" He saith to her
Whose lamp is dwindling towards
       the dark;
"My daughter, give thy heart to Me."
Awake, thou sluggard, watch and
       hark:
A cry is made, there comes a stir,
The Bridegroom comes and calls for
       thee.

13.   MS2: [Preceding line 13 are the
       following stanzas:]

God strengthen me to bear myself;
That heaviest weight of all to bear,
Inalienable weight of care.

All others are outside myself:
I lock my door and bar them out,
The turmoil, tedium, gad-about.

I lock my door upon myself
And bar them out: but who shall wall
Self from myself, most loathed of
       all?

If I could once lay down myself,
And start self-purged upon the race
That all must run! Death runs apace.

If I could set aside myself,
And start with lightened heart upon
The road by all men overgone!

God harden me against myself;
This coward with pathetic voice
Who craves for ease and rest and
       joys:
Myself, arch-traitor to myself;
My hollowest friend, my deadliest
       foe,
My clog whatever road I go.

[*Yet O*] [out to left margin]
       <Yet One> [indented two
       spaces] there is can curb
       myself,
Can roll the strangling load from
       me,
Break off the yoke and set me free.

13.   MS2: [*Lord, I*] [out to left
       margin] <Lord, I> [indented
       two spaces] had <> lot;

14.   MS2: well,

15.   MS2: Only [*t*]<T>hy choice for
       me is

16.   MS2: No different <diverse>
       lot in Heaven or Hell [The
       addition is in pencil in
       Christina's handwriting.]
       1885, 1886a: heaven and hell,

17.   MS2: me, rightly understood;
       1885, 1886a, 1904: me, fully

"WORSHIP GOD."

[Date of composition unknown. Editions: 1892, *1893*, 1904. In the 1892 text, line 13
is indented two spaces. In the 1904 text, lines 12 and 14 are indented two spaces.]

2.   1892: near"—
      1904: near':
9.   1892: said; "Worship Me: and
10.   1892: child";—now
      1904: child'; now

"AFTERWARD HE REPENTED, AND WENT."

[Date of composition unknown. Editions: 1885, 1886a, *1893*, 1904. In the 1885 and
1886a texts, line 7 is not indented, and lines 8 and 9 are indented two spaces.]

Title. 1885, 1886a: [untitled]
   1.   1885, 1886a: back,

"ARE THEY NOT ALL MINISTERING SPIRITS?"

[Date of composition unknown. Editions: 1892, *1893*, 1904. In the 1892 text, lines 3, 6, 9, 12, 15, and 18 are indented two spaces. In the 1904 text, line 2 is indented four spaces.]

Title. 1892: [untitled]
       1904: Are < > all Ministering
       Spirits?

11. 1892: death;
13. 1904: . . . Lo,

"OUR LIFE IS LONG. NOT SO, WISE ANGELS SAY"

[Composed April 14, 1856. Editions: 1885, 1886a, *1893*, 1896, 1904. The notebook MS (MS1) is in the Bodleian Library. A fair copy MS (MS2), signed "Christina Rossetti," is in the Rossetti Collection of Janet Camp Troxell, Princeton University Library.]

Title. MS1: How long?
       MS2: Time and Opportunity.
       1896: HOW LONG?

1. MS1: My life < > long—not so the Angels
    1885, 1886a: long—Not so wise < > say,
    1896: My life < > long—Not so the Angels

2. MS1, 1896: watch me waste < > trembling whilst they

3. MS1, 1896: eternity my lavished day.

4. MS1: My life < > long—not so the Saints in peace
    1885, 1886a: long—Not so the
    1896: My life< >long—Not so the Saints in peace

5. MS1, 1896: Judge, filled with plenitude that cannot cease:

6. MS1: Oh life was short which bought such large increase.
    1896: Oh life was short which bought such large increase!

7. MS1: My life < > long—Christ's Word is different:
    1885, 1886a: long—Christ's
    1896: My life < > long—Christ's word is different:

8. MS1, 1896: The heat and burden of the day were spent
    1885, 1886a, 1893, 1904: spent."

9. MS1: On Him, to me refreshing times are sent.
    1885, 1886a, 1893, 1904: today, work and repent.
    1896: On Him,—to me refreshing times are sent.

10. MS1, 1896: Give me an Angel's heart, that day
    1885, 1886a: like Thy Host, who

11. MS1: Rests not < > adoration its delight
    1896: Rests not < > adoration its delight,

12. MS1, 1896: Still crying "Holy holy" in

13. MS1: Give me the heart of Saints, who laid at rest
    1896: Give me the heart of Saints, who, laid at rest

14. MS1: In better Paradise than Abraham's breast
    1896: In better Paradise than Abraham's breast,
    1904: wrong,

15. MS1: In the Everlasting Rock have made their nest.
    1896: In the everlasting Rock have made their nest.

16. MS1: Give me Thy Heart O Christ, Who thirtythree
    1885, 1886a: like Thyself, for
    1896: Give me Thy heart, O

Christ, who thirty-three
1904: like Thyself; for
17.   MS1: of sorrow countedst short
for me
1885, 1886a: to Thee
1896: of sorrow countedst short
for me,

18.   MS1: art there Thy beloved
might
1885, 1886a, 1893, 1896, 1904:
art there

"LORD, WHAT HAVE I TO OFFER? SICKENING FEAR"

[Date of composition unknown. Editions: 1885, 1886a, *1893*, 1904.]

"JOY IS BUT SORROW"

[Date of composition unknown. Editions: 1885, 1886a, *1893*, 1904. In the 1885 and 1886a texts, lines 1, 3, 5, 6, 8, 10, 12, and 13 are not indented, and lines 2, 4, 9, and 11 are indented two spaces.]

14.   1885, 1886a: fair art thou as
moon-rise after

"CAN I KNOW IT?—NAY.—"

[Date of composition unknown. Editions: 1892, *1893*, 1904.]

1.   1904: 'Can < > it?'—'Nay.'—
2.   1904: 'Shall < > it?'—'Yea,
4.   1904: aye.'—
5.   1904: 'Why < > to-day?'—
6.   1904: 'Who
8.   1904: way.'—
9.   1904: 'Other < > gay.'—
10. 1904: 'Ask
12. 1904: bay.'—
13. 1892: past May day
1904: 'On

16. 1904: of May.'—
17. 1904: 'Dost
20. 1904: away.'—
21. 1904: 'Gone
24. 1904: to-day.'—
25. 1904: 'Dost
28. 1892: nay.—
1904: nay.'

"WHEN MY HEART IS VEXED I WILL COMPLAIN."

[Date of composition unknown. Editions: 1885, 1886a, *1893*, 1904.]

Title.   1885, 1886a: A DIALOGUE.
1904: When < > complain.
6.   1885, 1886a, 1904: "Ah woe

18.   1885, 1886a: That ever open
door

"PRAYING ALWAYS."

[Date of composition unknown. Editions: 1885, 1886a, *1893*, 1904.]

Title. 1885, 1886a: [untitled]
2. 1885, 1886a: one,—
6. 1885, 1886a: After midday, in

7. 1885, 1886a: one,—
8. 1885, 1886a: Day fall has

"AS THY DAYS, SO SHALL THY STRENGTH BE."

[Date of composition unknown. Editions: 1892, *1893*, 1904. In the 1892 text, lines 4, 8, 12, and 16 are indented two spaces. In the 1904 text, lines 4, 8, 12, and 16 are indented eight spaces.]

Title. 1892: [untitled]

"A HEAVY HEART, IF EVER HEART WAS HEAVY"

[Date of composition unknown. Editions: 1885, 1886a, *1893*, 1904.]

4. 1885, 1886a: bleed for Thee?—
5. 1904: Ah blessed heaviness if
6. 1904: leafy,
7. 1904: the fruit if

10. 1885, 1886a: The stript fruit-bearing
15. 1885, 1886a: loving for

"IF LOVE IS NOT WORTH LOVING, THEN LIFE IS NOT WORTH LIVING"

[Date of composition unknown. Editions: 1885, 1886a, *1893*, 1904.]

2. 1885, 1886a: forgot,

"WHAT IS IT JESUS SAITH UNTO THE SOUL?"

[Lines 1–7 composed March 2, 1850; date of composition of lines 8–14 unknown. Editions: 1885, 1886a, *1893*, 1904. The notebook MS (MS1) is in the Bodleian Library. Christina also included the poem in her manuscript notebook of *Maude: Prose and Verse* (MS2). MS2 is in the Huntington Library. In MS1, lines 11, 12, and 14 are not indented, and line 13 is indented two spaces. In MS2, lines 1, 4, 5, 8, and 10 are indented four spaces; lines 2, 3, 6, 7, and 12 are not indented; line 11 is indented two spaces; and line 13 is indented six spaces. In the 1885 and 1886a texts, lines 10 and 14 are not indented, and lines 11 and 12 are indented two spaces.]

Title. MS1: "Blessed are they that mourn for they shall be comforted."
1. MS1, MS2, 1885, 1886a: soul?—
2. MS1: the Cross and
   MS2: the Cross, and come, and
3. MS1, MS2: This word < > all; no man may

4. MS1: Without the Cross wishing to win the
   MS2: Without the Cross, wishing to win the
   1885, 1886a: a Cross yet
5. MS1, MS2: Then take it < > up, setting thy

7. MS1, MS2: Beyond thy utmost
    strength: take it; for He
8. MS1, MS2: Knoweth when thou
    art weak, and will control
9. MS1: The powers of darkness
    that thou need'st not fear:
    MS2: The powers of darkness
    that thou need'st not fear.
10. MS1: He will be with thee,
    helping, strengt[e]<h>ening,
    MS2: He will be with thee,
    helping, strengthening,
    1904: more.
11. MS1, MS2: Until it is enough:
    for lo, the day
12. MS1: Cometh when He shall call
    thee; thou shalt hear

    MS2: Cometh when He shall call
    thee: thou shalt hear
    1885, 1886a: morrow, go
13. MS1: His [v]<V>oice saying
    <[t]<T>hat says>: "Winter is
    passed, and Spring [The added
    words are in pencil in Christina's
    handwriting.]
    MS2: His Voice That says:
    "Winter is past, and Spring
    1885, 1886a: Suffer, and work,
    and
14. MS1: Is come; arise, My love,
    and come away."
    MS2: Is come; arise, My love,
    and come away."—

"THEY LIE AT REST, OUR BLESSED DEAD"

[Composed July 16, 1858. Editions: 1885, 1886a, *1893*, 1904. The notebook MS
(MS1) is in the British Library. A fair copy MS (MS2), signed "Christina G. Rossetti,"
is in the Open Collection, Princeton University Library. The poem originally formed
part of a poem entitled "A Burthen," which Christina never published as such.
"A Burthen" is presented in its own right in Volume III of the present edition. The
thirteenth and fourteenth stanzas of MS1 are printed in *Verses* as "'Then whose shall
those things be?'"]

Title. MS1: A Burthen.
       MS2: My old Friends.
1. MS1, MS2: rest asleep and dead,
    1885, 1886a: dead:
2. MS1: The dew is cool
3. MS1, MS2: when past summer
    fled— / *Amen.*
3. MS1: [After line 3 are the
    following stanzas:]

    They lie at rest and quite forget
    The hopes and fears that wring us
                yet;
    Their eyes are set, their heart is set—
                Amen.

    They lie with us, yet gone away
    Hear nothing that we sob or say
    Beneath the thorn of wintry may—
                Miserere.

    They lie asleep with us, and take
    Sweet rest altho' our heart should
                ache,
    Rest on altho' our heart should
                break—
                Miserere.

3. MS2: [After line 3 are the
    following stanzas:]

    They lie at rest and quite forget
    The hopes and fears that wring us
                yet;
    Their eyes are set, their heart is set—
                Amen.

    They lie with us, yet gone away
    Hear nothing that we sob or say
    Beneath the thorn of wintry [M]
                may—
                Miserere.

4. MS1, MS2: all yet < > alone,
    1885, 1886a: alone:
6. MS1, MS2: white appointed
    stone— / *Amen.* [indented thirty
    spaces]
7. MS1, MS2: our slumbers be so
8. MS1, MS2: And bleeding heart
    and
9. MS1, MS2: Lie lapped in < >
    sleep?— / *Miserere.* [indented
    thirty spaces]

9. MS1: [After line 9 are the
    following stanzas:]

    We dream of them: and who shall say
    They never dream while far away
    Of us between the night and day?—
                    Sursum corda.

    Gone far away: or it may be
    They lean toward us and hear and
        see
    Yea and remember more than we—
                    Amen.

    For wherefore should we think them
        far
    Who know not where those spirits
        are
    That shall be glorious as a star?—
                    Hallelujah.

    Where chill or change can never rise
    Deep in the depth of Paradise
    They rest world-wearied heart and
        eyes—
                    Jubilate.

    Safe as a hidden brooding dove,
    With perfect peace within, above,
    They love and look for perfect
        love—
                    Hallelujah.

    We hope and love with throbbing
        breast,
    They hope and love and are at rest;
    And yet we question which is best—
                    Miserere.

    Oh what is earth, that we should
        build
    Our houses here, and seek concealed
    Poor treasure, and add field to field

    And heap to heap and store to store,
    Still grasping more and seeking
        more
    While death stands knocking at the
        door?—
                    Cui bono?

    But one will answer: Changed and
        pale
    And sick at heart, I thirst I fail
    For love, I thirst without avail—
                    Miserrima.

    Sweet love, a fountain sealed to me:
    Sweet love, the one sufficiency
    For all the longings that can be—
                    Amen.

    Oh happy they alone whose lot
    Is love: I search from spot to spot;
    In life, in death, I find it not—
                    Miserrima.

Not found in life; nay, verily.
I too have sought: come sit with me
And grief for grief shall answer
    thee—
                Miserrima.

Sit with me where the sapless leaves
Are heaped and sere: to him who
    grieves
What cheer have last year's harvest
    sheaves?—
                Cui bono?

Not found in life: yet found in death.
Hush throbbing heart and sobbing
    breath:
There is a nest of love beneath

The sod, a home prepared before;
Our brethren whom one mother
    bore
Live there, and toil and ache no
    more—
                Hallelujah

9. MS2: [After line 9 are the
    following stanzas:]

    We dream of them: and who shall say
    They never dream while far away
    Of us between the night and day?—
                    Sursum corda.

    Gone far away: or it may be
    They lean toward us and hear and
        see
    Yea and remember more than we—
                    Amen.

    For wherefore should we deem them
        far
    Who know not where those spirits
        are
    That shall outshine both moon and
        star?—
                    Hallelujah.

    Where check or change can never
        rise
    Deep in recovered Paradise
    They rest world-wearied heart and
        eyes—
                    Jubilate.

    We hope and love with throbbing
        breast,
    They hope and love and are at rest:
    And yet we question which is best—
                    Miserere.

    Oh what is earth, that we should
        build
    Brief houses here, and seek
        concealed
    Poor treasure, and add field to field

And heap to heap and store to store,
Still grasping, ever grasping more,
While death stands knocking at our
  door?—
  Cui bono?

But one will answer: Changed and
  pale
And starved at heart, I thirst I fail
For love, I thirst without avail—
  Miserrima.

Sweet love, a fountain sealed to me:
Mere love, the sole sufficiency
For every longing that can be—
  Amen.

Oh happy those alone whose lot
Is love: I search from spot to spot;
In life, in death, I find it not—
  Miserrima.

Not found in life: nay, verily.
I too have sought: come sit with me
And grief for grief shall answer
  thee—
  Miserrima.

Sit with me where the sapless leaves
Are fallen and sere: to one who
  grieves
What cheer have last year's harvest
  sheaves?—
  Cui bono?

Not found in life: yet found in death.
Hush painful heart and labouring
  breath: <I sought life as
  but a breath> [The
  addition is in pencil in
  Christina's handwriting.]

There is a nest of love beneath
The sod, a home prepared before;
Our brethren whom one mother
  bore
Live there, and toil and ache no
  more—
  Hallelujah.

10. MS1: Our friends, our kinsfolk,
  great
  MS2: Dear friends and kinsfolk
  great < > small;

11. MS1: Our loved, our < > all:
  MS2: Not lost but saved both
  one and all:
  1885, 1886a: loves, our
  best-beloved of

12. MS1: They watch across the
  parting wall
  MS2: They w[illegible
  deletion]<a>tch across the
  parting wall

12. MS1, MS2: [After line 12 is the
  following stanza:]
  (Do they not watch?) and count the
    creep
  Of time, and sound the shallowing
    deep,
  Till we in port shall also sleep—
    Hallelujah, Amen.

12. 1885, 1886a: salt sea wall.

"YE THAT FEAR HIM, BOTH SMALL AND GREAT."

[Date of composition unknown. Editions: 1881, *1893*, 1904. In the 1881 text, the last line of each stanza is indented two spaces.]

Title. 1881: [The poem is untitled, but
  it appears in the chapter entitled
  "St. Philip and St. James the
  Less, Apostles."]

"CALLED TO BE SAINTS."

[Date of composition unknown. Editions: 1885, 1886a, *1893*, 1904. In the 1885 and 1886a texts, lines 4 and 8 are indented two spaces.]

Title. 1885, 1886a: [untitled]
  1904: Called < > be Saints.

"THE SINNER'S OWN FAULT? SO IT WAS"

[Lines 1–5 composed October 1, 1863. Date of composition of lines 6–10 unknown. Editions: 1885, 1886a, *1893*, 1904. The notebook MS is in the British Library. Lines 1–5 originally formed one stanza of a peom entitled "Margery," which Christina never published as such. "Margery" is presented in its own right in Volume III of the present edition.]

Title. MS: Margery.

1. MS1: [Preceding line 1 are the following stanzas:]

What shall we do with Margery?
  She lies and cries upon her bed,
  All lily-pale from foot to head,
Her heart is sore as sore can be;
Poor guileless shamefaced Margery.

A foolish girl, to love a man
  And let him know she loved him so!
She should have [*hel*] <trie>d a different plan;
  Have loved, but not have let him know:
  Then he perhaps had loved her so.

What can we do with Margery
  Who has no relish for her food?
We'd take her with us to the sea—
  Across the sea—but where's the good?
She'd fret alike on land and sea.

Yes, what the neighbours say is true:
  Girls should not make themselves so cheap.
But now it's done what can we do?
  I hear her moaning in her sleep,
  Moaning and sobbing in her sleep.

I think—and I'm of flesh and blood—
  Were I that man for whom she cares
I would not cost her tears and prayers
To leave her just alone like mud,
Fretting her simple heart with cares.

A year ago she was a child,
  Now she's a woman in her grief;
The year's now at the falling leaf,
At budding of the leaves she smiled;
Poor foolish harmless foolish child.

1. MS: It was her own fault? so it
2. MS: out
3. MS: and [*hedged*] <snared> us round [The deletion and addition are in pencil in Christina's handwriting.]
4. 1885, 1886a: take, because
5. MS: [After line 5 are the following stanzas:]

At any rate the question stands:
  What now to do with Margery,
A weak poor creature on our hands?
Something we must do: I'll not see
Her [*pine and*] <blossom> fade, sweet Margery. [The deletion and addition are in pencil in Christina's handwriting, written over by William Michael Rossetti.]

Perhaps a change may after all
  Prove best for her: to leave b[*l*]<e>hind
  These home-sights seen time out of mind;
To get beyond the narrow wall
Of home, and learn home is not all.

Perhaps this way she may forget,
  Not all at once, but in a while;
May come to wonder how she set
  Her heart on this slight thing, and smile
  At her own folly, in a while.

Yet this I say and I maintain:
  Were I the man she's fretting for
  I should my very self abhor
If I could leave her to her pain,
Uncomforted to tears and pain.

7. 1885, 1886a: pray,
8. 1885, 1886a: lagged, and

"WHO CARES FOR EARTHLY BREAD THO' WHITE?"

[Date of composition unknown. Editions: 1885, 1886a, *1893*, 1904.]

  9. 1886a: bid good-night to

"LAUGHING LIFE CRIES AT THE FEAST,—"

[Date of composition unknown. Editions: 1885, 1886a, *1893*, 1904. The notebook MS is in the Bodleian Library. In the MS notebook, the poem is the third in a group of ten poems entitled "Odds and Ends." At the end of the group is written, "Copied, September 1853."]

1. MS: Life is sitting in the hall,
2. MS: Death is knocking at the door:
3. MS: "Fill the cups, they sparkle all:"—
   1885, 1886a: feast?"—
   1904: 'Fish or fowl or
4. MS: me, fill up no more:"—
5. MS: "Pluck the roses:"—
   "[s]<S>ee they fade:"—

6. MS: "I am sunlight:"—"I <>
   shade;
   1885, 1886a: "I am sunlight."—
   "I
7. MS: "I <> the sun-sheltering west;
8. MS: am silence, I <> rest;
9. MS: "Come to me,

"THE END IS NOT YET."

[Date of composition unknown. Editions: 1885, 1886a, *1893*, 1904.]

Title. 1885, 1886a: [untitled]
  3. 1885, 1886a: old and <> small
  6. 1885, 1886a: Wind must blow and rain
 10. 1885, 1886a: wall

"WHO WOULD WISH BACK THE SAINTS UPON OUR ROUGH"

[Composed December 13, 1861. Editions: 1885, 1886a, *1893*, 1904. The notebook MS is in the British Library. The poem originally formed part of a poem entitled "Better so," which Christina never published as such. "Better so" is presented in its own right in Volume III of the present edition.]

Title. MS: Better so.
  1. MS: [Preceding line 1 are the following stanzas:]

Fast asleep, mine own familiar friend,
[F] [out to left margin] <F>ast [indented two spaces] asleep at last:
Tho' the pain was strong,
Tho' the struggle long,
It is past;

All thy pangs are at an end.
Whilst I weep, whilst death bells toll,
Thou art fast asleep,
With idle hands upon thy breast
And heart at rest:
Angels sing around thy singing soul.

  1. MS: wish thee back upon the rough
1885, 1886a: rough,

2. MS: Wearisome dangerous road?
3. MS: back thy toil-spent soul
4. MS: [*Now*] <Just> at [The deletion and addition are in pencil in Christina's handwriting.]
6. MS: For [*that*] <one> dear soul which hath enough. [The deletion and addition are in pencil in Christina's handwriting.]
7. MS: fetch thee back
8. MS: A sickening hope deferred,
9. MS: taste the cup
10. MS: From thirsty lips:
11. MS: Hast thou not
12. MS: What was to hear, and seen what was to see?
12. MS: [After line 12 is the following stanza:]

I would not speak the word if I could raise
My dead to life:
I would not speak
If I could flush thy cheek
And rouse thy pulses' strife
And send thy [illegible erasure] <feet> on the once-trodden ways.

13. MS: could I meet the dear rebuke
1885, 1886a: rebuke,
14. MS: If thou should'st say:
15. MS: <">O [The quotation marks are in pencil.]
16. MS: my lot of death,
18. MS: took"—?
1904: took'?

"THAT WHICH HATH BEEN IS NAMED ALREADY, AND IT IS KNOWN THAT IT IS MAN."

[Date of composition unknown. Editions: 1885, 1886a, *1893*, 1904. In the 1885 and 1886a texts, lines 4, 8, 12, and 16 are indented two spaces.]

Title. 1885, 1886a: [untitled]
1. 1893, 1904: seen":—yet
5. 1904: heard':—yet
9. 1885: yet hath man now
1886a: heart conceive:"—yet

hath man now
1904: conceived':—yet
11. 1885, 1886a: fired,
13. 1904: to deep':—man's
14. 1904: reap.

"OF EACH SAD WORD WHICH IS MORE SORROWFUL"

[Date of composition unknown. Editions: 1885, 1886a, *1893*, 1904.]

1. 1885, 1886a: word, which
2. 1885, 1886a: or "Disappointment?" I
3. 1904: inflections, baffling

5. 1904: lo a
10. 1885, 1886a: shape stepping-stone, or

"I SEE THAT ALL THINGS COME TO AN END." / I.

[Date of composition unknown. Editions: 1885, 1886a, *1893*, 1904.]

Title. 1885, 1886a: I. / "I see that all things come to an end."
1904: I <> end.

1. 1885, 1886a: fly
5. 1885, 1886a: roar
6. 1885, 1886a: cry

7.   1904: store,   9.   1904: Ah rosy
8.   1885, 1886a: silence bye and
     bye:—
     1904: and by:

"BUT THY COMMANDMENT IS EXCEEDING BROAD." / II.

[Date of composition unknown. Editions: 1885, 1886a, *1893*, 1904.]

Title. 1885, 1886a: 2. / "But Thy   2.   1885, 1886a: pain!—
        commandment is exceeding   9.   1885, 1886a: wane.
        broad."
        1904: But < > broad.

SURSUM CORDA.

[Date of composition unknown. Editions: 1885, 1886a, *1893*, 1904.]

Title. 1885, 1886a: [untitled]   7.   1885, 1886a: before now
  1.   1885, 1886a: hearts"—"We < >   1904: anew;
        them up"—Ah   9.   1885, 1886a: will and < > heart
  4.   1885, 1886a: heart"—I   and

"O YE, WHO ARE NOT DEAD AND FIT"

[Date of composition unknown. Editions: 1885, 1886a, *1893*, 1904.]

  3.   1885, 1886a: it,—   20. 1904: life, may
 16.   1885, 1886a: love; that   21. 1885, 1886a: love and
 19.   1885, 1886a: love; that

"WHERE SHALL I FIND A WHITE ROSE BLOWING?—"

[Date of composition unknown. Editions: 1885, 1886a, *1893*, 1904. A fair copy MS, signed "Christina G. Rossetti," is in the University of Kentucky Library. A copy of a separate printing of the poem on a single sheet is in the University of British Columbia Library; below the poem is added in pencil in William Michael Rossetti's handwriting: "Printed for Bazaar, June / 84, for Boys' Home at Barnet (Gillum)." In the textual notes, variants from that printing are designated "1884." In the MS, lines 5, 6, 11, 12, 17, 18, 23, and 24 are indented two spaces. In the 1884 text, lines 5, 6, 11, 12, 17, 18, 23, and 24 are indented four spaces. In the 1885 and 1886a texts, lines 6, 12, 18, and 24 are not indented.]

Title. MS: Roses and Roses.   11. 1884, 1885, 1886a: blushing;
        1884: ROSES AND   21. MS: tomorrow
        ROSES. / BY CHRISTINA G.
        ROSSETTI. / (*Copyright of the
        Author.*)

"REDEEMING THE TIME."

[Date of composition unknown. Editions: 1885, 1886a, *1893*, 1904.]

Title.   1885, 1886a: [untitled]
        1904: Redeeming the Time.

"NOW THEY DESIRE A BETTER COUNTRY."

[Date of composition unknown. Editions: 1885, 1886a, *1893*, 1904. In the 1885 and 1886a texts, lines 5 and 7 are not indented, and line 6 is indented two spaces.]

Title.   1885, 1886a: [untitled]
        1904: Now < > a Better
        Country.
  5.   1885, 1886a: pray:
  6.   1885, 1886a: praying:—
  9.   1885, 1886a: his dreamworld
        flushed

10.   1885, 1886a: weighing
11.   1885r: [In the upper left margin
      is added in pencil in Christina's
      handwriting:] My first roundel

A CASTLE-BUILDER'S WORLD.

[Date of composition unknown. Editions: 1885, 1886a, *1893*, 1904.]

Opening quotation. 1885,
      1886a: emptiness."—(ISAIAH
      xxxiv.II.)
      1904: The < > of Confusion,
      and < > emptiness.

2.   1885, 1886a: misty, gusty place;
7.   1885, 1886a, 1904: there

"THESE ALL WAIT UPON THEE."

[Composed January 22, *1853*. Editions: 1885, 1886a, *1893*, 1904. The notebook MS is in the Bodleian Library. The poem originally formed one stanza of a poem entitled "'To what purpose is this waste?'" which Christina never published as such. "'To what purpose is this waste?'" is presented in its own right in Volume III of the present edition. In the MS, no lines are indented. In the 1885 and 1886a texts, lines 1, 2, 4, 5, 7, 8, and 12 are indented two spaces.]

Title.   MS: "To what purpose is this
      waste?"
      1885, 1886a: [untitled]
      1904: These < > upon Thee.
  1.   MS: [Preceding line 1 are the
      following stanzas:]
      A windy shell singing upon the
          shore:
      A lily [illegible erasure] <b>udding
          in a desert place;
      Blooming alone
      With no companion

To praise its perfect plume and its
      grace:
A rose crimson and blushing at the
      core,
Hedged in with thorns behind it and
      before:
A fountain in the grass,
Whose shadowy waters pass
Only to nourish birds and furnish
      food
For squirrels of the wood:
An oak deep in the forest's heart, the
      house

Of black-eyed tiny mouse;
It's strong roots fit for fuel roofing in
The hoarded nuts, acorns and grains
       of wheat;
Shutting them from the wind and
       scorching heat,
And sheltering them when the rains
       begin:
A precious pear[e]<l> deep buried
       in the sea
Where none save fishes be:
The fullest merriest note
For which the skylark strains his
       silver throat,
Heard only in the sky
By other birds that fitfully
[illegible erasure] <Chase one
       another as they fly:>
The ripest plum down tumbled to
       the ground
By southern winds most musical of
       sound,
But by no thirsty traveller found:
Honey of wild bees in their ordered
       cells
Stored, not for human mouths to
       taste:—
I said, smiling superior down: What
       waste
Of good, where no man dwells.

This I said on a pleasant day in June
Before the sun had set, tho' a white
       moon
Already fla[sh]<k>ed the quiet blue
Which not a star looked thro'.
But still the air was warm, and
       drowsily
It blew into my face:
So since that same day I had
       wandered deep
Into the country, I sought out a place
For rest beneath a tree,
And very soon forgot myself in
       sleep:
Not so mine own words had
       forgotten me.
Mine eyes were opened to behold
All hidden things,
And mine ears heard all secret
       whisperings:
So my proud tongue that had been
       bold
To carp and to reprove,
Was silenced by the force of utter
       [l]<L>ove.

All voices of all things inanimate

Join with the song of Angels and the
       song
Of blessed Spirits, chiming with
Their Hallelujahs. One wind
       wakeneth
Across the sleeping sea, crisping
       along
The waves, and brushes thro' the
       great
Forests and tangled hedges, and calls
       out
Of rivers a clear sound,
And makes the ripe corn rustle on
       the ground,
And murmurs in a shell;
Till all their voices swell
Above the clouds in one loud hymn
Joining the song of Seraphim,
Or like pure incense circle round
       about
The walls of Heaven, or like a
       well-spring rise
In shady Paradise.

A lily blossoming unseen
Holds honey in its silver cup
Whereon a bee may sup,
Till being full she takes the rest
And stores it in her waxen nest:
While the fair blossom lifted up
On its one stately stem of green
Is type of her, the Undefil<e>d,
Arrayed in white, whose eyes are
       mild
As a white dove's, whose garment is
Blood-cleansed from all impurities
And earthly taints,
Her robe the righteousness of Saints.

1.   MS: And other eyes than our's
     1885, 1886a: ours,
2.   MS: Were made
4.   MS: The deep sun-blushing rose
     1885, 1886a: summer morn,
5.   MS: Round which the prickles
     close
7.   MS: The tiniest living thing
8.   MS: That soars on feathered
     wing,
9.   MS: Or crawls among the long
     grass out
     1885, 1886a: the grass-blades
     out
10. MS: Has just as good a
11. MS: To its appointed
     1885, 1886a: delight,

12. MS: As any King.
12. MS: [After line 12 are the
following stanzas:]

Why should we grudge a hidden
water stream
To birds and squirrels while we have
enough?
As if a nightingale should cease to
sing
Lest we should hear, or finch leafed
out of sight
Warbling its fill in summer light;
As if sweet violets in the spring
Should cease to blow, for fear our
path should seem
Less weary or less rough.

So every oak that stands a house
For skilful mouse,
And year by year renews its strength,
Shakes acorns from a hundred
boughs
Which shall be oaks at length.

Who hath weighed the waters and
shall say
What is hidden in the depths from
day?
Pearls and precious stones and
golden sands,
Wondrous weeds and blossoms rare,
Kept back from human hands,
But good and fair,
A silent praise as pain is silent
prayer.

A hymn, an incense rising toward
the skies,
As our whole life should rise;
An offering without stint from earth
below,
Which [*l*]<L>ove accepteth so.

Thus is it with a warbling bird,
With fruit bloom-ripe and full of
seed,
With honey which the wild bees draw
From flowers, and store for future
need
By a perpetual law.
We want the faith that hath not seen
Indeed, but hath believed His truth
Who witnessed that His work was
good:
So we pass cold to age from youth.
Alas for us: for we have heard
And known, but have not
understood.

O earth, earth, earth, thou yet shalt
bow
Who art so fair and lifted up,
Thou yet shalt drain the bitter cup.
Men's eyes that wait upon thee now,
All eyes shall see thee lost and mean,
Exposed and valued at thy worth,
While thou shalt stand ashamed and
dumb.—
Ah, when the Son of Man shall
come,
Shall He find faith upon the
earth?—

"DOETH WELL . . . DOETH BETTER."

[Date of composition unknown. Editions: 1885, 1886a, *1893*, 1904.]

Title. 1885, 1886a: "Doeth
well, . . . doeth better."—(I
COR. vii. 38.)
5. 1885, 1886a: her;

6. 1885, 1886a: "us," and
7. 1885, 1886a: substantial while
9. 1885: rest tho' < > her,
1886a: rest though < > her,

"OUR HEAVEN MUST BE WITHIN OURSELVES"

[Lines 1–4 composed January 25, 1854. Date of composition of lines 5–12 un-
known. Editions: 1885, 1886a, *1893*, 1904. The notebook MS is in the Bodleian Li-
brary. In the MS, line 4 is indented four spaces, and the revisions are in pencil in
Christina's handwriting. In the 1885 and 1886a texts, lines 4, 8, and 12 are indented
two spaces.]

Title.   MS: Our Heaven.
   2.   MS: Our only heaven < > faith,
   3.   MS: Thro' all the race < > life
       that shelves
   4.   MS: Downwards to
   4.   MS: [After line 4 are the
       following stanzas:]

The <That> calm blue heaven is
    built too far,
We cannot reach to hold it fast;
We cannot reach <touch> a single
    star

From first to last.
Our powers are strait to compass
    heaven,
   Our strength is weak to scale the
    sky;
There's not one day of all the seven
   That <can> bring[s] it nigh.
Our heaven must be within our
    heart,
   Unchangeable for night and day;
Our heaven must be the better part
   Not taken away.

"VANITY OF VANITIES."

[Composed August 6, 1858. Editions: 1885, 1886a, *1893*, 1904. The notebook MS is in the British Library. The poem originally formed part of a poem entitled "'Yet a little while,'" which Christina never published as such. "'Yet a little while'" is presented in its own right in Volume III of the present edition. The last two stanzas of the MS are printed in *Verses* as "Earth has clear call of daily bells." In the MS, the last two stanzas are deleted in pencil with a vertical line, and in the right margin the word "stet" is added in pencil in Christina's handwriting.]

Title.   MS: "Yet a little while."
     1885, 1886a: [untitled]
     1904: Vanity of Vanities.
   1.   MS: [Preceding line 1 are the
       following stanzas:]

These days are long before I die:
[*T*] [out to left margin] <To>
      [indented two spaces] sit
      alone upon a thorn
  Is what the nightingale forlorn
Does night by night continually;
She swells her heart to extasy
Until it bursts and she can die.

These days are long that wane and
    wax:
  Waxeth and wanes the ghostly
    moon
    Achill and pale in cordial June;
What is it that she wandering lacks?
She seems as one that aches and
    aches
Most sick to wane most sick to wax.

   1.   MS: all the sad sights in < >
     world
   2.   MS: The downfall of an
     [*a*]<A>utumn leaf
   3.   MS: Is grievous and suggesteth
     grief:

   4.   MS: thought when < > was
     fresh unfurled
   5.   MS: this? when Spring twigs
     gleamed impearled
   7.   MS: [The line is not in the text.]
   8.   MS: There are a
  10.   MS: A young fruit cankered
  11.   MS: A strong bird snared
  12.   MS: A nest that
  13.   MS: Yea sight and sound and
     silence
  14.   MS: [Line 14 is not in the text.
     After line 13 are the following
     stanzas:]

There is a lack in solitude,
  There is a load in throng of life;
   One with another genders strife,
To be alone yet is not good:
I know but of one neighbourhood
At peace and full; death's solitude.

Sleep soundly, dears, who lulled at
    last
  Forget the bird and all her pains,
  Forget the moon that waxes,
    wanes,
The leaf, the sting, the frostful blast;
Forget the troublous years that past
In strife or ache did end at last.

<[*We have clear call of daily bells,*
  A dimness where the anthems are,
  A chancel vault of sky and star,
  A thunder if the organ swells:
  Alas our daily life—what else?—
  Is not in tune with daily bells.]>
<[*You have deep pause betwixt the*
  chimes

Of earth and heaven, a patient pause
Yet glad with rest by certain laws:
You look and long; while oftentimes
Precursive flush of morning climbs
And air vibrates with coming chimes.]>

"THE HILLS ARE TIPPED WITH SUNSHINE, WHILE I WALK"

[Date of composition unknown. Editions: 1892, *1893*, 1904.]

10. 1904: Ah happy   14. 1892: song—

"SCARCE TOLERABLE LIFE, WHICH ALL LIFE LONG"

[Date of composition unknown. Editions: 1885, 1886a, *1893*, 1896, 1904. In the 1885 and 1886a texts, lines 12 and 13 are indented two spaces, and line 14 is not indented. In the 1896 and 1904 texts, lines 12 and 13 are not indented.]

Title. 1896: LIFE
1. 1885, 1886a: Scarce-tolerable
    life which
    1896: Oh intolerable life which
2. 1885, 1886a: death,—
    1896: Abidest haunted < >
    death—
3. 1885, 1886a: such life, life? If
    so,
    1896: such life life? When one
    considereth,
    1904: so who
4. 1896: Then black seems almost
    white, and discord
5. 1896: Alas this
6. 1896: grows, and < > by
    breath—

7. 1896: Slowly grows on us, and
    no
8. 1896: cords made long and all
    its
9. 1896: Life wanes apace—a< >
    deceives,
10. 1896: And works and reigns like
    life, and
11. 1885, 1886a: not, but
12. 1885, 1886a, 1896: life
    immortal,
13. 1886a: that woos us
    1896: The life < > tongue,
14. 1896: Whither? Much said, and
    < > unsaid. / *Circa* 1875.

"ALL HEAVEN IS BLAZING YET"

[Date of composition unknown. Editions: 1885, 1886a, *1893*, 1904. In the 1885 and 1886a texts, the poem is presented as two separate poems, the first comprising lines 1–8, the second, lines 9–16.]

Title. 1885, 1886a: [The first poem is
    numbered *1.*, and the second
    poem is numbered *2.*]
3. 1885, 1886a: Make haste, O sun,
    make
4. 1885, 1886a: [A stanza break
    follows the line.]

7. 1885, 1886a: knows,
12. 1885, 1886a: [A stanza break
    follows the line.]
14. 1885, 1886a: is Jesu's Will:

"BALM IN GILEAD."

[Date of composition unknown. Editions: 1885, 1886a, *1893*, 1904.]

Title. 1885, 1886a: [untitled]
        1904: Balm in Gilead.
   7.   1885, 1886a: binding things
        unbound.

   8.   1885, 1886a: succeeding,
        1904: Ah when < > fell, to < >
        succeeding,
  10.   1904: pleading;

"IN THE DAY OF HIS ESPOUSALS."

[Date of composition unknown. Editions: 1885, 1886a, *1893*, 1904.]

Title. 1885, 1886a: [untitled]
   1.   1885, 1886a: is Solomon's,

   9.   1885, 1886a: Birds in

"SHE CAME FROM THE UTTERMOST PART OF THE EARTH."

[Date of composition unknown. Editions: 1885, 1886a, *1893*, 1904.]

Title. 1885, 1886a: [untitled]
   5.   1885: Happy
   8.   1885: As < > moon, while
        1886a: moon, while

   9.   1885, 1886a: sun, is

"ALLELUIA! OR ALAS! MY HEART IS CRYING"

[Date of composition unknown. Editions: 1892, *1893*, 1904. In the 1892 text, lines 4 and 8 are indented two spaces.]

   1.   1892: crying:—
   2.   1892: sighing:

   5.   1904: 'Alas' grieves
   7.   1904: ascending.—

"THE PASSION FLOWER HATH SPRUNG UP TALL"

[Date of composition unknown. Editions: 1892, *1893*, 1904. In the 1892 text, lines 7 and 15 are not indented.]

GOD'S ACRE.

[Date of composition unknown. Editions: 1892, *1893*, 1904.]

Title. 1892: [untitled]
   2.   1892: cold:
   5.   1892: Balm, woodbine, and
        heliotrope,

   7.   1892: the Sun which

"THE FLOWERS APPEAR ON THE EARTH."

[Composed March 26, 1855. Editions: 1885, 1886a, *1893*, 1904. The notebook MS is in the Bodleian Library. The poem originally formed part of a poem entitled "'I have a message unto thee,'" which Christina never published as such. "'I have a message unto thee'" is presented in its own right in Volume III of the present edition.]

Title. MS: "I have a message unto
thee." / (written in sickness.)
1885, 1886a: [untitled]
1904: The < > the Earth.

1. MS: [Preceding line 1 are the
following stanzas:]

Green sprout the grasses,
  Red blooms the mossy rose,
Blue nods the harebell
  Where purple heather blows;
The water lily, silver white,
  Is living-fair as light;
    [Illegible erasure] <Sweet jasmine
      branches> trail
  A dusky star[illegible
    erasure]<ry> veil:
Each goodly is to see,
  Comely in its degree;
I, only I, alas that this should be,
  Am ruinously pale.

New year renews the grasses,
  The crimson rose renews,
Brings up the breezy bluebell,
  Refreshes heath with dews;
Then water lilies ever
  Bud fresh upon the river;
    Then jasmine lights its star
    And spreads its arms afar:
I only in my spring
  Can neither bud nor sing;
I find not honey but a sting
  Though fair the blossoms are.

For me no downy grasses,
  For me no blossoms pluck;
But leave them for the breezes,
  For honey bees to suck,
For childish hands to pull
And pile their baskets full:
  I will not have a crown
  That soon must be laid down;
Trust me, I cannot care
A withering crown to wear,
I who may be immortally made fair
  Where autumn turns not brown.

Spring, summer, autumn,
  Winter, all will pass,
With tender blossoms
  And with fruitful grass.
Sweet days of yore

Will pass to come no more,
  Sweet perfumes fly,
  Buds languish and go by:
Oh [illegible erasure] <bloom> that
    cannot last.
Oh blossom<s> [illegible erasure]
    <quite gone> past,
I yet shall feast when you shall fast.
  And live when you shall die.

Your workday fully ended,
  Your pleasant task being done,
You shall finish with the stars,
  The moon and setting sun.
You and these and time
Shall end with the last chime;
For earthly solace given,
But needed not in heaven.
  Needed not perhaps
  Thro' the eternal lapse:
Or else, all signs fulfilled,
What you foreshow may yield
Delights thro' heaven's own harvest
    field
  With undecaying saps.

2. MS: wreath;
5. MS: best?—
    1904: best—
7. MS: whose hoped for sweet
8. MS: feet?—
9. MS: Ah, what
    1904: Ah what
10. MS: ease—
11. MS: How long and deep that
    slumber is
16. MS: our happy dead.
18. MS: that slip away;
    1904: away;
19. MS: perfection
20. MS: And endless resurrection.
    1885, 1886a: love, and
21. MS, 1885, 1886a: fair
22. MS: air;
23. MS: For Angels, may be, finding
24. MS: [After line 24 are the
    following stanzas:]

A blessing on the flowers
  That God has made so good,

From crops of jealous gardens
    To wildlings of a wood.
They show us symbols deep
Of how to sow and reap;
    They teach us lessons plain
    Of patient harvest gain.
They still are telling of
God's unimagined love:—
"Oh gift," they say, "all gifts above,
    "Shall it be given in vain?—

"Better you had not seen us
    "But shared the blind man's night,
"Better you had not scented
    "Our incense of delight,

"Than o[*l*]<n>ly plucked to scorn
"The rosebud for its thorn:
"Not so the instinctive thrush
"Hymns in a holly bush.
    [illegible erasure] <"Be> wise
        betimes, and with the bee
    [illegible erasure] <"Suck> sweets
        from prickly tree
"To last when earth's are flown;
"So God well pleased will own
"Your work, and bless not time alone
    "But ripe eternity."

"THOU KNEWEST . . . THOU OUGHTEST THEREFORE."

[Date of composition unknown. Editions: 1892, *1893*, 1904.]

Title. 1892: [untitled]
  1.   1892: floating, dazzling
  9.   1892: low.

12.   1892: will I:
13.   1892: know;

"GO IN PEACE."

[Date of composition unknown. Editions: 1892, *1893*, 1904.]

Title. 1892: [untitled]
        1904: Go in Peace.
  2.   1892: perfume;

6.   1904: can.
8.   1904: brow.

"HALF DEAD."

[Date of composition unknown. Editions: 1892, *1893*, 1904. In the 1892 text, lines 2, 5, 8, 11, and 14 are indented four spaces.]

Title. 1892: [untitled]
        1904: Half dead.
  4.   1892: O Christ my life, pour
  9.   1893: [No stanza break follows
        the line.]

10.   1893: [A stanza break follows
      the line.]
14.   1892: now . . .

"ONE OF THE SOLDIERS WITH A SPEAR PIERCED HIS SIDE."

[Date of composition unknown. Editions: 1892, *1893*, 1904.]

Title. 1892: [untitled]
  1.   1904: Ah Lord,

7.   1892: love Thy face,

"WHERE LOVE IS, THERE COMES SORROW"

[Date of composition unknown. Editions: 1885, 1886a, *1893*, 1904.]

6.   1885, 1886a: measure

"BURY HOPE OUT OF SIGHT"

[Date of composition unknown. Editions: 1885, 1886a, *1893*, 1904.]

4.   1885, 1886a: well;   34.   1904: Lo the
19.   1885, 1886a: hour:

A CHURCHYARD SONG OF PATIENT HOPE.

[Date of composition unknown. Editions: 1892, *1893*, 1904. In the 1892 text, lines 4 and 8 are indented eight spaces.]

5.   1904: pain 'It   7.   1904: pain 'It

"ONE WOE IS PAST. COME WHAT COME WILL"

[Date of composition unknown. Editions: 1892, *1893*, 1904. In the 1892 text, lines 4 and 11 are indented four spaces.]

1.   1904: will,   10.   1892: heads: Come good,
7.   1892: overcast:

"TAKE NO THOUGHT FOR THE MORROW."

[Date of composition unknown. Editions: 1892, *1893*, 1904.]

Title.   1892: [untitled]   12.   1892: west
         1904: Take < > morrow.

"CONSIDER THE LILIES OF THE FIELD."

[Date of composition unknown. Editions: 1892, *1893*, 1904.]

Title.   1892: [untitled]   4.   1892: lilies thou accountest
         1904: Consider < > field.

"SON, REMEMBER."

[Date of composition unknown. Editions: 1892, *1893*, 1904.]

Title.   1892: [untitled]   2.   1904: not, I
   1.   1892: I, laid   8.   1904: And, be < > not seen, I
         1904: gate am   10.   1904: and trumpet-burst

"HEAVINESS MAY ENDURE FOR A NIGHT, BUT JOY COMETH IN THE MORNING."

[Date of composition unknown. Editions: 1885, 1886a, *1893*, 1904. In the 1885 and 1886a texts, the poem is presented as two separate poems, the first comprising lines 1–14, the second, lines 15–28. In the 1885 text, lines 13 and 28 are indented two spaces.]

Title.	1885, 1886a: [The first poem is numbered *1.*, and the second poem is numbered *2.*] 1904: Heaviness <> morning.	15.	1885, 1886a: anew,
		17.	1885: moon, 1886a: Sectral on <> moon,
5.	1885, 1886a: tidal wave becomes the	18.	1885, 1886a: last hint of
		20.	1885, 1886a: chirpings,—with
8.	1885, 1886a: game,—with	21.	1885, 1886a: doves,—a
12.	1885, 1886a: light shook off 1904: lo the	22.	1885, 1886a: answers, sweet
		26.	1885, 1886a: is,
13.	1885, 1886a: flashed carolling a lark,	27.	1885, 1886a: cares,

"THE WILL OF THE LORD BE DONE."

[Date of composition unknown. Editions: 1892, *1893*, 1904.]

Title.	1892: [untitled] 1904: The <> done.	8.	1892: song:
1.	1904: fulfil Thy Will,	12.	1904: still,

"LAY UP FOR YOURSELVES TREASURES IN HEAVEN."

[Date of composition unknown. Editions: 1885, 1886a, *1893*, 1904.]

Title.	1885, 1886a: [untitled] 1904: Lay <> in Heaven.	5.	1885, 1886a: pleasure
4.	1904: Ah my <> things!	7.	1885, 1886a: treasure

"WHOM THE LORD LOVETH HE CHASTENETH."

[Date of composition unknown. Editions: 1885, 1886a, *1893*, 1904.]

Title.   1885, 1886a: [untitled]
         1904: Whom <> chasteneth.

"THEN SHALL YE SHOUT."

[Date of composition unknown. Editions: 1885, 1886a, *1893*, 1904.]

Title.	1885, 1886a: [untitled]	10.	1885, 1886a: chime;
2.	1885, 1886a: sing, 1904: sing;	11.	1885, 1886a: sound:—
		13.	1885, 1886a: Cannot we sing

"EVERYTHING THAT IS BORN MUST DIE"

[Date of composition unknown. Editions: 1885, 1886a, *1893*, 1904.]

1. 1885, 1886a: die:
2. 1885, 1886a: sing:
3. 1885, 1886a: balance low < > high
5. 1885, 1886a: sting,

6. 1885, 1886a: sky,
8. 1885, 1886a: soul spread
9. 1885, 1886a: on homebound wing:

"LORD, GRANT US CALM, IF CALM CAN SET FORTH THEE"

[Date of composition unknown. Editions: 1892, *1893*, 1904.]

3. 1892: north;

4. 1892: sea

CHANGING CHIMES.

[Date of composition unknown. Editions: 1892, *1893*, 1904.]

Title. 1892: "THOU SHALT HEAR A VOICE BEHIND THEE."
3. 1892: cried, still

6. 1892: if ought was
9. 1892: alway.

"THY SERVANT WILL GO AND FIGHT WITH THIS PHILISTINE."

[Date of composition unknown. Editions: 1892, *1893*, 1904. In the 1893 text, line 10 is not indented.]

Title. 1892: [untitled]
1904: Thy < > this Philistine.

2. 1904: before,
13. 1904: but, proof < > grace,

"THRO' BURDEN AND HEAT OF THE DAY"

[Date of composition unknown. Editions: 1885, 1886a, *1893*, 1904.]

2. 1885, 1886a: feet,
8. 1885, 1886a: shadows grow lengthening
1885r: shadows [*grow*] <show>

lengthening [The revision is in pencil in Christina's handwriting.]
9. 1885, 1886a: complete:—

"THEN I COMMENDED MIRTH."

[Date of composition unknown. Editions: 1885, 1886a, *1893*, 1904.]

Title. 1885, 1886a: [untitled]
4. 1904: heart.

9. 1885, 1886a: mart:—

"SORROW HATH A DOUBLE VOICE"

[Date of composition unknown. Editions: 1885, 1886a, *1893*, 1904. In the 1885 and 1886a texts, lines 4, 8, and 12 are indented two spaces.]

"SHADOWS TODAY, WHILE SHADOWS SHOW GOD'S WILL"

[Date of composition unknown. Editions: 1892, *1893*, 1904.]

    7.   1892: not over bright;

"TRULY THE LIGHT IS SWEET."

[Date of composition unknown. Editions: 1892, *1893*, 1904.]

Title. 1892: [untitled]   12.   1892: Oh well <> thee and
       1904: Truly <> sweet.   1904: Oh well <> be.
  7. 1892: Light fountain <>
      delight

"ARE YE NOT MUCH BETTER THAN THEY?"

[Date of composition unknown. Editions: 1892, *1893*, 1904.]

Title. 1892: [untitled]   5.   1892: to-day,
       1904: Are <> they?   13.   1904: overflowing,

"YEA, THE SPARROW HATH FOUND HER AN HOUSE."

[Date of composition unknown. Editions: 1892, *1893*, 1904.]

Title. 1892: [untitled]
       1904: Yea, <> house.

"I AM SMALL AND OF NO REPUTATION."

[Date of composition unknown. Editions: 1892, *1893*, 1904.]

Title. 1892: [untitled]   6.   1892: cheer:
       1904: I <> reputation.   7.   1904: for I, who
  3. 1892: the Lamb,
  4. 1892: [No stanza break follows
      the line.]

"O CHRIST MY GOD WHO SEEST THE UNSEEN"

[Date of composition unknown. Editions: 1885, 1886a, *1893*, 1904.]

    5.   1885: O Thou who seest

"YEA, IF THOU WILT, THOU CANST PUT UP THY SWORD"

[Date of composition unknown. Editions: 1885, 1886a, *1893*, 1904.]

1.   1885, 1886a: up thy sword: 8.   1904: wanders canst

"SWEETNESS OF REST WHEN THOU SHEDDEST REST"

[Date of composition unknown. Editions: 1892, *1893*, 1904.]

4.   1892: men:

"O FOOLISH SOUL! TO MAKE THY COUNT"

[Date of composition unknown. Editions: 1892, *1893*, 1904. In the 1892 and 1904 texts, lines 4 and 8 are indented two spaces.]

"BEFORE THE BEGINNING THOU HAST FOREKNOWN THE END"

[Date of composition unknown. Editions: 1892, *1893*, 1904.]

2.   1892: birthday the deathbed was

"THE GOAL IN SIGHT! LOOK UP AND SING"

[Date of composition unknown. Editions: 1885, 1886a, *1893*, 1904.]

10.   1904: Hail Life

"LOOKING BACK ALONG LIFE'S TRODDEN WAY"

[Date of composition unknown. Editions: 1885, 1886a, *1893*, 1904. In the 1885 and 1886a texts, lines 4, 8, and 12 are indented two spaces.]

1.   1885, 1886a, 1904: way,   7.   1885: Evening harmonises all
2.   1885, 1886a: track: 11.   1885, 1886a, 1904: to-day,

Appendixes To Volume II

A. Tables of Contents from the English and American Editions

Sing-Song.
A Nursery Rhyme Book
(London: George Routledge and Sons; Boston: Roberts Brothers, 1872)

Sing-Song.
A Nursery Rhyme Book
(London and New York: Macmillan, 1893)

A Pageant and Other Poems
(London: Macmillan, 1881)

A Pageant and Other Poems
(Boston: Roberts Brothers, 1881)
and *Poems*
(Boston: Roberts Brothers, 1882, 1888)

Poems
(Boston: Roberts Brothers, 1888)

Poems, New and Enlarged Edition
(London and New York: Macmillan, 1890, 1891, 1892)

Verses. Reprinted from "Called to be Saints," "Time Flies," "The Face of the Deep"
(London: Society for Promoting Christian Knowledge; New York: E. and J. B. Young, 1893, 1894)

B. Table of Contents
from Christina Rossetti's Manuscript Notebook
of A Pageant and Other Poems

C. *Index of First Lines from* Verses

D. Corrections and Additions to Volume I

p. xviii
> Open Collection, Princeton University Library:
> The manuscript of "A Year's Windfalls" is in Christina's handwriting.

p. 244
> SONG. ["TWO DOVES UPON THE SELFSAME BRANCH"]
> [The notebook MS is in the Bodleian Library. The poem is the last in a group of ten poems entitled "Odds and Ends." At the end of the group is written, "Copied, September 1853."]
> Title. MS: [This section is untitled]
> 3. MS: flower;—
> 5. MS: in hand,
> 7. MS: in hand,

p. 275
> A YEAR'S WINDFALLS.
> [A later fair copy (MS3), signed "Christina G. Rossetti," is in the Open Collection, Princeton University Library.]
> 6. MS3: comes:
> 7. MS3: fire
> 8. MS3: And give him
> 10. MS3: Snow-flakes float
> 13. MS3: streams
> 16. MS3: be.—
> 18. MS3: down;
> 19. MS3: caterpillar-like;
> 22. MS3: And leaf buds by
> 24. MS3: day.—
> 30. MS3: pink
> 34. MS3: Besides pure < > flowers;
> 39. MS3: hawthorn [illegible deletion] <T>ops,
> 42. MS3: crop;
> 44. MS3: drop:
> 45. MS3: White-rose and yellow-rose
> 46. MS3: And moss-rose choice
> 47. MS3: the cottage-cabbage-rose
> 50. MS3: hail;
> 52. MS3: heaven, grown

53. MS3: ashore:
57. MS3: the parched August
58. MS3: head;
61. MS3: down,
62. MS3: breeze;
64. MS3: trees
68. MS3: shoots:
74. MS3: the Equinox,
76. MS3: rocks:
79. MS3: sea
82. MS3: shifts:
90. MS3: sands almost run,
92. MS3: the Sun:
94. MS3: low;

Indexes

INDEX OF TITLES

INDEX OF FIRST LINES